HANDEL

CHRISTOPHER HOGWOOD

HANDEL

Revised edition

Chronological table by
Anthony Hicks

With 100 illustrations,
10 in color

Thames & Hudson

clc

First published in the United States of America in 1985
by Thames & Hudson Inc., 500 Fifth Avenue,
New York, New York 10110

thamesandhudsonusa.com

Revised edition 2007

Library of Congress Catalog Card Number 2006909559

ISBN 978-0-500-28681-4

Printed and bound in Slovenia by
MKT Print d.d.

Contents

Europe after the Treaty of Utrecht (1713) and associated treaties
▬Boundary of the Holy Roman Empire

6

Preface

'One cannot always be praising Homer': thus the over-enthusiasm of nineteenth-century Handelians was countered, somewhat wearily, by Franz Liszt. Hagiography, posthumous fictions and picaresque novels are the legacy of these zealots in Handel's cause, for whom the Myth overshadowed attempts at studied biography and musical documentation which might have led them closer to Handel the Man. Even in his own lifetime Handel passed from being an individual to an institution, and eventually a complete industry; since his death, a reputation founded on endless repetitions of a small core of compositions has held Handel firmly captive. His compositions, according to Sir Donald Tovey's calculations, equal almost all those of Bach plus all of Beethoven – yet the overwhelming public preference for just one work has meant that most of this great output remains unfamiliar. 'His reputation is unshakably founded on one piece – *Messiah* – which represents an infinitesimal part of his enormous output, and yet which so comprehensively represents it that further exploration of his music never ultimately adds much' (*The Spectator*, 12 May 1984). Hallowed by the traditions of two centuries, misconceptions of this kind still represent the popular image of Handel today, totally ignoring the major arena of his work.

By vocation Handel was a man of the theatre. When thwarted in opera after thirty-six years, he turned to a form which he himself largely shaped – the oratorio – for the remainder of his life. This unique progression from the established, 'pure' form of *opera seria* to the novel and 'mixed' form of oratorio marks off Handel's career from those of his contemporaries, Bach and Scarlatti. He was also, unlike them, a traveller, the first truly cosmopolitan composer, with a staunch independence that prevented him from ever accepting the position of an employee and a pragmatic approach to composition that enabled him to excel in every chosen field, sacred or secular.

Burney describes him (admittedly in middle age) as 'studious and sedentary', and the evidence of his own manuscripts demonstrates his unflagging industry and also a constant curiosity and need to experiment, whether with his own works or the products of others. His technique of composing with borrowed material, ranging from small themes to complete movements, was noted during his lifetime (first by Mattheson in 1722) and has been a recurrent thorn to commentators ever since. To some nineteenth-century writers it was an issue of moral propriety which caused them a certain distress. Nowadays opinion is centred more on the musical value of such procedures, and the modern reader may more easily adopt the viewpoint of Handel's own century and perhaps accept the recommendation of John Potter, that a composer 'should examine every thing he can meet with and like *the curious bee, suck sweets from every flower*' (*Observations on the Present State of Music and Musicians*, 1762). Handel's borrowings are touched on from various standpoints in this volume; against any further objections Horace Walpole's rhetorical question might be enough defence: 'Ought one man's garden to be deprived of a happy object, because that object has been employed by another?' (*On Modern Gardening*). In Handel we find an identical philosophy, with 'every incident of view turned to advantage'.

As a public figure Handel is well documented, as an individual he remains hidden: his private life is rarely exposed, his letters are few and unrevealing, compared with those, say, of Mozart or Joshua Reynolds. This documentary biography therefore draws material from circles of evidence further removed from the subject himself – from the writings of contemporaries, both friends and enemies, the public press of London, the accounts of opera houses and noble patrons, the correspondence of librettists, and the flourishes of contemporary poets. Chief amongst eighteenth-century sources are the account of Handel's early life by Johann Mattheson (flawed though it is by later bitterness), who knew him as a young man, and the *Memoirs of the Life of the late George Frederic Handel*, compiled by the Rev. John Mainwaring (with contributions from James Harris and Robert Price) – the first biography of a composer ever published. Much of the information in Mainwaring was provided by Handel's assistant John Christopher Smith, who often appears to pass on what he had heard at first hand from the composer himself. Although the evidence is sometimes misconstrued, Mainwaring's account is less wayward than has often been supposed.

Both great eighteenth-century English historians of music had contact with Handel: Burney played in the opera orchestra and attended Handel's rehearsals at Carlton House; Sir John Hawkins reports verbatim conversations he had with the composer. The writings of both men reflect the differing tastes of a generation after Handel, and their views (particularly those of Burney on the operas, many of which he had never seen) should be read with appropriate allowance for the fast-moving and partisan feelings of the eighteenth-century artistic élite. It is Burney who reminds us that Handel, 'with his other excellencies, was possessed of a great stock of humour; no man ever told a story with more': a number of anecdotes, some plausibly fact, others surely myth, have been included as separate items in this text. True or untrue, they document a strongly-held view of Handel's character, and together with the evidence contained in the last chapter give some idea of how Handel's image has been reshaped from the time of his death until the present day.

Much of the documentary evidence from Handel's lifetime was gathered together by Otto Erich Deutsch: *Handel: a Documentary Biography*, first published by A. & C. Black in 1955, to which all later writers are indebted. Since that date new material has appeared, shedding light on some of the more shadowy patches of Handel's life: the Ruspoli archives, the Duke of Portland's papers, the correspondence between Charles Jennens and Edward Holdsworth, and several other collections of manuscripts. All these sources help us to reassess Handel's early years in Rome, the financial crises of the London opera, his problems with the dramatic oratorios and many other hitherto ambiguous incidents. As far as possible, documents in this volume are presented in chronological order. References by short-title are amplified in the Select Bibliography, with Deutsch as a constant recommendation for corroborative detail.

The writings of Winton Dean have proved a constant mine of information and pungent phraseology for which no Handelian can be too grateful. Particular thanks are due to Gerald Coke, for access to his unique collection of printed and pictorial material, Donald Burrows for information on Handel's church music, Robert Hume for sharing his latest discoveries in theatre documentation, Derek Drescher and Bennet Maxwell of the BBC for information on early recordings, Raymond Head for research in the library of the Royal Asiatic Society, and William B. Ober and Milo Keynes for diagnoses of Handel's medical condition. Richard Luckett, Heather Jarman and Simon Shaw take the credit for innumerable improvements and corrections to the typescript, and in addition to compiling the Chronological Table of Handel's life as traveller, performer and composer, Anthony Hicks has offered constant advice and information.

CHRISTOPHER HOGWOOD
Cambridge, 1984

Since 1984, the heightened awareness of Handel's operatic genius that we prayed for in the last century seems finally to have come about and many positions have changed, including my own. However, I am grateful to the many observant Handel-lovers who have communicated improvements to the old text, to Simon Shaw who fielded them, and to David Vickers, Teri Noel Towe and Heather Jarman for their assistance with the new Afterword and additional Bibliography (see pages 277 and 308) which attempt to record some of the recent endeavours and activities in this boundless territory. Meanwhile Handel still towers above us all, 'the more than Homer of his Age' (William Cowper, *The Task*, Book VI 1785).

CHRISTOPHER HOGWOOD
Cambridge, 2007

Marginal references in the text refer to the illustration sections: arabic numerals to the monochrome plates, roman to the colour.

George Friedrich Händel/
Der freyen Künste ergebener.

George Friedrich Händel,
dedicated to the liberal arts

(Handel's signature to a poem of mourning for his father,
written at the age of twelve)

1

Halle and Hamburg
1685–1706

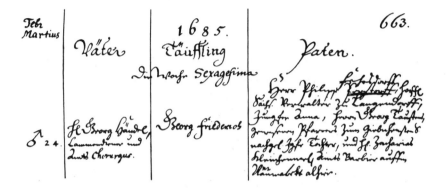

With this entry in the baptismal register of the Liebfrauenkirche in Halle, Handel entered the world of documentation, one day after his birth on 23 February 1685. Of the three relatives who signed as godparents, hardly any information survives. Seventy-four years later prayers were read in this same church when Handel died in a foreign capital, unmarried and without family; there again, the names that attended him, signed his will and codices are almost completely unidentifiable today. He was by then the most famous composer in his cosmopolitan world, and a public institution in his own right; yet the monument to his memory in Westminster Abbey was (and still is) inscribed with the wrong date of birth, so far was he from his origins. Even the various spellings of his name seem only to deepen the ambiguities of his life and to emphasize his international adaptability. Georg Friederich Händel at his christening, he first signed himself Georg Friedrich, adapted his surname to Hendel in Italy, is variously referred to as Haendel, Händeler, Hendler or Handell, and eventually settled on George Frideric Handel when he became a naturalized Englishman.

The origins of the Händel family are known only in outline. Middle-class tradespeople, as the surname would have implied originally, they were first represented in Halle by Valentin Händel, a coppersmith, who moved there in 1609. Georg Händel, his fifth son, was born into this staunchly Lutheran family in 1622. When his father died, Georg, aged fourteen, was apprenticed to become a 'surgeon–barber' (the two professions were normally associated), first to Andreas Berger, son-in-law of the English emigré musician William Brade,

11

and then to Christoph Oettinger. When this master died, Georg took over both his business and his wife, a marriage of convenience which produced two children who survived infancy, and propelled Georg into an appointment as surgeon and *valet de chambre* to the local court of Duke Augustus of Saxony. It was agreed at the Peace of Westphalia that Halle should come within the jurisdiction of Prussia, the emergent military state, and when the agreement came into operation on the death of Augustus in 1680, the centre of power moved to the Brandenburgs in Berlin. Georg was now employed by the local court of the new Duke of Weissenfels, some twenty miles from Halle. Johann Adolf I, a keen music-lover, took with him to the new establishment Johann Krieger, previously organist at the court of Halle. The extensive list of music that the well-travelled Krieger sold to the Liebfrauenkirche before he moved is still extant; it contains two thousand of his own works, and nearly five hundred pieces by German and leading Italian composers – a considerable resource for the musicians of Halle.

In 1682 Georg Händel's wife died, and (as was expected of a family man at the time) he remarried within a few months. He was sixty and his new wife, the daughter of the pastor of Giebichenstein, a suburb of Halle where he had worked, was thirty-two. Their first child, a son, died at birth; their second was Georg Friederich, who during the next five years acquired two sisters, Dorothea Sophia and Johanna Christiana.

The childhoods of the great tend to be forced into one of two patterns – angel or martyr. Handel's biographers have traditionally taken the latter stance, although the evidence is, to say the least, sketchy. Our picture must derive almost entirely from the account that John Mainwaring gives in his *Memoirs of the Life of the Late George Frederic Handel* (1760), which although fallible in chronology, stems from his conversations with Handel's amanuensis John Christopher Smith, who in turn reported what the composer himself remembered. Certainly for the early years, Mainwaring and Smith can have had no other source than Handel himself, and the earliest anecdotes, so frequently retold in the interests of martyrdom, can be simply interpreted as the reasonable fears of an elderly father. In a declining township with its court patronage now removed and the effects of the Thirty Years War still evident in its poverty and stricken economy, a preoccupation with music could be the start of a disastrous career, particularly if the young boy were not talented. Fortunately, he proved to have both talent and determination.

From his very childhood HANDEL had discovered such a strong propensity to Music, that his father, who always intended him for the study of the Civil Law, had reason to be alarmed. Perceiving that this inclination still increased, he took every method to oppose it. He strictly forbad him to meddle with any musical instrument; nothing of that kind was suffered to remain in the house, nor was he ever permitted to go to any other, where such kind of furniture was in use. All this caution and art, instead of restraining, did but augment his passion. He had found means to get a little clavichord privately convey'd to a room at the top of the house. To this room he constantly stole when the family was asleep. He had made some progress before Music had been prohibited, and by his assiduous practice at the hours of rest, had made such farther advances, as, tho' not attended to at that time, were no slight prognostics of his future greatness. (Mainwaring)

Another story probably originating with Handel concerns a visit to his half-brother Karl, nearly thirty years older than himself and a *valet de chambre* at the local court. Mainwaring states that he was under seven at the time, but this is unlikely; a more probable date for the incident would be 1696, when the boy was eleven. It is not impossible that Handel himself exaggerated his youthfulness in later storytelling, and that Smith and Mainwaring simply recorded what they remembered.

When he was yet under seven years of age, he went with his father to the Duke of Saxe-Weisenfels . . . His father intended to have left him behind, and had actually set out without him. He thought one of his age a very improper companion when he was going to the court of a Prince, and to attend the duties of his profession. The boy finding all his solicitations ineffectual, had recourse to the only method which was left for the accomplishment of his wish. Having watched the time of his father's setting out, and concealed his intention from the rest of the family, he followed the chaise on foot. It was probably retarded by the roughness of the roads, or some other accident, for he overtook it before it had advanced to any considerable distance from the town. His father, greatly surprised at his courage, and somewhat displeased with his obstinacy, could hardly resolve what course to take. When he was asked, how he could think of the journey, after such a plain refusal had been given him; instead of answering the question, he renewed his intreaties in the most pressing manner, and pleaded in language too moving to be resisted. Being taken into the chaise, and carried to court, he discovered an unspeakable satisfaction at meeting with his brother above-mentioned, whom till then he had never seen.

Arrived at the court, Handel's instincts had free rein, rather to his father's displeasure:

In such a situation it was not easy to keep him from getting at harpsichords, and his father was too much engaged to watch him so closely there as he had done at home. He often mentioned to his friends, this uncontroulable humour of his son, which he told them he had taken great pains to subdue, but hitherto with little or no success. He said it was easy to foresee, that if it was not subdued very soon, it would preclude all improvements in the science for which he intended him, and wholly disconcert the plan that had been formed and agreed on for his education.

The reasonableness of such apprehensions every one admitted, in case it was determined to adhere to the scheme above-mentioned. But the prudence of adhering to it was doubted by many. It was observed with reason, that where Nature seemed to declare herself in so strong a manner, resistance was often not only fruitless, but pernicious. Some said, that, from all the accounts, the case appeared so desperate, that nothing but the cutting off his fingers could prevent his playing; and others affirmed, that it was a pity any thing *should* prevent it. Such were the sentiments and declarations of the Doctor's friends in regard to his son. It is not likely they would have had any great effect, but for the following incident, which gave their advice all the weight and authority it seems to have deserved.

It happened one morning, that while he was playing on the organ after the service was over, the Duke was in the church. Something there was in the manner of playing, which drew his attention so strongly, that his Highness, as soon as he returned, asked his valet de chambre who it was that he had heard at the organ, when the service was over. The valet replied, that it was his brother. The Duke demanded to see him.

After he had seen him, and made all the inquiries which it was natural for a man of taste and discernment to make on such an occasion, he told his physician, that every father must judge for himself in what manner to dispose of his children; but that, for his own part, he could not but consider it as a sort of crime against the public and posterity, to rob the world of such a rising Genius!

The old Doctor still retained his prepossessions in favour of the Civil Law. Though he was convinced it was almost become an act of necessity to yield to his son's inclinations (as it seemed an act of duty to yield to the Prince's advice and authority) yet it was not without the utmost reluctance that he brought himself to this resolution. He was sensible of the Prince's goodness in taking such notice of his son, and giving his opinion concerning the best method of education. But he begged leave humbly to represent to his Highness, that though Music was an elegant art, and a fine amusement, yet if considered as an occupation, it had little dignity, as having for its object nothing better than mere pleasure and entertainment: that whatever degree of eminence his son might arrive at in such a profession, he thought that a much less degree in many others would be far preferable.

The Prince could not agree with him in his notions of Music as a profession, which he said were much too low and disparaging, as great excellence in any kind entitled men to great honour. And as to profit, he observed how much more likely he would be to succeed, if suffered to pursue the path that Nature and Providence seemed to have marked out for him; than if he was forced into another track to which he had no such bias; nay, to which he had a direct aversion. He concluded with saying, that he was far from recommending the study of Music in exclusion of the Languages, or of the Civil Law, provided it was possible to reconcile them together: what he wished was, that all of them might have fair play; that no violence might be used, but the boy be left at liberty to follow the natural bent of his faculties, whatever that might be.

All this while he had kept his eyes stedfastly fixed on his powerful advocate; and his ears were as watchful and attentive to the impressions which the Prince's discourse made upon his father.

The issue of their debate was this: not only a toleration was obtained for Music, but consent for a master to be employed, who should forward and assist him in his advances on his return to Hall. At his departure from Weisenfels, the Prince fill'd his pockets with money, and told him, with a smile, that if he minded his studies, no encouragements should be wanting.

Mainwaring's account, our only source, is quoted at length since although the debate is protracted and verbose, it suggests that in telling the story Handel emphasized the balance of both arguments, and was anxious to show sympathy with his father's dilemma. Although he never experienced them directly, the crises of parenthood appear frequently in the texts of Handel's dramatic music and found a ready response in him.

Back in Halle, his father followed aristocratic advice and filial pressure, and arranged for Handel to have lessons from the energetic Friedrich Wilhelm Zachow, who was organist at the Liebfrauenkirche and directed the local 'chorus musicus' in performances every third Sunday. He was an excellent teacher, intent on giving his pupil a solid, but not doctrinaire, foundation. As Mainwaring says:

The first object of his attention was to ground him thoroughly in the principles of harmony. His next care was to cultivate his imagination, and form his taste. He had a large collection of Italian as well as German music: he shewed him the different styles of different nations; the excellences and defects of each particular author; and, that he might equally advance in the practical part, he frequently gave him subjects to work, and made him copy, and play, and compose in his stead.

One manuscript volume from these lessons stayed with Handel all his life; he in his turn used it for teaching the young J. C. Smith; it is described in the *Anecdotes of George Frederick Handel* (p. 6) as 'a book of manuscript music, dated 1698, and inscribed with the initial G. F. H.' William Coxe, or possibly Smith himself, continues that 'the notes are characterized by a peculiar manner of forming the crotchets' and concludes that the greater part is in Handel's autograph. The composers represented in the book are listed as Froberger, Krieger, Kerll, Alberti, [Wolfgang] Ebner, Delphin [or Nicolaus Adam?], Strungk and Zachow himself; the pieces are described as 'various airs, choruses, capricios, fugues and other pieces of music'. The volume passed from Smith to his daughter-in-law, Lady Rivers, and has been missing since the nineteenth century. Its rediscovery would fill a gap in our knowledge not only of the music Handel studied as a child, but also of the extent to which he later borrowed from this repertory. The technique of 'easy borrowing' which he applied throughout his life may have been learned from Zachow at an impressionable age.

With Zachow's encouragement and with Krieger's library at his disposal Handel had ample opportunity to lay by the seeds of many later compositions. Zachow for his part was proud of his pupil's growing fame, and glad of an

15

assistant 'whenever he had an inclination to be absent, as he often was, from his love of company, and a chearful glass' (Mainwaring). From this time, we are told, Handel was allowed to follow his love of music without inhibition; the credit for this must rest with his mother, for on 11 February 1697 his father had died. The tombstone on the family grave carried an account of his life, transcribed by Chrysander before the stone was destroyed in 1860, which notes that he lived to see twenty-eight grandchildren and two great-grandchildren. In line with German custom, the funeral sermon was printed as a memorial to the deceased together with a selection of poems of mourning by relatives. The final tribute is a conventional series of metaphors signed by 'George Friedrich Händel, der freien Künste ergebener' – 'dedicated to the liberal arts'. While the poem may have been 'bought in', the signature is a sure sign of the twelve-year-old's personal ambitions.

For the next stage in Handel's career Mainwaring's account is defective. A trip to Berlin, where he had 'a friend and relation' at court, is dated 1698, but the confrontation which he describes between the Elector and Handel's father could only have occurred at latest in early 1697. His mention of a meeting with the composers Giovanni Bononcini and Attilio Ariosti sets the date after Georg Händel's death, since Ariosti arrived in Berlin only later in 1697, and Bononcini not until 1702. Mainwaring's account may be a conflation of more than one visit; alternatively Handel may have met the two Italians during his time in Hamburg. The description of the relationship between Handel and Bononcini is certainly coloured by hindsight, and the story of testing the competence of the young boy is too similar to many other legends to pass without some suspicion.

> This person [Bononcini] was in high request for his compositions, probably the best which that court had known. But from his natural temper, he was easily elated with success, and apt to be intoxicated with admiration and applause. Though HANDEL was talk'd of as a most extraordinary player on the harpsichord for one so young, yet on account of his years he had always considered him as a mere child. But as people still persisted in their encomiums, it was his fancy to try the truth of them. For this end he composed a Cantata in the chromatic style, difficult in every respect, and such as even a master, he thought, would be puzzled to play, or accompany without some previous practice. When he found that he, whom he had regarded as a mere child, treated this formidable composition as a mere trifle, not only executing it at sight, but with a degree of accuracy, truth, and expression hardly to be expected even from repeated practice; – then indeed he began to see him in another light, and to talk of him in another tone.

Comparing dates does nothing to clarify Mainwaring's chronology, but until a new source of information is found we have no choice but to reallocate the incidents he relates to the years when they most probably occurred. The proposals of the Elector (whom Mainwaring terms a king) and the counter-proposals of Handel's friend can in any case give us a clear picture of the young composer's future:

PLATE I Thomas Hudson's 1756 portrait of Handel in old age and blind was commissioned by Charles Jennens. More monumental than the earlier portrait of 1747 (see front cover), it also features a score of *Messiah*.

II

... the little stranger had not been long at court before his abilities became known to the King, who frequently sent for him, and made him large presents. Indeed his Majesty, convinc'd of his singular endowments, and unwilling to lose the opportunity of patronizing so rare a genius, had conceived a design of cultivating it at his own expence. His intention was to send him to Italy, where he might be formed under the best masters, and have opportunities of hearing and seeing all that was excellent in the kind. As soon as it was intimated to HANDEL's friends (for he was yet too young to determine for himself) they deliberated what answer it would be proper to return, in case this scheme should be proposed in form. It was the opinion of many that his fortune was already made, and that his relations would certainly embrace such an offer with the utmost alacrity. Others, who better understood the temper and spirit of the court at Berlin, thought this a matter of nice speculation, and cautious debate. For they well knew, that if he once engag'd in the King's service, he must remain in it, whether he liked it, or not; that if he continued to please, it would be a reason for not parting with him; and that if he happened to displease, his ruin would be the certain consequence. To accept an offer of this nature, was the same thing as to enter into a formal engagement, but how to refuse it was still the difficulty. At length it was resolved that some excuse must be found. It was not long before the King caused his intentions to be signified, and the answer was, that the Doctor [Handel's father] would always retain the profoundest sense of the honour done to him by the notice which his Majesty had been graciously pleased to take of his son; but as he himself was now grown old, and could not expect to have him long with him, he humbly hoped the King would forgive his desire to decline the offer which had been made him by order of his Majesty.

I am not able to inform the reader how this answer was relished by the King, whom we may suppose not much accustomed to refusals, especially of this sort. Such an incident made it improper for HANDEL to stay much longer at the court of Berlin, where the more his abilities should be known and commended, the more some persons would be apt to sift and scrutinize the motives of his father's conduct.

This early experience of court patronage, with its ties and obligations to a single master, might go a long way towards explaining Handel's lifelong avoidance of court appointments.

Whether or not Handel's father was actually involved in this tussle, the boy returned to his studies in Halle, and for several years we have no further information on his progress. To organ, harpsichord and composition lessons was now added violin tuition, and he soon surpassed his master; this, Mainwaring says, was the period when 'he began to feel himself more, to be conscious of his own superiority'. Berlin had opened his eyes to wider horizons, yet for the moment he was persuaded, perhaps by his mother, to follow the career advocated by his father.

PLATE II   View of London: 'Entrance to the Fleet River'. School of Samuel Scott (c. 1750).
PLATE III   In 'The Levée' from *The Rake's Progress*, 1733–4, Hogarth attacks the purveyors of aristocratic and foreign culture exemplified by the French dancing master and the Handel-like composer at the harpsichord.

Handel's signature in the register of Halle University on his entry as a student.

On 10 February 1702, at the age of seventeen, Handel enrolled in the new university at Halle; he signs himself 'Georg Friedrich Händel Hall Magdeburg', and there is no mention of which faculty he is to join. It can hardly have mattered much, since as Mainwaring pointedly remarks: 'From the few facts just related it is easy to guess, that from the time of HANDEL's having a master in form, the Civil Law could have had no great share of his attention'.

A major musical distraction presented itself scarcely a month later, when the Cathedral of Halle was obliged to sack its disreputable organist, Johann Christoph Leporin. Handel, who had been called in to deputize for him in the past, was now offered the position of organist on a year's probation. The doubts of the Pastors and Elders must surely have been doctrinal, rather than musical; the Cathedral was Calvinist and Handel was Lutheran, but there was no other 'reformiertes Subject' available. His salary was 50 thalers for the year, plus free lodging, for which he was required '. . . to play the organ fittingly at Divine Service, and for this purpose to prelude on the prescribed Psalms and Spiritual Songs, and to have due care to whatever might be needful to the support of beautiful harmony, to take heed to this end, that he be always in Church in good time and before the pealing of the bells ceases, and no less to take good care of the preservation of the organ and whatever appertains to the same . . .' ('Appointment of the organist, Hendel', 13 March 1702, records of Halle Cathedral). This was the only traditional musical post that Handel ever held in Germany; he had charge of a fine two-manual instrument with exceptional wind-supply (according to Dreyhaupt the bellows could sustain 180 bars at a measured tempo without refilling), and he organized a choir.

Also connected with the Cathedral was a 'Hautboistenbande', a consort of oboes run by the Hyntzsch family, from whom Handel may well have acquired his love of that instrument. The set of six so-called 'oboe trio sonatas' which are fondly quoted as Handel's earliest compositions cannot be connected with him, nor with this period, nor even with the combination of two oboes, since the second part goes down to A, contains double stopping, and is clearly intended for violin. The anonymous pieces were brought to England by Lord Polwarth and presented by him to his flute teacher, Weidmann. When Weidmann showed them to Handel, Burney reports, he 'seemed to look at them with much pleasure, and laughing said, 'I used to write like the D———l in those days, but chiefly for the hautbois, which was my favourite instrument' (*Sketch of the Life of Handel*, 1795, p. 3n). Slight evidence of authenticity! The only piece of Handel's which bears any ascription to his early years of composing is a single trio sonata (later op. 2 no. 2), which is stated on Jennens's copy of Handel's manuscript as having been 'Composed at the Age of 14'.

Another and more potent musical diversion from this time was his friendship with Telemann. Four years older than Handel and, like him, a reluctant lawyer, 5 Telemann had been sent to study in Leipzig, some twenty miles from Halle. The Kantor at the Thomasschule in Leipzig at that time was Kuhnau, who had recently published the *Biblical Sonatas* for keyboard by which he is best known today, and a comic novel *Der musicalische Quack-Salber* (The Musical Charlatan) which both Handel and Telemann probably read. Telemann was irked by the old-fashioned style of Kuhnau's teaching, though he paid his master some tribute in his autobiographical sketch for Mattheson's *Grundlage einer Ehren-Pforte* (1740): 'the pen of the excellent Kuhnau served me for a model in fugue and counterpoint; but in fashioning subjects of melody, HANDEL and I were continually exercising our fancy, and reciprocally communicating our thoughts, both by letter and conversation, in the frequent visits we made to each other'. Telemann remembered Handel as being 'already of some importance even in those days', and the two remained friends all their lives: more than fifty years later Handel remembered to send Telemann a case of exotic plants for his collection. Telemann's greatest service to Handel was introducing him to the delights of opera, an entertainment unknown in Halle. Although nothing like as elaborate or as well funded as the opera of free Imperial cities such as Hamburg, Leipzig boasted a small house under the direction of Nicolaus Strungk, and the tireless Telemann became much involved in its activities. 'I composed many dramas', he wrote, 'not only for Leipsic, . . . but for Sorau, Frankfort, and the court of Weissenfels'.

The contact with opera was to prove instantly infectious for Handel. Halle was now too small for him, the university held no charms and his one-year contract with the Cathedral was due to expire. Allowing for Mainwaring's confused chronology, it is possible that another trip to Berlin occurred at this time, when he could reasonably have met Bononcini and Ariosti – though at the age of eighteen one would hardly expect to find him sitting on Ariosti's knee, as

6   Mainwaring relates. Handel's eventual destination was Hamburg, 'the Venice of the Elbe', a free and prosperous Hanseatic city with a public opera house controlled by the famous and dissolute Reinhard Keiser.

On what terms Handel arrived in Hamburg is not known; 'it was resolved', says Mainwaring, 'to send him thither on his own bottom, and chiefly with a view to improvement'. (Then follows a lengthy paragraph extolling Handel's freedom from exploitation, liberty of employment and, in the same breath, immunity to the charms of women.) A second source of documentation exists

4   for Handel at this period, in the account given by Johann Mattheson, a musician we might today describe as 'too clever by half'. Four years older than Handel, he was already established in Hamburg as composer, singer, actor, harpsichord player and writer. At nine he had been able to sing his own compositions to his own accompaniment on the organ in the local churches; at eighteen he had taken the title role in an opera of his own composition, *Die Plejades*. He later went on to be secretary to the English Resident [= consul], lawyer, diplomat, translator, Anglophile, and bore. At the age of twenty-two he struck up an immediate friendship with Handel.

Handel came to Hamburg in the summer of 1703, rich only in ability and goodwill. I was almost the first with whom he made acquaintance. I took him round to all the choirs and organs here, and introduced him to operas and concerts, particularly to a certain house [the English ambassador's?] where everything was given up to music. At first he played ripieno violin in the opera orchestra, and behaved as if he could not count to five, being naturally inclined to a dry humour. . . . But once when the harpsichord player failed to appear he allowed himself to be persuaded to take his place, and showed himself a man – a thing no one had before suspected, save I alone. At that time he composed very long, long airs, and really interminable cantatas, which had neither the right kind of skill nor of taste, though complete in harmony, but the lofty schooling of opera soon trimmed him into other fashions. He was strong at the organ, stronger than Kuhnau in fugue and counterpoint, especially *ex tempore*, but he knew very little about melody till he came to the Hamburg operas.   (*Grundlage einer Ehren-Pforte*)

Mattheson has a tendency to treat his public writing as though it were private correspondence; the stories he adds to prove Handel's dry sense of humour, for instance, give us a lively picture of the two youths, but can have meant very little to anyone other than the participants in 1740.

I know well enough that he will laugh heartily when he reads this, though as a rule he laughs but little. Especially if he remembers the pigeon-fancier, who travelled with us by the post to Lübeck, or the pastrycook's son who blew the bellows for us when we played in the Maria Magdalena Church here. That was 30 July, and on the 15th we had been for a water-party, and hundreds of similar incidents come back to me as I write.

Handel's journey to Lübeck in August 1703 foundered on the same condition as Bach's two years later – that the price for succeeding Buxtehude as organist at the Marienkirche was to marry his daughter. As Mattheson relates:

On 17 August in the same year we journeyed to Lübeck, and in the carriage made many double fugues *da mente non da penna*. I had been invited by Magnus von Wedderkopp, the president of the council, to compete for the post of successor to the renowned organist Dietrich Buxtehude, and I took Handel with me. We played on almost all the organs and harpsichords in the place, and made an agreement, which I have mentioned in another place, that he should only play the organ and I only the harpsichord. However, it turned out that there was some marriage condition proposed in connection with the appointment, for which we neither of us felt the smallest inclination, so we said goodbye to the place, after having enjoyed ourselves extremely, and received many gratifying tributes of respect.

One of the best introductions that Mattheson had made for Handel was to the English Resident in Hamburg, John Wyche, whose cellar had been praised by John Addison earlier in the year. Wyche's was a musical household, and Handel was employed for a while to give harpsichord lessons to the Ambassador's son, Cyril. This improved his financial position (he returned the money that his mother sent him), and, more important, it gave him a first opportunity of exploring an international milieu, and his first taste of the possibilities of becoming a European rather than a German musician.

Mattheson anticipated Handel's aspiration towards an international life, claiming: 'My inclination was always to England'. In 1704 he was en route and had reached Amsterdam when, as he says, 'I received on 21 March such an obliging and emphatic letter from *Händel* in Hamburg, that it moved me, principally, to make the journey back home again'. The portion of the letter he then quotes, the first we have from Handel, does little to explain the reasons for this about-turn: '. . . I wish very much to have the pleasure of seeing you and talking with you, and this is likely to be achieved soon, for the time is coming when nothing can be done at the Opera in your absence. I beg you respectfully to let me know when you leave, so that with Mlle Sbülens I may perform the pleasurable duty of meeting you . . .'. Perhaps Mlle Sbülens was at the bottom of it (her name occurs twice in later letters of Handel), or perhaps Handel's own plans for composing an opera demanded Mattheson's assistance: Mattheson claims that Handel 'used to bring me his first opera scene by scene, and every evening would take my opinion about it – and the trouble it cost him to conceal the pedant!'

Their friendship may have clouded slightly when Mattheson took up a position as tutor to Cyril Wyche, thus doing Handel out of a teaching job. Feelings darkened even more during the famous incident at the opera, recounted by Mattheson thirty-five years later:

On 5 December [1704] . . . when my third opera, *Cleopatra*, was being performed, with Handel at the harpsichord, a misunderstanding arose: such a thing is nothing new with young people who strive after honour with all their power and very little consideration. I, as composer, directed, and at the same time sang the part of *Antonius*, who, about half-an-hour before the end of the play, commits suicide. Now until that occasion I had been accustomed, after this action, to go into the orchestra and accompany the rest myself: which unquestionably the author can do better than anyone else; this time, however, Handel refused to give up his place. Incited by several people who were present, we fought a duel at the exit of the Opera House, in the open market place and with a crowd of onlookers. Things might have passed off very unfortunately for both of us, had God's guidance not graciously ordained that my blade, thrusting against the broad, metal coat-button of my opponent, should be shattered. No harm came of the affair, and through the intervention of one of the most eminent councillors in Hamburg, as well as of the manager of the Opera House, we were soon reconciled again; and I had the honour, on the same day, 30 December, of entertaining *Handel* to dinner after which we went in the evening to the rehearsal of his *Almira*, and became better friends than before.

Mainwaring makes a curious mélange of this story, getting Handel's age wrong again and adding confusion to what Handel probably recounted to Smith in his old age. In Mainwaring's version, Mattheson attacked the 'stripling' as he came out of the orchestra, with no warning and with the sword 'aimed full at his heart'. All would have been lost 'but for the friendly *Score*, which he accidentally carried in his bosom'. Mattheson was incensed when this interpretation reached his ears, and protested that in this version the duel had 'more the appearance of *assassination* than of a *rencounter*'. As for being taken unawares, Mattheson claims, his opponent was perfectly able to look after himself: 'HANDEL, at the time of the quarrel, was twenty years of age; tall, strong, broad-shouldered, and muscular; consequently, well able to defend himself . . . a dry slap on the face was no assassination, but rather a friendly hint, to put him on his guard'.

Probably neither side was blameless for the incident, but the peevish tone of Mattheson's history, which he claims was provoked by Handel's later reluctance to communicate with him and co-operate on his collection of biographies, sullies this first attempt to write Handel's life.

No Handel autographs survive from this period of his life, and yet we have his own word that he 'composed like the Devil'. Mainwaring, in a tone that suggests verbatim reporting of the composer's words, says: 'During his continuance at Hamburgh, he made a considerable number of Sonatas. But what became of these pieces he never could learn, having been so imprudent as to let them go out of his hands'. Speculation must fill the gap, with a limited amount of keyboard music ascribed to Handel both on stylistic evidence and on his own comment to J. W. Lustig that five keyboard pieces published by Witvogel in 1732 had been written 'in his early youth' (reported by Marpurg in *Kritische Briefe*, 1763). Several suites and partitas and two of his largest sets of chaconne variations, one designed for a two-manual harpsichord, can be assigned to Hamburg; many of them contain ideas refined and reused later, and a few of them may even date from Halle.*

In 1773 Burney picked up a manuscript in Hamburg which contained two cantatas attributed to Handel 'which I never saw elsewhere . . . One of these has a spirited accompaniment for the harpsichord, *obligato*' (*Sketch of the Life of Handel*, p.*7n), but there is no evidence that either of these compositions dated from Handel's time in Hamburg. Until recently a sonata for viola da gamba and obbligato harpsichord, containing an ingenious *arpeggiando* accompaniment to one movement fully written out, was thought to be Handel's; this ascription is now accepted as spurious, and the work was probably written by Johann Matthias Leffloth. Both the cantata 'Ach Herr, mich armer Sünder' and the setting of the St John Passion, for long described as Handel's earliest masterpiece, must also be deleted from the canon. The Passion setting to a text by Postel, first performed in Hamburg on Good Friday 1704, is now thought to be the work of Keiser, director of the opera house.

The development of opera in Germany had been seriously impeded by the financial losses of the Thirty Years War, which meant that smaller and private establishments such as those at Brunswick and Weissenfels had attempted to cultivate a native German style, without recourse to the expensive importation of grand singers from beyond the Alps. Only gradually were the specialist

---

*For a complete listing see Terence Best, 'Handel's harpsichord music', pp. 171 ff.

theatres established; first in Hamburg (1678), described by Berthold Feind in his *Deutsche Gedichte* (1708) as 'the most enterprising', followed by Hanover (1687), Brunswick (1690) and Leipzig (1692). It was to the north that the enterprising composers were drawn – Kusser, Strungk, Theile, Franck, Conradi, and eventually Keiser, who took over direction of the Hamburg house in 1696. By this time the ideal of a naturalized German opera had given way to a composite recipe whose three ingredients were German *lied*, Italian aria, and French dance. Each was played out in its own language: airs in Italian were connected by recitatives sung in German, while stage descriptions and balletic scenes were often in French. Many of the plots were heavily historical or mythological (Venetian libretti had a head start in this direction), with scenes of violence and spectacle emphasized for German taste and moderated by sub-plots of homely comedy. (Both the violence and the comic relief were also to the fore in productions of Shakespeare's plays given in Hamburg at this time by visiting English companies.)

In the course of some eighty operas Keiser, the most gifted opera composer in Germany, managed to impart conviction and individuality to this amalgam. By his own admission (in the *Avertissement* to *La fedeltà coronata*, 1706), he included the comic element for commercial reasons – Hamburg had no royal patronage and relied on middle-class support – but denied that this ever involved any concessions, as he put it, 'um den mauvais goût du Parterre'. Keiser was sensitive to the flow of the drama, and wary of the German partiality for elaboration and counterpoint. His use of instrumental colour for dramatic effect reflected the resources of the Hamburg Opera; in wind instruments in particular the Germans had the advantage over the Italians, and Keiser's scores show a strategic use of trumpets and horns, not merely for fanfares but as symbolic ingredients in an aria. Scorings for five bassoons (in *Octavia*) and five flutes (in *Orpheus*) reveal how extensive were the theatre's means.

In *Almira* Handel had a text typical of the most colourful Hamburg repertory. Partially adapted into German by Friedrich Christian Feustking from a Venetian libretto by Giulio Pancieri (already set to music in 1691 by Boniventi), its full title was *Der in Kronen erlangte Glückwechsel, oder: Almira, Königin von Kastilien* (The Vicissitudes of Royalty, or; Almira, Queen of Castile). The opera opens with the spectacle of a coronation, to a chorus with three trumpets and drums, followed by a ballet for the Spanish court to a chaconne and saraband. Act III includes another sequence of dances, for a masque of the continents: according to the libretto Europe, in Roman dress, is preceded by an oboe band, Africa is carried by twelve Moors to the sound of trumpets and drums, and Asia, with bow and arrows, is drawn by lions to an accompaniment of cymbals, side-drums and fifes. The 'Danse des Asiates', a saraband, became one of Handel's most famous melodies when he reused it six years later, with some alterations, as 'Lascia ch'io pianga', Almira's aria in *Rinaldo*. (It had meanwhile done duty as 'Lascia la spina' in *Il Trionfo del Tempo* of 1707). The distinctive rhythm of the saraband and something of its melodic contours can also be found in a minor-key version in Act I, where it serves as an instrumental dance. This formula, together with two distinctive cadence figures which occur

26

frequently in *Almira* but disappear almost completely from Handel's music after 1710, can reasonably be looked on as Hamburg characteristics, and help in the allocating of undated (keyboard) music to this same time, as well as indicating when Handel may have borrowed earlier material in his later works.*

Almira opened on 8 January 1705 with an epilogue, *The Genius of Europe*, supplied by Keiser. Mattheson sang the principal tenor part (presumably that of Fernando), and the opera ran for some twenty nights. (Mainwaring's claims that the opera ran for 'thirty nights' and that its composer was 'not much above fourteen' are false.) While the music was successful, there appears to have been some criticism of Feustking's libretto, to judge from the tone of a pamphlet he issued in reply, in which Handel's name is mentioned for the first time publicly in print. 'To censure Almira, which receives *approbation* from reasonable people as much for its verses as for the artistic music by Herr Hendel, and up to the present is honoured with such approbation, is a sign of *malicious* unreasonableness or unreasonable *malice*' (*Der Wegen der 'Almira' Abgestriegelte Hostilius* [Hostilius given a dressing-down on account of 'Almira'], Hamburg, 1705).

Handel, alive to the main chance, immediately pursued his first stage success with another opera, again with a book by Feustking: *Die durch Blut und Mord erlangte Liebe, oder: Nero* (Love obtained by Blood and Murder, or: Nero). The music to this, and to Handel's next Hamburg opera, is lost, but from the extant libretto we find that the cast was even larger than in *Almira* and a high proportion of ballet was included; dances for Combatants or Fencers, Priests, Harlequins and Pulcinelles, Murderers, Cavaliers and Ladies. *Nero* was first performed on 25 February, but had no more than three performances. This time Handel himself is thought to have voiced the complaint about the quality of the libretto, which appeared the same year in Hunold's *Theatralische, Galante und Geistliche Gedichte* (Dramatic, Elegant and spiritual Poems): 'How is a musician to create anything beautiful if he has no beautiful words? Therefore, in the case of the composition of the *Opera Nero*, someone has not unjustly complained: There is no spirit in the *verse*, and one feels vexation in setting such to *music*'.

This history of *Almira* is inextricably bound up with Keiser's fortunes as manager of the opera at Hamburg. Handel's chance to compose *Almira* came because Keiser (as Mainwaring indicates) left Hamburg for Weissenfels in the spring of 1704 to escape his creditors. He was then no longer manager of the opera and his partner, Drusike, gave Handel the libretto to set. Keiser had already set the libretto once and although his original setting was never performed, he composed a revised version for Weissenfels and published the arias of the first two acts of his original setting in his *Componimenti musicali*. There is some reason to think Keiser was resentful of Handel when he returned to Hamburg in August 1705; Handel however remained indebted to Keiser for the remainder of his life.

---

ibid.

The debt was recognized even during his lifetime by Johann Scheibe, who in his *Critischer Musikus* (2nd edition, Leipzig, 1745) noted that 'Händel, although many times developing not his own thoughts but those of others, especially the inventions of *Reinhard Kaiser*, has manifested all the time a great understanding and a powerful deliberation . . .'. With the publication of Keiser's *Octavia* in 1902 as a supplementary volume to Chrysander's projected Handel complete edition, the extent of Handel's borrowing from that one opera was revealed – the germ of 'Comfort ye my people', for instance, can be detected there. More recent work shows that Handel kept copies of, and quarried from, many more Keiser operas. Even so typically Handelian a number as 'O ruddier than the cherry' stems almost note for note from an ostinato bass in Keiser's *Janus*.

In 1706 Handel set to work on a libretto supplied by Hinrich Hinsch. Again the music is lost, but some confirmation of Mattheson's complaint that Handel was too long-winded is contained in the preface that accompanied the libretto when the work was eventually performed in 1708:

> Since the admirable *music* with which this *Opera* is adorned has turned out to be rather long, and might put the audience out of humour, it has been considered necessary to arrange the complete work in two parts, of which the *first* presents the feast *Pythia*, arranged to the honour of *Apollo*, and occurring on the same day, the betrothal of *Florindo* with *Daphne*; it receives, therefore, on account of this prominent part of the plot, the name *Happy* FLORINDO. *The second part* will represent the stubbornness of *Daphne* against the love of *Phoebus*, and also the repugnance she feels for all love, and finally her transformation into a laurel-tree, and hence it will receive the name *Transformed* DAPHNE. (Preface to *Florindo*, January 1708)

It is likely that some of the music from the lost Hamburg operas would have been recycled by Handel, and some of the pieces now in an Aylesford volume in the British Library have putatively been connected with certain numbers in *Florindo* and *Daphne*.[*]

By 1706, however, with the public demanding comedies on the one side and the Pietists a purge of all theatre on the other, the future of opera in Hamburg was becoming unstable. Because of administrative problems and Keiser's general dissipation, and despite the success of *Almira*, the lease of the Hamburg theatre was eventually handed over to J. H. Saurbrey in 1707, and Keiser left for employment in smaller Holstein households. For Handel, working with Keiser was his first experience of the vicissitudes that attend the life of manager–impresario–composer and one that plainly did not deter him. Mattheson, having taken the title role in *Nero* 'amid general applause' (on his own estimation), had left the theatre 'to consider something more solid and lasting', and had become tutor and Hofmeister, and eventually secretary, to

---

[*]See Bernd Baselt, 'Wiederentdeckung'.

Sir John Wyche. Handel, after flexing his wings in the theatre, left Hamburg for the only destination a fledgling opera composer could contemplate. By the time the prolix *Florindo* and *Daphne* were holding the boards in January 1708, in company with a local farce called *Die lustige Hochzeit*, Handel was well established in the far south.

2

The Italian Years
1706–1710

Handel, non può mia Musa
Cantare in un istante
Versi che degni sian della tua lira,

My Muse, O Handel, is not so wise
Thus instantly to improvise
Verse worthy of thy Muse's art,

> From a poem by Cardinal Pamphili
> in praise of Handel (and set to music
> by the composer)

There is certainly no Place in the World where a Man may travel with greater Pleasure and Advantage than in Italy. One finds something more particular in the Face of the Country, and more astonishing in the Works of Nature, than can be met with in any other Part of Europe. It is the great School of Musick and Painting, and contains in it all the noblest Productions of Statuary and Architecture both Ancient and Modern. It abounds with Cabinets of Curiosities, and vast Collections of all kinds of Antiquities. No other Country in the World has such a Variety of Governments, that are so different in their Constitutions, and so refined in their Politicks. There is scarce any Part of the Nation that is not Famous in History, nor so much as a Mountain or River that has not been the Scene of some extraordinary Action.

Joseph Addison's preface to the account of his travels in Italy,* undertaken some three years before Handel's visit, gives the standard motivation of every connoisseur who felt the obligation to look south. As far as the arts were concerned, all northern capitals, except Paris, would readily have confessed themselves satellites of Italy and concurred with Dr Johnson that 'a man who has not been in Italy is always conscious of an inferiority, from his not having seen what it is expected a man should see. The grand object of travelling is to see the shores of the Mediterranean'.

---

*Remarks on Several Parts of Italy &c. (1705).

Handel at first seems to have been a reluctant traveller, if we can trust Mainwaring's account of his conversations with Prince Ferdinand de' Medici of Florence, who was staying in Hamburg at the same time Handel was there. Mainwaring's story gives a picture of an arrogant, enthusiastic young German prodigy, not yet twenty-one, tactfully put down by a worldly Italian patron:

> The Prince was a great lover of the art for which his country is so renowned. Handel's proficiency in it, not only procured him access to his Highness, but occasioned a sort of intimacy betwixt them: they frequently discoursed together on the state of Music in general, and on the merits of Composers, Singers, and Performers in particular. The Prince would often lament that Handel was not acquainted with those of Italy; shewed him a large collection of Italian Music; and was very desirous he should return with him to Florence. Handel plainly confessed that he could see nothing in the Music which answered the high character his Highness had given it. On the contrary, he thought it so very indifferent, that the Singers, he said, must be angels to recommend it. The Prince smiled at the severity of his censure, and added, that there needed nothing but a journey to Italy to reconcile him to the style and taste which prevailed there. He assured him that there was no country in which a young proficient could spend his time to so much advantage; or in which every branch of his profession was cultivated with so much care. Handel replied, that if this were so, he was much at a loss to conceive how such great culture should be followed by so little fruit. However, what his Highness had told him, and what he had before heard of the fame of the Italians, would certainly induce him to undertake the journey he had been pleased to recommend, the moment it should be convenient. The Prince then intimated, that if he chose to return with him, no conveniences should be wanting. Handel, without intending to accept of the favour designed him, expressed his sense of the honour done him. For he resolved to go to Italy on his own bottom, as soon as he could make a purse for that occasion. This noble spirit of independency, which possessed him almost from his childhood, was never known to forsake him, not even in the most distressful seasons of his life.

Mattheson, in his embittered style, simply states that 'the opportunity arose of setting out on a free journey to Italy with *Binitz*' – an unknown companion ennobled by later biographers to 'von Binitz' and presented as Handel's patron. This misconception may be discounted in favour of Mainwaring's more convincing version – that Handel managed to save 200 ducats while still sending remittances from time to time to his mother: the sort of circumstantial detail that surely only Handel could have passed on.

Until recently, Handel's itinerary in Italy has been obscure; in twenty pages of fact and fable Mainwaring garbles the chronology so that no coherent picture of Handel's musical development can be deduced. Discoveries made in the archives of the Ruspoli family, notably the household accounts of Handel's main Roman patron the Marchese Francesco Ruspoli, and the manuscripts and

31

autographs in his library, now make it possible to reconstruct a chronology (albeit with gaps) covering the period between the productions of *Almira* and *Nero* in 1705 and *Agrippina* in Venice in 1709–10. Many of the new details emerge from the listings of fees paid to copyists who produced material for Ruspoli's weekly concerts. From these dated payments, which usually mention either the title or the scoring of the work copied, it is possible to deduce the patterns of Handel's employment and his travels within Italy.

His first stop is undocumented, but there seems every likelihood that in the autumn of 1706 he travelled to Florence, as Mainwaring states, on the invitation of Ferdinand de' Medici. Ferdinand was himself an accomplished musician – it was said that he could sightread a difficult harpsichord sonata and immediately afterwards play it from memory – and if we hear nothing more about the young Handel for a while, it could well be that the Prince's daily concerts and his library of 390 volumes of music (now lost) sufficiently claimed his attention.

His arrival in Rome can be dated from an entry in the diary of Valesio for 14 January 1707: 'A German ['Sassone'] has arrived in this city who is an excellent player of the harpsichord and composer. Today he exhibited his prowess by playing the organ in the church of St John [Lateran] to the admiration of everybody.'

Handel's first patrons were the leading men of the Church; of the Cardinals Colonna, Pamphili and Ottoboni mentioned by Mainwaring, the last was the most wealthy and active though hardly the most clerical in character. The French diplomat de Brosses remembers him as being *'sans moeur, sans crédit, débauché, ruiné, amateur des arts, grand musicien'*, while de Blainville records: 'His Eminence keeps in his Pay, the best Musicians and Performers in Rome, and amongst others, the famous Archangelo Corelli, and young Paolucci, who is reckoned the finest Voice in Europe; so that every Wednesday he has an excellent Concert in his Palace. . .'.*

7

Corelli had been resident in Ottoboni's 'Palazzo della Cancelleria' since 1690 as director of these weekly concerts and his presence there undoubtedly influenced Handel's development.† Handel's writing for the violin (in the accompanied cantatas and *La Resurrezione* for example) now shows the influence of Corelli's playing and is, interestingly, more extrovert than anything in Corelli's own published violin sonatas. Although the most crucial development in Handel's composing during his time in Italy was primarily a refining and softening of his vocal style, his experiments with string sonorities, particularly their use for dramatic ends, were also seminal.

It was at one of Ottoboni's gatherings that Mainwaring placed the famous meeting between Handel and Domenico Scarlatti – two of the world's greatest keyboard virtuosi, born in the same year.

As he was an exquisite player on the harpsichord, the Cardinal was resolved

---

Travels through Holland . . . (Eng. trans., London, 1743–5).
†The Ottoboni household accounts from this period, which could tell us so much, have yet to be located.

to bring him and HANDEL together for a trial of skill. The issue of the trial on the harpsichord hath been differently reported. It has been said that some gave the preference to SCARLATTI. However, when they came to the Organ there was not the least pretence for doubting to which of them it belonged. SCARLATTI himself declared the superiority of his antagonist, and owned ingenuously, that till he had heard him upon this instrument, he had no conception of its powers. So greatly was he struck with his peculiar method of playing, that he followed him all over Italy, and was never so happy as when he was with him. . . .

Though no two persons ever arrived at such perfection on their respective instruments, yet it is remarkable that there was a total difference in their manner. The characteristic excellence of SCARLATTI seems to have consisted in a certain elegance and delicacy of expression. HANDEL had an uncommon brilliancy and command of finger: but what distinguished him from all other players who possessed these same qualities, was that amazing fulness, force, and energy, which he joined with them. And this observation may be applied with as much justness to his compositions, as to his playing.

One of Handel's first major Roman compositions (for which a copyist's bill was paid on 14 May 1707) was the oratorio *Il trionfo del Tempo e del Disinganno* (The Triumph of Time and Truth) to a text by Cardinal Pamphili and presumably performed in his own palace. Since there was a papal ban on the production of opera in Rome, resulting from a carnival scandal in 1677, the princely establishments of the city vied with each other in the elaborate staging of cantatas and oratorios that were operas in all but name. Leading singers and players took part, but there was no acting. The orchestra for *Il trionfo* was led by Corelli, who, according to Mainwaring, had some difficulty in playing Handel's French-style overture.

Indeed there was in the whole cast of these compositions, but especially in the opening of them, such a degree of fire and force, as never could consort with the mild graces, and placid elegancies of a genius so totally dissimilar. Several fruitless attempts HANDEL had one day made to instruct him in the manner of executing these spirited passages. Piqued at the tameness with which he still played them, he snatches the instrument out of his hand; and, to convince him how little he understood them, played the passages himself. But CORELLI, who was a person of great modesty and meekness, wanted no conviction of this sort; for he ingenuously declared that he did not understand them; *i.e.* knew not how to execute them properly, and give them the strength and expression they required. When HANDEL appeared impatient, *Ma, caro Sassone* (said he) *questa Musica è nel stylo Francese, di ch' io non m' intendo* [But my dear Saxon, this music is in the French style, which I do not understand].*
*The Overture for IL TRIONFO DEL TEMPO was that which occasioned CORELLI the greatest difficulty. At his desire therefore he made a symphony in the room of it, more in the Italian style.

Mainwaring's story, together with his footnote to the effect that Handel eventually replaced the overture with a 'symphony . . . more in the Italian style', cannot easily be dismissed as myth. An overture in B flat (which appeared in a collection of Handel overtures in 1758) contains passagework peculiar to Handel's compositions of this year, and uses the same fugal theme as the sinfonia we know today. Its standard French-style opening makes it plausibly the very piece to which Corelli objected.

The allegorical story of Truth and Time tempted by Beauty and Pleasure excited Handel less than the large orchestra of virtuosi available to him, and elaborate solo passages are worked in for violin, viola, cello, oboes and for solo organ (in a sonata interrupted by Bellezza's 'Taci, qual suono ascolto' [Hush! What sounds do I hear?]). The famous sarabande from *Almira* also turns up in its first vocal form, 'Lascia la spina'.

Handel's more strictly liturgical works began with the dramatic splendour of *Dixit Dominus*, composed in April, and it has been suggested that they culminated in a collection of seven settings for the celebrations on the Feast of Our Lady of Mount Carmel on 16 July.* Handel's easy absorption of the emotionally charged Italian church style is remarkable; to effectively continue, rather than merely imitate, the expressionism of Carissimi and Stradella argues a rapidity of musical digestion that we associate with Mozart. But any suggestion from his patrons that he might give up his Lutheran faith was met with a characteristic stubbornness.†

Being pressed very closely on this article by one of these exalted Ecclesiastics, he replied, that he was neither qualified, nor disposed to enter into enquiries of this sort, but was resolved to die a member of that communion, whether true or false, in which he was born and bred. No hopes appearing of a real conversion, the next attempt was to win him over to outward conformity. But neither arguments, nor offers had any effect, unless it were that of confirming him still more in the principles of protestantism. (Mainwaring)

As a refuge from religious pressures, Handel had as his most regular patron in Rome the secular prince Francesco Maria Ruspoli. A series of documents from the Fondo Ruspoli (now held in the Archivio Segreto Vaticano) informs us of Handel's activities during most of 1707 and 1708, outlines the Marchese's arrangements for weekly concerts in the Palazzo Bonelli (he did not move to the present Palazzo Ruspoli in via del Corso until 1713), and enables us to date many compositions. (Although Handel's name is rarely mentioned in the documents, the copyist Angelini normally included the first words of works with his account.)

---

*Recently discovered manuscript partbooks confirm a connection between five of the Latin settings and the Carmelite feast; if normal liturgical practice was being followed, however, the performances would have been spread over two or three services (but see p. 278).
†Could this stubbornness be the 'malizzia' mentioned by Mannucci (see p. 44)?

PLATE IV   The building erected in Green Park for the firework display to celebrate the Treaty of Aix-la-Chapelle, 1749.
PLATE V   *The Rehearsal of an Opera*, attributed to Marco Ricci (1676–1729). The figure standing in the centre directing the proceedings is possibly intended to be Nicolini, singing a duet with Mrs Katherine Tofts.

Ruspoli had no regular *Maestro di capella* until Caldara was appointed in 1709. Handel's employment was on a 'regulated' basis (similar to the congenial arrangement he was to enjoy later in England with Burlington and Chandos): he was resident in Ruspoli's palace for specified periods with an obligation, as Mainwaring puts it, 'to furnish his quota' of vocal works. Since there are no records of a salary being paid to him, his household position was probably somewhere between a protégé and a favoured guest.

Judging from slightly later documents, the routine seems to have included a weekly *conversazione*, held every Sunday during the late afternoon and evening. The small number of house musicians would perform cantatas with continuo accompaniment only, and outside players would be hired for the *cantate con stromenti*; they were paid at the rate of one *scudo* per performance ('funtione'), and half a *scudo* (50 *baiocchi*) for a rehearsal ('prova'). When the Marchese moved to his *castello* at Vignanello during May and June 1707, the accounts show not only the transfer of his whole household (cooks, huntsmen and musicians), but also payment 'al Cimbolaro per accomodatura del Cimbolo per Vignanello' ('for the transport of a harpsichord'), and the copying of an appropriate new cantata 'della caccia', *Diana Cacciatrice*. Back in Rome, the pattern of weekly cantatas in Italian was broken by payments for a 'Cantata francese' (*Sans y penser*) and the curious 'Cantata Spagnuola' *No se emenderá jamás*, written in archaically long notes and with guitar accompaniment. In both cases, it is interesting to note, Handel took the precaution of writing the foreign text himself into the performing copy, obviously not trusting the house copyist. From an adjacent payment we see that the famous soprano Margarita Durastante, with whom Handel was to be associated for many years, was expected to sing in both languages.

The first break in Handel's period of residence with Ruspoli came in the autumn of 1707, when he returned to Florence for the production of his first Italian opera *Rodrigo*. How this had been arranged, when and where Handel received the libretto, and who sang in the production are still open questions. The Florentine libretto, recently discovered by Reinhard Strohm, shows that the piece was performed under the patronage of Prince Ferdinand, at the theatre in via del Cocomero, rather than at a private performance in the Pitti Palace as had previously been suggested. The overture (the opening of which was borrowed from *Almira*) and succeeding dances, which could equally well have been written during Handel's Hamburg days, eventually made their way to England before him, and shorn of the concluding Passacaille were used as incidental music to a London revival of Ben Jonson's *The Alchemist* in 1710. From Mainwaring's apologetic tone one can deduce that Handel was unhappy with the stilted characterization of the libretto and with his own musical contribution, but with typical economy he used much of the remaining music in later operas. For the Florentine performance, Handel was presented with 100 *sequins* and a silver (or porcelain) dinner service, which, says Mainwaring, 'may serve for a sufficient testimony of its favourable reception'. (Handel received several such cumbersome rewards over the course of three years travelling in Italy, and brought at least one home with him to present to his mother.)

PLATE VI Portrait of Handel attributed to Balthasar Denner, 1726–8, showing the composer in his prime. Apparently the picture passed to J. C. Smith the younger who in turn left it in his will to William Coxe, the early chronicler of Handel's life.

The problems of being an 'Italian' composer are highlighted by Robert Price, the writer of the *Observations on the Works of George Frederic Handel* that accompany Mainwaring's *Memoirs*. Although the *Observations* reflect a later critical aesthetic, Price nevertheless describes conditions very similar to those that faced Handel on his entry into the theatre.

The Italian Composers have two things strongly against them, and which I conceive to be the cause of all the trifling, frothy Music we have at this time. The one is, the little time they have for composing. For as soon as any rising genius has given some striking proof of his abilities, the Managers of almost every Opera in Italy, want to engage him to compose for them. The young fellow thinks his reputation is established, and endeavours to make the most of it, by undertaking to compose as much as it is possible to do in the time. This obliges him to write down any thing that first presents itself: and thus his Opera is chiefly made up of old worn-out passages hastily put together, without any new turn of expression, or harmony. . . . The other difficulty the Italian Opera-composers have to struggle with, is the undue influence of the Singers over them. A good Singer (which is equally applicable to both the sexes) seldom fails to make such a party in his favour, as it would not be prudent in the Composer to disoblige. This in some degree puts him under the Singer's direction in relation to his own Songs; which is in fact the being directed in his compositions by a person that knows very little of Music, and that wants to shine by playing all the tricks he has been able either to invent or to learn.

Throughout his career, Handel himself could hardly be called blameless when it came to making a new opera hastily from 'old passages' – in fact he was almost more involved in travelling with the nicely termed 'arie di bagaglio' ('baggage arias', singers' favourite pieces which travelled around with them) than his most complacent prima donnas. The second difficulty seems to have been circumvented on this occasion by an apparent romance with his leading lady. Mainwaring tells the story with tact:

VITTORIA, who was much admired both as an Actress, and a Singer, bore a principal part in this Opera. She was a fine woman, and had for some time been much in the good graces of his Serene Highness. But, from the natural restlessness of certain hearts, so little sensible was she of her exalted situation, that she conceived a design of transferring her affections to another person. HANDEL's youth and comeliness, joined with his fame and abilities in Music, had made impressions on her heart.

Vittoria Tarquini, familiarly known as 'la Bombace', was one of Ferdinand's favourite singers, and it seems unlikely that Handel would have engaged with her on any other than professional terms. Further doubt is cast on Mainwaring's story by the fact that her name does not appear on the cast list printed in the libretto. But the rumour revives with the recent discovery by

Anthony Hicks of a letter written in 1710 by the Electress Sophia of Hanover, referring to Handel as 'a good-looking man and the talk is that he was the lover of Victoria . . .'.

A bill of 26 February 1708 for the copying of a cantata indicates that Handel was once more in Rome and resident with Ruspoli. His main commission for this period, probably reflecting the success of *Rodrigo*, was the nearest thing to a full-scale opera that Rome was allowed to offer. *La Resurrezione*, Handel's first sacred oratorio and the most elaborate and expensive of all the entertainments that Ruspoli presented, was to be given on Easter Sunday. The ostentation was partly to attract the favours of Pope Clement XI, who was a lover of oratorio, and partly to compete with, or to complement, Alessandro Scarlatti's *Passione* which Cardinal Ottoboni had scheduled for the Wednesday of Holy Week. Preparations for the Marchese's spectacular were made well in advance: Handel was resident at least seven weeks before, allowing ample time for composition and revision (as evidenced by the conducting score, identified in 1960 in the Santini Collection*), and he was allowed the unusual luxury of three rehearsals, the first a full week before Easter. Durastante was to lead the team of five solo voices, and there was to be a repeat performance the following day, Easter Monday.

The staging and decorations were also to be more impressive than any previous spectacle, as the following paraphrase† of original documents shows:

A stage was prepared in the *Stanzione delle Accademie*, on the first floor of the Marchese's Palazzo, but as the audience threatened to be too large, was transferred to the main hall on the ground floor. Here was built a 'teatro a scalinata', a series of four terraced rows of seats for the orchestra, just over 12 m wide, slightly curved towards the audience and rising to the back wall. Between the orchestra and the audience was a barrier with a raised podium in the middle for the 'Concertini de' Violini' (the leader and his second violin), and perhaps for Handel also with his harpsichord. Twenty-eight music stands were built, the desks and legs in the shape of fluted cornucopiae, half to be painted with the coat of arms of the Marchese, half with that of his wife, all in gold *chiaroscuro*. Three rows of the orchestral seats were also to be painted yellow. Above the proscenium was hung a long cartoon from one side of the hall to the other, decorated with cherubs, palm trees and foliage in yellow and crimson *chiaroscuro*, and in the middle a plaque with the title of the oratorio on it – forty-six letters on four lines, each letter about 18 cm [7 in.] high; these letters, cut out and backed with transparent paper, were lit from behind with seventy light pans. Damask, crimson, yellow and red velvet with taffeta and velvet rosettes engulfed the decorative arch, and a taffeta curtain, worked by seven wooden pulleys, concealed the stage. The whole 'church or hall', lavishly decorated with red and yellow taffeta and velvet trimmed with gold, was lit by sixteen candelabra. The pièce de résistance of the decorators' art was the painted canvas

---

*See R. Ewerhart, 'Die Händel-Handschriften'.
†Derived from 'The Ruspoli Documents on Handel' by Ursula Kirkendale, which contains a transcription of the bill of the carpenter, Crespineo Pavone, itemizing the work.

backdrop, nearly 4 m square, representing the *dramatis personae* of Handel's oratorio. Within the square was a round frame in yellow *chiaroscuro*; in the four corners were smaller square frames in similar colouring containing the Ruspoli coat of arms. At the centre, painted 'al naturale', was depicted the resurrection of our Lord with a 'gloria' of *putti* and cherubim, the angel sitting on the tomb announcing the resurrection to Mary Magdalene and Mary Cleophas, with John the Evangelist by a mountain, and demons plunging into an abyss.

To complement this visual feast, a mammoth orchestra was engaged, led from the podium by Corelli. From the list of payments, and remembering that the players mentioned were employed *in addition* to Ruspoli's house musicians, we can reconstruct the exact proportions of the ensemble: 23 *violini* (including Corelli), 4 *violette*, 6 *violoni*, 6 *contrabassi*, 1 bass viol, 2 trumpets, 1 trombone and 4 oboes. A number of the back-desk *violini*, *violoni* and *contrabassi* attended only two rehearsals, suggesting that a reduced string group was used in some numbers. Corelli was paid by separate contract (20 *scudi* as opposed to the maximum orchestral rate of 4.50) and the copyist Angelini was reimbursed 30 *scudi* for copying 300 *fogli* (2400 pages), including a full score of each act for Corelli. Only Handel's name is nowhere to be found in the accounts; we have no evidence what (or even whether) he was paid for the composing of the oratorio that marks the summit of his Italian development.

8   The work treats the events between Good Friday and Easter Sunday on two levels. In agitated recitative and brilliant (sometimes almost comic) arias, Lucifer and an Angel dispute Christ's power of redeeming the souls of mortals in Hell. Mary Magdalene (sung by Durastante), Mary Cleophas and St John the Evangelist lament the events on Earth and then move from despondency to joyful elation as the resurrection is announced.

For the characterization of mortal passions, Handel uses his large forces with great aptness and control. Mary Magdalene's lament at the entrance to the tomb opens with solo viola da gamba and violin, to which Handel adds the eerie sonority of a single melodic line played by 'tutti flauti e un oboe sordo' (all the recorders and a muted oboe). St John's 'simile' aria of the dove pursued by hawks is a Largo in *siciliano* rhythm with flute, gamba and theorbo, interrupted by violent predatory scales from the entire body of strings (Handel may have had doubts about this device, since the scales are cancelled in the conducting score). Mary Magdalene's light, affectionate aria 'Ho un non so che nel cor', which became an immediate hit, reappears in several later operas, and was sung as a street ballad in England; it consists of nothing but a vocal melody, doubled at the unison by violins.

With the simplest scoring Handel keeps a sense of advancing drama. St John's description of the sunrise that opens the second part (after an orchestral *Introduzione* found only in the conducting score) is accompanied by a rising ostinato for continuo alone; his grief-laden 'Quando è parto dell'affetto' features a solo viola da gamba, a sonority reminiscent of the aria 'Es ist vollbracht' in Bach's St John Passion. When mortal and immortal worlds meet, the Angel announces the resurrection in recitative and addresses the weeping Marys in the lightest of continuo-arias with dancing coloratura. It is answered by an equally buoyant and light-headed aria, in varying metres, from Mary Magdalene. The delicacy of Handel's dramatic control is impeccable in these transitions, and his portrayal of real human reactions, as opposed to Biblical formulae, transmits emotion rather than observing and mirroring it.

Sadly, in this wealth of documentation there is only a small entry in Valesio's diary for Easter Sunday recounting the actual event: 'This evening the Marchese Ruspoli had a very fine musical oratorio performed in the Bonelli palace at the SS Apostoli, having set up in the great hall a well-appointed theatre for the audience. Many of the nobility and a few cardinals were present.'

Only one hitch seems to have marred the magnificence of La Resurrezione: after the first performance the Pope issued an admonition to Ruspoli 'for having used a female singer in the oratorio of the previous evening'. For the second performance it seems that Durastante was replaced by one 'Filippo' in deference to papal prejudice.

Before the end of the month, Handel left the Ruspoli household again. Bills for 'the return of the Jew's bed hired for Monsù Endel' were paid on 30 April, together with the account of Ruspoli's dispensatore for food 'per Monsù Endel e Comp:ᵒ' – an alarming 38.75 scudi, which compared with a prima donna's salary of 20 scudi or the annual 10 scudi for the bassist would seem to lend substance to the tales of Handel's gargantuan appetite. But 'Comp:ᵒ' may be more than 'companion', and Handel could well have been entertaining the entire company.

> HANDEL, with many virtues, was addicted to no vice that was injurious to society. Nature, indeed, required a great supply of sustenance to support so huge a mass, and he was rather epicurean in the choice of it; but this seems to have been the only appetite he allowed himself to gratify.
>
> (Charles Burney, 1785)

His next stop was Naples, where he produced a cantata and the serenata Aci, Galatea e Polifemo at the house of the Duke of Alvito (both autographs are dated). Again, the occasion was not right for a full opera, although they were legal and flourishing in Naples, and Handel's one-act pastoral setting of the mythological tale was the nearest he could achieve within the commission for a marriage celebration.* The story is shared with his later masque Acis and Galatea, but the music is totally different – a rare instance of Handel not reusing material. The role of Polifemo calls for a bass of prodigious range, who in 'Fra l'ombre e gl'orrori' is asked to negotiate jumps of two and a half octaves from top A to bottom D. Neither the horror of the giant's demands, nor the emotional response between the two lovers is as subtly conveyed as in the later masque, but individual dramatic moments have great beauty, in particular Aci's death and Galatea's first lament 'Sforzano a piangere', with its yearning chromaticism set against an accompaniment in six parts – an earnestly Teutonic

---

*Mainwaring misremembered the occasion, and attempted to implicate another affair in with it, this time with a Donna Laura who commissioned the work.

touch. Most dramatically apt are the trio 'Proverà lo sdegno', with all three characters carefully distinguished, and the love duet 'Dolce, caro' which is interrupted by indignant recitative from Polifemo. Although there is no evidence that the piece was intended for staging, such encounters have a theatrical quality the more remarkable since Handel had had small opportunity prior to this commission of experimenting with such forces. *Clori, Tirsi e Fileno*, the most impressively operatic of the cantatas, datable to 1707, is the only real precedent.

In pastoral convention, on the other hand, he was by this time totally at home. The formal properties of 'Arcadia' to which all his Roman patrons subscribed had been self-consciously realized at the end of the previous century in the literary Accademia degli Arcadi, a private club of noblemen and artists with the avowed aim of rescuing Italian poetry from involved, artificial mannerism and restoring it to simplicity and naturalness. Their fiction of the Golden Age included all the members of the group as 'shepherds', each under an appropriate pseudonym: amongst the musicians were Arcimelo (Corelli), Terpando (Alessandro Scarlatti) and Protico (Pasquini). Their meetings were held in each others 'capanne' and 'boschi' ('cabins' and 'woods'), in reality their palaces and gardens, and to avoid the hardships of celebrating Christmas (an essential date in the shepherd's calendar) in the open air during winter, the feast was moved to their summer season. The position of 'host' of this almost Masonic gathering was rotated annually, and on Handel's return to Rome in July, Ruspoli had just succeeded Prince Giustiniani.

Handel's first contribution to Ruspoli's Arcadia was the cantata for two sopranos and instruments, *Arresta il passo* (identified in the accounts by its first aria, 'Fiamma bella'). A mention of 'il Dio bambin' in the text has led to the supposition that this is actually a Christmas cantata (to be compared with Alessandro Scarlatti's more familiar *Cantata pastorale* written for a similar occasion).*

The accounts for the next few months correlate with Handel's 'quota' of weekly cantatas; fifteen new cantatas were copied, and there were fifteen Sundays between the performance of *Arresta il passo* and the end of October (the conclusion of Ruspoli's summer season). One of the cantatas can be dated to 9 September, the brilliant 'cantata a tre con stromenti Il Tebro', in which Ruspoli himself was glorified under his Arcadian name of Olinto. The other two singers, 'Il Tebro' and 'La Gloria', proclaim the glories of their hero and his return; a far from rural trumpet is introduced in the final flamboyant aria to remind Ruspoli's pastoral friends of his recent (and less Arcadian) military successes on the Pope's behalf at the siege of Ferrara.

A rather unexpected piece of personal flattery from this same series is the cantata in praise of Handel himself, on a text apparently recited extempore by Cardinal Pamphili. Pamphili's verses, complimentary though they are, do not represent quite the extremes of praise that Mainwaring inferred: 'He was

---

*See U. Kirkendale, 'The Ruspoli Documents'.

compared to ORPHEUS, and exalted above the rank of mortals'. A marginal note made much later by Handel's librettist Charles Jennens in his copy of Mainwaring's *Life* indicates that some thirty-five years on, the comparison of himself to Orpheus seemed ridiculous to Handel: 'Handel told me that the words of Il Trionfo &c. were written by Cardinal Pamphilii, & added "an old Fool!" I ask'd "why Fool? because he wrote an Oratorio? perhaps you will call *me* fool for the same reason!" He answer'd "So I would, if you flatter'd me, as He did"'.

Recitative

Handel, non può mia Musa
Cantare in un istante
Versi che degni sian della tua lira,
Ma sento che in me spira
Sì soave armonia che a' tuoi
   concenti
Son costretto cantare in questi
   accenti:

My Muse, O Handel, is not so wise
Thus instantly to improvise
Verse worthy of thy Muse's art,
Yet now thy harmonies impart
Sounds to me so persuasive sweet,
   that I
Perforce with words must match
   thy melody.

Aria

Puote Orfeo, con dolce suono
Arrestar d'augelli il volo
  E fermar di belva il piè,
Si muovèro a un sì bel suono
Tronchi e sassi ancor dal suolo,
  Ma giammai cantar li fè

Orpheus with music and with lay
Made pause the prowling beasts of
   prey
  And charmed birds on the wing;
Stones, tree-trunks rooted in the
   ground,
All moved at his Lyre's compelling
   sound,
  But he never made them sing.

Recitative

Dunque, maggior d'Orfeo, tu sforzi
  al canto
La mia Musa all'ora che il plettro
  appeso avea
A un tronco annoso, e immobile
  giacea.

O greater, then, than Orpheus, thou
Hast from my Muse such
  inspiration wrung,
Long after on an aged bough
My harp unused and lifeless I had
  hung.

Aria

Ognun canti e all'armonia
Di novello Orfeo si dia
Alla destra il moto, al canto
  Voce tal che mai s'udì,
E in sì grata melodia
Tutta gioia l'alma sia:
Ingannando il tempo intanto
  Passi lieto e l'ore e il dì.

Sing all and raise each voice
To strains of new beauty,
And let your fingers play
  To this new Orpheus' tune.
Let every heart rejoice
In so sweet melody,
And make the time of day
  Pass happily but not soon.

Handel's setting is appropriately occasional. In this summer context one might insert the bill for the delivery of 45 lb of 'snow' (i.e. ice) to 'Monsù Endel', doubtless to chill the local wine.

Documents from the Ruspoli archives clearly define the system of patronage under which Handel was working, the conditions of performance and the dates of several of the weekly cantatas (a corpus that invites comparison with the routine of Bach, despite the differences of genre and intent). But many of the most impressive works still have no documentary context, which prevents a full analysis of Handel's 'Italianization'. *Sento là che ristretto, Sarei troppo felice, Se pari è la tua fe* and *O Numi eterni* (*La Lucrezia*) were evidently popular pieces, since they are found in a large number of early copies; a copy of *Armida abbandonata* exists in Bach's handwriting; yet the neglect of this exceptional repertoire in performance means that a modern audience is almost totally unaware of the greater part of Handel's work in Italy.

Still more shamefully neglected are the continuo cantatas, every one an operatic *scena* in embryo. More than the fully accompanied works, they provided a storehouse of musical and dramatic ideas on which Handel was to draw and improve for the next forty years. His compositional style developed through improvisation, and in these early works the different stages of his decision-making can be isolated, his motives dissected and his growth to a musical maturity closely watched. Questions of his indebtedness to Alessandro Scarlatti, Stradella, Caldara, Gasparini and many other proposed influences must rest until we have a firmer grasp of what music he actually came into contact with during his years in Rome.*

> *The out of the way bits of Handel are like the little side bits in such a town as Verona.* (Samuel Butler, *Notebooks* 1874–1902)

From the autumn of 1708 we re-enter the shadows of Handel's journey; there is no recorded return of bed to terminate his stay in Rome, and we are left to assume that he vacated the Ruspoli household at some point during the autumn. Certainly by March the following year, when Caldara was appointed to control the Ruspoli music, Handel had rejoined the court of Prince Ferdinand. Our only documentary source for the next eight months is a retrospective mention in the diary of Francesco Mannucci that at the funeral of Francisco Maria Medici on 15 February 1711, Prince Ferdinand, the composer Perti and several other musicians from the Florentine court talked about Handel: they discussed his musical 'borrowings', his 'malizzia' ('mischievousness' rather than 'malice'?) and more specifically *Il Pianto di Maria*, composed 'per il Venerdì Santo di Siena' in 1709. Five manuscripts exist of this piece for soprano and strings, all ascribed to Handel; but since its style is implausibly

---

*Much of the music from which he was able to 'borrow' (several operas by Keiser, as well as some by Alessandro Scarlatti) is still being identified; see *Handel Sources Series* ed. John Roberts.

Handel's, and the copies all stem from a single source, the attribution must be treated with suspicion. There is no reason for Handel *not* to have visited Siena, but we cannot document his movements until he left Florence on about 9 November, armed with a letter of recommendation from Prince Ferdinand to Prince Karl von Neuberg in Innsbruck. He intended eventually to turn north again; but his immediate destination was Venice. There, according to Addison, operas were a 'great Entertainment. . . The Poetry of them is generally as exquisitely ill, as the Musick is good. The Arguments are often taken from some celebrated Action of the ancient *Greeks* or *Romans*, which sometimes looks ridiculous enough; for who can endure to hear one of the rough old *Romans* squeaking thro' the Mouth of an Eunuch, . . .' (*Remarks on Several Parts of Italy &c.*, 1705)

Had Addison attended the opera in Venice some seven years later, he might have revised his peremptory, though not unsympathetic opinion. Opening after Christmas and running for an unprecedented twenty-seven consecutive performances, Handel's *Agrippina* was a black comedy, based loosely, it is true, on ancient Roman history, but composed to an expert libretto laced with cynicism and irony: in place of the 'rough old Roman', a comic bass portrayal of the pompous and amorous Emperor Claudius; the only 'squeaking Eunuch' a virtuoso singer in the part of Nero as an ambitious adolescent, not yet the power-drunk monster of history; the one tragic and heroic figure in an otherwise dissipated company, Ottone, sung by a woman; a pair of unscrupulous henchmen; the sex-kitten Poppea with three suitors at one moment hidden behind screens in her bedroom; and towering over all, the dominating and amoral figure of the Empress Agrippina,* devoting a complete *scena* to plans for a triple murder.

Handel's librettist for *Agrippina* was the Cardinal Vincenzo Grimani, a Venetian who had recently been appointed Viceroy of Naples. The opera was produced in his family theatre, Teatro di San Giovanni Crisostomo, described as 'the finest and richest of the city', and boasting a huge chandelier bearing the arms of the Grimani family, which was lowered from the ceiling an hour before each performance took place.†

Since the theatre had been shut up for a long time and two other opera houses, one directed by Gasparini and the other by Lotti, were in full swing at the same time, the success of *Agrippina* was all the more remarkable. As Mainwaring recounts:

The audience was so enchanted with this performance, that a stranger who should have seen the manner in which they were affected, would have imagined they had all been distracted.

The theatre, at almost every pause, resounded with shouts and acclamations of *viva il caro Sassone!* and other expressions of approbation too extravagant to be mentioned. They were thunderstruck with the grandeur

*Sung by Margarita Durastante and Elena Croce on alternate nights.
†The Teatro Malibran occupies the site today.

and sublimity of his stile: for never had they known till then all the powers of harmony and modulation so closely arrayed, and so forcibly combined.

The audience were not to know that the opera they applauded for its novelty contained only five arias written specifically for the occasion. More than forty numbers are based on earlier material, from the opening bars of the Overture* (taken from a sacred cantata, *Donna che in ciel*, probably written three years earlier to celebrate Rome's deliverance from an earthquake) to the final aria of Juno who descends to bless the one happy couple that the librettist could rescue from the intrigue (a mixture of themes drawn from *Rodrigo* and a Ruspoli cantata).

Not all the borrowings were from Handel's own music; some stem from Keiser; and one blatant example drew a sharp response in print from Mattheson in 1722, the first public mention of Handel's borrowings.

> In the *opera Porsenna*, of my composition, as it was performed here 20 years ago [actually 1704], and *accompanied* by *Haendel* under my *Direction*, is found an *Aria* whose opening words run: *Diese Wangen will ich küssen (These cheeks I would kiss)*. It can well be that the melody may have seemed not unacceptable to *Haendel*: for not only in his *Agrippina*, which appeared in Italy, but also in another, new *opera*, recently performed in England and treating of *Mutio Scaevola*, he has chosen just this same melody, almost note for note. (*Critica Musica*, Vol. 1)

Freed from Mattheson's justifiable sense of pique, our attitude to Handel's borrowings can be more positive, particularly during this period when he was spreading his wings in opera. We can analyze the changes he made to his own compositions: for example, in borrowing the A section of an aria, but supplying a new B section to reinforce (or sometimes to obliterate) the tension and contrast between the sections; and we can observe a similar process, usually involving a simplification of repetitive rhythm or predictable passagework, in the changes made to ritornelli as they pass from piece to piece.

Another approach is to ask why, from all the musical resources available to him, Handel chose to re-use *this* aria, *this* ritornello, rather than another? To follow the subtleties of his selective process is a route towards understanding the insight he had achieved into the kinds of psychological interplay that the operatic matrix could contain. *Agrippina* is the first totally successful demonstration of this genius; it is a summary, rather than the summit, of his Italian compositions.

Almost as great as Handel's musical successes in Venice were his social conquests. According to Mainwaring, 'He was first discovered there at a Masquerade, while he was playing on a harpsichord in his visor. SCARLATTI happened to be there, and affirmed that it could be no one but the famous

---

*Mainwaring claims that 'the two first Movements of HANDEL's seventh Suite in the 1st Vol of his [harpsichord] Lessons formerly stood for the Overture in his famous Opera AGRIPPINA'.

Saxon, or the devil.' Amongst the foreign diplomats impressed by *Agrippina* were Baron Kielmansegge, Master of the Horse to the Elector of Hanover, and Charles Montagu, Earl of Manchester, the British Ambassador. Discovering that Handel was bound for Innsbruck, they each extended a counter-invitation to their respective courts. The Hanoverian case was supported by Prince Ernst, the Elector's younger brother, who is supposed to have attended every performance of the opera; and a view of England may well have been expressed by Joseph Smith, the banker and patron of Canaletto, who had been resident in Venice for some years (and was later used as an Italian contact by Handel).

Handel dealt with the offers in sequence, and it is fair to assume that his evaluation of the courts he visited rested on their potential for opera. Innsbruck had been the first German-speaking town to have a permanent company for opera, but by 1710 its music was in decline. We have no date for his arrival, but from a letter that Prince Karl in Innsbruck sent to Ferdinand de' Medici we learn that Handel had left the city by 9 March 1710.

Hanover was more promising, with its magnificent Opernhaus, famous for stage machinery and effects. Agostino Steffani, who had written at least eight Italian operas there before turning first to diplomacy (in Düsseldorf) and then to the Church, was warm in his greetings to Handel. It is possible that the two had met in Rome, where Steffani had worked as a diplomat between 1708 and 1709. Hawkins reports Handel's memories of this period in the composer's own words:

'When I first arrived at Hanover I was a young man, under twenty; I was acquainted with the merits of Steffani, and he had heard of me. I understood somewhat of music, and,' putting forth both his broad hands, and extending his fingers, 'could play pretty well on the organ; he received me with great kindness, and took an early opportunity to introduce me to the princess Sophia* and the elector's son, giving them to understand that I was what he was pleased to call a virtuoso in music; he obliged me with instructions for my conduct and behaviour during my residence at Hanover; and being called from the city to attend to matters of a public concern, he left me in possession of that favour and patronage which himself had enjoyed for a series of years.'

Mainwaring continues the story with Baron Kielmansegge recommending Handel to the Elector, who 'immediately offered him a pension of 1500 Crowns per annum as an inducement to stay'. Handel explained to the Baron that such a post would inhibit his freedom to travel (he mentions a promise to visit the Elector Palatine in Düsseldorf), and with Kielmansegge as an intermediary, it was agreed that 'he had leave to be absent for a twelve-month or more, if he chose it; and to go whithersoever he pleased'. On such easy terms Handel at the age of twenty-five was appointed Kapellmeister on 16 June, and left Hanover almost immediately, bound via Halle for the far more brilliant court at Düsseldorf. In Mainwaring's words:

---

*The Elector's mother.

He considered it as his first and principal engagement to pay a visit to his Mother at Hall[e]. Her extreme old-age, and total blindness, tho' they promised him but a melancholy interview, rendered this instance of his duty and regard the more necessary. When he had paid his respects to his relations and friends (among whom his old Master ZACKAW was by no means forgot) he set out for DÜSSELDORF. The Elector Palatine was much pleased with the punctual performance of his promise, but as much disappointed to find that he was engaged elsewhere. At parting he made him a present of a fine set of wrought plate for a desert, and in such a manner as added greatly to its value.

The letters of the Electress to her brother, the Crown Prince of Tuscany, mention the brilliance of Handel's harpsichord playing during the months he stayed at Düsseldorf, and the advice he gave about the purchase of a harpsichord for the count at Florence. But he was impatient to visit England, where (as Burney says) 'a passion for dramatic Music had already manifested itself in several awkward attempts at operas', and thus drawn on, he made his way through Holland to embark on the first sea voyage of his life.

3

London: the Heyday of Opera
1710–1728

Crown'd by the gen'ral Voice, at last you shew
The utmost Length that *Musick*'s Force can go:
What Pow'r on Earth, but Harmony like Thine,
Cou'd *Britain*'s jarring Sons e'er hope to join?
Like *Musick*'s diff'ring Sounds we all agree,
Form'd by thy skilful Hand to *Harmony*:
Our Souls so tun'd, that *Discord* grieves to find
A whole fantastick Audience of a Mind:
The Deaf have found their Ears, – their Eyes the Blind.

(Anonymous, *An Epistel to Mr. Handel,*
upon His Operas of Flavius and Julius Caesar, 1724)

Handel first set foot on English soil towards the end of 1710, 'one of the most memorable years of that longest, but most prosperous war . . . which England had ever waged with a foreign power' (Mainwaring). Despite (and because of) Marlborough's triumphs over the French, the national debt was enormous, and Harley (inspired by Defoe) was already hatching his plans for 'The Great Swindle', the South Sea Company. Sarah, Duchess of Marlborough, who wielded much power with Queen Anne, remarked tartly that, 'Painters, poets and builders have very high flights but must be kept down'. She detested both the scale and style of Blenheim Palace, built by Vanbrugh to her husband's orders.

London, where St Paul's Cathedral ('the only building that could challenge Europe') had just been completed after thirty-five years of building, had become according to some 'for sweetness, cleanness, and for salubrity . . . not only the finest but the most healthy city in the World' (Dr Woodward, letter to Wren). Others with rather closer knowledge of the state of political chicanery and administrative corruption might rather have seen it as Dr Johnson did some twenty-eight years later:

London, the needy Villain's gen'ral Home,
The Common Sewer of *Paris* and of *Rome*

(*London: A Poem*)

49

After three years of life in a Mediterranean climate, Handel surely shared the misgivings of his compatriot Baron von Pollnitz, who decided that London, despite its 'magnificent Structures, both sacred and profane, cannot be rank'd among the finest Cities; for many of its Streets being dirty and ill-paved, its Houses of Brick, not very high, nor adorn'd with Architecture, but blacken'd with unmerciful Smoke of Coal-fires, gives it a dark Hue, which renders it far less agreeable than it would be otherwise' (*Memoirs*, Vol. II).

There is no evidence that Handel contemplated an extended stay in England. 'His curiosity was not yet allay'd', says Mainwaring, 'nor likely to be so while there was any musical court which he had not seen', and an exploratory season in England was all that his year's leave of absence would allow. The growing links between Hanover and London would have encouraged the venture, but Handel appears to have arrived in the country without any commission or offer of patronage; Mainwaring mentions 'strong invitations' from the opera-loving Earl of Manchester, but he was still engrossed with diplomatic tangles in Venice.

For a fully accredited opera composer, England, of all European countries, was the least exploited and, in that sense, the most challenging. Although Italian singers, including castrati, had aroused favourable comment, opera 'after the Italian manner' – that is, entirely sung – was for the most part held to be 'nonsense well-tun'd'. One reason for English resistance was the long association of music with the spoken play. Both in masques and in the so-called 'semi-operas', London audiences had been accustomed to an equal balance of drama and music, delivered in their own tongue, often by actors who were also singers. When *Dido and Aeneas*, the most immediate candidate for the title of 'English opera', was revived in part in 1700 and 1704, it served as musical interlude in a spoken drama. There was, however, criticism of the form. 'Semi-operas' suffered, as Roger North put it, 'by an error of mixing 2 capitall entertainments. . . . For some that would come to the play, hated the musick, and others that were very desirous of the musick, would not bear the interruption that so much rehearsall [i.e. recitation] gave, so that it is best to have either by itself intire' (*Roger North on Music*, ed. Wilson).

Between 1704 and 1710, two London theatres had been vying with each other to present a compatible version of 'all-sung' opera to the public. Christopher Rich, at the Theatre Royal, Drury Lane, led with *Arsinoe, Queen of Cyprus* on 16 January 1705, a confection of weak plot and Italian tunes 'borrowed' by Thomas Clayton, which ran for thirty-five performances in all. Though sung throughout in English by an all-English cast, the music was sometimes preceded by an act of spoken drama to conform with established English taste.* A few months later, Vanbrugh and Congreve opened their new Queen's Theatre in the Haymarket with *The Loves of Ergasto*, an Italian pastoral set by one Jakob Greber (a German!) and 'Perform'd by a new Sett of Singers, Arriv'd from Italy; (the worst that e're came from thence) . . . and they being lik'd but indifferently

---

*See Curtis Price, 'The Critical Decade'.

by the Gentry; they in a little time marcht back to their own Country' (John Downes, *Roscius Anglicanus*).

In contrast to this costly failure, Drury Lane mounted one of the century's greatest successes, *Camilla*, in March 1706. The music, adapted by Haym, was by Giovanni Bononcini, and the text was translated by Owen Swiney, who was eventually to become manager of both theatres in quick succession (and dubious circumstances). According to the anonymous author of *A Critical Discourse upon Operas in England*, *Camilla* had an instantaneous effect:

> before this every man that had the least smattering in music undertook to compose an opera, but upon the appearance of *Camilla* all their projects vanished into nothing: they who before bragged of their undertakings were now ashamed to own 'em, and they who had valued themselves upon having almost finished their work began now to deny they had so much as set about it, so that at least six or seven embryos of operas that had no being but in the airy conceptions of their pretended composers became abortive, and everyone joined in the admiration of *Camilla*.

Two of the operas that remained unstaged because of the success of *Camilla* were *Semele* by Congreve and Eccles, and Pepusch's *Venus and Adonis*. Either of them might have done much to establish English opera in London prior to the efforts of Arne much later in the century. But the tide was turned decisively towards Italian singers by the arrival in London of the castrato Nicolini (Nicolino Grimaldi), as great an actor as he was a singer. 'Every limb and every finger contributes to the part he acts', exclaimed Steele in *The Spectator* (December 1708), 'inasmuch that a deaf man may go along with him in the sense of it . . . He performs the most ordinary action in a manner suitable to the greatness of his character, and shows the prince even in the giving of a letter, or the despatching of a messenger'.

He appeared at the Queen's Theatre in December 1708 in a half-Italian, half-English version of Alessandro Scarlatti's *Pirro e Demetrio*, the recitative and arias sung in either Italian or English according to the nationality of the singer. Nicolini's fight with a lion in *Hydaspes* (*L'Idaspe Fedele* by Mancini, performed entirely in Italian) was the hit of the next season at the Queen's Theatre – Addison's only complaint was that the lion would not be revived for an encore. It was clear to both theatres that the public would pay to hear the best Italian voices in heroic opera, though they may well have been aware of 'the difference between an Italian opera and an opera in Italy' (as Richard Estcourt put it in a note to his satiric *pasticcio Prunella*).

The reservations which remained to the eighteenth-century public, and which are largely shared by a twentieth-century audience, concern the expectations and conventions of *opera seria*. The da capo aria, the secco recitative, the conventions of exit and entrance, the exploitation of a singer's agile gullet and the convenience of a magical conversion: these were the chosen materials of all composers of *opera seria*. It is imprudent to suggest that Handel, the greatest of them all, found these ingredients a restriction or, as has been seen in modern productions, a mere source of amusement. Handel was not fettered by the rules; we need to note when he flouts convention, and why. We need to look, with him, beyond the predictability of forms to the development of human characters and emotional situations, and to the manipulation of a musical architecture serving dramatic ends. The essence of the Baroque is to stretch the forms but not to break them.

The greatest complaints with *opera seria* were its dramatic incoherence, the predictability of the constant da capo aria form, and the hierarchical demands made on a composer by the star singers, especially the imported (and expensive) castrati. Goldoni summarizes the last point, and establishes the etiquette ruling both librettist and composer:

The three principal personages of the drama ought to sing five airs each; two in the first act, two in the second, and one in the third. The second actress and the second soprano can have only three, and the inferior characters must be satisfied with a single air each, or two at the most. The author of the words must furnish the musician with the different shades which form the *chiaroscuro* of music, and take care that two pathetic airs do not succeed one another. He must distribute with the same precaution the bravura airs, the airs of action, the inferior airs, and the minuets and rondeaus. He must, above all things, avoid giving impassioned airs, bravura airs, or rondeaus, to inferior characters. (*Memoirs*, Vol. 1)

Add to such requirements a mythological story-line, and it is no surprise that Handel's audience equipped itself with a bilingual libretto, often containing a commentary and summary which could be followed during the performance. Even so, one seventeenth-century librettist felt obliged to end his text of Cavalli's *Veremonda* with a 'Summary of the opera for those who cannot understand it after having heard and read the same'.

If a certain lack of intelligibility was a generic fault of *opera seria*, the da capo aria was one of its essential virtues. For one thing, it was the perfect vehicle for demonstrations of individual virtuosity, with its A-B-A form giving appropriate scope for a singer's powers of extempore decoration. More important, it became, especially for Handel, the primary dramatic medium. Duets, trios and other ensembles are rare in *opera seria*, not because they are musically inappropriate, but because they create a communal sentiment rather than an individual *Affekt*. In Handel's operas, the tensions between characters are worked out in succeeding arias, rather than simultaneously declaimed. Only in a final chorus do all the singers appear together, occasionally out of character.

Of the singers themselves – their techniques, physiques, fees and foibles – the eighteenth-century press gives ample evidence. It was generally agreed that Italian singers were better trained and more talented than local products: 'though the opera in Italy is a monster', admits John Dennis (*Essay on the Operas*, 1706), ''tis a beautiful harmonious monster, but here in England 'tis an ugly howling one'.

1 A putative early portrait of Handel by Christoph Platzer, dated *c.* 1710, towards the end of his visit to Italy.

2 Engraving of Handel's father, c. 1690.

3 Halle market-place, c. 1715, showing the Liebfrauenkirche and its library and, on the right, the Red Tower.

4, 5 Telemann and Mattheson were both instrumental in launching Handel on his international operatic career. The friendship with the latter was clouded over at least temporarily when the two young men fought a duel over who should play the continuo in Mattheson's opera *Cleopatra*. Fifty years later Handel was still in touch with Telemann, an avid horticulturalist, sending him a crate of exotic plants.

6 View of Hamburg, where Handel's first two operas, *Almira* and *Nero*, were performed.

7 Arcangelo Corelli, who directed Cardinal Ottoboni's private orchestra in Rome and led the oratorio *La Resurrezione* in the performance at Ruspoli's palace (1708).

8 Lucifer's aria 'O voi dell'Erebo' in *La Resurrezione* exemplifies the bold sweep of Handel's calligraphy at this time. He reused the same music (with different words) in the opera *Agrippina* the following year.

9 Portrait said to be of Handel, after Bartholomew Dandridge.

10 Handel took London by storm with *Rinaldo*, his first Italian opera to be staged in England; it received fifteen performances in its first season at the Queen's (later King's) Theatre, Haymarket.

13, 14 (opposite) King's Theatre, Haymarket: cross-section by Dumont (1764), showing (*from left to right*) the comparatively small auditorium, the shallow orchestra pit, the boxes encroaching on the fore-stage, and the depth of stage available for perspective sets (as below); proscenium arch and stage, *c.* 1725.

11, 12 The manager of the Haymarket Theatre was the dramatist Aaron Hill, who provided the scenario for *Rinaldo*. The assistant manager was John James Heidegger, 'the most ugly man that was ever formed', who subsequently went into partnership with Handel.

SONG's *in the* OPERA *of* Rinaldo Compos'd by Mr Hendel

London Printed for J Walsh Servant in Ordinary to her Britanick Majesty, at ÿ Harp & Hoboy in Katherine street near Somerset House in ÿ Strand, & J Hare at ÿ Viol & Flute in Cornhill near the Royall Exchange.

Mr AARON HILL.

Ætatis Suæ 24 A. Domi 1709

H Hulsbergh Sculp.

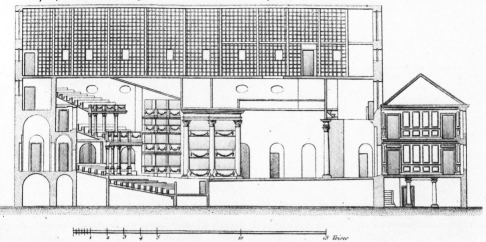

1 2 3 4 5   *10*   *15 Toises*

15–17 For three years (1713–16) Handel lived with Lord Burlington at his house in Piccadilly. Burlington (*left*, attrib. J. Richardson) was a noted patron of the arts and the stimulating intellectual company he kept included Alexander Pope (*right*, Pond/Houbraken), John Gay and John Arbuthnot.

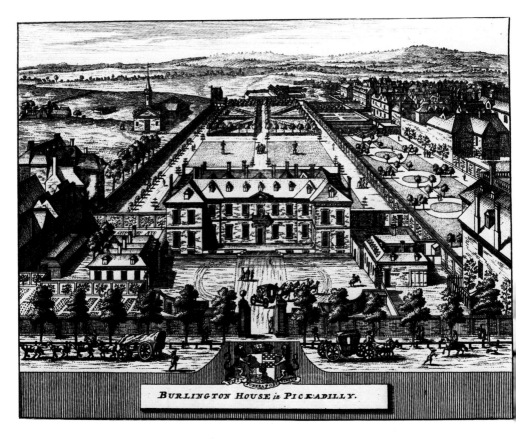

BURLINGTON HOUSE in PICCADILLY.

So the costly importation of castrati began, involving, North noted, 'immense charges in profuse salarys, pensions, subscriptions, and promiscuous courtship and flatterys into the bargain. These farr fecht and dear bought gentlemen return home rich, buy fine houses and gardens, and live in admiration of English wealth and profusion' (*Roger North on Music*, ed. Wilson). But these 'Semivirs', 'Vocal Unspecificates', or 'squeaking shadows of men' (however disparagingly described) were as essential to Italian *opera seria* as the da capo aria, and with them came the end of the polyglot compromise that had tried to sustain English singers as the equal of the foreigners. 'At length', Addison satirically wrote, 'the audience got tired of understanding half the opera, and therefore, to ease themselves entirely of the fatigue of thinking, have so ordered it at present that the whole opera is performed in an unknown tongue'.

Addison was at this time smarting from the failure of his own opera *Rosamond*, set by Clayton, which had folded after three performances. His subsequent sallies at the Italian opera derive from his firm opinion that a genuine English opera could be both intelligible and dramatic. Italian opera *per se* did not offend him – in fact he admits to open admiration of what he heard in Italy between 1701 and 1703: 'the Musick is good', and thanks to the language 'the *Italian* Opera, . . . amidst all the Meanness and Familiarity of the Thoughts, has something beautiful and sonorous in the Expression' (*Remarks*, pp. 65–6). But setting the English language according to an Italian model did offend, since the inflection of the phrase was rendered unnatural:

> For this reason, the recitative musick, in every language should be as different as the tone or accent of each language; for otherwise, what may properly express a passion in one language, will not do it in another. Everyone who has been long in *Italy* knows very well, that the cadences in the *Recitativo* bear a remote affinity to the tone of their voices in ordinary conversation, or, to speak more properly, are only the accents of their language made more musical and tuneful.
>
> Thus the notes of interrogation, or admiration, in the *Italian* musick (if one may so call them) which resemble their accents in discourse on such occasions, are not unlike the ordinary tones of an *English* voice when we are angry; insomuch that I have often seen our audiences extremely mistaken as to what has been doing upon the stage, and expecting to see the hero knock down his messenger, when he has been asking him a question; or fancying that he quarrels with his friend, when he only bids him good-morrow. (*The Spectator*, 3 April 1711)

Translation, so Addison's argument runs, can hardly avoid traducing the original:

> It happened also very frequently, where the sense was rightly translated, the necessary transposition of words, which were drawn out of the phrase of one tongue into that of another, made the musick appear very absurd in one tongue that was very natural in the other. I remember an *Italian* verse that ran thus, word for word,

> *And turn'd my rage into pity;*
> which the *English* for rhyme sake translated,
> *And into pity turn'd my rage.*
> By this means the soft notes that were adapted to *pity* in the *Italian*, fell upon the word *rage* in the *English*; and the angry sounds that were turned to *rage* in the original, were made to express *pity* in the translation. It oftentimes happened likewise, that the finest notes in the air fell upon the most insignificant words in the sentence. I have known the word *and* pursued through the whole gamut, have been entertained with many a melodious *the*, and have heard the most beautiful graces, quavers, and divisions bestowed upon *then*, *for*, and *from* to the eternal honour of our *English* particles. (*The Spectator*, 21 March 1711)

The argument leads naturally to the tenet, as valid today as in 1711, that 'The great pleasure in hearing vocal music arises from the association of ideas raised at the same time by the expressions and sound'.

How far things stood from this case at that time was clearly stated by Mainwaring: 'it is plain that, what with the confusion of languages, and the transposition of passions and sentiments owing to that cause, the best Composer could hardly be distinguished from the worst. The arrival of HANDEL put an end to this reign of nonsense'.

Handel was not unknown in London. Those who had made the Grand Tour would have come across his music, perhaps in Hanover or more probably in Italy, and London audiences had themselves been exposed (albeit unwittingly) to his works. The overture and dances from *Rodrigo* (which had been used as incidental music for a revival of Ben Jonson's *The Alchemist* at the Queen's Theatre in January 1710) were published by Walsh as the work of 'an Italian Master', while during a revival of *Pirro e Demetrio*, Francesca Vanini included 'Ho un non so che nel cor', which she had heard Durastanti sing when she appeared with her in *Agrippina* in Venice. More excerpts from *Agrippina* were to find their way into London operas during the next season.

The catalyst of Handel's first London triumph was the young manager Aaron Hill, who had moved from Drury Lane to the Haymarket when the Queen's Theatre obtained a monopoly of opera productions. He sketched out a libretto based on the story of Rinaldo and Armida from Tasso's *Gerusalemme Liberata*, which was realized by the theatre's librettist, Rossi, in great haste – 'the delivery of but a few evenings'. The composer worked with even greater speed: 'Mr. *Hendel*, the *Orpheus* of our century, while composing the music, scarcely gave me time to write, and to my great wonder I saw an entire Opera put to music by that surprising genius, with the greatest degree of perfection, in only two weeks' ('The Poet to the Reader'). Rossi's irony was probably inspired by Handel's normal working habits: some fifteen numbers in *Rinaldo* are derived either whole or in part from the scores of *Almira*, *La Resurrezione*, *Agrippina*, and other Italian works. They include the saraband air 'Lascia ch'io pianga', 'Bel piacere' (taken over words and all from *Agrippina*), and Armida's concluding aria in Act II, 'Vo' far guerra', in which Handel delighted the London audience with 'the

11
13, 14

lightness and elasticity of his finger' in improvised breaks for the harpsichord.*
For Nicolini Handel wrote afresh. From the tenderness of 'Cara sposa', 'which
the author would frequently say was one of the best he ever made' (Hawkins), to
the bravura of 'Venti, turbini', Rinaldo's arias were calculated to test the full
range of the great castrato's style.

On the first night Aaron Hill published a complete word-book of the opera
with a dedication to the Queen in which he expressed a hope, with her support,
'to see the *English* OPERA more splendid than her Mother, the Italian'. In his
Preface, aimed at the public, Hill was rather more critical:

> The Deficiencies I found, or thought I found, in such ITALIAN OPERA'S as
> have hitherto been introduc'd among us, were, *First*, That they had been
> compos'd for Tastes and Voices, different from those who were to sing and
> hear them on the *English* Stage; And *Secondly*, That wanting the Machines
> and Decorations, which bestow so great a Beauty on their Appearance, they
> have been heard and seen to very considerable Disadvantage.
>
> At once to remedy both these Misfortunes, I resolv'd to frame some
> Dramma, that, by different Incidents and Passions, might afford the Musick
> Scope to vary and display its Excellence, and fill the Eye with more delightful
> Prospects, so at once to give Two Senses equal Pleasure . . .
>
> Mr. *Hendel*, whom the World so justly celebrates, has made his Musick
> speak so finely for its self, that I am purposely silent on that Subject; and shall
> only add, That as when I undertook this Affair, I had no Gain in View, but
> That of the Acknowledgment and Approbation of the Gentlemen of my
> Country; so No Loss, the Loss of That excepted, shall discourage me from a
> Pursuit of all Improvements, which can possibly be introduc'd upon our
> *English* Theatre.

Since both the music and the singing were a total success, the critics were left
with Hill's scenic effects as their only target:

> An Opera may be allowed to be extravagantly lavish in its Decorations, as its
> only Design is to gratify the Senses, and keep up an indolent Attention in the
> Audience. Common Sense however requires, that there should be nothing in
> the Scenes and Machines which may appear Childish and Absurd. How
> would the Wits of King *Charles's* Time have laughed to have seen *Nicolini*
> exposed to a Tempest in Robes of Ermin, and sailing in an open Boat upon a
> Sea of Paste-Board?
>
> . . . As I was walking in the Streets about a Fortnight ago, I saw an ordinary
> Fellow carrying a Cage full of little Birds upon his Shoulder; and, as I was
> wondering with my self what Use he would put them to, he was met very
> luckily by an Acquaintance, who had the same Curiosity. Upon his asking
> him what he had upon his Shoulder, he told him, that he had been buying
> Sparrows for the Opera. Sparrows for the Opera, says his Friend, licking his

---

*Those published later by William Babell are probably exaggerations of Handel's style.

Lips, what,? are they to be roasted? No, no, says the other, they are to enter towards the end of the first Act,* and to fly about the Stage.

This strange Dialogue awakened my Curiosity so far, that I immediately bought the Opera [i.e. libretto], by which means I perceived that the Sparrows were to act the part of Singing Birds in a delightful Grove: though upon a nearer Enquiry I found the Sparrows put the same Trick upon the Audience, that Sir *Martin Mar-all* practised upon his Mistress; for, though they flew in Sight, the Musick proceeded from a Consort of Flageletts and Birdcalls which was planted behind the Scenes ... The Opera of *Rinaldo* is filled with Thunder and Lightning, Illuminations, and Fireworks; which the Audience may look upon without catching Cold, and indeed without much Danger of being burnt; for there are several Engines filled with Water, and ready to play at a Minute's Warning, in case any such Accident should happen. However, as I have a very great Friendship for the Owner of this Theatre, I hope that he has been wise enough to *insure* his House before he would let this Opera be acted in it ... (Addison, *The Spectator*, 6 March 1711)

Addison's colleague Steele took up the same theme in the next issue:

... We had also but a very short Allowance of Thunder and Lightning; th' I cannot in this Place omit doing Justice to the Boy who had the Direction of the Two painted Dragons, and made them spit Fire and Smoke: He flash'd out his Rasin in such just Proportions and in such due Time, that I could not forbear conceiving Hopes of his being one Day a most excellent Player. I saw indeed but Two things wanting to render his whole Action compleat, I mean the keeping his Head a little lower, and hiding his Candle.

As to the Mechanism and Scenary ... at the *Hay-Market* the Undertakers forgetting to change their Side-Scenes, we were presented with a Prospect of the Ocean in the midst of a delightful Grove; and th' the Gentlemen on the Stage had very much contributed to the Beauty of the Grove by walking up and down between the Trees, I must own I was not a little astonished to see a well-dressed young Fellow, in a full-bottom'd Wigg, appear in the midst of the Sea, and without any visible Concern taking Snuff.

But no carping could take away the fact that *Rinaldo* was the success of the season, running for fifteen nights (and incidentally totalling a record number of fifty-three performances in Handel's lifetime). Walsh published the songs 'together with their Symphonys and Riturnels in a Compleat Manner' and 'got fifteen hundred pounds by the printing it' (Hawkins). It was the first English publication to identify the composer, still in his German livery: 'Mr. Hendel, Chapple Master to ye Elector of Hanover'.

Apart from this triumph, which in retrospect can be said to have settled the course of Handel's career and the future of opera in England, little is known

10

---

*Almirena's aria 'Augelletti', with its extended introduction for two *flauti* and 'flageoletto' (sopranino recorder).

of Handel's early English experiences. He was introduced at Court, and a 'Dialogue in Italian, in Her Majesty's Praise, set . . . by the famous Mr. Hendel' and sung by Nicolini was given on the Queen's birthday at St James's Palace (reported in *The Political State of Great Britain*). According to Hawkins, Handel took part in the musical evenings organized by Thomas Britton, the musical small-coals (i.e. charcoal) seller, and although there is no verification of this story, it is endearing to think of him taking turns at the harpsichord with Pepusch in the impromptu concerts held in the loft over the charcoal store, 'with a window but very little bigger than the Bunghole of a Cask'. Britton's library (listed in detail by Hawkins) would have attracted Handel, and together with Pepusch's antiquarian collection could well have provided the basis of his continuing musical self-education in England.

On a more intimate level, Handel made the acquaintance of a young girl of ten, Mary Granville, who as Mrs Pendarves and later Mrs Delany was to remain a lifelong friend and a valuable (if partisan) source of information on Handel's affairs. In her own words:

> In the year '10 I first saw Mr. Handel who was introduced to my uncle [Sir John Stanley, a commissioner of customs] by Mr. Heidegger, the . . . most ugly man that was ever formed. We had no better instrument in the house than a little spinet of mine, on which the great musician performed wonders. I was much struck with his playing, but struck as a child, not a judge, for the moment he was gone, I seated myself at my instrument and played the best lessons I had then learnt. My uncle archly asked me if I thought I should ever play as well as Mr. Handel. 'If I did not think I should,' cried I, 'I would burn my instrument!' Such was the innocent presumption of childish ignorance.*

John James Heidegger, a Swiss emigré and opportunist, was at this time assist-ant manager of the Haymarket Theatre, and was throughout his life associ-ated with the most proper entertainments (Handel's included) as well as scandalous and lewd ridottos and masquerades.

At the close of the London season, Handel returned to his employer in Hanover, staying a few days in Düsseldorf on his way at the behest of the Elector Palatine 'in order to show him several *Instrumenta* and other things, and to learn his opinion of them'.

Without an opera house to engage his enthusiasm, Handel's life fell into a quieter pattern. One of his royal duties was to provide a set of twelve vocal duets for the Princess Caroline (later Queen), who was congratulated by Haym on her 'perfetta e giudiziosa conoscenza della musica'. Only four or five of the duets were newly composed for the Princess. Mainwaring also mentions an unspecific 'variety of other things for voices and instruments'. A letter from Handel to Andreas Roner, a fellow German working in London, shows that before leaving

---

*All quotations from Mary Granville-Pendarves-Delany in this text come from the *Autobiography and Correspondence of Mary Granville, Mrs Delany* (London, 1861–2).

England he had met the poet John Hughes, and was hoping to collaborate with him: '. . . Please convey my best compliments to Mr Hughes. I shall take the liberty of writing to him at the earliest opportunity. If however he wishes to honour me with his commands and add thereto one of his charming poems in English, that will afford me the greatest possible pleasure. Since I left you, I have made some progress in that language . . .' The only certain outcome of this plan was Handel's setting of Hughes's *Venus and Adonis*, from which only two arias survive. Hughes also wrote the text of 'Would you gain the tender creature' in *Acis and Galatea*.

In the context of the hoped-for 'English Opera', Hughes's early death in 1720 marks another of Handel's 'missed opportunities'. Hughes, although as staunch as Addison in his view on the suitability of English as a vehicle for music, was more congenial and showed a studied sympathy for music, which might have won Handel over from his refusal to be associated with English on stage:

> As Theatrical Musick expresses a Variety of Passions, it is not requisite, even for the Advantage of the Sound, that the Syllables shou'd every where Languish with the same loose and vowelly Softness. But what is certainly of much more Consequence in Dramatical Entertainments, is, that they shou'd be perform'd in a Language understood by the Audience. One wou'd think there shou'd be no need to prove this. (Preface to *Calypso and Telemachus*, 1712)

Handel was the one composer who could have turned the enthusiasm of such people as Pepusch, Galliard, Hughes and Haym into national opera; had he done so, Dr Johnson's famous epithet on Italian opera (included in his life of Hughes, see p. 103 below) would have required some amendment.

In the autumn of 1712, Handel asked permission of his Elector to return, and was allowed 'on condition that he engaged to return within a reasonable time' (Mainwaring). Handel's objectives on his second visit to England were patent enough – to follow up his first operatic success, and to establish relations with a patron who would allow the same type of 'regulated employment' that he had enjoyed with Ruspoli. But with the Hanoverian succession in prospect, he had to move with political circumspection and his stay lengthened in proportion to the certainty of the patronage he attracted.

Of his first supporter we have only a name and address: one Mr Andrews of Barn-Elms (now Barnes), who also had a town residence. A connection with the Kit-Cat Club, the most eminent of the Whig groups that combined politics with the arts, can be speculated, since the instigator of the Club, the publisher Jacob Tonson, had built a special meeting-room for its members in his house at Barn-Elms. Theatre was a particular interest of the group – the Queen's Theatre had been founded by two of them, Vanbrugh and Congreve – and Handel may well have been cultivated by them in the same manner as they drew in his compatriot, Godfrey Kneller, to paint portraits of the leading members (the stock canvas size that he used has ever since been known as a 'kit-cat').

Handel's first venture of the operatic season was not well-judged. *Il Pastor Fido*, or *The Faithful Shepherd*, which was finished on 24 October and opened less than a month later, received short shrift in an opera register (attributed to Francis Colman but undoubtedly by other hands, since it continues during the period he spent as a diplomat in Florence): 'The Scene represented only ye Country of Arcadia. ye Habits were old. – ye Opera Short'. The cast list shows that neither Nicolini nor Boschi was in England, which must have meant a major public disappointment; the music, written in Handel's deliberately simplified pastoral style, with none of the flamboyance of *Rinaldo*, a reduced number of arias (many of these both borrowed and monothematic) and very abbreviated recitative, represents an Italian ideal, less compelling and more stereotyped than English pastoral precedents of which Handel was probably ignorant.

Finding he had misjudged public taste, Handel was quick to make amends: *Teseo*, finished a month after *Pastor Fido*'s opening, was high tragedy in no less than five acts. Medea is one of Handel's best character types – the impassioned sorceress – and Burney records for us the powers of Handel's accompanied recitative 'in which the wild and savage fury of the enraged sorceress . . . and her incantations, are admirably painted by the instruments'. His only regret is that after five acts of strong contrast, 'the usual opera *denouement* advances happily' with a light gavotte. But while the opera was running to full houses, the *Opera Register* (c.15 January 1713) reveals a major crisis backstage:

> Mr O. Swiny ye Manager of ye Theatre was now setting out a New Opera, Heroick. all ye Habits new & richer than ye former with 4 New Scenes, & other Decorations & Machines. Ye Tragick Opera was called Theseus. Ye Musick composed by Mr Handel . . . ye Opera being thus prepared Mr Swiny would have got a Subscription for Six times, but could not. – he then did give out Tickets at half a Guinea each, for two Nights ye Boxes lay'd open to ye Pit, ye House was very full these two Nights.
>
> after these Two Nights Mr Swiny Brakes & runs away & leaves ye Singers unpaid ye Scenes & Habits also unpaid for. The Singers were in Some confusion but at last concluded to go on with ye operas on their own accounts, & divide ye Gain amongst them.

The vacancy left by Swiney's defection with the cashbox was quickly filled by Heidegger – an astute move that was to keep him in business as an opera impresario for the next thirty years.

The libretto of *Teseo* (by Haym) carries a dedication to the young Lord Burlington, who now became Handel's patron and offered Burlington House as   15, 17
a residence. In Hawkins's words:

> Into this hospitable mansion was Handel received, and left at liberty to follow the dictates of his genius and invention, assisting frequently at evening concerts, in which his own music made the most considerable part. The course of his studies during three years residence at Burlington-house, was very regular and uniform: his mornings were employed in study, and at dinner he sat down with men of the first eminence for genius and abilities of any in the kingdom.

Handel's contribution to this society was specifically mentioned by Gay:

> There *Hendel* strikes the Strings, the melting Strain
> Transports the Soul, and thrills through ev'ry Vein;
> There oft' I enter (*Trivia*, Bk II)

Richard Boyle, Earl of Burlington, was a youth of barely nineteen at the time he met Handel. He was energetic, enthusiastic and still under the watchful eye of his mother, the Countess Juliana. The company he kept in the Piccadilly mansion (of which very little is retained in the present-day Burlington House) included Alexander Pope, John Gay, Dr Arbuthnot and, eventually, most of the leading architects and painters of the day. 'He possessed', Walpole declared, 'every quality of a genius and artist except envy', and the spread of Palladianism in England was largely due to his active support and finance. As a noble amateur (though himself an architect of some competence), he preferred to initiate rather than execute. Amongst his circle of designers, the most favoured was William Kent, whom he met in Rome during his first Italian visit in 1714. 'Kentino' moved into Burlington House on his return to England and lived with the Earl for the remainder of his life; according to John Harris (*The Palladians*, p. 18), 'There is no reason not to presume a close homosexual relationship'.

16

The atmosphere at Burlington House must have been familiar to Handel from his first Italian residence with Ferdinand de' Medici. His private life here, however, remains private even today; from his youth he retained an enigmatic aloofness in matters of sex, politics and religion.

Of Handel's London activities at this time, Hawkins records his visits to St Paul's to play the Father Smith organ after evening services, and later to the Queen's Arms Tavern for an evening of refreshment and musical entertainment. A large room with a harpsichord served for informal concerts, and it was here that when Handel heard of the publication of Mattheson's *Pièces de Clavecin*, he sent for a copy, and 'without hesitation, played it through'.

Although never servile, Handel had learned to be a courtier in Italy, and from his newly-won position as Burlington's 'artistic pensioner' set out to pay his respects both to Queen Anne and the traditions of English church music. His first opportunity came with the official Thanksgiving Service for 'Marlborough's Wars', concluded with the treacherous Treaty of Utrecht, that 'indelible blot on the age', as Lord Chatham later described it, for which Handel supplied a setting of the Te Deum and Jubilate. How a subject of the Hanoverian Court came to be celebrating a treaty that the Elector himself had opposed is not easily explained. There is no record of a direct commission from the English Court – and in any case William Croft, the principal composer for the Chapel Royal, would have been the obvious choice.

The score of the Utrecht Te Deum was completed well in advance of the official celebrations, which took place on 14 January – a day when Handel would also have been directing the second performance of *Teseo*. Either an earlier peace settlement was expected, or Handel was writing in the hope that his aristocratic supporters could press his case at court. Possibly to strengthen his chances, Handel produced at the same time an *Ode for the Birthday of Queen Anne*, intended for a performance at court on 6 February which may not have taken place. Its debt to Purcell is apparent in the opening bars of duet between obbligato trumpet and countertenor, 'Eternal source of light divine'; its connection with the Treaty is emphasized in a repeated refrain celebrating 'the day that gave great Anna birth, that fix'd a lasting peace on earth'.

Handel must have learned something from Purcell's accentuation, since neither this *Ode* nor the Te Deum and Jubilate shows any sign of awkwardness in its setting of English. But the scale of Handel's design is larger and his scoring (particularly for the winds) more independent. Thomas Tudway, who had been a friend of Purcell, found the style 'too theatrical'; 'Mr. Purcell keeps a Nobler, & more Elevated style . . . & has not so much of ye flutter &c'.*

The Queen rewarded Handel with a pension of £200 a year for life, an act of bounty 'the more extraordinary, as his foreign engagements were not unknown' (Mainwaring). Normally the Queen took little interest in her composers and, wrote the Duke of Manchester, was 'too busy or too careless to listen to her own band, and had no thought of hearing and paying new players however great their genius or vast their skill'. Her motive in this case was surely to detach Handel from his foreign engagements (if, as documents in Hanover suggest, he had not already been suspended from his position).

For Mainwaring Handel's truancy was a joking matter: 'whether he was afraid of repassing the sea, or whether he had contracted an affection for the diet of the land he was in . . . the promise he had given at his coming away, had somehow slipt out of his memory'. But throughout this year the Queen's constant ill-health reminded the nation that the House of Hanover might be required to provide a new monarch at any moment. When the expected happened, and Handel's Hanoverian employer arrived as George I in September 1714, one of his first engagements was to attend morning service at the Chapel Royal, where a '*Te Deum* was sung, composed by Mr. Handel' (presumably the 'Caroline' setting) – hardly a mark of royal disfavour. The scenario of resentment and reconciliation devised by Mainwaring with the aid of the *Water Music* legend, and later expanded by Hawkins to include a surprise appearance at court as Geminiani's accompanist, seems improbable – certainly it anticipates other reports of the water party by three years, during which time the royal family had been regular attenders at the opera, and the King had added a further £200 per annum to Handel's pension.

At the renamed King's Theatre, *Rinaldo* was being revived 'With all the proper Decorations as Originally'. In January 1715, Nicolini returned to the title role; the *Opera Register* reports 'ye King, Prince & Princesse present, & a full House'. A warning notice issued by the managers of the theatre probably relates to Nicolini's return: 'Whereas by the frequent calling for the songs again the Operas have been too tedious, therefore the singers are forbidden to sing any song above once; and it is hoped nobody will call for 'em or take it ill when not obeyed'.

---

*BL Harl. 3782, f.86, quoted by C. Hogwood in *Music in Eighteenth-Century England*, p. 30.

The libretto of Handel's next opera, *Amadigi*, has a dedication (by Heidegger) thanking Burlington for 'that Generous Concern Your Lordship has always shown for the promoting of Theatrical Musick, but this Opera more immediately claims Your Protection, as it is compos'd in Your own Family...': evidence that Handel was still resident in Piccadilly, and possibly a reminder to the Earl that much of the music of *Amadigi* was taken from a short opera, *Silla*, which may have been presented privately on 2 June 1713 (though there is no evidence of a performance in Burlington House, as frequently proposed). So much emphasis was placed on the machinery and effects (including a 'practicable' fountain) that on 25 May the 'Daily Courant' had to announce, tactfully: '... whereas there is a great many Scenes and Machines to be mov'd in this Opera, which cannot be done if Persons should stand upon the Stage (where they could not be without Danger), it is therefore hop'd no Body, even the Subscribers, will take it Ill that they must be deny'd Entrance on the Stage'.

In spite of these allurements, Handel's operas were not drawing as well as revivals of Mancini's *Idaspe*, or even the evergreen *Camilla*; attendances were upset by indisposed singers, the King's birthday, the hot summer and Jacobite threats. The *Opera Register* records: 'No Opera performed since ye 23 July, ye Rebellion of ye Tories and Paptists being ye cause – ye King and Court not liking to go into such Crowds these troublesome times'.

Although the theatres closed for autumn and part of the winter, Handel's achievements that year were already substantial. He had not recaptured the éclat of *Rinaldo*, it is true, and although *Pastor Fido*, *Teseo* and *Amadigi* could all be criticised (too short, too long and too muddled, respectively), he showed growing confidence in the treatment of strong human emotion, and in the integration of drama with musical effects. In simple financial terms, he was able to invest £500 in the South Sea Company.

In June 1716 Handel requested a dividend from the Company, probably drawn to finance his return to Germany with the King in July. The trip is not documented, but Handel is assumed to have used his time visiting his relatives in Halle, and calling on an early acquaintance, Johann Christoph Schmidt at Ansbach; there was little call for his services at court, where George was amply amused by a troupe of French comedians. Schmidt, now a flourishing wool-merchant, had been a fellow student with Handel at the University of Halle, and was persuaded to return with him to England as amanuensis and musical assistant, which he remained for the rest of his life. His son tells us in addition that his father 'regulated the expences of his public performance, and filled the office of treasurer with great exactness and fidelity' (*Anecdotes of George Frederick Handel and John Christopher Smith*, 1799). As the output of Handel's 'studio' increased, Schmidt's son, also John Christopher, followed his father into Handel's service (in 1720). The handwriting of the Smiths, together with various copyists engaged under them, provides invaluable clues in the dating and unravelling of Handel's compositions, revisions and borrowings from this period onwards.

Handel's only essay in German oratorio style, a setting of a poem by Brockes on the Passion, is also allocated to this period, although its first documented performance did not take place until 23 March 1719 in Hamburg. Keiser, Telemann and Mattheson all made use of the same text in different years, and, since they were all acquainted, an element of competition may have been involved; Mattheson himself states that Handel composed the piece in England, and sent it to Germany 'by post in an uncommonly close-written score', but gives no date. Bach (with Anna Magdalena) made a copy of the complete score for use at Leipzig, where its uncommitted operatic tone and simple chorale setting were in strong contrast to the usual repertoire, and Telemann also performed the work in 1722. For Handel it was almost the last time he set the German language. From 1717, when he had returned to England to revise *Rinaldo* and *Amadigi*, he intended to be an Englishman, and therefore looked to secure his sources of patronage.

The King had also returned, reluctantly, openly flaunting his mistress, Madame Schulenberg ('The Maypole') and with his half-sister Madame Kielmansegge ('The Elephant').* Within his own family feelings were not cordial. 'The King', declared one English wit, 'was undoubtably of an affectionate nature for of all the people in the world he hated only three: his mother, his wife and his son'. With an open rift between himself and the Prince of Wales, and a swiftly deteriorating public opinion of his intelligence (he refused to speak a single word of English, and, as Lady Mary Wortley Montague bluntly expressed it: 'In private life he would have been called an honest block-head'), George decided on a modest display of public mollification. His plans were recorded in detail by Friedrich Bonet, the Prussian Resident in London.

A few weeks ago the King expressed to Baron Kilmanseck His desire to have a concert on the river, by subscription, similar to the masquerades this winter which the King never failed to attend. The Baron accordingly applied to Heidecker, – a Swiss by origin, but the cleverest purveyor of entertainments to the Nobility. The latter replied that, much as he would wish to comply with His Majesty's desires, he must reserve subscriptions for the great events, namely the masquerades, each of which brings him in three or 400 guineas net. Observing His Majesty's chagrin at these difficulties, M. de Kilmanseck undertook to provide the concert on the river at his own expense. The necessary orders were given and the entertainment took place the day before yesterday [17 July]. About eight in the evening the King repaired to his barge, into which were admitted the Duchess of Bolton, Countess Godolphin, Mad. de Kilmanseck, Mrs. Were and the Earl of Orkney, the Gentleman of the Bedchamber in Waiting. Next to the King's barge was that of the musicians, about 50 in number, who played on all kinds of instruments, to wit trumpets, horns, hautboys, bassoons, German flutes, French flutes, violins and basses; but there were no singers. The music had been composed specially by the famous Handel, a native of Halle, and His Majesty's principal

---

*Mme Kielmansegge was not, as previously thought, the King's mistress. See R. Hatton: *George I*, pp. 23–4.

Court Composer. His Majesty approved of it so greatly that he caused it to be repeated three times in all, although each performance lasted an hour – namely twice before and once after supper. The [weather in the] evening was all that could be desired for the festivity, the number of barges and above all of boats filled with people desirous of hearing was beyond counting. In order to make this entertainment the more exquisite, Mad. de Kilmanseck had arranged a choice supper in the late Lord Ranelagh's villa at Chelsea on the river, where the King went at one in the morning. He left at three o'clock and returned to St James' about half past four. The concert cost Baron Kilmanseck £150 for the musicians alone. Neither the Prince nor the Princess took any part in this festivity.

The *Celebrated Water Musick* as published by Walsh (1733) included only ten pieces from Handel's original sequence. A theory that the traditional movements are an amalgam of three separate suites was proposed in the 1950s, but disproved by the discovery (2004) of the earliest manuscript score which confirms the sequence of 22 pieces as published by Chrysander, with the novel sonorities of the horn numbers contrasted with the interlocking music for trumpets (in D) and for quieter instruments (flute, recorder and bassoons) to create an unprecedented hour-long suite of instrumental music without voices (see p. 284).

Handel's willingness to oblige the King is a revealing contrast to Heidegger's curt refusal on commercial grounds. While the 'Swiss Count' wooed the public on their terms, however base, Handel required the security of a discriminating patron to give him freedom to experiment on his terms.

19
20   James Brydges, Earl of Carnarvon (and from 1719 Duke of Chandos) was the next to offer Handel security and a refuge: a Palladian palace (as yet unfinished) near the village of Edgware, some nine miles from the centre of London, and 'remarkable for having much more of art than nature, and much more cost than art' (Mainwaring). As Paymaster-General to Marlborough's armies overseas, Brydges had so successfully profiteered, by judicious investment of public funds and acceptance of 'gratifications' that, despite being implicated in the total losses of £35 million, he managed to quit office after eight years £600,000 the richer. The building of Cannons, under the successive directions of Vanbrugh, Talman, John James and Gibbs, cost him some £230,000 and defeated the descriptive powers of Defoe: '. . . so Beautiful in its Situation, so Lofty, so Majestick the Appearance of it, that a Pen can but ill describe it, the Pencil not much better; 'tis only fit to be talk'd of upon the very Spot, when the Building is under View, to be consider'd in all its Parts'. In *A Journey Through England* (1722) John Macky, less thunderstruck, gives a more specific account:

> The Disposition of the Avenues, Gardens, Statues, Paintings, and the House of *Cannons*, suits the Genius and Grandeur of its great Master. The Chapel, which is already finished, hath a Choir of Vocal and Instrumental Musick, as the Royal Chapel; and when his Grace goes to Church, he is attended by his *Swiss* Guards, ranged as the Yeomen of the Guards: his Musick also play when he is at Table, he is served by Gentlemen in the best

Order; and I must say, that few German Sovereign Princes, live with that Magnificence, Grandeur and good Order . . .

The Chapel is incomparably neat and pretty, all finely plaistered and gilt by *Pargotti*, and the Cielings and Niches painted by *Paulucci*; there is a handsome Altar Piece, and in an Alcove above the Altar a neat Organ; . . . In the Windows of this Chapel, are also finely painted some Parts of the History of the New Testament.*

In that Court, which opens into the *Area*, is the dining room, very spatious . . . and at the End of it, a Room for his Musick, which performs both Vocal and Instrumental, during the Time he is at Table; and he spares no Expense to have the best . . .

Handel was invited to join Cannons not as director of the music, since that position was already held by Dr Johann Pepusch, but as composer-in-residence – another example of the 'regulated employment' that he had found with Ruspoli and Burlington, but even further from the public eye. Between the account of the water party in 1717 and February 1719 there is not a single mention of his activities in the London press. The Opera House had been given over to the more profitable masquerades, as Heidegger tried to recoup his finances, and Handel's life remains undocumented save for a mention in the newly-discovered diary of Henry Brydges indicating the composer's presence at Cannons on 4 August 1717 and an invitation that Brydges extended to John Arbuthnot in a letter dated 25 September 1717: 'Mr Handle has made me two new Anthems very noble ones & most think they far exceed the two first. He is at work for 2 more & some Overtures to be plaied before the first lesson. You had as good take Cannons in your way to London'.

Since neither the chapel nor the music room of Cannons was finished until 1720, the performances of these pieces (the first of the *Chandos Anthems*) probably took place in the small church of St Lawrence, Whitchurch (still standing). 'Princely Chandos' maintained a small band of musicians, who were expected not only to sing and play, but to double in other domestic roles; one player was recommended because 'He shaves very well & hath an excellent hand on the violin & all necessary languages'. Handel's scoring shows the limitations of the Cannons band, at least in its early days. The list of instruments drawn up by Pepusch in 1720 includes only four violins (all by Stainer), one cello, one double bass and a number of keyboard instruments, one of which was a chamber organ by Jordan with '3 rows of keys, 18 stops'. Handel's anthems are without viola and have a chorus of either one or two tenor parts, but no alto. In line with normal eighteenth-century practice, the two oboists doubled on the flute and recorder.

The eleven *Chandos Anthems* (one a distillation of the Utrecht Jubilate) and the Te Deum in B flat, designed for the leisurely time-scale of a princely court, were too elaborate and too full of 'symphonies' to enter the normal

---

*The stained glass and one of the panels by 'Paulucci' (i.e. Bellucci) can still be seen in Great Witley Church, Worcestershire, the wrought-iron gates at Hampstead Parish Church, London.

cathedral repertoire. Several were later recast for use in the Chapel Royal, and most were quarried for ceremonial music. They provide one of the most fruitful sources of information on Handel's descriptive powers and eclecticism; Italy, Germany and the England of Purcell all contribute to the overall style.

Two larger works better survive their origins, since both drew directly on Handel's dramatic experience, and can retrospectively be seen as pivotal points in his development. The two masques, *Acis and Galatea* and *Esther*, present the secular and sacred sides of a coin that Pepusch had long wished to see in circulation – the all-sung, all-English dramatic entertainment. Pepusch had already produced a fine example, *Venus and Adonis* (the text by John Hughes), which Handel surely knew, and the libretto for *Acis*, the work of John Gay (plus a few other friends from Burlington House days including Pope and Hughes) offered Handel a similarly unpretentious but superbly 'visual' pastoral story of the type that always ignited his inspiration. In its original version, *Acis and Galatea* was cast in one act, without the chorus 'Happy we'. Some of the finest touches are the caricature of a pastoral air in Polyphemus's 'O ruddier than the cherry', the abrupt change of mood with the chorus 'Wretched lovers', the profoundly moving death of Acis (*adagissimo e piano*) and the transformation of 'Heart, the seat of soft delight', where expectations of a da capo form are wonderfully unfulfilled: with such strokes Handel disarms criticism and comparison.

The libretto for *Esther* (possibly by Pope, or a syndicate with Arbuthnot and Gay) was less inspiring. The drama and motivation are ragged, though individual characters shine through (the arrogant Haman in particular), and the strength of the Jewish choruses looks forward to Handel's later innovations. But it remains a puzzling question why he found such differences between the 'private' taste of his Cannons circle and that of the London public that neither *Acis* nor *Esther* should have been introduced to the larger audience until the 1730s – and even then by accident. To a modern listener, who can find the emotional conviction of Galatea or Esther as compelling as the dilemmas of Tamerlano or Medea, Handel's addiction to *opera seria* can seem inexplicable. But we have never seen Italian operas as Handel saw them, and never will; 'our business', as Mainwaring puts it, 'is not to play the panegyrist, but the historian'.

Handel's other activities at Cannons are obscure. Some teaching was involved, because the Duke was later able to recommend one of his pages, George Monroe, for an organist's post in London saying that 'he hath been so successful in his improvement under Mr. Handel & Dr. Pepusch that he is become, though young, a perfect master both for composition & performance on the organ & harpsichord'.* Possibly as a result of these lessons, keyboard music by Handel began to circulate in manuscript and within two years he was obliged to publish his own edition of *Suites de Pièces pour le Clavecin* (preferring the French title to the normal 'Harpsichord Lessons') with the preliminary note:

I have been obliged to publish Some of the following Lessons, because Surrepticious and incorrect copies of them had got abroad. I have added

---

*Baker, *The Life and Circumstances of James Brydges*, p.130.

Folio of autograph manuscript showing Handel's first, second and final attempts at the opening of the F minor harpsichord suite.

several new ones to make the Work more usefull which if it meets with a favourable reception: I will still proceed to publish more reckoning it my duty with my Small talent to Serve a Nation from which I have receiv'd so Generous a protection.

Amongst these suites is the set of variations to which the nineteenth century attached the title of 'The Harmonious Blacksmith', a mythical melodist said to have been resident at Whitchurch, close to Cannons.

> *Handel's jig in the ninth Suite de Pieces, in G minor, is very fine but it is perhaps a little long. Probably Handel was in a hurry, for it takes much more time to get a thing short than to leave it a little long. Brevity is not only the soul of wit, but the soul of making oneself agreeable and of getting on with people, and, indeed, of everything that makes life worth living. So precious a thing, however, cannot be got without more expense and trouble than most of us have the moral wealth to lay out.*
>
> (Samuel Butler, *Notebooks* 1874–1902)

After two seasons without Italian opera on the London stage, moves were afoot to revive an opera company. On 20 February 1719 Handel wrote a guarded letter to his brother-in-law in Halle, postponing an expected visit: '. . . it is greatly to my regret that I find myself kept here by affairs of the greatest moment, on which (I venture to say) all my fortunes depend; but they have continued much longer than I had anticipated.' The affairs, Mainwaring explains, were as follows:

> a project was formed by the Nobility for erecting an academy at the Haymarket. The intention of this musical Society, was to secure to themselves a constant supply of Operas to be composed by HANDEL, and performed under his direction. For this end a subscription was set on foot: and as his . . . Majesty was pleased to let his name appear at the head of it, the Society was dignified with the title of the Royal Academy.*

The enterprise was a great deal more cumbersome and less businesslike than Mainwaring's précis suggests, but the nation was mad for speculation – the South Sea Bubble had not yet burst – and despite past experiences, could even be persuaded that opera might show a profit to shareholders.

The noble promoters of the venture, many from the Burlington/Chandos circle and closely tied to the Kit-Cat Club, appointed a Governor, Deputy-Governor and twenty Directors – all amateurs. At the nominal head was the twenty-six-year-old Lord Chamberlain, Thomas Pelham-Holles, Duke of Newcastle: 'nervous, pompous, always in a hurry, and always behindhand: ignorant of common things, and not learned in any way'. Robert Benson, Lord Bingley, a tricky politician, was Deputy; and amongst the Directors only two had any qualification for dealing with opera: Sir John Vanbrugh and Colonel Blathwayte, who had studied with Alessandro Scarlatti as a prodigy harpsichordist at the age of twelve. Fortunately, the manager was the experienced Heidegger; Handel was named 'master of the Orchestra with a Sallary' (the figure is nowhere mentioned).

A formal 'Proposal for carrying on Operas by a Company and a Joynt Stock', published in April, intended a capital of £10,000, each subscriber to contribute £200 and be liable to annual 'calls' on money pledged. In fact sixty-three subscribers were listed in May, some contributing up to £1000 for their share in the venture. In return they each received two silver tickets of admission to the opera for, so the charter stated, twenty-one years. This plan was later modified to fourteen years, and eventually, despite twenty-one calls on subscribers over the next nine seasons, the enterprise ran out of money in 1728. Blame for the bankruptcy has been laid on the extortionate and unforeseen demands of the foreign stars, on the fickleness of the public, on the financial collapse of many subscribers after the South Sea Bubble and on the inadequacy of the royal subsidy of £1000 (which was equalled by several of the nobility). But from the minutes and estimates of the Academy recently rediscovered in the Duke of

---

*The title was chosen in imitation of the French Académie Royale de Musique, which controlled the Paris Opéra.

Portland's papers (now in Nottingham University), it is clear that the scheme was known to be financially untenable from the start.* Promises of a 25 per cent return on capital were, if not downright dishonest, at least wild figments of an opera-besotted imagination.

Sample budgets drawn up by the Duke of Portland reveal the gap between hope and reality. His rough estimate for a thirty-night season for 1720 includes:

Expences for 30 nights att 50£. a night.	1500
Dancers	300
for scenes & Cloaths.	1000
Operas	200
Poetts	100
Sallarys. Mr Herder, dore keeper secretary.	300
Rent & old scenes.	
Ye patent.	150

Compared with the nightly cost of £75 incurred by Vanbrugh ten years earlier (recorded in the Vice-Chamberlain Coke's Theatrical papers) none of these figures appears realistic. In addition Handel's salary is not mentioned in the estimate, and neither are costs of copying, rehearsing or preparing the house for a first season, although the Duke jotted down a few omissions later, without costs:

Ye alteration of ye House.
Painting of ye scenes.
Contracting with ye Painter
To come to a resolution about dancers.

Against a background of such ingenuous calculations the flowery wording of the 'Proposal' has a hollow ring:

Opera's are the most harmless of all publick Diversions. They are an Encouragement and Support to an Art that has been cherished by all Polite Nations. They carry along with them some Marks of Publick Magnificence and are the great Entertainment which Strangers share in. Therefore it seems very strange that this great and opulent City hath not been able to support Publick Spectacles of this sort for any considerable time . . . To Remedy which Inconveniency for the future it is proposed

That there be subscribed by the Undertakers a Joynt Stock of Ten thousand Pounds Divided into Shares of Two hundred Pounds apeice . . .

---

*Judith Milhous and Robert Hume, 'New Light on Handel', from which the following extracts are taken.

This Project would be attended with the following good Effects. It would ease People of Quality of the exorbitant Burthen of Subscriptions instead of which it may be reasonably Expected that it will turn very much to the Profit of the Subscribers. And tho' it is impossible in a matter subject to so many Casualtyes to form an Exact Judgment of the Advantages likely to arise thereby yet that they will be very considerable may be inferred from the following Considerations.

1st That in Citys farr less able to support any publick Entertainment Operas are carryed on with great Magnificence and produce very great Gain to the Undertakers.

2dly That the Money comeing in dayly to Answer the Expences there can in all Probability be no occasion to raise any great Summe upon the Subscribers. And tho' a Call will be necesary to sett the Project a going Twenty per Cent on Ten thousand Pounds is generally supposed to be as much as the Service can require. . .

As the Operas themselves will be in greater Perfection that [sic] what have hitherto appeared (Joyning what is excellent both in the French and Italian Theatre) so they will undoubtedly procure better Audiences And by the Constancy and Regularity of the Performance the Taste rendred more universall.

On 14 May 1719 Handel received his warrant to travel abroad in search of singers for the opening season. One voice in particular was imperative, that of the great but temperamental castrato Senesino.

21, 29

Instructions to Mr Hendel.
That Mr Hendel either by himself or such Correspondenc^s as he shall think fit procure proper Voices to Sing in the Opera.

The said Mr Hendel is impower'd to contract in the Name of the Patentees with those Voices to Sing in the Opera for one Year and no more.

That Mr Hendel engage Senezino as soon as possible to Serve the said Company and for as many Years as may be.

That in case Mr Hendel meet with an excellent Voice of the first rate he is to Acquaint the Govr and Company forthwith of it and upon what Terms he or She may be had. . .

Holles Newcastle.

After a (putative) trip to his family in Halle (legend maintains that Bach just missed meeting him there), Handel made his way to Dresden, where Lotti was director of the King of Saxony's opera. Lotti's *Teofane*, produced for a marriage celebration in September, starred the castrati Berselli and Senesino, as well as Durastante and Boschi with whom Handel had worked before. While waiting for a chance to induce them to leave Dresden, he wrote in French to Lord Burlington, with whom he was still obviously on good terms in spite of the move to Cannons:

It is always as much with deep gratitude as in duty bound that I have the honour to assure you of my zeal and devotion towards your person. I further owe you an exact account of what I have undertaken and of the successful outcome of my long voyage.

I am waiting here for the engagements of Sinesino, Berselli and Guizzardi to be concluded and for these gentlemen (who are, I may add, favourably disposed) to sign contracts with me for Great Britain. Everything will be decided in a few days' time; I have good hopes, and as soon as I have concluded something definite, I shall inform you of it, My Lord, as my benefactor and patron. Pray continue, My Lord, your favours; they will be precious to me, and I shall always exert myself in your service to carry out your commands with zeal and fidelity.

In the event only Durastante was able to come to England for the Academy's first season, a catch sneered at by the Academy's appointed poet and librettist, Paolo Rolli: 'It is said for certain that Durastanti will be coming for the Operas: Oh! what a bad choice for England! I shall not enter into her singing merits but she really is an Elephant!' The nickname stuck, and it is small wonder that Handel was never on good terms with Rolli (he was in any case a poor dramatist), and preferred to work with Nicola Haym, who had begun as a cellist in the service of the Duke of Bedford before becoming both librettist and impresario.

So firmly was attention riveted on the singers that contemporary sources of information on the orchestral contribution to Handel's operas are few and far between. Amongst the papers of the Duke of Portland which deal with the first season of the Royal Academy are several lists of orchestral players, with their gradings for payment. The names include most of the finest performers in London, and comprise in all 34 players: 8 first violins, 5 seconds, and 4 '3d Rank of violins', 2 violas, 4 cellos, 2 double basses, 4 oboes, 3 bassoons, a theorbo and a trumpet (Committee Minutes, 15 February 1720).* In 1728 a French visitor to London, Pierre-Jacques Fourgeroux, recorded his impressions of the final season at the King's Theatre in his manuscript account of his 'Voiage d'Angleterre'. He noted the divine voices of Faustina, Cuzzoni and Senesino, and the fees they were paid ('C'est un prix exorbitant'). 'The orchestra was made up of twenty-four violins [including violas], led by the brothers Castrucci, two harpsichords – one of them played by the German "Indel", a great performer and a great composer – an archlute, three violoncellos, two double-basses, and occasionally flutes [traversi or recorders?] and trumpets. This orchestra makes a great din . . . there is only one cello, the two harpsichords and the archlute for the recitatives'. Fourgeroux also comments on the way the chords in recitative are cut off – invaluable evidence for a modern player, although Fourgeroux calls it in his opinion 'a bad style of accompanying'.

Thanks to the energy that Handel invested in the enterprise over the next eight years, the Academy, though financially disastrous, was an artistic triumph.

---

*ibid.

Other composers were drawn in – Bononcini (on Burlington's suggestion) in 1720 and three years later, Ariosti – but the bulk of the musical output, and the overall artistic control, was always Handel's. Of 487 performances, Chrysander calculates 245 were of Handel, 108 of Bononcini, 55 of Ariosti and 79 made up of other composers or *pasticcii*.

Contemporary accounts give only the external aspect of Handel's engagement with the many-headed monster of *opera seria*. His struggles with the form itself must be read in the music. There was, first, his attitude to libretto and characterization: all but one of the Academy operas are dynastic, epic and, it is suggested, symbolic of the ruling order, reflecting what one feels as Handel's own desire for stability, hierarchy and succession. Second, his insistence on harnessing the best possible vocal talents to his ideas, underlining the force that sheer vocal virtuosity exerted on his inspiration. But he was never tyrannized by either the voice or the singer; his stubbornness and his revisions were always at the service of the drama, never the glory of the gullet. Even Cuzzoni came to see the reasons for her threatened defenestration (see p. 83). Third, there was the perennial battle between a constant curiosity towards what other composers were doing and his own stubborn individuality. Bononcini's softer elegance and lyricism, for instance, which can be traced in Handel's style from the third Academy season onwards, combine with stylistic elements deriving from material of his earlier days: the task of describing Handel's stylistic development cuts across chronological analysis.

Public reaction to the new Academy is well documented. The first season opened (with a makeshift team of singers) on 2 April 1720; Handel's new opera was held back until the King was ready to attend, so the first opera was Porta's *Numitore*.* The excitement was all the greater, Mainwaring tells us, when *Radamisto* finally appeared.

> If persons who are now living, and who were present at that performance may be credited, the applause it received was almost as extravagant as his AGRIPPINA had excited: the crowds and tumults of the house at Venice were hardly equal to those at LONDON. In so splendid and fashionable an assembly of ladies (to the excellence of their taste we must impute it) there was no shadow of form, or ceremony, scarce indeed any appearance of order or regularity, politeness or decency. Many, who had forc'd their way into the house with an impetuosity but ill suited to their rank and sex, actually fainted through the excessive heat and closeness of it. Several gentlemen were turned back, who had offered forty shillings† for a seat in the gallery, after having despaired of getting any in the pit or boxes.

Radamisto, 'more solid, ingenious, and full of fire than any drama which Handel had yet produced' (Burney), was the most fully scored of Handel's

---

*Handel directed the performance and presumably kept a copy of the score, from which he quarried later on in his career (see p. 171).
†The advertised price was five shillings.

works to date and included horns, for the first time in the theatre, in 'Alzo al volo'. Even without the greatest Italian singers, Handel had proved that his music could draw; spirits were high, and opera might even yet prove profitable, as a note in *The Theatre* on 8 March records: 'At the Rehearsal on *Friday* last, Signior NIHILINI BENEDITTI rose half a Note above his Pitch formerly known. Opera Stock from 83 and a half, when he began; at 90 when he ended'.

But the metaphor was ill-chosen: in the summer of 1720, the Bubble burst. Rolli's letters to Riva of 23 September and 18 October, while signalling the arrival of Handel's chosen voices, shows the effect of the crash on London society and the Academy:

> On Monday last Senesino arrived in company with Berselli and Salvai. . . . I am delighted to find this famous artist a man well-mannered, well-read, extremely kind and endowed with the noblest sentiments. . .
>
> My dear Riva, what ruination has the Southsea crash caused! The whole nobility is at its last gasp; only gloomy faces are to be seen. Great bankers are going bankrupt, great shareholders just disappear and there is not an acquaintance or friend who has escaped total ruin. These rogues of Company Directors have betrayed everybody and I assure you the tragic worst is feared. They ought to be gibbeted these South Sea Directors, who have ruined all my friends – and I very much fear that they will in consequence have ruined the Academy. God damn 'em. . .

Nevertheless, after many changes to the Directorate in the aftermath of the South Sea scandal, the Academy's second season opened on 19 November. 'The stage was never so well served as it is now', wrote Mrs Pendarves (Handel's friend Mary Granville), 'there is not one indifferent voice, they are all Italians. There is one man called Serosini [*sic*] who is beyond Nicolini both in person and voice'.

Senesino remained with the Academy as *primo uomo* until its fall, his fee reaching £2000 a year. He was never easy to deal with, and according to Rolli's letters there was animosity between him and Handel from the start (which Rolli helped to foment). His singing, according to Quantz, was beyond reproach:

> He had a powerful, clear, equal and sweet contralto voice, with a perfect intonation and an excellent shake [trill]. His manner of singing was masterly and his elocution unrivalled. Though he never loaded adagios with too many ornaments, yet he delivered the original and essential notes with the utmost refinement. He sang allegros with great fire, and marked rapid divisions, from the chest, in an articulate and pleasing manner. His countenance was well adapted to the stage, and his action was natural and noble. To these qualities he joined a majestic figure; but his aspect and deportment were more suited to the part of a hero than of a lover.

Others, such as Zambeccari, the impresario who had worked with him some years earlier in Italy, were less flattering about his acting ability:

> Senesino continues to comport himself badly enough; he stands like a statue, and when occasionally he does make a gesture, he makes one directly the opposite of what is wanted. He expresses himself abominably in recitatives, unlike Nicolino who used to do them admirably; as for the arias, he sings them well when in voice. But yesterday evening, in the best aria, he was two beats ahead of time.

Senesino made his début in the work of another new arrival, Bononcini, whose opera *Astarto* (libretto by Rolli) ran for twenty-four performances in the season – a record that Handel never equalled. It was followed by a revival of *Radamisto*, much revised and with Senesino in the title role, which played for only seven nights. This element of competition between Academy composers was heightened by a curious ploy of the Academy later in the season when, probably to save time, *Muzio Scevola* was written by three composers simultaneously: Act I by Filippo Amadei, the principal cellist of the Opera, Act II by Bononcini and Act III by Handel, 'who easily triumphed over the others', according to the courtier De Fabrice.

After a number of calls on the Academy's subscribers (answered none too promptly), the new season included a second revival of *Radamisto*, followed by a new Handel opera *Floridante*, which was dedicated, perhaps tactlessly, to the Prince of Wales. The story hinges on the imprisonment of a rightful heir who nevertheless triumphs in the end; a contemporary report states that at this 'last circumstance, there happened to be very great and unreasonable clapping, in the presence of great ones'. Apart from the fugue of the overture based 'upon a convulsive and unpleasant theme', Burney was impressed by its lyricism: 'I mention the slow songs in this opera as superior in every respect to those of Bononcini, who has frequently been extolled by his admirers for unrivalled excellence in airs of tenderness'.

Handel could not have kept the Academy supplied with sufficient operas single-handed, and his chief support came from Bononcini, who in any case drew better: he had sixty-three performances in his first two seasons against Handel's twenty-eight. The idea of the two men locked in battle stems in fact from the partisan spirit of contemporary audiences rather than the feelings of the composers. Singers and subscribers were grateful to both, and the divisions amongst the nobility became comically irrelevant:

> Some say, compar'd to Bononcini,
> That Mynheer Handel's but a Ninny;
> Others aver, that he to Handel
> Is scarcely fit to hold a candle:
> Strange all this Difference should be
> 'Twixt Tweedle-dum and Tweedle-dee!

> John Byrom, *Epigram on the Feuds*
> *Between Handel and Bononcini*

James Ralph, the American author of a pamphlet called *The Touchstone: or, . . . Essays on the Reigning Diversions of the Town* (1728), picked what he considered to be the particular excellence of each of the Academy composers. Handel should express 'the Rage of Tyrants, the Passions of Heroes and the Distresses of Lovers in the Heroick Stile', Bononcini 'sighing Shepherds, bleating Flocks, chirping Birds and purling Streams in the *Pastoral*', and the almost forgotten Ariosti 'good Dungeon Scenes, Marches for a Battel, or Minuets for a Ball, in the *Miserere*. H—l would warm us in Frost or Snow, by rousing every Passion with Notes proper to the Subject: Whilst B—ni would fan us, in the *Dog-Days*, with an *Italian* Breeze, and lull us asleep with gentle Whispers'.

The main attraction of the Academy's fourth season was the arrival of a new soprano from Italy, announced in *The London Journal* on 27 October 1722:

> There is a new Opera now in Rehearsal at the Theatre in the Hay-Market, a Part of which is reserv'd for one Mrs. *Cotsona*, an extraordinary Italian Lady, who is expected daily from Italy. It is said, she has a much finer Voice and more accurate Judgment, than any of her Country Women who have performed on the English Stage.

Francesca Cuzzoni, although 'short and squat, with a doughy cross face' (Horace Walpole), made an instant success in *Ottone*: 'the house was full to overflowing', wrote De Fabrice, '. . . and there is such a run on it that tickets are already being sold at 2 and 3 guineas which are ordinarily half a guinea, so that it is like another Mississippi or South Sea Bubble'.

The slow aria that 'fixed her reputation as an expressive and pathetic singer' (Burney) draws from Mainwaring a famous anecdote describing Handel's dictatorial government of his prima donnas at rehearsal.

> *Having one day some words with* CUZZONI *on her refusing to sing* Falsa imagine *in* OTTONE; *Oh! Madame (said he) je scais bien que Vous êtes une véritable Diablesse: mais je Vous ferai sçavoir, moi, que je suis Beelzebub le* Chéf des Diables. *With this he took her up by the waist, and, if she made any more words, swore that he would fling her out of the window.*

Not only were the Nobility so transported that they eventually 'gave her 50 Guineas a Ticket', but even the gallery (where footmen and servants were admitted free) was carried away, and was issued with a warning: 'Upon Complaint to the Royal Academy of Musick, that Disorders have been of late committed in the Footmen's Gallery, to the Interruption of the Performance; This is to give Notice, That the next Time any Disorder is made there, that Gallery will be shut up.' The threat evidently went unheeded, for at a later performance a groom in the gallery shouted: 'Damn her! she has got a nest of nightingales in her belly!'.

Opera fever gripped the town: 'folks, that could not distinguish one tune from another, now daily dispute about the different styles of Handel,

Bononcini, and Attilio [Ariosti]', wrote Gay to Jonathan Swift on 3 February; 'Senesino is daily voted to be the greatest man that ever lived'. As a result, although Cuzzoni's starting price of £1500 was almost double the Duke of Portland's original estimate, the Academy was able to offer a surprising dividend of 7 per cent on 6 February 1723. There was even a plan, which never materialized, to take the company to Paris for twelve performances.

Three days after Cuzzoni's début, Ariosti's first Academy opera, *Coriolano*, opened, to the (by now) familiar scenes of wild enthusiasm for Senesino and Cuzzoni. It was followed by Bononcini's *Erminia*; both were heroic, neither distinctive. Handel, with the true showman's instinct for surprise, finished the season with a parody of the heroic manner, *Flavio*, an opera that is by turns comic, sentimental, ironic and politically satirical. Handel is said to have accompanied one of Ugone's arias so flamboyantly in rehearsal that the singer, a young Scottish tenor named Gordon, threatened to jump into the harpsichord if Handel persisted. His reply shows a characteristically dry humour: 'let me know when you will do that, and I will advertise it; for I am sure more people will come to see you jump, than to hear you sing'.

23   Handel wrote only a single opera for the next season, *Giulio Cesare in Egitto*, perhaps his most fully wrought example of the true heroic ideal, a consolidation of all he had learned to date in the theatre and one for which he allowed himself an unusual amount of composing time. It was started in the summer of 1723, and opened on 20 February 1724. With eight principal characters (four Roman, four Egyptian) and an orchestration more colourful and varied than any since *La Resurrezione*, Handel was aiming at a magnificence more exotic than in any of his previous operas. Cleopatra's aria 'V'adoro, pupille', featuring a double orchestra (including a stage band with muted strings, theorbo, harp and concertante viola da gamba), exemplifies the kind of spacious sensuality with which the opera is imbued, far removed from the heroic brilliance of *Rinaldo* that could be turned out in two weeks. *Giulio Cesare* was a great success: 'the house was just as full at the seventh performance as at the first', noted De Fabrice. It was also Handel's most successful export, with forty performances in Hamburg alone between 1725 and 1737, although one in August 1735 was cancelled because 'no one came'. The translation was prepared by Thomas Lediard, who also designed the sets. As was common in Hamburg operas by then, the composer's score was heavily supplemented: in the first performance by six ballets and in later versions by comic peasants and a chorus of concubines and eunuchs. The most spectacular performance was given in honour of George I's birthday in 1727 by the English envoy Wyche and his secretary, the multi-talented Lediard, who supplied illuminations and fireworks, wrote the libretto for an extra Prologue and Epilogue called *The Joy and Happiness of the British Nation* and commissioned Telemann to write the music.

Encouraged by his operatic fortunes, Handel moved at about this time to the

32   house in Lower Brook Street* near Hanover Square which he was to occupy for the rest of his life. St George's Church in Hanover Square where, although

*After Handel's death the house was numbered 57 Brook St, altered later to its present 25.

Lutheran, he became a regular worshipper, was completed in the following year.

Opera left Handel with little spare time, and all we know of his other musical activities during the season is that he was paid 'Three Pounds Eighteen Shillings and Six pence for Writing the Anthem* which was perform'd at St James before His Ma^{ty}' in January to celebrate the King's return to England; and that on 24 August, according to Applebee's *Original Weekly Journal*, '. . . the Royal Highnesses, the Princess Anne and Princess Caroline, came to St. Paul's Cathedral, and heard the famous Mr. Hendel, (their Musick Master) perform upon the Organ'. This is the first mention of Handel's appointment as music master to the Princesses, the only regular position he ever held in the King's Music. Handel later maintained that Princess Anne was his only pupil (see p. 120).

The sixth opera season opened on 31 October with a discreet act of political affiliation by Handel. Three anniversaries in the following month held traditional monarchist overtones – the birthday of William of Orange, the royalist landings of 1688 and, of course, Guy Fawkes Day on 5 November. The theatre world normally marked this month with a performance of Nicholas Rowe's pro-William, anti-Louis XIV play *Tamerlane*, and Handel correspondingly obliged the court with an operatic version, *Tamerlano*, performed nine times in October and November.

Francesco Borosini, a tenor, was engaged for the part of the hero Bajazet; an unusual casting in the heyday of castrati, and a chance for innuendo that the press could not resist: 'It is commonly reported this Gentleman was never *cut out for a Singer*' (*Weekly Journal*, 17 October 1724). The choice caused Handel much unexpected work; a revised libretto brought by Borosini from Gasparini's setting of 1719 acted as a catalyst for him to refashion much of Bajazet's music, lowering the tessitura to suit Borosini's voice – there are five versions of the Act I prison scene. The music of the arias was published by Cluer with the unusual addition of an English translation, made by Henry Carey.

Handel's second opera of the season, *Rodelinda*, opened on 13 February 1725 and also featured Borosini, but the major impact on the public was made by Cuzzoni's costume: 'on her appearing in this opera, in a *brown silk gown*, trimmed with silver, with the vulgarity and indecorum of which all the old ladies were much scandalized, the young adopted it as a fashion, so universally, that it seemed a national uniform for youth and beauty' (Horace Walpole).

At the end of the season Handel wrote one of his formal, unrevealing letters to his brother-in-law, apologizing for his failure again to visit Halle: 'I had hoped to be able to renew our friendship in person by a visit to your parts when the King departs for Hanover, but my hopes cannot be fulfilled this time, and the state of my affairs deprives me of that happiness despite all my expectations. However I do not despair of being so fortunate one day'. His worries are explained by a note in the *London Journal* of 4 September: 'Signiora *Faustina*, a famous Italian Lady, is coming over this Winter to rival Signiora

---

*The music performed was probably *Let God arise* and the Te Deum in A, both based on Chandos material.

Cuzzoni; the Royal Academy of Musick has contracted with her for Two Thousand Five Hundred Pound'. The Directors of the Academy had finally gone too far. To engage the world's two greatest sopranos simultaneously was certainly a coup, but psychologically and financially it was sheer folly.

28, 29   Faustina Bordoni was a foil to Cuzzoni, both in voice and temperament. Burney claims that 'she in a manner invented a new kind of singing, by running divisions with a neatness and velocity which astonished all who heard her. She had the art of sustaining a note longer, in the opinion of the public, than any other singer, by taking her breath imperceptibly'. Coupled with her ability as an actress, she had intelligence, a sweet disposition, good looks and the advantage of being unmarried (she became the wife of the composer Hasse in 1730).

For a short while the confrontation of Cuzzoni and 'La Nuova Sirena' was delayed; Faustina did not arrive to dazzle London until May 1726. In the meantime Handel, operating almost single-handed, started the season with revivals and hastily produced *Scipione*. The score was finished on 2 March and the opera opened ten days later; its introductory March, reflecting the military confidence of the time, was subsequently taken up by the Grenadier Guards. Six days later the Academy, its financial balance increasingly precarious, announced its seventeenth distress call of 5 per cent, and looked anxiously to the combination of Cuzzoni, Faustina and Senesino for rescue.

Handel rose to the musical and diplomatic challenge posed by his triumvirate of singers with *Alessandro*, in which both ladies were allocated the same number of arias, both had a duet with the hero Senesino, with whom they were both in love and, most daring of all, both together sang the duet, 'Placa l'alma', with exactly balanced parts. *Alessandro* ran for eleven nights, so successfully that the normal pattern of two performances a week had to be broken, and would have run longer had not Senesino, probably feeling neglected, announced himself 'indisposed' before the final night, and returned to Italy for the sake of his health. The prima donnas continued in an atmosphere of growing hostility.

Senesino's continued 'convalescence' prevented a new season from opening at the Haymarket in the autumn of 1726. Christopher Rich, manager of the rival Lincoln's Inn Fields Theatre, seized the opportunity to revive the old favourite, *Camilla*, which was sung in English, ran for twenty-three performances (ten more than either of Handel's last operas), and was introduced with a Prologue both satirical and ominous:

> Ye British Fair, vouchsafe us your Applause,
> And smile, propitious, on our English Cause;
> While Senesino you expect in vain,
> And see your Favours treated with Disdain:
> While, 'twixt his Rival Queens, such mutual Hate
> Threats hourly Ruin to yon tuneful State.
> Permit your Country's Voices to repair,
> In some Degree, your Disappointment there:

Here, may that charming Circle Nightly shine;
'Til Time, when That deserts us, to resign.

The battle of the Italian singers resumed in January 1727 with a new Handel opera, *Admeto*. Quantz, debating whether to live in London rather than Berlin, was present and commented that the opera, which includes some of Handel's finely calculated atmospheric settings, 'had magnificent music. *Faustina*, *Cuzzoni* and *Senesino*, all three virtuosos of the front rank, were the chief performers in it, the rest were middling. . . . The orchestra consisted for the greater part of Germans, several Italians, and a few Englishmen. *Castrucci*, an Italian violinist, was the leader. All together, under *Händel's* conducting, made an extremely good effect' (*Autobiography*, 1754). But it was ruined for him by the audience: 'the violence of party for the two singers . . . was so great that when the admirers of one began to applaud, those of the other were sure to hiss'.

Animosity reached a head during a performance of Bononcini's last London opera *Astianatte*. The *British Journal* for 10 June reported:

On Tuesday-night last [6 June], a great Disturbance happened at the Opera, occasioned by the Partisans of the Two Celebrated Rival Ladies, Cuzzoni and Faustina. The Contention at first was only carried on by Hissing on one Side, and Clapping on the other; but proceeded at length to Catcalls, and other great Indecencies: And notwithstanding the Princess Caroline was present, no Regards were of Force to restrain the Rudenesses of the Opponents.

Nor was the violence limited to the audience: 'who would have thought the Infection should reach the Haymarket, and inspire two Singing Ladies to pull each other's coiffs?' asked John Arbuthnot in his pamphlet, *The Devil to Pay at St. James*, published that year; '. . . it is certainly an apparent Shame that two such well bred Ladies should call Bitch and Whore, should scold and fight like any Billingates'.

The town satirists quickly capitalized on the scandal. A hastily published skit, called *The Contre Temps; or, Rival Queans*, gives a replay of the action set in the Temple of Discord, with Handel standing fatalistically by as the two ladies maul each other:

I think 'tis best – to let 'em fight it out:
Oil to the Flames you add, to stop their Rage;
When tir'd, of Course, their Fury will assuage.
(*Faustina lays flat Cuzzoni's nose with a sceptre, Cuzzoni breaks her head with a gilt leather crown: Handel, desirous to see the end of the battle, animates them with a kettledrum: a globe thrown at random hits the High Priest on the temples: he staggers off the stage.*)

Within days of the fight between his leading singers Handel and London society were deflected to matters of more moment. News arrived that on

11 June (22nd according to the Continental calendar)* George I had died of
apoplexy at Osnabrück. One of the last functions he had performed before
leaving England had been to put his signature to 'An Act for naturalizing
Louis Sechehaye, George Frideric Handel, and others'. Handel's first commission
as a naturalized citizen of Britain was to write the music for the Coronation
Service of the new sovereign George II (Heidegger was asked to organize the
illuminations). The four anthems *Zadok the Priest, My Heart is Inditing, Let
Thy Hand be Strengthened* and *The King shall Rejoice* were on a larger scale than
anything of this kind Handel had previously essayed, and even their rehearsals
aroused public excitement; 'the Time will be kept private', announced *Parker's
Penny Post* on 4 October, 'lest the Crowd of People should be an Obstruction
to the Performers', who themselves constituted a fair crowd, 'there being
40 Voices, and about 160 Violins, Trumpets, Hautboys, Kettle-Drums, and
Bass's proportionable; besides an Organ, which was erected behind the Altar'
(*Norwich Gazette*, 14 October).

Though in rehearsal 'both the Musick and the Performers, were the
Admiration of all the Audience', the actual ceremony seems to have gone off
badly. An authority no less than the Archbishop of Canterbury jotted on his
Order of Service that 'by the Negligence of the Choir of Westmʳ' one anthem
was entirely omitted; *Zadok the Priest* was sung during rather than after the
Anointing; and in sum, he found 'The anthems in confusion; all irregular in the
music [i.e. orchestra]'. This may not have been Handel's fault. John Alcock,
who was a choirboy at the coronation service, later paid this testimony to
Handel's skill and discipline as a choirmaster: 'Handel was the only Master of
Music that ever cou'd govern a set of Singers: and he himself was often obliged
to use very rough means, as well as bitter words, before he cou'd accomplish it.'
But *Zadok the Priest*, with its inspired opening crescendo and breathtaking entry
of the seven-part chorus with trumpets, became and has remained ever since a
public favourite, reappearing in every succeeding coronation service.†

Back in the opera house, Senesino and the two sirens had been contracted
for one more season. But public tolerance for the antics of Italian opera was
spent: 'I doubt operas will not survive longer than this winter, they are now
at their last gasp', wrote Mrs Pendarves to her sister; 'the subscription is
expired and nobody will renew it. The directors are always squabbling, and
they have so many divisions among themselves that I wonder they have not
broke up before; Senesino goes away next winter, and I believe Faustina, so
you see harmony is almost out of fashion'.

Handel made a massive effort with three new operas: the patriotic *Riccardo
Primo, Rè d'Inghilterra; Siroe;* and *Tolomeo.* With its recitative much reduced for
an English audience, *Siroe* received nineteen performances, and the Gigue that
ends the Overture, one of Handel's best perpetual motion movements, lived on

*Until 3 September 1752, the British calendar lagged eleven days behind the Continental calendar. In this book all the dates subsequent to Handel's arrival in England (1710) are given according to the former, except where the latter is indicated by 'NS' (New Style).
†Burney recalls that he played *Zadok* in a keyboard arrangement to demonstrate Kirckman harpsichords in his youth.

long after the opera – Burney remembers hearing the composer 'play it by memory as a lesson at Mrs. Cibber's, with wonderful neatness and spirit near twenty years after it was composed'.* But the dedication of *Tolomeo* to the Earl of Albemarle, imploring his protection for operas in general as 'being on the decline', marks the end of the enterprise with which Handel had been associated for the past eight years. Despite the presence of three of Europe's finest singers and the support of the Royal Family, the opera ran for only seven nights.

At Lincoln's Inn Fields, a hastily mounted novelty shadowed these last few days of the Academy's existence. *The Beggar's Opera*, a satirical play with ballad tunes hurriedly inserted to support Gay's lyrics, attacked politicians, corruption, 'good taste', speculation and the affectations of Society. Some risible elements of opera libretti – the 'simile' aria ('The Swallow, The Moth, The Ship, The Bee, The Flower'), the sudden happy ending, the high moral tone – were ready victims, and the loyal subscribers (Mrs Pendarves among them) were understandably upset: 'the taste of the town is so depraved, that nothing will be approved of but the burlesque. The Beggars' Opera entirely triumphs over the Italian one'.

The triumph of 'burlesque' was a result, rather than the cause, of the Academy's collapse. Even before its doors opened in 1720 Vanbrugh had pinpointed its inherent failings; the extravagance of the venture, he noted, 'would bring the Expences to about twice as much as the Receipts'. And in its final year the diagnosis was the same. According to James Ralph, who reissued his pamphlet of 1728 with a new title, *The Taste of the Town*, in 1731, they could not 'with the highest Prices be certain of coming off Clear one Season unless they have crowded houses every Night'. Ralph also suggested the only possible cure:

> I have often heard it very publickly whisper'd, that some great People intended to have a larger Opera-House built; but what obstructed so noble and laudable a Design, I could never learn. Had it been carried on, and executed, according to the Plans of some Theatres in Italy, which are capa[b]le of containing an Audience of several Thousands, the Advantages resulting from so great an Undertaking would prove infinite.
>
> An Opera-House so contriv'd as to allow a Number of Spectators, would admit of several Degrees of Seats, suited in their prices to all Ranks of People, from the highest to the lowest Station of Life: And from an Audience so numerous, might be rais'd all Sums necessary to defray the greatest Expences; as the heaviest Taxes are made easy, by being made general.

His advice, even had it been practical, came too late. A General Court was held to consider 'proper Measures for recovering the Debts due to the Academy, and discharging what is due to performers, Tradesmen, and others and also to determine how the Scenes, Cloaths, etc. are to be disposed of' (*Daily Courant*, 31 May), and the doors closed with a final performance of *Admeto* on 1 June.

---

*The keyboard arrangement published by Walsh, however, is certainly not by Handel.

4

London: the Decline of Opera
1729–1737

In Days of Old when *Englishmen* were *Men*,
Their Musick like themselves, was grave, and plain . . .
But now, since *Brittains* are become polite,
Since some have learnt to *read*, and some to write . . .
Since *Masquerades* and *Opera*'s made their Entry,
And *Heydegger* and *Handell* rul'd our Gentry;
A hundred different Instruments combine,
And foreign *Songsters* in the Concert join . . .
In unknown Tongues mysterious Dullness chant,
Make Love in *Tune*, or *thro' the Gamut rant*.

James Miller, *Harlequin-Horace:
or the Art of Modern Poetry* (1731)

The collapse of a company, the ruin of an enterprise, the disposing of effects, the closing of theatre doors – these may often be more emotive descriptions in the hands of a historian than the events ever were to the actors in the drama. The end of a régime means (for the historian) a hunt for lost threads, enabling him to piece together the fabric of the old and the new; to the participants the 'tragedy' was a momentary hiccup, and a chance to shake the dice once more. As the Earl of Shaftesbury so bluntly put it: 'the Fund for maintaining Opera's being exhausted, they ceased of course, – and the Singers left England'. But no one was ruined by the demise of the Royal Academy of Music, and (this time at least) there was no physical collapse. Every singer, player, painter and mechanic was paid off – no one could get away with notes of credit (except Handel in his later life) – and the young bloods amongst the Directorate had had the pleasure of seeing their outlay give more general and lasting satisfaction than a similar expenditure on Newmarket or the *ridotto*. Now that the initial thrill of running their own opera had worn off, and the difference between commitment and true business sense been made quite clear, they were happy to hand over their facilities to the professionals. Viscount Percival, a Director since 1719, noted in his diary on 18 January:

I went to a meeting of the members of the Royal Academy of Musick: where we agreed to prosecute the subscribers who have not yet paid; also to permit

Hydeger and Hendle to carry on operas without disturbance for 5 years and to lend them for that time our scenes, machines, clothes, instruments, furniture, etc. It all past off in a great hurry, and there was not above 20 there.

From Rolli we learn how the new company was put in motion. Heidegger, the impresario, was granted £2200 by Lord Bingley, who was at the head of the new project, with which to provide theatre, scenery and costumes. Handel was to be allowed £1000 for each opera, to be written by himself or whoever he chose. A subscription system would be initiated, offering fifty performances a season for 15 guineas per person. As for the singers, by whom the fate of the new venture would be decided, a total of £4000 was allocated, the two *primarii* to be offered £1000 each plus the usual benefit concert and the remainder all to be secured for a total of £2000. Since Heidegger had apparently just returned empty-handed from a trip to Italy, Handel was to be sent to find fresh singers, accompanied by three representatives of the subscribers, 'in order to examine them'. Farinelli and Cuzzoni were the favourites, although Handel preferred to work with new (and presumably less temperamental) singers. Haym was to circulate all the appropriate candidates, to advise them of Handel's visit.

Yesterday Morning Mr. Handell, the famous Composer of the Italian Musick, took his Leave of their Majesties, he being to set out this Day for Italy, with a commission from the Royal Academy of Musick. (*Daily Post*, 27 January 1729)

A mist descends over all Handel's movements outside the confines of London, whether he merely made the journey up the Edgware Road to Cannons, or crossed Europe to hear Farinelli in Venice. His one surviving letter from this trip to his former brother-in-law (Michael Michaelsen, since remarried) places him in Venice during Carnival time.

Venice, 11 March 1729.

Honoured Brother,
. . . I beg you to continue to send me your news from time to time while I am travelling in this country, since you cannot but know the interest and satisfaction that I take in them. All you have to do is to address letters each time to Mr Joseph Smith,* Banker, at Venice (as I have already mentioned), who will send them on to me at the various places in Italy where I shall be.

Two more of Handel's 'various places' in Italy can be fixed. Rolli had heard that Senesino gave him a cold reception and reported back to Senesino 'that he was complaining and protesting about it, adding that Princes have a long reach'; but after a reconciliation, Handel promised 'to come to Siena on his return from Naples'. Whether he did or not is unknown. 'On his arrival at Rome', Mainwaring says, 'he received a very friendly and obliging letter of invitation

---

*Joseph Smith, the patron of Canaletto, had married the soprano Catherine Tofts, who had played the title roles in *Arsinoe* and *Camilla*, early Italian operas in London

from Cardinal COLONNA, with a promise of a very fine picture of his Eminence. But, hearing that the Pretender was then at the Cardinal's, he prudently declined accepting both the invitation and the picture'. It was politic not to risk his Hanoverian support by associating with Jacobites.

As for the return trip through Germany, we have only the despatch from Hanover of 16 June (printed in the *London Gazette*) that 'Mr. Hendel passed this Place some Days ago, coming from Italy and returning to England'. We assume, indeed hope, that he visited his mother in Halle (a month earlier than he had estimated), but there are no grounds for the story that he turned down an invitation to visit Johann Sebastian Bach in Leipzig, delivered by his son Wilhelm Friedemann, who was living in Halle at that time.

The facts of Handel's talent-hunting expedition were filled in by the *Daily Journal* immediately on his return to London.

Mr. Handel, who is just returned from Italy, has contracted with the following Persons to perform in the Italian Opera's, vz.

Signor Bernachi, who is esteem'd the best Singer in Italy.

Signora Merighi, a Woman of a very fine Presence, an excellent Actress, and a very good Singer – A Counter Tenor.

Signora Strada, who hath a very fine Treble Voice, a person of singular Merit.

Signor Annibal Pio Fabri, a most excellent Tenor, and a fine Voice.

His wife, who performs a Man's Part exceeding well.

Signora Bartoldi, who has a very fine Treble Voice; she is also a very genteel Actress, both in Men and Womens Parts.

A Bass Voice [Riemschneider] from Hamburgh, there being none worth engaging in Italy.

'Thus embarqued on a new bottom', as Mainwaring put it, Handel opened with *Lotario*, which he had completed on 16 November; 2 December was, by any standards, a late start to the season, but it still gave only a fortnight for preparation. It was probably at a final rehearsal that Mrs Pendarves had a chance to judge the new team:

Bernachi has a vast compass, his voice mellow and clear, but not so sweet as Senesino, his manner better; his person not so good, for he is as big as a Spanish friar. Fabri has a tenor Voice, sweet, clear and firm, but not strong enough, I doubt, for the stage: he sings like a gentleman, without making faces, and his manner is particularly agreeable; he is the greatest master of musick that ever sang upon the stage. The third is the bass, a very good distinct voice, without any harshness. La Strada is the first woman; her voice is without exception fine, her manner perfection, but her person *very bad*, and she makes *frightful mouths*.* La Merighi is the next to her; her voice is not

---

*Others were less restrained about Strada's appearance and christened her 'The Pig'. She was the only one of Handel's singers who remained with him to the end of the 1738 season.

```
┌─────────────────────────────────────┐
│                                      │
│   PARTHENOPE                         │
│           an                         │
│   OPERA                              │
│   as it was Perform'd                │
│           at the                     │
│   KINGS Theatre                      │
│         for the                      │
│   Royal Accademy                     │
│      Compos'd by                     │
│                                      │
│   Mr Handel.                         │
│   ─────────────────────────────     │
│         LONDON.                      │
│   Printed for and fold by I:Walfh    │
│   fervant to his Majefty at the Harp │
│   and Hoboy in Catherine ftreet in   │
│   the Strand. and Iofeph Hare at     │
│   the Viol and Hoboy in Cornhill     │
│   near the Royal Exchange.           │
│                                      │
└─────────────────────────────────────┘
```

Title-page of Partenope, *published by Walsh in 1730.*

extraordinarily good or bad, she is tall and has a very graceful person, with a tolerable face; she seems to be a woman about forty, she sings easily and agreeably. The last is Bertoli, she has neither voice, ear, nor manner to recommend her; but she is a perfect beauty, quite a Cleopatra, that sort of complexion with regular features, fine teeth, and when she sings has a smile about her mouth which is extreme pretty, and I believe has practised to sing before a glass, for she has never any distortion in her face.

Lotario was not popular, and Rolli was expectedly critical: 'Everyone considers it a very bad opera . . . they are putting on *Giulio Cesare* because the audiences are falling away fast'. He was less harsh on the singers: 'Strada pleases mightily'. 'Fabri is a great success . . . Would you have believed that a tenor could have such a triumph here in England?' – a reminder that in the eighteenth century, adulation fixed on the soprano voice, artificial or natural, rather than the tenor; half of Handel's operas have no tenor part at all. The bass 'sings sweetly in his throat and nose, pronounces Italian in the Teutonic manner, acts like a sucking-pig, and looks more like a *valet* than anything . . .' Mrs Pendarves was more sympathetic to Handel:

The opera is too good for the vile taste of the town: it is condemned never more to appear on the stage after this night. I long to hear its dying song, poor dear swan. We are to have some old opera revived, which I am sorry for, it will put people upon making comparisons between these singers and those that performed before, which will be a disadvantage among the ill-judging multitude. The present opera is disliked because it is too much studied, and they love nothing but minuets and ballads, in short the *Beggars' Opera* and *Hurlothrumbo** are only worthy of applause.

Flexible as ever, Handel changed his approach with *Partenope*, possibly realizing that a lighter, more tuneful style was wanted. In mock-heroic manner, it pokes fun at the heroic conventions used in *Lotario* and the earlier Academy operas. The stock 'woman-disguised-as-man' situation, for instance, is reduced to near-farce when the hero agrees to fight his supposed adversary (the heroine, naturally) only if both contestants strip to the waist, and the sheer quantity of incidental military and battle music makes it hard to take seriously. The more introspective moments, such as Arsace's *sommeil* in Act III scored for muted strings, two flutes, pizzicato bass-line and theorbo, are delicately handled, and the aria 'Ch'io parta' earlier in the act (also for Arsace) is one of the line of 'other-worldly' slow movements in E major that lead to 'I know that my Redeemer liveth'. It was a key in which Handel found a fatalistic quality, and Burney admits that this aria has 'no fault but brevity'.

Despite this change of style, the new company was not a success and Handel's stop-gap measure of a *pasticcio* called *Ormisda* – the music by Vinci, Hasse and other 'moderns' laced together with recitative by himself – was declared 'very heavy' by Mrs Pendarves.

It was clear that Bernacchi could not fill the gap left by Senesino, and for the next season Handel was obliged to reopen negotiations for his former star, through the intermediary of Francis Colman, the British Envoy in Florence.† and via Owen Swiney, who had settled in Italy after decamping in 1713. A letter from Handel to Colman in Florence instructs him to engage a soprano as well, who 'should be equally good at male and female parts'. He also requests Colman 'once again that no specific mention be made in the contracts of *prima, seconda* or *terza donna*, since that embarrasses us in the choice of the opera and in any case is a source of great inconvenience'.

In July Swiney wrote from Bologna to Colman in Florence:

I am favoured wth y^rs of ye 15th instant, & shall Endeav^r to observe punctually w^t you write about. I find y^t *Senesino* or *Carestini* are desired at 1200 G each, if they are to be had; Im'e sure that *Carestini* is Engaged at Milan, & has been so, for many Months past: and I hear y^t *Senesino*, is Engaged for ye ensuing Carnival at Rome.

---

*A popular comedy (with music) by one Samuel Johnson of Cheshire.
†He was also (partially) the writer of the *Opera Register* from which we quote.

If *Senesino* is at liberty (& will accept ye offer) then the affair is adjusted if Sig^{ra} Barbara Pisani accepts the offer I made her, which I really believe she will.

If we can neither get *Senesino*, nor *Carestini*, then Mr Handel desires to have a man (Soprano) & a woman contrealt, & y^t the price (for both) must not exceed *one Thousand* or *Eleven hundred* Guineas, & that the persons must sett out for London ye latter end of Augt or beginning of Septemb^r, and y^t no Engagem^t must be Made wth one with^t a certainty of getting the other.

Several of the persons recommended to Mr Handel (whose names he repeats in ye letter I received from him this Morning) are I think exceedingly indifferent, & Im'e persuaded wou'd never doe in England: & I think shou'd never be pitch'd on, till nobody else can be had.

I have heard a *Lad* here, of a^{bt} 19 years old, wth a *very good soprano voice* (& of whom there are vast hopes) who Im'e persuaded, would do very well in London, and much better than any of those mentioned in Mr Handel's letter who are not already engaged in case you cannot get *Senesino* . . .

Having no time to answer Mr. Handel's Letter, this day, I hope you will be so good as to let him know y^t I shall Endeav^r to serve him to the utmost of my power, & y^t I shall do nothing but w^t shall be concerted by you.

The upshot was that Senesino made the most of his advantage and accepted an offer of 1400 guineas – a great advance on the original budget, and a considerable risk for Handel, who, no longer having the financial backing of a Directorate, relied directly on the public. In the middle of October Handel reported back to Colman:

Sir,

I have just had the honour of receiving your letter of the 22nd past [NS], from which I see the reasons which determined you to engage Signor Senesino at a salary of 1400 guineas, which we agree to; and I most humbly thank you for all the trouble which you have been kind enough to take in this matter. Signor Senesino arrived here twelve days ago and I have not omitted to pay him on the presentation of your letter the hundred guineas of his salary on account, as you had promised him.

When the season opened with *Scipione* on 3 November, 'Senesino being return'd charm'd much' (Colman).

But the year ended in sorrow for Handel, with his mother's death on 16 December. The funeral sermon preached on the 22nd, later printed at Handel's expense, referred to him as standing 'in especial grace, by reason of his exceptional knowledge of music, as Director of Music to the reigning Majesty in England and Elector of Hanover, George II'. An over-elaborate poem of condolence also found its way to Handel, as he mentions to Michael Michaelsen in a distraught letter written in awkward German mixed with French:

Honoured Brother,

I have received your most honoured letter of 6 January in good order, whence in several ways I perceive the carefulness which you took to inter my blessed mother with propriety, and in compliance with her last wishes. Here I cannot restrain my tears. Yet it has pleased the Almighty, to whose Holy Will I submit myself with Christian resignation. Her memory will, however, never become obliterated for me, until after this life, we are again united, which may the beneficent God grant, in his grace.

Against this background, Handel finished *Poro*, composing the second act in a week. The Metastasio libretto dealt in a rather superior way with lofty issues remote to Handel's sensibilities; he needed human drama and emotional response, and did his best to shift the emphasis of the book. Senesino had the best air in the piece, 'Dov'è? Si affretti', which Burney described as 'in a grand style of theatrical pathetic'.

Rinaldo and *Rodelinda* (both much better operas) were revived, and the season ended with enough time spare to offer subscribers two extra performances, to make up for a shortfall the previous season. Handel, who was a shrewd dealer in stocks and shares throughout his life, and kept a number of banking friends, also had time to invest in more South Sea Annuities and to wind up the business of his mother's funeral costs. To Michaelsen he wrote at the beginning of August:

Honoured Brother,

From the letter which you did me the honour of writing to me on 12 July [NS], in reply to my previous letter, and from the list which you enclosed, I am aware of all that you did on the occasion of the burial of my dear mother.

Furthermore I am much obliged to you for the copies of the funeral oration which you sent me . . .

I shall have occasion later to repay in part the obligations under which I stand towards you.

Two other events of 1731 bear on Handel's future. One was the disgrace and departure of his old rival Bononcini over a scandal at the Academy of Ancient Music, a professional club. He had claimed to be the author of a madrigal sung at one of its meetings, 'In una siepe ombrosa', which some time later Bernard Gates, Master of the Children of the Chapel Royal, discovered in a printed collection by Lotti. After much acrimonious debate – it was, after all, common practice of the period to 'borrow' musical ideas if not whole pieces – Bononcini was discredited.

The second, and far more innocent event, was the first public performance of *Acis and Galatea* at a benefit concert presented by John Rich in the Theatre Royal, Lincoln's Inn Fields; Handel was not involved, and as far as we can tell, failed to see the implication of this venture.

For the new season at the King's Theatre, Antonio Montagnana made his début, a true bass (as opposed to Boschi, who was a baritone) with a remarkable range of more than two octaves and coloratura to match. Handel made his audience for *Ezio* wait until the second act for an aria that really exploited his *abilità*, though musically this number is overshadowed by an accompanied recitative for Fulvia in the anguished key of E flat minor. The King came to four of the five performances, but according to the *Opera Register* 'the piece did not draw much company'.

Giulio Cesare, a standard favourite, was revived to give time for *Sosarme, rè di Media*, finished on 4 February, to be rehearsed for the 15th. Handel originally called it *Fernando, rè di Castiglia* but altered both cast and title when he reached Act III – change of nationality is of little consequence in *opera seria* (though Winton Dean argues that the original Portuguese setting could have been politically embarrassing to George II*). At the same time, and more puzzlingly, Handel abbreviated many of the recitatives, either because rehearsal time was too short, or as a reaction to the failure of *Ezio* and the English distaste for long stretches of Italian (even when without them the plot makes no sense). One aria ('Fra l'ombre') was borrowed from the Naples serenata *Aci, Galatea e Polifemo* for Montagnana, although even he was not asked to cope with the extreme leaps of the original. Handel also adapted the scoring, eliminating the two 'flauti' and re-establishing the banished continuo. Burney was impressed by the bass singer's 'depth, power, mellowness, and peculiar accuracy of intonation in hitting distant intervals'.

The opera was a success: Viscount Percival noted that it 'takes with the town, and that justly, for it is one of the best I ever heard', and Colman that it was 'for many nights much crowded to some peoples admiration'.

But the performance of the year that was to prove most revolutionary took place (perhaps not accidentally) on Handel's forty-seventh birthday. An entry in Viscount Percival's diary on 23 February 1732 recorded: 'From dinner I went to the Music Club, where the King's Chapel boys acted the *History of Hester*, writ by Pope, and composed by Hendel. This oratoria or religious opera is exceeding fine, and the company were highly pleased, some of the parts being well performed'. According to a manuscript copy of the score, Bernard Gates directed three private performances of *Esther* at the 'Crown and Anchor' Tavern in the Strand 'with the Children of the Chapel-Royal, together with a Number of Voices from the Choirs of St. James's, and Westminster, join'd in Chorus's, after the Manner of the Ancients, being placed between the Stage and the Orchestra; and the Instrumental Parts (two or three particular Instruments, necessary on the Occasion, Excepted) were perform'd by the Members of the Philarmonick Society, consisting only of Gentlemen'.

These were the first London performances of an oratorio, and the lead was quickly followed. Even before Handel could comply with Princess Anne's request to have the piece put on at the Haymarket Theatre complete with action, a public performance was announced in the Great Room, York Buildings. The organizers are not named, though it would not be unreasonable to suspect Thomas Arne senior, or even John Rich. Handel's reaction to this

*Winton Dean, 'Handel's "Sosarme"'.

form of competition was as pragmatic as his slashing of *Sosarme* had been hardly a month earlier; meet public demand, but offer it something new. The *Daily Journal* announced:

By His MAJESTY'S *Command*.

At the King's Theatre in the Hay-Market, on Tuesday the 2d Day of May, will be performed, *The Sacred Story* of ESTHER: an *Oratorio* in *English*. Formerly composed by Mr. *Handel*, and now revised by him, with several Additions, and to be performed by a great Number of the best Voices and Instruments.

N.B. There will be no Action on the Stage, but the House will be fitted up in a decent Manner, for the Audience. The Musick to be disposed after the Manner of the Coronation Service.

Tickets to be delivered at the Office of the Opera house, at the usual Prices.

The lack of action, which the Princess had particularly asked for, was, according to Burney, *force majeure*; 'Dr. Gibson, then bishop of London, would not grant permission for its being represented on that stage, even with books in the children's hands'. We have no other evidence for the Bishop's intervention, nor, indeed, any proof that Handel had intended action in London or incorporated it at Cannons. His additions were substantial, involving twelve extra numbers, some taken from *La Resurrezione*, the *Ode for the Birthday of Queen Anne* and *Zadok the Priest*, others newly composed, and using forces dramatically larger and more exotic than had been available to him at Cannons. 'Tutti bassi del concertino Cembali Teorba Harpa Violoncelli due Contrabassi due Bassoni senza Organi e Ripieno' in the 'Alleluia' aria gives some idea of the wealth of continuo support, both there and elsewhere. The arrangement of these forces 'after the Manner of the Coronation Service' was in a horseshoe layout, with the singers 'in a sort [of] Gallery', according to Colman. 'Was performed six times and very full' summarizes Handel's success, and he was able to invest £700 in South Sea Annuities after only the third performance.

But Handel seems to have been supremely untouched, at both this and other points of his career, by the success of *Esther* and the open enthusiasm for dramatic works in England. He had placed his faith in Italian opera and Italian voices, and could only be dislodged by a direct invasion of his own territory. Before the run of *Esther* had ended, *Acis and Galatea* was again being offered to the public – and again, as the *Daily Post* reported, the initiative came from elsewhere: 'We hear that the Proprietors of the English Opera will very shortly perform a celebrated pastoral Opera call'd Acis and Galatea, compos'd by Mr. Handel, with all the Grand Chorus's and other Decorations, as it was perform'd before his Grace the Duke of Chandos at Cannons, and that it is now in Rehearsal'.

The instigators of the English Opera were Thomas Arne, father of the composer, and J. F. Lampe, together with Arne junior and Henry Carey. *Acis and Galatea*, the piece they chose, was the only remaining possibility from Handel's Cannons repertoire, and had already been tested on the public the previous year. Between them, they made a not unreasonable three-act version of the piece, and, for the second time within a month, Handel found himself in competition with Handel.

This time his response to piracy was to get the best of both worlds, English and Italian. By interleaving his 1708 *Aci, Galatea e Polifemo* with the Cannons masque, he too produced a three-act piece with several impressive choruses, eight soloists and very little new music to be written. His two English soloists (Mrs Robinson and Mrs Davis) sang English arias in English, the impressive list of Italians (with Senesino as Acis and Montagnana as Polifemo) all sang in Italian, and only the chorus had to be bilingual.* Such a macaronic arrangement was not new; it had happened before Handel, he had adopted it in earlier operas of his own, and it even persists in this century in some major opera houses of the world.

As to the staging, the *Daily Courant* announced: 'There will be no Action on the Stage, but the Scene will represent, in a Picturesque Manner, a rural Prospect, with Rocks, Groves, Fountains and Grotto's; amongst which will be disposed a Chorus of Nymphs and Shepherds, Habits, and every other Decoration suited to the Subject'. Satisfied with this show of strength, Handel rashly removed his attention from the threat of English Opera and turned it to the new Italian season.

On 25 November *Alessandro* was revived, with Senesino, the only survivor from the 1726 cast, in the title role. Strada and Gismoni took over from the warring Faustina and Cuzzoni, and Montagnana sang the bass part of Clito, created originally by Boschi. It was a good first night, 'The King &c all at ye Opera a full House', but 'A thin house' was all the *Register* could note on the second night. The English Opera was winning hands down, and it must have been particularly galling to Handel to see Lincoln's Inn Fields offering *Teraminta*, a pastoral piece (set in Cuba, curiously enough) with music by the young John Christopher Smith, his own pupil and protégé, then just twenty.†

The campaign to sustain an 'English Opera', which had begun with Lampe's *Amelia* in March, ended with Arne's burlesque version of Fielding's *The Tragedy of Tragedies*, confidently titled *The Opera of Operas*, given the following year. Smith junior also contributed *Ulysses*, a remarkably well-scored work for so young a composer, although hampered by a pedestrian libretto by Samuel Humphreys; and Addison's *Rosamond* was set for the third time since its inauspicious start in 1707 (such is the power of the critic), this time by Arne. Again, a talented composer and a perceptive writer failed to generate the spark that might have ignited a national opera. The plot fails to engage the attention (and the composer), in spite of its blatant patriotism, because very little happens; as Burney put it, 'the loss of Rosamond in the second act is not compensated by a single interesting event in the third'.

---

*Whether the whole constitutes a 'German pastoral' as suggested by Ellen Harris in *Handel and the Pastoral Tradition* is more debatable.

†A theory that the opera was the work of John Stanley (Mollie Sands, 'The Problem of "Teraminta"') on the grounds of one possible 'borrowing' is difficult to sustain (see Fiske, *English Theatre Music*, pp. 135–6).

After seven attempts at full-length English operas 'after the Italian manner', it was clear that the best music the Arnes had offered was their piracy from the very man who refused to be connected with opera in English. 'See and Seem Blind', an anonymous pamphlet ostensibly addressed to 'A—— H—— Esq.' tried to drum home the message.

> . . . I left the *Italian* Opera, the House was so thin, and cross'd over the way to the *English* one, which was so full I was forc'd to croud in upon the Stage . . .
>
> This alarm'd *H*——*l*, and out he brings an *Oratorio*, or Religious *Farce*, for the duce take me if I can make any other Construction of the Word, but he has made a very good *Farce* of it, and put near 4000*l*. in his Pocket, of which I am very glad, for I love the Man for his Musick's sake.
>
> This being a new Thing set the whole World a Madding; Han't you be at the *Oratorio*, says one? Oh! If you don't see the *Oratorio* you see nothing, says t'other; so away goes I to the *Oratorio*, where I saw indeed the finest Assembly of People I ever beheld in my Life, but, to my great Surprize, found this Sacred *Drama* a mere Consort, no Scenary, Dress or Action, so necessary to a *Drama*; but *H*——*l*, was plac'd in Pulpit, (I suppose they call that their Oratory), by him sate *Senesino, Strada, Bertolli,* and *Turner Robinson,* in their own Habits; before him stood sundry sweet Singers of this poor *Israel,* and *Strada* gave us a *Halleluiah* of Half an Hour long; *Senesino* and *Bertolli* made rare work with the *English* Tongue you would have sworn it had been *Welch*; I would have wish'd it *Italian*, that they might have sung with more ease to themselves, since, but for the Name of *English*, it might as well have been *Hebrew* . . .*

The addressee may have been Aaron Hill, who twenty-two years earlier had espoused the cause of an English opera in his dedication of the word-book to *Rinaldo* (see p. 63). It is not known whether he had had much contact with the composer since their first early collaboration, having deserted theatre management for speculative ventures in the wool and timber trades, and attempting 'to bring to perfection the *Art of making potash*, bought with vast sums from Russia'. Mainwaring remarked with sarcasm that 'from composing Dramas to be set, to the extracting oil from Beechnuts, was a transition quite peculiar to such a versatile genius as Mr. HILL. The connection betwixt the orchestra and the alembic it is difficult to discover'.

Still a supporter of Handel, he would have attended both the English Opera and *Alessandro* and been painfully aware of the need for co-operation. In December 1732 he wrote to Handel forcefully putting the case for English Opera:

> Sir,
>
> . . . Having this occasion of troubling you with a letter, I cannot forbear to tell you the earnestness of my wishes, that, as you have made such considerable

---

*Mrs Thrale reported the 'good & comical' story concerning one of the Italian singers, 'set to sing these English Words – *I come my Queen to Chaste Delights* – He sung and pronounced them thus. *I comb my Queen to catch* [*sic* for 'chase'] *the Lice.*' (G. Dorris, *Paolo Rolli*, p. 101n).

steps towards it, already, you would let us owe to your inimitable genius, the establishment of *musick*, upon a foundation of good poetry; where the excellence of the *sound* should be no longer dishonour'd, by the poorness of the *sense* it is chain'd to.

My meaning is, that you would be resolute enough, to deliver us from our *Italian bondage*; and demonstrate, that *English* is soft enough for Opera, when compos'd by poets, who know how to distinguish the *sweetness* of our tongue, from the *strength* of it, where the last is less necessary.

I am of opinion, that male and female voices may be found in this kingdom, capable of every thing, that is requisite; and, I am sure, a species of dramatic Opera might be invented, that, by reconciling reason and dignity, with musick and fine machinery, would charm the *ear*, and hold fast the *heart*, together.

Such an improvement must, at once, be lasting, and profitable, to a very great degree; and would, infallibly, attract an universal regard, and encouragement.

Handel refused to rise to the bait. The vision of an English opera, so vivid to Addison, Hill, Carey and Arne (as it had been to Congreve and John Hughes), could not tempt him from the old form that he understood nor the new one that he had created. Despite a willing public, available theatres, congenial backers and an enthusiastic press, Handel turned his back on the vision. In the opinion of the two great eighteenth-century music historians, it was a grave mistake. Burney noted 'a manifest inferiority in design, invention, grace, elegance and every captivating requisite' in these later operas, but attributed it to the growing animosity between Handel and Senesino. Hawkins preferred to blame their lack of success on the composer's temperament:

Such as are not acquainted with the personal character of Handel, will wonder at his seeming temerity, in continuing so long an opposition which tended but to impoverish him; but he was a man of a firm and intrepid spirit, no way a slave to the passion of avarice, and would have gone greater lengths than he did, rather than submit to those whom he had ever looked on as his inferiors: but though his ill success for a series of years had not affected his spirit, there is reason to believe that his genius was in some degree damped by it; for whereas of his earlier operas, that is to say, those composed by him between the years 1710 and 1728, the merits are so great, that few are able to say which is to be preferred; those composed after that period have so little to recommend them, that few would take them for the work of the same author. In the former class are Radamistus, Otho, Tamerlane, Rodelinda, Alexander, and Admetus, in either of which scarcely an indifferent air occurs; whereas in Parthenope, Porus, Sosarmes, Orlando, Aetius, Ariadne, and the rest down to 1736, it is a matter of some difficulty to find a good one. (*History*)

It is disconcerting to find eighteenth-century opinion, particularly when it is expressed by two men who were acquainted with Handel, so different from our own. Perhaps it should be taken as fair warning against passing judgment on opera from the printed page, although Burney's description of *Orlando* shows that he at least consulted the manuscript, not merely the Walsh edition. The same opera, to modern eyes after the experience of twentieth-century revivals, is 'one of Handel's richest and most rewarding operas' (Andrew Porter, *The New Yorker*, 14 March 1983) and to Winton Dean a 'masterpiece . . . musically the richest of all his operas' (*Handel and the Opera Seria*, p. 91), comparable on several counts with *The Magic Flute*. What do we see that Burney missed? Or what are we prepared to accept that he found unworthy?

These questions are best answered by looking at how an eighteenth-century audience considered opera. It was, unquestionably, most interested in the activities of the *primarii*; arias for lesser characters, and recitative in general offered an opportunity to discuss the merits of the prima donna, the machinery, the costumes and the assembled *haute monde*. Of a like mind, Burney treats each act as a string of arias, dealt out according to strict rules of protocol. Significantly he never refers to the characters in the plot, but only to the singers ('a cavatina for Senesino', 'an air for Strada'), and he is dismayed to find a 'subaltern or cadet' singer being overemployed or overextended; 'The second act begins with a very elegant and pleasing pastoral air: *Quando spieghi*, for Celeste [Gismondi, who sang Dorinda], which seems to require greater abilities in the execution, than are usually found in a singer of the second or third class'.

There is no evidence that Handel wrote down to his audience, however, nor that he deliberately wrote badly for a singer he disliked, as Burney maliciously suggested. On the contrary, there is every sign that he worked to curb the excesses of his prime singers in the interests of continuity of drama – as Burney himself noted from the manuscript of *Orlando*, he pruned Montagnana's great solo in Act III, 'Sorge infausta', of much gratuitous passage-work.

It was chiefly their concentration on set pieces that makes the commentaries of both Burney and Hawkins on Handel's later operas defective. *Opera seria* originated in the word-book, and a study of this reveals levels of the composer's creative intentions which escaped them: the 'Argument', the allocation of *arioso* and accompanied recitative in place of *secco* (for an increase in intensity that did not imply an obligatory exit for the character), the introduction of *sinfonie* and above all, the consistent development of a psychological thread and the *exploitation* (rather than simply the creation) of situations. Throughout *Orlando* Handel disrupts the traditional mould of the da capo aria with action: Orlando's attempted suicide breaks an aria off in mid-stream, in his madness dance-metre and recitative alternate, and the crazed vision of Charon's boat rocking on the waters of the Styx is interrupted by fragments of scales in 5/8, 'a division of time which can only be bourne in such a situation', Burney primly observes.

For connoisseurs and friends like Mrs Pendarves or James Harris, who could recognize 'a Charming peice of Recitative', the opera contains much to admire. The gentle irony as well as the anguish of Ariosto's original is reflected in *Orlando* by more varied accompaniments than appear in any other of his operas. For those wearied of female sorceresses, Zoroastro is the one example in

Handel of a bass wielding the powers of destiny and magic, and there is no operatic opening more sublime than his invocation to the stars, an arioso with 'a wild grandeur in it of a very uncommon kind' (Burney). Orlando's relapse from fury into sleep is accompanied by two 'violette marine' (a type of viola d'amore?) played by the two Castrucci brothers,* with a spell-binding accompaniment of *violoncelli pizzicati*.

The opera opened on 27 January: Colman voted the piece 'extraordinary fine & magnificent' and the Queen attended the second night: her sedan chair came to grief as she left. Worse upsets were waiting for Handel. The Earl of Delawar informed the Duke of Richmond:

> There is a Spirit got up against the dominion of Mr. Handel, a subscription carry'd on, and Directors chosen, who have contracted with Senesino, and have sent for Cuzzoni, and Farinelli, it is hoped he will come as soon as the Carneval of Venice is over, if not sooner. The General Court gave power to contract with any Singer Except Strada, so that it is Thought Handel must fling up, which the Poor Count [i.e. Heidegger] will not be sorry for, There being no one but what declares as much for him, as against the Other, so that we have a Chance of seeing Operas once more on a good foot. Porpora is also sent for. We doubt not but we shall have your Graces Name in our Subscription List. The Directrs. chosen are as follows. D. of Bedford, Lds. Bathurst, Burlington, Cowper, Limmerick, Stair, Lovel, Cadogan, DeLawarr, & D. of Rutland, Sir John Buckworth, Henry Furnese Esq., Sr. Micl. Newton; There seems great Unanimity, and Resolution to carry on the Undertaking comme il faut.

With this first shot, the final round of operatic warfare was announced. It signalled the desertion of many of Handel's friends and colleagues: not only had five of the new directors been on the board of the original Academy (including Handel's patron, Burlington), but almost all his singers were to defect to the enemy, except for Strada who remained faithful to Handel for the rest of her career. Senesino was one of the prime instigators of the new scheme, which was variously known as 'Senesino's Opera' or 'The Opera at Lincoln's-Inn Fields', although never, apparently, by the title now accepted for it, the 'Opera of the Nobility'. Five years (and twelve Handel operas) later both sides withdrew from the fray defeated; from which perspective Dr Johnson viewed Italian opera not only as an 'exotic and irrational entertainment', but one 'which has been always combated and always has prevailed' (*Lives of the English Poets*: John Hughes).

Handel ignored the threat of rivalry, but immediately tested public reaction to the new oratorio idea with *Deborah*; choruses and heavy drama were the recipe, and it was noted by the public. 'It was very magnificent, near a hundred performers, among whom about twenty-five singers', wrote the Earl of Egmont after the second performance on 27 March – a size of chorus which might give

---

*Pietro Castrucci, leader of the opera orchestra, is said to be the model for Hogarth's *Enraged Musician* (see ill. 31).

modern choral societies pause for thought. It had been hastily put together, largely from earlier church music: the Brockes Passion, Chandos Anthems and two of the Coronation Anthems, plus Italian airs. The music might be ill-assorted and the libretto (by Humphreys again, who had dealt *Ulysses* a fatal blow) pedestrian, but it was the right piece at the right time. With three operas so far in one year (revivals of *Tolomeo* and *Floridante* had flanked *Orlando*), Senesino still tractable and public curiosity still warm from *Esther*, Handel had to seize his moment. To wait longer for a better word-book or to take time off composing afresh would be to lose the advantage over the rival houses, perhaps to lose his star castrato, and certainly to miss the possibility of introducing London to the idea of an oratorio season. *Deborah* had to appear speedily, and *Esther* would follow (on 14 and 17 April). Handel, in his enthusiasm and confidence, went too far. With noble support for the opera slipping away from him, he now managed to offend his subscribers with 'Tickets . . . at One Guinea each, Gallery Half a Guinea', double the normal prices. On 31 March Lady Irwin wrote to Lord Carlisle:

Last week we had an Oratorio, composed by Hendel out of the story of Barak and Deborah, the latter of which name[s] it bears. Hendel thought, encouraged by the Princess Royal, it had merit enough to deserve a guinea, and the first time it was performed at that price, exclusive of subscribers' tickets, there was but a 120 people in the House. The subscribers being refused unless they would pay a guinea, they, insisting upon the right of their silver tickets, forced into the House, and carried their point. This gave occasion to the eight lines I send you, in which they have done Hendel the honour to join him in a dialogue with Sir Robert Walpole. I was at this entertainment on Tuesday [the 27th]; 'tis excessive noisy, a vast number of instruments and voices, who all perform at a time, and is in music what I fancy a French ordinary in conversation.

To a hostile press, the analogy between the extortionate world of the opera and the machinations of the Prime Minister's Tobacco Excise Bill, which brought England to the verge of civil war, provided perfect copy. The eight-line epigram that Lady Irwin saw was nothing compared to the bitter extended attack to which it was appended in *The Craftsman*:*

---

*Handel = Walpole
The Opera = the State
Orchestra = civil servants and Parliament
Montagnana = George II
Performers = foreign powers
Door-keepers = tax-collectors
Constant attenders at opera = small government majority
His own country = Germany (Handel), Norfolk (Walpole)
'Si caro, si' = arias in *Rinaldo* (Act III) and *Admeto*
   (Act III)
The two seconds = the dissolute Lord Hervey and the ugly Heidegger

The Rise and Progress of Mr. H——l's Power and Fortune are too well known for Me now to relate. Let it suffice to say that He was grown so insolent upon the sudden and undeserved Increase of both, that He thought nothing ought to oppose his imperious and extravagant Will. He had, for some Time, govern'd the *Opera's*, and modell'd the *Orchestre*, without the least Controul. No *Voices*, no *Instruments* were admitted, but such as flatter'd his Ears, though They shock'd those of the Audience. *Wretched Scrapers* were put above the *best Hands* in the *Orchestre*. No *Musick* but *his own* was to be allow'd, though every Body was weary of it; and he had the impudence to assert, *that there was no Composer in* England *but Himself*. Even *Kings* and *Queens* were to be content with whatever low Characters He was pleased to assign Them, as is evident in the Case of Seignor *Montagnana*; who, though a *King*, is always obliged to act (except an angry, rumbling Song, or two) the most insignificant Part of the whole Drama. This Excess and Abuse of Power soon disgusted the Town; his Government grew odious; and his *Opera's* grew empty. However the Degree of Unpopularity and general Hatred, instead of humbling Him, only made Him more furious and desperate. He resolved to make one last Effort to establish his Power and Fortune by Force, since He found it now impossible to hope for it from the good Will of Mankind. In order to do This, He form'd a *Plan*, without consulting any of his *Friends*, (if He has any) and declared that at a proper Season He would communicate it to the Publick; assuring us, at the same Time, that it would be very much for the Advantage of the Publick in general, and of *Opera's* in particular. . . . Notwithstanding all these and many more Objections, Mr. H——l . . . at last produces his *Project*; resolves to cram it down the Throats of the Town; prostitutes *great* and *aweful Names*, as the Patrons of it; and even does not scruple to insinuate that They are to be Sharers of the Profit. His *Scheme* set forth in Substance, that the late decay of *Opera's* was owing to their *Cheapness*, and to the great *Frauds* committed by the *Door-keepers*; that the *annual Subscribers* were a parcel of *Rogues*, and made an ill Use of their Tickets, by often *running* two into the Gallery; that to obviate these Abuses He had contrived a Thing, that was better than an *Opera*, call'd an *Oratorio*; to which none should be admitted, but by *printed Permits*, or Tickets of one Guinea each . . .; and lastly, that as the very Being of *Opera's* depended upon *Him singly*, it was just that the Profit arising from hence should be for his *own Benefit*. He added, indeed, one Condition, to varnish the whole a little; which was, that if any Person should think himself aggrieved, and that the *Oratorio* was not worth the Price of the *Permit*, he should be at Liberty to appeal to three *Judges of Musick*, who should be obliged, within the Space of seven Years at farthest, finally to determine the same; provided always that the said *Judges* should be of his Nomination, and known to like no other Musick but his.

The Absurdity, Extravagency, and Oppression of *this Scheme* disgusted the whole Town. Many of the most constant Attenders of the *Opera's* resolved absolutely to renounce them, rather than go to them under such Extortion and Vexation. They exclaim'd against the *insolent and rapacious Projector of this Plan*. The King's old and sworn Servants, of the two Theatres of *Drury-Lane* and *Covent-Garden*, reap'd the Benefit of this general Discontent, and were resorted to in Crowds, by way of Opposition to the *Oratorio*. Even the fairest Breasts were fired with Indignation against this *new Imposition*. Assemblies, Cards, Tea, Coffee, and all other Female Batteries were vigorously employ'd to defeat the *Project*, and destroy the *Projector*. These joint Endeavours of all Ranks and Sexes succeeded so well, that the *Projector* had the Mortification to see but a very thin Audience at his *Oratorio*; and of about two hundred and sixty odd, that it consisted of, it is notorious that not ten paid for their *Permits*, but, on the contrary, had them given Them, and Money into the Bargain, for coming to keep Him in Countenance.

This Accident, They say, has thrown Him into a *deep Melancholy*, interrupted sometimes by *raving Fits*; in which He fancies he sees ten thousand *Opera* Devils coming to tear Him to Pieces; then He breaks out into frantick, incoherent Speeches; muttering *sturdy Beggars, Assassination*, &c. In these delirious Moments, He discovers a particular Aversion to the City. He calls Them all a Parcel of *Rogues*, and asserts that the *honestest Trader among them deserves to be hang'd* – It is much question'd whether He will recover; at least, if He does, it is not doubted but He will seek for a Retreat in his *own Country* from the general Resentment of the Town.

I am, Sir, Sir

Your very humble Servant,

P—LO R—LI.

O.

P.S. Having seen a little Epigram, lately handed about Town, which seems to allude to the same Subject, I believe it will not be unwelcome to your Readers.

EPIGRAM

Quoth *W——e* to *H——l*, shall We Two agree,
And *excise* the whole Nation?
      H. si, Caro, si.
Of What Use are *Sheep*, if the *Shepherd* can't shear
      them?
At the *Hay-Market* I, you at *Westminster* –
      W. Hear Him!
Call'd to Order, their *Seconds* appear in their Place;
One fam'd for his *Morals*, and one for his *Face*.
In half They succeeded, in half They were crost.
The EXCISE was obtain'd, but poor DEBORAH lost.
  O.

Although the prime victim of the attack was clearly supposed to be Walpole, it is a measure of Handel's unpopularity that he could have sustained the metaphor.*

Whether the 'deep melancholy' of the final paragraph was fact or fiction, there are signs from this period that Handel's health, along with his public reputation, was deteriorating under stress. On 4 May 1733, Count Ludwig von Pöllnitz wrote to a friend from London: '. . . They have an *Italian* Opera, which is the best and most magnificent in *Europe* . . . The Music of these Operas is generally composed by one *Hendel*, who is esteemed by a great many People beyond all Expression, but others reckon him no extraordinary Man; and for my own Part, I think his Music not so affecting as 'tis elegant'. This feeling had hardened into definite personal antagonism a year later, when an anonymous ill-wisher declared in December 1734: 'I don't pity Handell in the least, for I hope this mortification will make him a human creature; for I am sure before he was no better than a brute, when he could treat civilized people with so much brutality as I know he has done'. So far Handel's 'brutality' had only extended to sacking the overbearing Senesino; a bad move commercially, but one made inescapable by the clash of personalities.

> *Handel's general look was somewhat heavy and sour; but when he did smile, it was his sire the sun, bursting out of a black cloud. There was a sudden flash of intelligence, wit, and good humour, beaming in his countenance, which I hardly ever saw in any other.* (Burney, 1785)

At this point it was Handel's loyalty to the Crown that indirectly brought respite from such attacks. Dr William Holmes, a staunch Hanoverian and Vice-Chancellor of Oxford University proposed a revival of the 'Publick Act', an elaborate degree-giving ceremony held in the Sheldonian Theatre, and invited Handel to take part.

Great Preparations are making for Mr. Handel's Journey to Oxford, in order to take his Degree of Musick; a Favour that University intends to compliment him with, at the ensuing Publick Act. The Theatre there is fitting up for the Performance of his Musical Entertainments, the first [of] which begins on Friday Fortnight the 6th of July. We hear that the Oratorio's of Esther and Deborah, and also a new one never performed before, called Athaliah, are to be represented two Nights each; and the Serenata of Acis and Galatea as often. That Gentleman's Great *Te Deum*, *Jubilate*, and *Anthems*, are to be vocally and instrumentally performed by the celebrated Mr. Powell, and others, at a solemn Entertainment for the Sunday. The Musick from the Opera is to attend Mr. Handel; and we are informed, that the principal Parts

---

*George Dorris (*Paolo Rolli*) has suggested that Rolli wrote the piece in Italian and Bolingbroke translated it; his distinguishing mark 'O' appears at the end of both letter and epigram. But the Italian translation now in the Senesino archives on which Dorris rests his case is unlikely to be Rolli's original, and his involvement in the matter appears only as conjecture.

in his Oratorio's, &c. are to be [sung] by Signora Strada, Mrs. Wright, Mr. Salway, Mr. Rochetti, and Mr. Wartzs. (*The Bee*)

Because of the scale of the occasion, Holmes arranged for the performances to be given in the Sheldonian rather than the 'Musick School' of the Bodleian Library.

Controversy, parochial though it was, still dogged Handel. The traditionalists objected to 'a forreigner . . . being desired to come to Oxford to perform in Musick this Act'; Dr Thomas Hearne in his diary (6 July 1733) referred to 'Handel and (his lowsy Crew) a great number of forreign fidlers . . .'.

The first performance of Handel's 'spick and span new Oratorio *Athalia*' could not take place on 9 July as planned since 'the Solemnity in conferring the Degrees . . . engag'd the Theatre to a very late Hour of that Afternoon', but had to be deferred to the following day, '. . . when it was performed with the utmost Applause, and is esteemed equal to the most celebrated of that Gentleman's Performances: there were 3700 Persons present' (*The Bee*). The *London Magazine* also estimated 'an Audience of near 4000', but these figures must surely represent the total attendance at the two performances.*

Thanks to Racine's original play (rather than Humphreys' treatment of it), Handel at last had the auspicious ingredients of a strong dramatic thread, with particularly well placed double choruses for the Priests of Baal, and a credible tragic heroine in Athalia herself (sung by Mrs Wright). With the exception of Strada, all his singers were now English, and included the boy alto Goodwill, who sang the part of Joas. Even the overture struck a new note; for the first and last time Handel forewent the traditional French overture format in favour of a three-movement (fast–slow–fast) Italian overture. As with so many of his innovations, English composers were slow to follow his lead (contrary to the theory of national dependence on the Handelian model). Boyce first used the form in *Peleus and Thetis* (1736), and Thomas Arne (who attended the Sheldonian performance together with Michael Festing) followed in 1740 with his masque *Alfred*.

Sumptuous scoring for 'about 70 voices and Instruments of Musick' (*Norwich Gazette*) included horns doubling the trumpets, solos for cello (still a novelty), flute, two recorders (for the bird-song of 'Through the land so lovely blooming') and a precisely indicated continuo line: 'archilute' to accompany the solo cello, for example, and the organ admitted only in certain numbers, and then with strict control ('not very loud', 'tasto solo', 'Loud left hand right hand soft').† The solo for the boy Joas, 'Will God, whose mercies ever flow', is without continuo throughout.

---

*The present-day audience capacity of the Sheldonian Theatre is set at 800.
†These indications, plus the extant organ part to *Alexander's Feast*, give a clear notion of the severe restraint a continuo organist should employ.

18 Frontispiece of *Alexander's Feast*, published by Walsh in 1738. The scene from the
work beneath the portrait was designed by Gravelot. Portrait of Handel by the Dutchman
Jacob Houbraken, the only likeness known to have been approved for publication by Handel.

19, 20 From the summer of 1717 Handel spent a period as composer-in-residence to the 1st Duke of Chandos at his extravagant new palace of Cannons. The works Handel composed there included *Acis and Galatea*, *Esther* (first version) and the 11 *Chandos Anthems*.

The South Front of Cannons in Middlesex the Seat of his Grace James Duke of Chandos &c

To whom this Plate is most Humbly Inscrib'd by his Graces most Obed.t Servant John Price. Architect Built, Anno 1720.

21, 22 Senesino, the celebrated male mezzo-soprano. One of his most popular roles was Caesar in *Giulio Cesare*, but his arrogant manner earned him admiration rather than love. At one performance he was the object of ridicule when, having just sung the words 'Caesar does not know what fear is', he was visibly terror-struck by a falling piece of scenery. *Right*, page from Bickham's *Musical Entertainer*, 1738–40 (note the two boys loading his 'Ready Money' on board). *Below*, caricature of Senesino, Cuzzoni and Berenstadt in *Flavio*, performed at the King's Theatre in 1723.

23 Title-page of the first edition of *Giulio Cesare*, published by Cluer and Creake in 1724. It was advertised as 'Curiously engrav'd on Copper Plates Corrected and Figur'd by Mr. Handel's own Hands'.

24 'Farinelli in an oriental role', by Marco Ricci. Although one of the most sought-after castrati of his day, Farinelli sang with Handel's rivals rather than with him. Of Farinelli and Senesino it was said that they carried sacks of gold with them when leaving England (see ill. 21).

25 When in 1733 Senesino defected to the new Opera of the Nobility, Giovanni Carestini was one of two castrati Handel engaged for a revival of *Ottone* and two *pasticcii*.

26, 27 A passage from the aria 'Scherza infida' from Act II of *Ariodante*: *above*, Handel's autograph (full score); *below*, detail of a contemporary manuscript, with written-out ornaments which it is believed may indicate how Carestini embellished the aria in performance (both vocal parts are written in the soprano clef). Such evidence suggests that ornamentation may be exuberant while preserving the basic contour of the melody.

28, 29 Although it was considered quite a coup for the Academy to engage the world's two leading sopranos – Faustina Bordoni (*left*) and Cuzzoni – in the same season, the move was not only a financial but also a diplomatic disaster: the two ladies eventually came to blows on the stage. *Below*, Faustina and Senesino by Marco Ricci.

30 *Rich's Glory, or his Triumphant Entry into Covent Garden*, by an unknown engraver, after Hogarth. The impresario John Rich opened a new opera house in Covent Garden in 1732 on the proceeds from Gay's highly popular *Beggar's Opera*. The success of the latter coincided with the temporary sinking of Handel's fortunes and the demise of the Academy. **31** Another aspect of musical London is depicted by Hogarth in *The Enraged Musician* (1741). According to Burney, the musician was Pietro Castrucci, leader of Handel's opera orchestra.

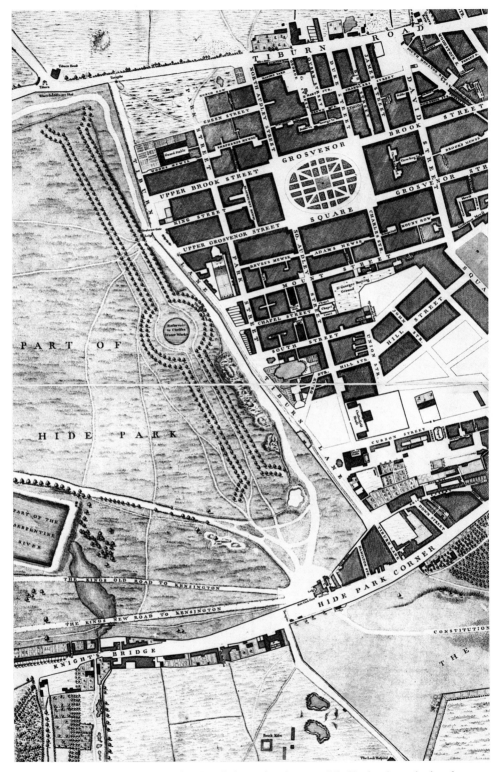

32 From c.1724 Handel lived in Brook Street (modern no. 25). His local parish church was St George's, Hanover Square, and as the contemporary map shows he was only a short walk from Hyde Park.

Handel's doctorate remains a mystery; it is possible that it was never offered, although all the periodicals jumped to the obvious conclusion. *The Craftsman* reported that 'Mr. Handel has not accepted his Degree of Doctor of Musick, as was reported, that Gentleman having declin'd the like Honour when tender'd him at Cambridge',* while Prévost (in *Le Pour et Contre*, August 1733) hazards the unlikely guess that it was modesty that made him 'refuse the marks of distinction that were proposed for him' at the ceremonies the day before *Athalia*. Although later in the century, Haydn was to complain about the expense of taking his honorary degree under the same circumstances, Handel would hardly have been deterred, since Hearne noted 'that 'twas computed, that Mr Handel cleared by his Musick at Oxford upwards of 2000£'. Handel's own explanation in a letter of May 1744 (now lost) reveals little: 'I neither could nor would accept the Doctor's degree, because I was overwhelmingly busy'.† He can hardly have meant pressure of rehearsals, since *Athalia* was actually postponed by a day. Could it be that *Athalia* (despite its choruses in eight parts) was not considered academic enough as an Exercise, and that Handel refused to submit some dry display of counterpoint? For the rest of his life he is referred to stubbornly as 'Mr. Handel' except, curiously enough, in the subscription list of Telemann's 1733 *Musique de Table*, for which he was the only English subscriber and from which he borrowed wholeheartedly, where he is 'Mr. Hendel, Docteur en Musique, London'.

Back in London, Handel was able to attend to family business, but did not make the trip to Germany that Hawkins, and following him, Chrysander, suggested. Again he pleaded overwork. Referring to the domestic receipts and expenditures which Michaelsen had continued to take in hand, he wrote:

> My honoured brother mentions that it might well be necessary that I personally should inspect such, but however much I long to pay a visit to the people of your place, nevertheless the imminent and inevitable matters of business, which indeed quite overwhelm me, do not allow me such a pleasure; I will, however, bear in mind to send in writing what I feel about it.
>
> My honoured brother has done well in remembering to take heed of my dear, blessed mother's last wishes with regard to her tombstone,‡ and I hope that he himself will fulfil those same wishes.
>
> I perceive from the transmitted account that Frau Händel, who resides in the house,§ pays six Reichsthaler for a year's rent; I could wish that in the future she might be absolved from paying such, as long as she likes to remain in occupation.

---

*Handel had never been offered a degree from Cambridge, and according to Burney, thought little of Maurice Greene ('my *pellows-plower*' because he had blown the organ at St Paul's for Handel in about 1715) who had accepted both a doctorate and the Professorship there.

†This fragment only of the letter is quoted by L. C. Mizler in *Neu eröffnete Musikalische Bibliothek* (Leipzig, 1736–54).

‡The text of the tombstone of his parents is given in Mueller von Asow, pp. 30–31.

§The house, 'Zum gelben Hirschen', is still pointed out as Handel's birthplace, although he was actually born in the house next door. Frau Händel may have been the daughter-in-law of Karl, Handel's half-brother.

In June Senesino had publicly defected to the new Opera of the Nobility, taking with him Montagnana, Bertolli and Gismondi. London anxiously awaited the new operatic season:

> Winter is coming on. You already know how there was an irreconcilable rupture between Senesino and Handel, and how the former produced a schism in the company and hired a separate theatre for himself and his partisans. His enemies sent for the best voices in Italy; they pride themselves on keeping going despite his machinations and those of his clique. So far the English nobility has been divided; victory will remain in the balance a long time if they have enough determination not to change their minds. But it is expected that the first few performances will put an end to the quarrel, since the better of the two theatres cannot fail to attract very soon the support of them all. (*Le Pour et Contre*, October 1733)

Handel and Heidegger worked fast to assemble a new company and repertoire. Durastante (now a mezzo soprano) returned from Italy, despite having ended her 1724 season in London by singing:

> But let old charmers yield to the new
> Happy soil, adieu, adieu!

25 Two new castrati, Carlo Scalzi and Giovanni Carestini, were engaged. The problem of instant repertoire was solved by reviving *Ottone* and devising two *pasticcii*, for which Handel simply wrote the (short) recitatives: *Semiramide* (music mostly by Vinci, Handel's favourite source for *pasticcii*) and *Cajo Fabricio* (music mostly by Hasse).

Handel's strategy was to strike the first blow, and keep on striking. He opened two months before the rival company, even though he had new singers, and they his old team. He chose to open on 30 October, the King's birthday, when it was usual for a royal ball to be given in St James's; however, the whole court decided to attend the opera, and even the Prince of Wales was present, despite his open support for the Nobility Opera. A first tactical victory, therefore, to Handel. But the second night, according to Lady Bristol, was less propitious:

> I am just come home from a dull empty opera, tho' the second time; the first was full to hear the new man [Carestini], who I can find out to be an extream good singer; the rest are all scrubbs except old Durastante, that sings as well as ever she did.

King, Queen and Prince also supported the opening of *Ottone*, but by Christmas the Nobility Opera was under way, and according to the *Daily Post*, Frederick was offering it more than usually direct help: 'Last Night there was a Rehearsal of a new Opera at the Prince of Wales' House in the Royal Gardens in Pall Mall, where was present a great Concourse of the Nobility and Quality of both Sexes:

some of the choicest Voices and Hands assisted in the Performance'. (Christmas Day, 1733)

The new opera was *Arianna in Nasso* by Porpora, and the choicest voices included Senesino, Montagnana and Gismondi, but not Cuzzoni, who did not arrive until the following spring. The King of Prussia received an account of the opening from his Minister in London couched in overtly political terms:

Last Saturday [29 December 1733] the opening of the new *Opera-house* took place, which the *Noblesse* has undertaken since they were not satisifed with the *Conduite* of the *Directeur* of the old *Opera*, *Händel*, and, to abase him, planned a new one, to which over two hundred people *subscribed*, and each one contributed 20 *guineas*. The premier singer, *Senesino*, is stamped on the *Piquet* of the subscribers, and has the superscription: *Nec pluribus impar.** It was this *Opera-house* which was first called the *Opera-house* of the rebels. Since the whole court, however, was present at the first *Ouverture* it has become thereby *legalised* and *loyal*. In this the *genius* of the nation has shown itself, namely, how very inclined it is to *novelties* and *factions*. In the *preliminary treaties* which were drawn up for this *foundation*, the first article runs: Point d'accommodement à jamais avec le Sr Händel.

By a genuine coincidence, Handel's first new opera of 1734 also treated Ariadne (but the score of *Arianna in Creta* was dated 5 October); 'a new Opera & very good', said Colman, '– Sigr Cerestino sung surprizingly well: a new Eunuch – many times performed' – in fact, the opera had seventeen performances.

Although he had fewer subscribers than the Nobility Opera, feelings seemed to be turning once more towards Handel. An enthusiastic pamphlet appeared, entitled *Harmony in an Uproar*, which offered him some public compensation for the insinuations of *The Craftsman*.

Wonderful SIR!
The mounting Flames of my Ambition having long aspir'd to the Honour of holding a small Conversation with you; but being sensible of the almost insuperable Difficulty of getting at you, I bethought me, a Paper Kite might best reach you, and soar to your Apartment, though seated in the highest Clouds; for all the World knows, I can top you, fly as high as you will.

But all preliminary Compliments, and introductory Paragraphs laid aside, let us fall to Business – You must know then, Sir that I have been told, and made to understand by your Betters, Sir that of late you have been damn'd *Insolent*, *Audacious*, *Impudent* and *Saucy*, and a thousand things else, Sir (that don't become you) worse than all that –

... I am humbly of the Opinion, before I hear you, that you are certainly in the wrong: But to shew my Impartiality, since I am declared Umpire in this weighty Cause, I solemnly cite you before my Tribunal ...

... Therefore proceed we now without more delay to your Trial. – *Cryer* – O yes? – O yes? – &c.

---

*'Not unequal to most'.

This is to give Notice, to all Directors of Operas, Masters of Play-houses, Patentees with Patents or without, Composers, Performers, or other Masters that neither Compose nor Perform, all Dancing-Masters, Exhibiters of Poppet-Shews, Presidents of Bear-Gardens, Rope-Dancers, but particularly all Judges of Musick and others – That they now appear and produce their several Complaints against the Prisoner at the Bar, in order to bring him to speedy Justice.

Court. *Frederick Handel*, Hold up your Hand. Know you are here brought to answer to the several following high Crimes and Misdemeanors, committed upon the Wills and Understandings, and against the Peace of our Sovereign Lord the Mobility of *Great-Britain*, particularly this Metropolis: To which you shall make true and faithful Answer – So help you Musick – Swear him upon the two Operas of *Ariadne*, alias the *Cuckoo* and the *Nightingale*.

Imprimis, You are charg'd with having bewitch'd us for the Space of twenty Years past; nor do we know where your Inchantments will end, if a timely Stop is not put to them; they threatning us with an entire Destruction of Liberty, and an absolute Tyranny in your person over the whole Territories of the *Hay-Market*.

Secondly, You have most insolently dar'd to give us good Musick and sound Harmony, when we wanted and desir'd bad; to the great Encouragement of your Opera's, and the Ruin of our good Allies and Confederates, the Professors of bad Musick.

Thirdly, – You have most feloniously and arrogantly assum'd to yourself an uncontroul'd Property of pleasing us, whether we would or no; and have often been so bold as to charm us, when we were positively resolv'd to be out of Humour.

Besides these, we can, at convenient Time or Times, produce and prove five hundred and fifteen Articles of lesser Consequence, which may in the whole, at least, amount to accumulative Treason – How say you, Sir, are you guilty of the said Charge or no?

Prisoner. – *Guilty of the whole Charge*. . .

Also taking Handel's part against the Nobility Opera were patrons of the highest order: the King and Queen, and Princess Anne, Handel's royal pupil – the one person whom Handel was induced to teach, according to Jacob Lustig (*Inleidung tot de Muziekkunde*, 1771), and whom he called 'the flower of princesses'. Relations between the Princess and her brother, Prince Frederick, were strained on this and other accounts, as Lord Hervey recalled in his *Memoirs*:

Another judicious subject of his enmity was her supporting Handel, a German musician and composer (who had been her singing master, and was now undertaker of one of the operas), against several of the nobility who had a pique to Handel, and had set up another person to ruin him; or, to speak more properly and exactly, the Prince, in the beginning of his enmity to his sister, set himself at the head of the other opera to irritate her, whose pride and passions were as strong as her brother's (though his understanding was so much weaker), and could brook contradiction, where she dared to resist it, as little as her father.

What I had related may seem a trifle, but though the cause was indeed such, the effects of it were no trifles. The King and Queen were as much in earnest upon this subject as their son and daughter, though they had the prudence to disguise it, or to endeavour to disguise it, a little more. They were both Handelists, and sat freezing constantly at his empty Haymarket Opera, whilst the Prince with all the chief of the nobility went as constantly to that of Lincoln's Inn Fields. The affair grew as serious as that of the Greens and the Blues under Justinian at Constantinople. An anti-Handelist was looked upon as an anti-courtier, and voting against the Court in Parliament was hardly a less remissible or more venial sin than speaking against Handel or going to Lincoln's Inn Fields Opera. The Princess Royal said she expected in a little while to see half the House of Lords playing in the orchestra in their robes and coronets; and the King (though he declared he took no other part in this affair than subscribing £1,000 a year to Handel) often added at the same time he did not think setting oneself at the head of a faction of fiddlers a very honourable occupation for people of quality; or the ruin of one poor fellow so generous or so good-natured a scheme as to do much honour to the undertakers, whether they succeeded or not; but the better they succeeded in it, the more he thought they would have reason to be ashamed of it.

The alleged hostility with which the Prince of Wales viewed Handel derives almost exclusively from this single source. A recently discovered set of the Prince's household accounts offers a contrasting picture, however, of Frederick's role as patron of Handel's operas.* In the 1733–4 season, bounties of £250 were given to both Handel and the rival Nobility Opera; whilst this was given only to the Nobility in the next two seasons, payment to Handel resumed in 1736–7, continued in the next season, and for all subsequent seasons from 1738 to 1744 the Prince's accounts show regular attendance at, and payment for, Handel's opera, oratorio and other musical entertainments. In a total of eight seasons, Handel benefited from Frederick's patronage to the tune of £1120 10s; the Nobility and Lord Middlesex's ventures had £1000 and £1042 in four and three seasons, respectively. The Prince's support for Handel's rivals cannot be disputed, but his treatment of Handel was patently not as hostile as Hervey recounted.

In March, the wedding of Princess Anne and Prince William of Orange, which had been postponed from the previous year because of his illness, was celebrated in the French Chapel at St James's with a Wedding Anthem by the Princess's music-master (*This is the day* . . .). On the eve of the wedding celebrations, Handel offered a serenata, *Parnasso in Festa*, in the Haymarket

---

Household Accounts of Frederick Louis, Prince of Wales (Duchy of Cornwall Office), quoted by Carole Taylor, 'Handel and Frederick, Prince of Wales'.

Theatre; there was one set, and the characters were 'emblematically dress'd, the whole Appearance being extreamly magnificent. The Musick is no less entertaining, being contrived with so great a Variety, that all Sorts of Musick are properly introduc'd in single Songs, Duetto's, &c. intermix'd with Chorus's, some what in the Style of Oratorio's. People have been waiting with Impatience for this Piece, the celebrated Mr. Handel having exerted his utmost Skill in it' (*Daily Journal*). In fact, any people who had attended the Oxford celebrations would have recognized the greater part of it as being taken from *Athalia* (which Handel also quarried for the Wedding Anthem).

During this beleagured period Handel was working out in public a distinction between true oratorio and the semi-staged world of masque and serenade. The action of *Athalia* could not be emblematically treated on stage, and despite its obviously stronger sense of drama, Handel never repeated it in more than twenty years after his London performances of 1735; *Parnasso in Festa*, its mythological gloss, however, was seen again in 1737, 1740 and 1741. At the same time, he seems to have remained untouched by rival attempts at the oratorio form; neither Defesch's *Judith*, which appeared in the field immediately after *Esther* (and imitated Handel's presentation with 'scenes and other decorations'), nor Porpora's *Davide e Bersabea*, which was given by the rival team one day before *Parnasso*, had any effect on his decisions and development. He was, in any case, better off with English singers and an English text – even allowing that the theme of David and Bathsheba was not ideally suited to the eve of royal matrimony – and his grasp of drama as a musical force was patently superior to all competition. On 28 March Mrs Pendarves wrote to her sister:

> Yesterday in the afternoon Phil and I went to the oratorio at Lincoln's Inn, composed by Porpora, an Italian, famous for church music, who is now in England: it is a fine solemn piece of music, but I confess I think the subject too solemn for a theatre. To have words of piety made use of *only* to introduce good music, is *reversing* what it ought to be, and most of the people that hear the oratorio make no reflection on the meaning of the words, though God is addressed in the most solemn manner; some of the choruses and recitatives are extremely fine and touching, but they say it is not equal to Mr. Handel's oratorio of *Esther* or *Deborah*.

To that pertinent critique of oratorio, Mrs Pendarves adds a rare glimpse of Handel the man, freed from the tension of professional life:

> I must tell you of a little entertainment of music I had last week; I never wished more heartily for you and my mother than on that occasion. I had Lady Rich and her daughter, Lady Cath. Hanmer and her husband, Mr. and Mrs. Percival, Sir John Stanley and my brother, Mrs. Donellan, Strada and Mr. Coot. Lord Shaftesbury begged of Mr. Percival to bring him, and being a *profess'd friend* of Mr. Handel (who was here also) *was admitted*; I never was so *well* entertained at *an opera*! Mr. Handel was in the best humour in the world, and played lessons and accompanied Strada and all the ladies that sang from

seven o'the clock till eleven. I gave them tea and coffee, and about half an hour after nine had a salver brought in of chocolate, mulled white wine and biscuits. Everybody was easy and seemed pleased, Bunny staid with me after the company was gone, eat a cold chick with me, and we chatted till one o'the clock.

Most of the guests were amateur musicians (the sort of company one does not readily associate with Handel), and Lady Sunderland lent a harpsichord for the party. Philip Percival played the viola (and composed), Lady Hanmer sang and her husband (Thomas Hanmer of Fenns MP) played the violin. Bernard Granville ('Bunny') was brother to Mrs Pendarves, and later to become a close friend of Handel and a collector of his music. Just as Rebecca Schroeter's letters offer us such tantalizing glimpses of Haydn's private life in London, it is equally frustrating that Handel's near neighbour in Brook Street, with whom he was so at ease, leaves so few accounts of him. She was, however, a loyal supporter of every public performance, and on 30 April and 28 May respectively, reported on revivals of *Sosarme* and *Il Pastor Fido*, the latter much expanded and 'intermixed with choruses'.

These operas ended the season, and also terminated Heidegger's contract with Handel. Theirs was not a partnership; Handel was employed as musical director and composer, but the manager was free to re-let his theatre to a more profitable concern – which Heidegger did, to the Nobility Opera. Handel reacted quickly and approached John Rich, who had profited so famously from *The Beggar's Opera* and with the proceeds had built the new Theatre Royal in Covent Garden. The architect of this new venture was Edward Shepherd, who had completed Cannons for the Duke of Chandos; in spite of the showy exterior ('an Ionick expensive portico', William Kent called it), the interior, with the usual fan-shaped auditorium, was based on that of Lincoln's Inn Fields and with its extended apron stage was equally well suited to oratorio performance and opera. Handel saw its potential, and Rich was agreeable to alternating operas with his plays and pantomimes. 30

In spite of Prévost's gloomy prognostications – 'he has incurred so much ruinous expense and [written] so many beautiful operas that were a total loss, that he finds himself obliged to leave London and return to his native land' – Handel remained in England, but went to take the waters 'to get rid of that dejection of mind, which his repeated disappointments had brought upon him' (Hawkins).

The cure was so effective that by 12 August he was already at work on a new opera, *Ariodante*. The first surviving personal letter in English from Handel dates from this summer (27 August), apologizing to Sir Wyndham Knatchbull for not being able to make the trip from Tunbridge Wells to Ashford; his grammar is not perfect.

Sir

At my arrival in Town from the Country, I found my self honored of your kind invitation.

I am sorry that by the situation of my affairs I see my self deprived of receiving that pleasure being engaged with Mr. Rich to carry on the Operas at Covent Garden.

I hope at your return to Town, Sir, I shall make up this loss . . .

At the opening of the new season, the dice were heavily loaded in favour of the Nobility. They had taken the best theatre, the greatest number of subscriptions, the best of Handel's earlier team of singers, and – the crowning stroke – they now produced the most famous vocal virtuoso in the world: Carlo Broschi, known everywhere as Farinelli. Lord Cowper had first heard him in Venice, during his Grand Tour; now, as Director of the new Opera, he observed his effect on the London musicians. In Burney's words: 'On his arrival here, at the first private rehearsal at Cuzzoni's apartments, Lord Cooper, then the principal manager of the opera under Porpora, observing that the band did not follow him, but were all gaping with wonder, as if thunder-struck, desired them to be attentive; when they all confessed, that they were unable to keep pace with him: having not only been disabled by astonishment, but overpowered by his talents.'

Burney goes on to list Farinelli's virtues: the 'force, extent and mellifluous tones' of his voice, the rapidity of his coloratura, and, in particular his 'messa di voce, or swell' in which he surpassed all other singers and astonished the public: '. . . by the natural formation of his lungs, and artificial œconomy of breath, he was able to protract to such a length as to excite incredulity even in those who heard him; who, though unable to detect the artifice, imagined him to have had the latent help of some instrument by which the tone was continued, while he renewed his powers by respiration.' Most convincing of all, however, is the praise of Rolli, who, as a close friend of Senesino would have been the first to find fault. 'However, I must have you know – for it deserves to be known – that Farinello was a revelation to me, for I realised that till then I had heard only a small part of what human song can achieve, whereas I now conceive I have heard all there is to hear. He has, besides, the most agreeable and clever manners, hence I take the greatest pleasure in his company and acquaintance' (letter to Riva, 9 November 1734).

The Nobility opened on 29 October at the Haymarket with *Artaserse*, the music by Hasse (who had refused to come to England for the Nobility when he learned that Handel was still alive) and Farinelli's brother, Riccardo Broschi. Even on stage Farinelli's colleagues were apparently overwhelmed: 'Senesino had the part of a furious tyrant', Burney reported, 'and Farinelli that of an unfortunate hero in chains; but in the course of the first air, the captive so softened the heart of the tyrant, that Senesino, forgetting his stage-character, ran to Farinelli and embraced him in his own'. The audience were equally extreme: 'One God one Farinelli', a lady of quality shouted, and the phrase was fixed by Hogarth (in *Marriage à la Mode*, IV).

24

Handel could manage only a modest answer to such adulation: 'A Scholar of Mr Gates, Beard, (who left the Chappell last Easter) shines in the Opera of Covent Garden & Mr Hendell is so full of his Praises that he says he will surprise the Town with his performances before the Winter is over', reported Lady Elizabeth Compton to the Countess of Northampton. The other novelty, and one that coloured the next three operas he was to write, was the celebrated dancer Mlle Sallé, 'the muse of gracious, modest gesture' who had been engaged by Rich for his pantomimes. 'She has dared to appear . . . without pannier, skirt, or bodice, and with her hair down', wrote the London correspondent of the *Mercure de France*: 'Apart from her corset and petticoat she wore only a simple dress of muslin draped about her in the manner of a Greek statue'. Others less refined asserted that the looseness extended beyond her costume. For her and her company of dancers, Händel yet again revised *Il Pastor Fido*, this time adding dance music to each act, and preceded it by 'a new Dramatic Entertainment (in Musick) call'd, TERPSICHORE' (*Daily Post*) – his only French-style opera–ballet.

Already there was comment on the expense of having two opera companies: 'We hear that both Operas (occasion'd by their dividing) are at a vast expence to entertain the Nobility and Gentry for the ensuing Season; the Opera House in the Haymarket are reckon'd to stand near 12000*l*. and Mr. Handell at near 9000*l*. for the Season' (*Ipswich Gazette*).* Handel nevertheless retaliated to the long-running *Artaserse* with a revival of *Arianna*, and *Oreste*, a *pasticcio* made out of his own music, before deciding it was time to launch his new *Ariodante* in February. In all such tactics, he was prepared to wait (or rush) for the right moment, and by choosing February he hoped that the initial Farinelli fever would have abated, while anticipating the Nobility's second production, *Polifemo*, by nearly a month.

Rather than fight them with even more heroic opera, Handel had chosen (again from Ariosto) a low-key story, also used by Shakespeare in *Much Ado About Nothing*; pastoral, sensual and reflective, to which Handel introduced the idea of a moonlight scene, which is not suggested in Salvi's libretto. Burney calls the first act 'monotonously happy', and is scornful of Waltz, the bass with whom Handel had to replace Montagnana ('his manner was coarse and unpleasant'); he also points out that the rival theatre had not only stolen singers but also players from Handel's orchestra, including the trumpeter, Valentine Snow, 'who had the brighest tone, and most accurate intonation, of any performer I ever heard on that instrument'.

A recently discovered manuscript version of 'Scherza infida' from Act II of *Ariodante* contains elaborate ornamentation which may reflect the performance of Handel's new star, Carestini. If so, his challenge to Farinelli's decorative style was beaten off:

> On the 15th of last Month the famous Signor *Farinelli*, the Singer, had his Benefit Night at the Opera-House in the Hay-Market, when there was a most

27

---

*This figure of £9000 accords well with the minimum budget of £8500 calculated by Judith Milhous and Robert Hume ('Handel's Opera Finances in 1732–3') on the basis of a newly discovered summary of income for Handel's opera season of 1732–3.

numerous Audience; for the Pit and Galleries were full by four o'clock, and the Stage being done up without any Scenes, as at a Ridotto, and curiously adorned with gilt leather, there were several hundreds of People in the Seats erected there; so that it is reckoned that he had a most extraordinary Benefit; for besides the usual Price of Tickets, his Royal Highness the Prince of *Wales* gave him 200 Guineas, the *Spanish* Ambassador 100, the Emperor's 50, his Grace the Duke of *Leeds* 50, the Countess of *Portmore* 50, the Lord *Burlington* 50, his Grace the Duke of *Richmond* 50, the Hon. Col. *Paget* 30, the Lady *Rich* 20, and most of the other Nobility 50, 30, or 20 each; In the whole, it is computed he made by his Benefit 2000 l. and as he has besides a Salary of 1500 l. for each Season, and has got several other Presents upon extraordinary Occasions, it may be reckoned he has got at least 4 or 5000 l. for this season in *England*, which will be a lasting Monument to the Politeness and Generosity of the Persons of Quality and Distinction of this Age. (*The Political State of Great Britain*, April 1735)

III The irony of the last remark is set off with more spleen by Hogarth, in *The Rake's Progress*, where Tom Rakewell joins the adulators with a present of 'A gold-snuff-box, chased with the story of Orpheus charming the Brutes'. The bewigged harpsichordist is said by some to be Handel, though others suggest Porpora; in any case, Handel seemed impervious to Farinelli's success, as Prévost reported:

Signor Farinelli, who came to England with the highest expectations, has the satisfaction of seeing them fulfilled by generosity and favour as extraordinary as his own talents. The others were loved: this man is idolized, adored; it is a consuming passion. Indeed, it is impossible to sing better. Mr. Handel has not omitted to produce a new *Oratorio*, which is given on Wednesdays and Fridays, with chorus and orchestral accompaniments of great beauty. Everyone agrees that he is the Orpheus of his age and that this new work is a masterpiece. He plays the organ himself in it, with consummate skill. He is admired, but from a distance, for he is often alone; a spell draws the crowd to Farinelli's (*Le Pour et Contre*, May 1735)

Organ concertos were included in the oratorio performances as a last-minute addition. Burney claims that Handel had started the practice in 1733, at a revival of *Esther*, and Arne and Festing told him that when Handel again included a concerto (probably also in *Esther*) at the Oxford Act, they had never heard better playing either extempore or 'premeditated'. Mrs Pendarves considered 'his playing on the organ in Esther, where he performs a part in two concertos, . . . the finest things I ever heard in my life'. Because these works were primarily designed as vehicles for Handel's improvisations, they were notated in shorthand or skeletal form, solo sections and even complete movements being indicated simply by *organo ad libitum*; they present problems of reconstruction today if we are to hear anything like the effects produced by Handel's extempore and 'volant touch'.

> When he gave a concerto, his method in general was to introduce it with a
> voluntary movement on the diapasons, which stole on the ear in a slow and
> solemn progression; the harmony close wrought, and as full as could
> possibly be expressed; the passages concatenated with stupendous art, the
> whole at the same time being perfectly intelligible, and carrying the appearance
> of great simplicity. This kind of prelude was succeeded by the concerto itself,
> which he executed with a degree of spirit and firmness that no-one ever
> pretended to equal.   (Sir John Hawkins, 1776)

In spite of this extra attraction, however, 'so strong is the Disgust [probably in
the sense of 'change of taste' rather than 'revulsion'] taken against him, that even
this has been far from bringing him crowded Audiences. . . . *Handel* whose
excellent Compositions have often pleased our Ears and touched our Hearts,
has this Winter sometimes performed to an almost empty Pitt . . . His Loss is
computed for these two Seasons at a great Sum'. (*Old Whig*)

Handel's finest offering of the season was *Alcina*, the third of the Ariosto
trilogy, more fierily dramatic than *Ariodante* and in the opinion of Mrs
Pendarves 'so fine I have not words to describe it. Strada has a whole scene of
charming recitative* – there are a thousand beauties. While Mr. Handel was
playing his part, I could not help thinking him a necromancer in the midst of his
own enchantments'. Possibly to compensate for their attendance at the Nobility
Opera, the King and Queen gave particular support to *Alcina*, which had
eighteen performances, 'always by command of their Majesties, till the King
went to Hanover, and then by command of her Majesty alone' (Burney). It was
Handel's last great operatic triumph. Alcina, queen and sorceress, is a character
of extraordinary intensity; hypnotically evil, moving in her doomed passion
and pathetically deserted by her kingdom and her magic, while her victims
rejoice. The most famous air from the opera was at first turned down by
Carestini, as Burney reports:

> . . . *Verdi prati*, which was constantly encored during the whole run of *Alcina*,
> was, at first, sent back to HANDEL by Carestini, as unfit for him to sing; upon
> which he went, in a great rage, to his house, and in a way which few
> composers, except HANDEL, ever ventured to accost a *first-singer*, cries out:
> 'You toc! don't I know better as your seluf, vaat is pest for you to sing? If
> you vill not sing all de song vaat I give you, I will not pay you ein stiver.'
> (Sketch, p.*24n)

Marie Sallé also featured in the extended ballet sections of *Alcina*, but too
daringly for English taste; she was hissed at one of the last performances, since
'she cast herself for the role of Cupid and took upon herself to dance it in male
attire. This, it is said, suits her very ill and was apparently the cause of her
disgrace' (*Le Pour et Contre*, June 1735). She withdrew to Paris and never danced
in England again.

---

*'Ah, Ruggiero crudel!' (Act III).

Alcina also saw the end of Handel's *primo uomo*: 'Yesterday Signor Caristina, a celebrated Singer in the late Opera's in Covent Garden Theatre, embarqued on Board a ship for Venice' (*Daily Post*). Handel had lost his only possible answer to Farinelli, and given the losses incurred that season, to retrench would seem the only possibility. 'Mr. Handel . . . is to have Concerts of Musick next Season, but no Opera's', announced the *General Evening Post* (20 May 1735).

Loss of the opera, coupled with threatened loss of health, meant that Handel was in no mood to write his autobiography for his Hamburg acquaintance, Johann Mattheson, whose *Die Wol-klingende Finger-Sprache* (Burney calls it 'the well-sounding finger-language'), a collection of keyboard fugues, had arrived with a dedication describing Handel as 'the nobly-born, deeply learned, and world famous gentleman'. With it also came a request to contribute details of his life for Mattheson's next publication, *Grundlage einer Ehren-Pforte*. Handel replied in French on 29 July, but we only have the censored version of his letter that Mattheson chose to reprint. Burney's *Life* includes a translation, plus Mattheson's peevish response:

> . . . I only wish *that I was in more favourable circumstances* for manifesting my inclination to serve you. The work is well worthy the attention of the curious; and for my own part, I am always ready to do you justice.
>
> As for drawing up memoirs concerning myself, I find it utterly impossible, on account of my being continually occupied in the service of the court and nobility, which puts it out of my power to think of any thing else.
>
> Since which time, says Mattheson, till 1739, when the court and first nobility, and, indeed, the whole nation, were more attentive to a ruinous war, than to places of public entertainment, this could be no excuse. I therefore repeated my request, inforced by all the arguments I could devise, but still to no purpose.

Had Handel obliged, his biographers would no doubt be grateful; but there were far vaster musical benefits implicit in a letter to the wealthy, ostentatious VII and eccentric author, Charles Jennens, which he wrote ten days later, on 28 July:

> Sr
>
> I received your very agreable Letter with the inclosed Oratorio. I am just going to Tunbridge [Wells], yet what I could read of it in haste, gave me a great deal of Satisfaction. I shall have more leasure time there to read it with all the Attention it deserves. There is no certainty of any Scheme for next Season, but it is probable that some thing or other may be done, of which I shall take the Liberty to give you notice, beeng extreamly obliged to you for the generous concern you show upon this account. The Opera of Alcina is a writing out and shall be send according to your Direction . . .

Of Handel's surviving letters, the nine to Jennens are the largest number to any one correspondent, and, with the exception of this single example, fall between the years 1741 and 1749. Jennens may already have been acquainted with

Handel for some time – he was certainly a subscriber to all his published music – but this letter would seem to start his collaboration as a librettist. If the 'inclosed Oratorio' was in fact the libretto of *Saul*, it must have been pushed from Handel's mind for several years by dissension over the opera and the continual temptation to return to the theatre to demonstrate how, despite public indifference, operas *could* be written. One can sympathize with Lord Hervey's frustration at the beginning of the new season:

> ... I am this moment returned with the King from yawning four hours at the longest and dullest Opera that ever the enobled ignorance of our present musical Governors ever inflicted on the ignorance of an English audience; who, generally speaking, are equally skilful in the language of the drama and the music it is set to, a degree of knowledge or ignorance (call it which you please) that on this occasion is no great misfortune to them, the drama [*Adriano in Siria*] being composed by an anonymous fool, and the music by one Veracini, a madman, who to show his consummate skill in this Opera has, among half a dozen very bad parts, given Cuzzoni and Farinelli the two worst. The least bad part is Senesino's, who like Echo reversed, has lost all his voice, and retains nothing of his former self but his flesh . . . Handel sat in great eminence and great pride in the middle of the pit [i.e. auditorium], and seemed in silent triumph to insult this poor dying Opera in its agonies, without finding out that he was as great a fool for refusing to compose, as Veracini had shown himself by composing, nobody feeling their own folly, though they never overlook other people's, and having the eyes of a mole for the one, with those of a lynx for the other.

Handel was the last man who would have wanted pity; he was free from operatic worries until strategy demanded a return, and the waters of Tunbridge Wells would seem to have improved his condition, if we are to judge from a heartening marginal note which he scribbled about this time:

> 12 Gallons Port
> 12 Bottles French   Duke Street, Meels.

Refreshed, he started work on a setting of Dryden's 1697 St Cecilia Day Ode *Alexander's Feast*, described both by Newburgh Hamilton, who adapted the words, and the Earl of Egmont, who attended the first performance, as an 'Entertainment'; to the Purcellian concept of a Cecilian ode, Handel added all his experience of drama and orchestral colouring. He (or Hamilton) ignored the conventional calls for a chorus at the close of every stanza, and offset the danger of static description with startling recitatives, and orchestral colouring (recorders, oboes, bassoons in three parts, trumpets, drums and seven-part choruses) appropriate to the poem's subtitle, 'The Power of Music'. In his will, Handel described Hamilton as having 'assisted me in adjusting words for some of my compositions'; according to Hamilton himself, in the verbose Preface to *Alexander's Feast*, 'I was determined not to take any unwarrantable liberty with that poem, which has so long done honour to the nation, and which no man can add to or abridge in anything material, without injuring it. I therefore confined

129

> *The late Mr. Brown, leader of his majesty's band, used to tell me several stories of HANDEL's love of good cheer, liquid and solid, as well as of his impatience. Of the former he gave an instance, which was accidentally discovered at his own house in Brook-street, where Brown, in the Oratorio season, among other principal performers, was at dinner. During the repast, HANDEL often cried out – 'Oh – I have de taught;' when the company, unwilling that, out of civility to them, the public should be robbed of any thing so valuable as his musical ideas, begged he would retire and write them down; with which request, however, he so frequently complied, that, at last, one of the most suspicious had the ill-bred curiosity to peep through the key-hole into the adjoining room; where he perceived that dese taughts, were only bestowed on a fresh hamper of Burgundy, which, as was afterwards discovered, he had received in a present from his friend, the late lord Radnor, while his company was regaled with more generous and spirited port.*   (Charles Burney, 1785)

myself to a plain division of it into airs, recitatives, or choruses, looking upon the words in general so sacred as scarcely to violate one in the order of its first place'.

The first performance was well attended; there were 'at least 1300 Persons present; and it is judg'd that the Receipt of the House could not amount to less than £450' (*Daily Post*). The only complaint was that the performers were too far away from the audience, perhaps on account of the large orchestra, but this was rectified at the second performance by flooring the pit over into the boxes. The two sopranos were Strada and Cecilia Young (shortly to marry Thomas Arne); Beard, Handel's new discovery and still not twenty, was the tenor, and a 'Mr Erard', the bass, was the first to revel in 'Revenge, Timotheus cries'.

Alexander's Feast achieved the unusual distinction of being published complete in full score by Walsh two years later, together with a portrait of the composer engraved by Houbraken and a scene from the Ode beneath, which was delivered afterwards to the 150 subscribers. Handel was paid the extraordinary sum of £105, compared with the 25 guineas that was standard for an opera (and only 20 for an oratorio). Only a few days after *Alexander's Feast* was first heard, John Walsh senior died, 'worth £30,000'. Since Handel himself left only £22,000 at his death, there may have been reason for his supposed remark that in future he would publish works if Walsh would write them.

What the published score did not include were the various concertos that Handel introduced into the piece. In Part I there was a concerto for 'Harp, Lute, Lyricord, and other Instruments' after the recitative 'Timotheus, plac'd on high', which is conjectured to be a version of the published Organ Concerto op. 4 no. 6, while Part II ended with an organ concerto (op. 4 no. 1) before an additional chorus with words by Newburgh Hamilton.* In the interval, Handel

---

*See Donald Burrows, 'Handel and "Alexander's Feast"'.

gave the Concerto Grosso in C major (now known as the *Concerto in Alexander's Feast*) plus an Italian cantata (which Walsh did include) to satisfy Strada, also on a Cecilian text: 'Cecilia, vogli un sguardo'.

Another royal marriage was now in prospect; the Prince of Wales was to be married at last to Augusta, Princess of Saxe-Gotha, and Handel saw his chance to gain once more substantial royal patronage. The King was already tired of the squabbles. Around 15 May 1736, Benjamin Victor wrote to the violinist Matthew Dubourg in Dublin: '. . . As to the Operas, they must tumble, for the King's presence could hardly hold them up, and even that prop is denied them, for his Majesty will not admit his royal ears to be tickled this season. As to music, it flourishes in this place more than ever, in subscription concerts and private parties, which must prejudice all operas and public entertainments'. The presentation of a wedding opera would therefore draw the only remaining royal patron to Handel's party. It was not an unreasonable tactic in view of the Prince's support for both parties; he was sensitive to the arts, he played the cello (as shown by Mercier) and his greatest motive had been to annoy his father. The Earl of Egmont noted in his diary the interest that the royal couple took in Handel's music: the day after the Princess landed, 'they passed the evening on the water with music' (very possibly one of Handel's *Water Music* suites), and the following day at the wedding 'There was a prodigious crowd . . . The chapel was finely adorned with tapestry, velvet, and gold lace . . . Over the altar was placed the organ, and a gallery made for the musicians. An anthem* composed by Hendel for the occasion was wretchedly sung . . .'

The opera, *Atalanta*, was a pastoral, almost masque-like creation, calculated to flatter the Prince of Wales. Spectacular scenery and machinery were a feature of the production, and the *Daily Post* reported: 'as the Wedding was solemnized sooner than was expected, great Numbers of Artificers, as Carpenters, Painters, Engineers, &c. are employed to forward the same, in order to bring it on the Stage with the utmost Expedition, and [we hear] that several Voices being sent for from Italy, for that purpose, are lately arrived, who as we are informed, will make their first Appearance, in the Opera of *Ariodante*'.†

Handel's new star was Conti, a soprano (Senesino and Carestini had been altos), and from London the poet Thomas Gray reported on the proceedings to Horace Walpole in Cambridge:

It was hardly worth while to trouble you with a letter till I had seen somewhat in town; not that I have seen anything now but what you have heard of before, that is, *Atalanta*. There are only four men and two women in it. The first is a common scene of a wood, and does not change at all till the end of the last act, when there appears the Temple of Hymen with illuminations; there is a row of blue fires burning in order along the ascent to the temple; a fountain of fire spouts up out of the ground to the ceiling, and two more cross each other obliquely from the sides of the stage; on the top is a wheel that

---

*'Sing unto God'.

†As an emergency measure, Handel for the first time allowed the insertion of arias by other (unidentified) composers.

whirls always about, and throws out a shower of gold-colour, silver, and blue fiery rain. Conti I like excessively in everything but his mouth which is thus, ⊟; but this is hardly minded, when Strada stands by him.

Gray, who was not normally partial to Handel's music, asked to purchase a score of *Atalanta*. Conti's 'square cavernous mouth, in outline like a knuckle-bone', obviously worried him, and he was still referring to it in 1742.

Burney noticed that Handel adopted a new style for Conti, and picked out 'Non saria poco' in the first act where, he says, 'the base and the accompaniments are of a modern cast, and, except the closes and two or three of the divisions, the whole seems of the present age' (i.e. 1789). Few of Handel's contemporaries appreciated his judiciousness in adapting his style to the taste and talents of the performers, without compromising his dramatic ideals. Benjamin Victor wrote that although at Handel's appearance in the pit 'there was so universal a clap from the audience that many were surprized', nevertheless when it came to the opera 'the critics say, it is too like his former compositions, and wants variety'. Even so, the elaborate scenes, the transparencies and the fireworks, in addition to the music of *Atalanta*, not only gave 'uncommon Delight and Satisfaction', but fulfilled Handel's hopes, at least in part, since the Prince remained a staunch Handelian, and, after eight performances that season, demanded a revival the following November.

The surviving correspondence of the summer months suggests relaxation. From a letter he wrote in June to the Earl of Shaftesbury, Handel evidently stayed in the country, though it is not known where:

> At my return to Town from the Country (where I made a longer stay than I intended) I found my self honoured with Your Lordships Letter. I am extremly obliged to Your Lordship for sending me that Part of My Lord Your Fathers Letter* relating to Musick. His notions are very just. I am highly dilighted with them, and can not enough admire 'em.

To Michael Michaelsen, who had informed him of the impending marriage of Handel's niece to a professor of law at Halle University, he wrote in August:

> Honoured Brother,
> As I now have no nearer relative than my dear niece and have always loved her particularly, you could not apprise me of more welcome news than that she is to marry a person of such distinguished character and attainments. Your agreement alone would have sufficed to place her on the pinnacle of happiness, so I take the request that you make for my approval as a further proof of your condescension. The sound upbringing which she owes to you will assure not only her own happiness, but also afford you some consolation; and you will not doubt but that I shall add my voice thereto to the best of my ability.

---

*This was the 'Letter relating to Musick' from *Soliloquy, or Advice to an Author* (1710) by Anthony, Third Earl of Shaftesbury.

PLATE VII   Charles Jennens, Handel's arrogant, irascible collaborator who provi
the word-book for *Messiah* and S

ennens Efq.^r
l uncle to
ther Curzon.

VIII

I have taken the liberty of sending the bridegroom as a small wedding-present a gold watch by Delharmes, with a gold chain, and two seal-rings, one of amethyst and the other of onyx. I trust you will approve my sending on the same occasion as a small wedding-present to the bride, my dear niece, a solitaire diamond ring; the stone weighs a little over 7½ grains, is of the first water and quite perfect. I shall despatch both to Mr. Sbüelen in Hamburg for delivery to you . . .

Handel approached the 1736/7 season with the same strategy he had used two years earlier: revivals before Christmas and new pieces for the New Year. But as Benjamin Victor had pointed out in a letter to Dubourg, predictions were not good: 'It is the confirmed opinion that this winter will compleat your friend *Handel's* destruction, as far as loss of money can destroy him'. The Theatre Royal hoped to maintain the festive atmosphere of the wedding, not only with the royal command revival of *Atalanta*, but with suitable decorations for other operas. At *Alcina*, for example,

. . . The Box in which their Royal Highnesses sat, was of white Satin, beautifully Ornamented with Festons of Flowers in their proper Colours, and in Front was a flaming Heart, between two Hymeneal Torches, whose different Flames terminated in one Point, and were surmounted with a Label, on which were wrote, in Letters of Gold, these Words, MUTUUS ARDOR. (*Daily Post*).

For a report on the rival company, which opened a fortnight after Handel, and on Handel's future plans, we turn to a letter from Mrs Pendarves to her sister:

Bunny came from the Haymarket Opera, and supped with me comfortably. They have Farinelli, Merighi, with *no sound* in her voice, but thundering action – a beauty with *no other merit*; and one Chimenti, a tolerable good woman with a pretty voice and Montagnana, who *roars as usual*! With this band of singers and dull Italian operas, such as you almost fall asleep at, *they presume* to rival Handel – who has Strada, that sings better than ever she did; Gizziello, who is much improved since last year; and Annibali who has the best part of Senesino's voice and Caristini's, with a prodigious fine taste and good action! . . . Mr. Handel has two new operas ready – Erminius and Justino. He was here two or three mornings ago and *played to me both the overtures*, which are charming.

Neither *Arminio* nor *Giustino*, nor the talents of Conti and the new contralto Annibali, could save Handel; even the 'modernizing' of his style, which Burney is always so keen to discover, extends only to him using 'more bases and accompaniments in iterated notes, in this opera, than in any preceding work'. The Nobility showed more initiative, and finding that Farinelli's charms were wearing thin at last, added comic *intermezzi* between the acts of the *opera seria*. *Il*

Giocatore, introduced between the acts of Hasse's *Siroe* on New Year's Day 1737 with all the royal family present (except the King, who was becalmed on the Dutch coast), was the first Italian comic opera to be heard in London. Yet even these desperate measures could not draw an audience, and Colley Cibber wrote, 'we have seen . . . even *Farinelli* singing to an Audience of five and thirty Pounds' (*Apology*, II, p. 88).

Handel, with *Berenice* still up his sleeve, attempted to swamp the market with performances throughout Lent, and advertised a plan for two opera days a week. A ban (the *London Daily Post* does not say by whom) forced him to change direction: 'We hear, since Operas have been forbidden being performed at the Theatre in Covent Garden on the Wednesdays and Fridays in Lent, Mr. Handel is preparing Dryden's Ode of Alexander's Feast, the Oratorios of Esther and Deborah, with several new Concertos for the Organ and other Instruments; also an Entertainment of Musick, called Il Trionfo del Tempo e della Verita, which Performances will be brought on the Stage and varied every Week'.

Within two weeks, Handel had produced a rewritten version of his very first essay in oratorio form, *Il Trionfo del Tempo e del Disinganno*, from about 1707. It was the only pertinent work which had not already been quarried extensively, and could therefore appear 'new'. (*La Resurrezione*, written in Italy one year after *Il Trionfo*, called for an unusually large and varied orchestra, besides presenting the Easter story in a style incompatible with English taste; it had, in any case, contributed to *Esther*.) Many of his alterations simply pruned the piece of its early excesses, in particular the over-strained chromaticism, which he had retained from his earliest days in Germany. This heavily revised version, with much new music in it (yet to be published, such is the randomness of Handel editions) was rechristened *Il Trionfo del Tempo e della Verità*.*

Some idea of the way Handel drove himself during these months can be gathered from a timetable of works and performances leading up to Easter – a list that does not include the rehearsals for each oratorio which Handel directed in person, nor the concertos with which he supplemented each performance. (The Prince of Wales may not have realized the strain he was unwittingly placing on the composer on 16 March by commanding a repeat of 'Mr. Handel's Concerto on the Organ'.)

February 25	*Giustino*
March 2	*Giustino*
4	*Giustino*
9	*Parnasso in Festa*
11	*Parnasso in Festa*
16	*Alexander's Feast*
18	*Alexander's Feast*
23	*Il Trionfo*

*It is perhaps symbolic that this same piece, much adapted and translated, was to become Handel's last work: *The Triumph of Time and Truth*.

| 25 | Il Trionfo |
| 30 | Alexander's Feast |

April 1	Il Trionfo
4	Il Trionfo
5	Alexander's Feast
6	Esther
7	Esther

Few men could have stood the strain; still fewer would have dared propose a continuation of operas immediately after Easter; on the Wednesday, a *pasticcio*, *Dido* (music mostly by Vinci, but recopied by J. C. Smith with alterations in Handel's hand), on 4 May *Giustino* and on 18 May the premiere of *Berenice*.

The performances did take place – but without Handel. On 13 April he became ill (a stroke has been suggested). The papers at first minimized the seriousness of his condition: 'Mr. Handel, who has been some time indisposed with the rheumatism . . .' (*London Daily Post*, 30 April), but then admitted it was more grave: 'The ingenious Mr. Handell is very much indispos'd, and it's thought with a Paraletick Disorder, he having at present no Use of his Right Hand, which, if he don't regain, the Publick will be depriv'd of his fine Compositions' (*London Evening Post*, 14 May). The Earl of Shaftesbury, in his *Memoirs of Handel*, was more specific: 'Great fatigue and disappointment, affected him so much, that he was this Spring (1737) struck with the Palsy, which took entirely away, the use of 4 fingers of his right hand; and totally disabled him from Playing: And when the heats of the Summer 1737 came on, the Disorder seemed at times to affect his Understanding'.

His friend James Harris, having heard of Handel's illness from the Earl of Shaftesbury, also feared that he might never compose again, and in a letter of 5 May to the Earl tells us what little we know of Handel's treatment.

Y^r Lord$^{p's}$ information concerning Mr Handel's Disorder was y^e first I received – I can assure Y^r Lord^p it gave me no Small Concern – when y^e Fate of Harmony depends upon a Single Life, the Lovers of Harmony may be well allowed to be Sollicitous. I heartily regrett y^e thought of losing any of y^e executive part of his meritt, but this I can gladly compound for, when we are assured of the Inventive, for tis this which properly constitutes ye Artist, & Separates Him from ye Multitude. It is certainly an Evidence of great Strength of Constitution to be so Soon getting rid of So great a Shock. A weaker Body would perhaps have hardly born ye Violence of Medicines, wch operate So quickly.

. . . If Mr Handel gives off his Opera, it will be the only Pleasure I shall have left in ye musicall way, to look over his Scores, and recollect past Events – Here Strada used to shine – there Annibale – This was an Excell^t Chorus, and that a Charming peice of Recitative – In that I shall amuse my Self much in the Same manner as Virgil tells of ye Trojans . . .

Berenice opened on 18 May with all the royal family present, but Handel appears to have taken no part in the performance. Neither is there any contemporary account of its reception, though Burney, in tune with most modern listeners, declares the minuet 'happy and pleasing to an uncommon degree'. Even without the dampening effect of Handel's illness on his supporters, there is every sign that both public and performers were exhausted and satiated by the season, and *Berenice* held the stage for only four nights, the shortest run of any Handel opera.

Even so, he had managed to outrun his opponents, if only by four days. Despite the novelty of Italian *intermezzi*, the Nobility Opera came to a premature close on 11 June; Farinelli had been 'indisposed' earlier in the season, and the final performance of *Sabrina* (based on Milton's *Comus*, with words and music adapted by Rolli) was cancelled when he developed a cold. 'With so little eclat did this great singer quit the English stage, that the town seems rather to have left him, than he the town!' (Burney). Farinelli himself later assured Burney (in 1770) that before he left he had been negotiating with the Nobility to return for the following season, had not the deranged King of Spain, Philip V, discovered that three airs sung daily by Farinelli (always the same three) were the perfect cure for his melancholy: 'Advices from Madrid inform us, that his Catholic Majesty has settled a pension of 14,000 pieces of eight on Signor Farinelli, to engage him to stay at that court, besides a coach, which the King will keep for him at his own charge. This is important intelligence for the Hay-market' (*Daily Post*).

Handel, had he been in London to read the news, might well have envied the cure as well as the resources that made it possible. But after a final command performance of *Alexander's Feast* on 25 June, which he may have rallied sufficiently to direct, his friends decided that Handel had taken enough punishment. The Nobility, according to Burney, had lost £12,000 on their season, and Handel's deficits were computed at £10,000. He was not bankrupt, either at this period or any other time, as his Bank of England accounts show, but he may have temporarily lost both health and clarity of mind in the struggle.

In this melancholic state, it was in vain for him to think of any fresh projects for retrieving his affairs. His first concern was how to repair his constitution. But tho' he had the best advice, and tho' the necessity of following it was urged to him in the most friendly manner, it was with the utmost difficulty that he was prevailed on to do what was proper, when it was any way disagreeable. For this reason it was thought best for him to have recourse to the vapor-baths of Aix la Chapelle, over which he sat near three times as long as hath ever been the practice. Whoever knows any thing of the nature of those baths, will, from this instance, form some idea of his surprising constitution. His sweats were profuse beyond what can well be imagined. His cure, from the manner as well as from the quickness, with which it was wrought, passed with the Nuns for a miracle. When, but a few hours from the time of his quitting the bath, they heard him at the organ in the principal church as well as convent, playing in a manner so much beyond any they had ever been used to, such a conclusion in such persons was natural enough. Tho' his business was so soon dispatched, and his cure judged to be thoroughly effected, he thought it prudent to continue at Aix about six weeks, which is the shortest period usually allotted for bad cases. (Mainwaring)

Farinelli, Senesino, Cuzzoni had all left the country; Porpora had returned to Italy some time earlier; Conti and Strada had sung for the last time for Handel in *Berenice*. For a few months the country was as empty of its stars as it had been at the beginning of 1729.

5

London: the Oratorios 1737–1759

Strong in new Arms, lo! Giant Handel stands,
Like bold Briareus, with a hundred hands;
To stir, to rouze, to shake the Soul he comes,
And Jove's own Thunders follow Mars's Drums.
Arrest him, Empress; or you sleep no more' –
She heard, and drove him to th'Hibernian shore.

(Alexander Pope, *The Dunciad*, Book IV, 53–70)

Handel's enforced stay at Aix-la-Chapelle gave him the time to reflect on his position which the cut-and-thrust of the previous seasons in London had denied him. There was much to absorb his thoughts: the failure of the opera; the change in public taste and patronage; his own standing with both public and performers; the new leads that seemed to be opening up with the success of opera in English; and the consistent good fortune that had attended his own ventures away from the operatic stage.

His own future as a performer seemed assured, thanks to the 'miracle' of his cure, and his iron constitution. Current medical analysis has offered various explanations of Handel's illnesses. The most popular diagnosis is cerebral thrombosis, with a quick recovery due to efficient vascularity.* Recurrent muscular rheumatism is also a candidate† and could more readily explain Handel's brisk recovery. The particular association of Aix with cures for venereal disease in the eighteenth century is insufficient basis for the theory that Handel was suffering from syphilis.

More difficult to diagnose is the state of Handel's mind over Italian opera. He was too much a pragmatist not to have taken account of the fact that English taste was changing, and that his own operas were 'too good for the vile taste of the town', as Mrs Pendarves bemoaned. But Handel had a natural and justified sense of superiority when it came to musical values, and it would take more than a fickle public to sway his faith in the dramatic concept of Italian opera. If he allowed traits from Bononcini and the lighter *intermezzi* into his own highly

---

*See Percy Young, *Handel* and, more recently, William Ober, who (in a private communication of 1982) points out the comparable case of Woodrow Wilson, who survived his first 'minor stroke' at the age of forty in 1896 to suffer his well-known 'major stroke' in 1919.
†Milo Keynes, 'Handel's Illnesses'.

developed idea of *opera seria*, this was the maximum compromise to which he would extend. But there was another consideration, just as important in 1737 as when Rolli had first raised it in a letter to Riva: 'I shall speak only of Results, that is whether the theatre was full or empty, on which all depends, be it good or bad' (6 November 1729).

There are few facts to illuminate this crucial question of finance. Recent discoveries (particularly in the Duke of Portland's papers) and the work of Robert Hume and Judith Milhous put Handel's position in a clearer light, and on a sounder basis than was previously thought.* While the Royal Academy was financially desperate from its formation (see pp. 76–7), a rough analysis of the finances for the 1732–3 season shows that both Handel and Heidegger could have continued in business with the opera, thanks to their outside emoluments – Heidegger's from his masquerades, which are said to have netted him more than £2000 a year, and Handel from his profitable concert work (the massive returns on *Athalia*, for instance), his royal pension and his commissions (*Water Music*, and odes for special occasions such as weddings and funerals).

As long as Handel was not himself one of the prime undertakers of the venture, his financial security was not at risk. But the closer he was forced to management, as in the second venture with Heidegger, the more did he invite the 'disgust' of the public and accusations of 'tyranny' from the singers he employed. The fate of an opera could not be left, as Walpole put it of Lord Middlesex's later company, to 'the improbability of eight thoughtless young men of fashion understanding economy'. For his part, Handel had only his stubbornness and natural musical fecundity to recommend himself as a prime undertaker. Tolerance was not one of his virtues, and a man who could declare that a Royal Prince was no longer in *his* good graces could only react badly to the artistic excesses of the 'farr fetched and dear bought gentlemen' who made up his casts. And yet, as Colley Cibber put it:

> The truth is that this kind of entertainment being so entirely sensual, it had no possibility of getting the better of our reason but by its novelty, and that novelty could never be supported but by an annual change of the best voices, which, like the finest flowers, bloom but for a season and, when that is over, are only dead nosegays. (*Apology for His Life*, 1740)

Handel's failure could certainly not be blamed on a lack of patronage from above. The King, the Queen and (as shown above) the Prince of Wales all gave consistent support to Handel's ventures. 'If everyone were as well satisfied with the company as is the Royal Family, we should have to admit that there never had been such an Opera since Adam and Eve sang Milton's hymns in the Garden of Eden', Rolli wrote sarcastically in 1729. An analysis of figures for the 1732–3 season shows that out of the total income for the year, some 23 per cent came from subscribers (or in some distinguished cases, failed to come); 50 per

---

*See 'Handel's Opera Finances in 1732–3'.

cent from sales of tickets, reflecting the marked increase in 'walk-in' support for individual operas; 7 per cent from box rental; and an impressive 20 per cent of the whole income from the Royal Family.

The crux of the dilemma was the fact that there were now two opera companies in London. One company might have found enough support to survive financially; two meant that each quickly became ruinously unprofitable. Their joint demise can only have been hastened by the unseemly squabbles that accompanied it:

> Our operas have given much cause of dissension. Men and women have been deeply engaged, and no debate in the House of Commons has been urged with more warmth. The dispute of the merits of the composers and singers is carried to so great a height, that it is much feared by all true lovers of music that operas will be quite overturned. I own I think we make a very silly figure about it. (Mrs Pendarves to Swift, May 1735)

Competition and rivalry were compounded by the demand of the London public for Sense, as well as for sight and sound. Handel had remained obdurate in his refusal to listen to the pleas of Aaron Hill and other supporters of an English opera; now the public had been drawn off by burlesques and satires. *The Beggar's Opera* had killed not the Italian opera but the chances of serious English opera. All Handel could see now was that the new popular English entertainment it had demanded was already in the hands of the London public. It was not in the form that he (or Arne or Hill) would have wished; but the opportunity had been missed.

I have heard it related, that when Handel's servant used to bring him his chocolate in a morning, he often stood with silent astonishment (until it was cold) to see his master's tears mixing with the ink, as he penned his divine notes; which are surely as much the pictures of a sublime mind as Milton's words. (William Shield, 1800)

Against the failure of his operatic ventures, Handel had to balance the success of *Athalia* and *Esther*, *Alexander's Feast* and *Acis and Galatea*. Although he was not yet convinced of the musical potential of oratorio, his public evidently had their suspicions that a conjunction of Mr Handel's 'sublime and noble' style with comparable measures from Dryden, Milton or the Bible would supply the missing link between the manner of his occasional State music, with its long pedigree of English church idiom, and the masterly but over-specialized dramas of his *opera seria*.

The one danger with oratorio, as Handel had already seen, was that of public animosity – opera might well be attacked as absurd and extravagant, but oratorio had to face the sterner charge of blasphemy. A compromise, based on his successes with Dryden and his earliest essays at Cannons with *Acis and*

Galatea, was the English ode or pastoral. Rather less adventurous, but a sure financial success in the hands of a business-like publisher, was the field of instrumental music. As far as the public were concerned, a concerto could be in no better hands than Handel's, and although editions of instrumental music did not carry the prestige of operas, neither did they have its pitfalls.

While two opera companies existed in London, therefore, Handel's dilemma would seem to resolve into a choice between concerto, ode or oratorio – in his newly fortified state he might even attempt more than one.

So much for speculation. Whatever shape Handel's career is given in retrospect, one thing always stands out – his stubborn refusal to be deflected from his vocation to the theatre. Neither financial nor physical disasters overcame it, and he would persist in the face of an apathetic public, an altered musical taste, and rumours of a decline in his powers. Word had even spread to Germany that 'Hendel's great days are over, his inspiration is exhausted and his taste behind the fashion' (Prince Friedrich of Prussia to Prince William of Orange, 8 October 1737).

But almost before his six weeks convalescence were up, Handel defied such defeatist rumour by undertaking to provide for the five hundredth anniversary of the town of Elbing on the Baltic (close to present-day Gdansk) a *pasticcio* opera based on seven of his own compositions. A libretto of *Hermann von Balcke* (founder of the town in 1237) is still preserved in the Municipal Library there, but the music of the *pasticcio* is not extant. If Handel actually journeyed to Elbing to supervise the production, it says much for his amazing powers of recuperation, and one can more readily credit Mainwaring's somewhat patronizing story of the nuns at Aix-la-Chapelle, amongst whom Handel's cure passed 'for a miracle'. In his *Memoirs of Handel*, written in autumn 1760, the Earl of Shaftesbury records a variant of the story in evidence of a total cure; in his account the incident takes place on Handel's journey homewards:

His recovery was so compleat, that on his Return from thence to England, he was able to Play long Voluntaries upon the Organ. In one of the great Towns in Flanders, where he had asked Permission to Play, the Organist attended him, not knowing who he was; and seem'd Struck with Mr Handell's Playing when he began: But when he heard Mr Handell lead off a Feuge, in Astonishment he ran up to him, & embracing him, said 'You can be no other but the great Handell'.

The figure of Handel was large, and he was somewhat corpulent, and unwieldy in his motions; but his countenance, which I remember as perfectly as that of any man I saw but yesterday, was full of fire and dignity; and such as impressed ideas of superiority and genius. He was impetuous, rough, and peremptory in his manners and conversation, but totally devoid of ill-nature or malevolence. (Charles Burney, 1785)

Reinstated to the position of 'the Composer of the Italian Music' by the *Daily Post* (28 October 1737), which ten days later described him as 'greatly recovered in his Health', Handel arrived home to find himself, for the first time in his career, an outsider to the opera season which had just opened. It was a season with a difference. The Licensing Act, coming into operation that summer, had given the two patent theatres, Covent Garden and Drury Lane, a monopoly of dramatic (other than musical) entertainment. John Rich capitalized on the break-up of the fringe theatres by acquiring the burlesque opera *The Dragon of Wantley* for Covent Garden, recouping his losses and securing the one musical attraction that could fill the building. It earned sixty-nine performances in its first season, seven more than *The Beggar's Opera*, and drove the final nail into the coffin of the Italian opera.

The libretto was a bawdy affair by Henry Carey, set to music throughout (including recitatives) by John Lampe. 'Many joyous Hours have we shared during its Composition', wrote Carey in the Preface, 'chopping and changing, lopping, ekeing out, and coining of Words, Syllables, and Jingles, to display in *English* the Beauty of Nonsense, so prevailing in the *Italian Operas*'. Although aimed at Italian opera in general, its specific target was Handel's *Giustino*; the Dragon of the title pilloried Handel's sea monster, and was sung by one of his regular basses, Reinhold, described in the text as 'Sigr. Furioso (his other Name to be conceal'd)'. Burney found it 'an excellent piece of humour', the King attended it several times, keeping the ailing Queen Caroline from her bed with his interminable tales of the Dragon's antics, and (according to the young Lord Wentworth in a letter to his father written on 14 January 1738) even 'Mr. Handel owns he thinks the tunes very well composed'.

At the Haymarket, Heidegger, the last surviving professional from the failed Nobility Opera, had opened the new season with a *pasticcio*, *Arsace*. Although Shaftesbury mentions 'the Gentlemen at the Haymarket', and Mainwaring names Lord Middlesex as the new Director, it seems probable that Heidegger floated this season on his own account. His substitute for Farinelli, who had left London for good that summer, was the haughty Caffarelli, a great singer by contemporary accounts, but with a capricious temper and uncontrollable arrogance, who was later imprisoned in Italy for humiliating a *prima donna* on stage with obscene gestures. Heidegger had announced Pescetti as house composer, but he can hardly have intended him to supply the whole season, and must have hoped that Handel would find the bait irresistible. Less than a fortnight after his return, Handel came to an arrangement with Heidegger to supply to his company two new operas, one *pasticcio* and his services as musical director for a fee of £1000. Caffarelli in comparison had got 1000 guineas plus another 150 for travelling expenses. Handel began work on *Faramondo* on 15 November. All plans and performances were suddenly interrupted, however, by the death of Queen Caroline on 20 November, and the theatres were closed for six weeks' mourning.

Handel felt the death of the Queen as a personal loss; he had known her from the age of eleven, when she was Caroline of Ansbach, and in 1711 had written duets for her in Hanover as the new bride of Georg Augustus. She had faithfully given him her support in England, subscribing to the operas with her daughters, engaging him as music master and softening where she could the antagonism shown towards him by her husband and son. The King, according to Hawkins, commissioned a funeral anthem on 7 December, and by the 12th Handel had completed *The Ways of Zion do Mourn*. It was rehearsed on the 14th in the Banqueting House Chapel, Whitehall, with the Royal Family present incognito, where the combination of Handel's music with Rubens's ceiling drew an ecstatic reponse from John Lockman:

Writ after the rehearsal (in the Banqueting-House, Whitehall) of the Anthem,
composed by Mr. Handell for her late Majesty's Funeral

> Struck with the Beauties form'd by magic Dyes,
> From Group to group, the Eye in Transport flies;
> Till Seraph-accents, solemn, deep, and slow,
> Melt on the Ear, in soft, melodious Woe.
>
> Such Charms the two contending Arts dispense;
> So sweetly captivate each ravish'd Sense,
> We n'er can fix; but must by Turns admire
> The mimic Pencil, and the speaking Lyre.

(Old Whig, 4 January 1738)

The anthem uses the large-scale forces that Handel reserved for great moments of State or for outdoor celebrations, with 'near 80 vocal performers, and 100 instrumental from his Majesty's band, and from the Opera, &c.' (*Grub-Street Journal*, 22 December 1737). As with the Coronation Service, it was probably limited rehearsal time that jeopardized the execution, and the service itself in Henry VII's Chapel of Westminster Abbey on 17 December drew a critical comment from the Duke of Chandos in a letter to his nephew the following day:

> The Solemnity of the Queen's Funeral was very decent, and performed in more order than any thing I have seen of the like kind . . . It began about a quarter before 7, & was over a little after ten; the Anthem took up three quarter of an hour of the time, of which the composition was exceeding fine, and adapted very properly to the melancholly occasion of it; but I can't say so much of the performance.

The extended anthem refers in various ways to Handel's (and the Queen's) Lutheranism, for example in quoting a motet by Jacob Handl (*Ecce quomodo moritor justus*), still in regular use in Germany as funeral music, and in a literal quotation of the chorale melody 'Du Friedefürst Herr Jesu Christ' in the section of the anthem 'She deliver'd the poor that cried'. The gravity of earlier English church music is also there, although even in the section 'Their bodies are buried in peace', where the influence of Gibbons is most obvious, the mood is jolted by

surprising shifts of harmony. Significantly, Handel completely avoids any conventional *operatic* symbols of grief, which in his mind were connected with
personal anguish; a declaration of national grief should forego the drooping
appoggiaturas and the overwrought chromatic descent. For similar reasons he
avoids the use of soloists; only when reworking the piece later (in the
Foundling Hospital Anthem, for instance) did he allocate sections to single
voices, in the manner of a verse anthem.*

> *Dr. Maurice Greene, whose compositions, whether for the church or the
> chamber, were never remarkably mellifluous, having solicited Handel's
> perusal and opinion of a solo anthem, which he had just finished, was
> invited by the great German to take his coffee with him the next morning,
> when he would say what he thought of it. The Doctor was punctual in his
> attendance, the coffee was served, and a variety of topics discussed; but not
> a word said by Handel concerning the composition. At length Greene,
> whose patience was exhausted, said, with eagerness, and an anxiety which
> he could no longer conceal, 'Well, Sir, but my anthem – what do you think
> of it?' 'Oh, your antum – ah – why I did tink it vanted air, Dr. Greene.'
> 'Air, Sir?' 'Yes, air; and so I did hang it out of de vindow.'*

A week after the funeral, on 24 December, Handel completed *Faramondo*.
Giving himself a day off for Christmas, he notes on the manuscript of the next
opera, *Serse*, 'angefangen den 26 Decembr 1737 od Montag, den 2 X tag'
[begun on Monday 26 December 1737, being the second day of Christmas].
One can hardly ask for more evidence of the composer's resilience, stamina
and stubbornness despite the intimations of a jotting at the foot of the air
'Vanne, che piu ti miro' from *Faramondo*: 'Mr Duval medecin in Poland St.'.

When Court mourning ended on 3 January, *Faramondo* went immediately
onto the stage. 'It being the first Time of Mr Handel's Appearance this Season,
he was honour'd with extraordinary and repeated Signs of Approbation',
enthused the Press the day after. Lord Wentworth (not yet sixteen) wrote to his
father after the rehearsal on the 3rd, 'To be sure it will be vastly full, since there
has not been one for so long a time, and a new person to sing into the [bargain]'.
The newcomer was the soprano, Elisabeth Duparc, known as 'La Francesina',
who became one of Handel's regular singers. Also in the cast was an English
countertenor – William Savage, who later sang as a bass. The countertenor
voice was not typical of *opera seria*, and Savage perhaps took the small soprano
part of Childerico because of the problems Heidegger encountered in casting
it. It is certainly no historical precedent; in a similar dilemma Handel would
normally have transposed or transferred a castrato part to a female singer.

In the event, Handel's opera could not compete with *The Dragon of Wantley*,
and on 14 January Lord Wentworth was forced to revise his prediction to his
father: 'The poor operas I doubt go on but badly, for tho' every body praises

---

*The list of soloists ascribed by Chrysander and Deutsch to the funeral service actually applies to
the Te Deum composed 'for the arrival of Princess Caroline' (c. 1714).

both Cafferielli and the opera yet it has never been full, and if it is not now at first it will be very empty towards the latter end of the winter'. His latest fears were realized, for *Faramondo* had only eight nights: 'which', remarked Burney, 'reflects more disgrace on the public than the composer'.

With many of his debts still outstanding, Handel was more than usually anxious to capitalize on his work by seeing it into print. On 23 January, 'Proposals for Printing by Subscription, The Opera of *Faramondo*, in Score' were announced in the *Daily Post*.

1. The Work will be printed on good Paper.
2. The Price to Subscribers is Half a Guinea to be paid at the Time of Subscribing.
3. The whole will be corrected by the Author.
4. The Lovers of Musick, who are willing to subscribe, are desired to send in their Names immediately, the Work being in such Forwardness, that it will be ready to be deliver'd to Subscribers by the 4th of February next.
   Subscriptions are taken in by John Walsh . . . and by most Musick-Shops in Town.

Four days later the Advertisement was altered to admit subscriptions being taken in 'by the Author' – a significant change, since this was the first time Handel had admitted the public (those of them, at least, who purchased his music) into his house. Perhaps the move was contrived as much to soften his image as to bring in more hard cash.

By February the score was ready to deliver to subscribers; that of *Alexander's Feast*, already subscribed for, was ready a month later. Here again there appears to have been a business realignment between Handel and John Walsh, who is described as 'the Undertaker of this Work for the Author'. Handel may have anticipated a quicker return by attempting to set up as his own publisher, but the arrangement (if it ever was ratified) proved temporary. On the heels of *Alexander's Feast* came the songs from *Alessandro Severo*, an all-Handel *pasticcio* which drew on ten earlier Academy operas, to which Handel added new recitatives and an overture. Running for six nights from 25 February, it did little to replenish his resources; his financial position, as Burney reports, was still precarious:

Handel had been so great a loser by striving against the stream of fashion and opposition the preceding season, that he was obliged to sell out of the funds the savings of many former years, to pay his performers, and was still in some danger of being arrested by the husband of Strada, for the arrears of her salary. It was at this time that his friends with great difficulty persuaded him to try public gratitude in a benefit, which was not disgraced by the event; for on Tuesday, in Passion-week, March 28th, was advertised at the Opera-house in the Hay-market, an ORATORIO, with a CONCERT on the organ, for the benefit of Mr. Handel; pit and boxes put together at half a guinea each ticket, and 'for the better conveniency, there will be benches on the stage'. The theatre, for the honour of the nation, was so crouded on this occasion, that he is said to have cleared £.800.

Other estimates were even higher: the Earl of Egmont, who was present, 'counted near 1,300 persons besides the gallery and upper gallery', and concluded, in his diary entry for 28 March, 'I suppose he got by this night 1,000 *l*'; Mainwaring suggests £1500.

Although called an 'Oratorio', the benefit concert was in fact a *pasticcio* containing the separate elements of oratorio without any dramatic continuity. Airs from *Esther* and *Athalia* together with a handful of Italian arias were interwoven in a potted version of *Deborah*, reduced to thirty numbers. An organ concerto between the acts and *Zadok the Priest* as a final chorus, sung to the words 'Blessed are all they that fear the Lord', completed the illusion. Reluctant though Handel may have been to condone such a *mélange*, he can hardly have missed making some obvious deductions. First, without composing a single new bar, he had netted as much as Heidegger offered for two new operas and a *pasticcio*. Second, despite the prevailing opinion of Italian opera as an absurdity, the London public was now prepared to accept him as a classic figure of the musical establishment. Third, the concept and title of 'oratorio' were clearly not a deterrent to English taste, even when it was void of dramatic credibility.

Against this strong case for oratorio, he could set the failure of his new opera, *Serse*, which opened two weeks later and limped through five performances despite a prestigious cast and (for the first time in Handel) some overtly comic action. It is doubly ironic that an opera opening with 'Ombra mai fù' should flop so instantaneously and that from so sensual an air, marked 'Larghetto' and sung by the hapless Xerxes in praise of a tree, should evolve the sentimental nineteenth-century *tombeau* of 'Handel's Largo'.

While the fortunes of the opera sank Handel, with divided feelings, could watch his rise. Freed at last from the importunings of Strada (or her husband) for back-payments, he now saw himself elevated to classic status in the finest of London's pleasure gardens:

34

33 We are informed from very good Authority; that there is now near finished a Statue of the justly celebrated Mr. Handel, exquisitely done by the ingenious Mr. Raubillac, of St. Martin's-Lane, Statuary, out of one entire Block of white Marble, which is to be placed in a grand Nich, erected on Purpose in the great Grove at Vaux-hall-Gardens, at the sole Expence of Mr. Tyers, Undertaker of the Entertainment there; who in Consideration of the real Merit of that inimitable Master, thought it proper, that his Effigies should preside there, where his Harmony has so often charm'd even the greatest Crouds into the profoundest Calm and most decent Behaviour; it is believed, that the Expence of the Statue and Nich cannot cost less than Three Hundred Pounds; the said Gentleman likewise very generously took at Mr. Handel's Benefit Fifty of his Tickets. (*Daily Post*, 18 April 1738)

Jonathan Tyers, who had taken over and upgraded the Gardens in 1732, was a discriminating businessman, complimented by Fielding in *Amelia* for his 'truly elegant taste'. The Gardens were designed to supply evening entertainment of a decorous nature during the summer season, and Tyers equipped them with supper-boxes, decorated by Francis Hayman, and a bandstand ('the Orchestra') which together formed the focal point of the walks and colonnades. Although contemporaries complained that the ham served was so thinly sliced that the programme could be read through it, the musical entertainment was usually lavish, with 'a Band consisting of above thirty of the ablest Performers' (*Daily Post*, 17 May 1736). Handel's music would have been frequently played, especially as vocal items were not included before 1745; but to be publicly represented in marble while still alive, by way of 'apotheosis, or laudable idolatry', was unique. Not until 1770, when a statue of Voltaire was commissioned by a group of 'philosophes' in Paris, was a comparable distinction conferred on a living artist or writer. Tyers was astute in his choice of the young Louis François Roubiliac, then an assistant to the sculptor Henry Cheere who recommended him to Tyers as 'an uncommonly clever fellow . . . employ him, and he will produce you a fine statue'. It was his first important commission (his last was to be the Handel monument in Westminster Abbey), and his choice of an informal pose (Handel wears a nightcap, one slipper lies discarded, the other dangles from his left foot) created much comment, and attracted many visitors.

There was some uncertainty amongst the first viewers as to whether Handel was represented in the character of Orpheus or of Apollo (the latter is correct). Impressed but a little inaccurate, the *Daily Post* described him as 'represented in a loose Robe, striking the Lyre, and listening to the Sounds; which a little Boy, carv'd at his Feet, seems to be writing down on the back of the Violoncello' – actually a sheaf of pages supported on a viol. The *London Magazine* published a number of verses by Lockman, the poet of the Gardens, and others to mark the event.

> *Seeing the Marble Statue (carv'd by Mr. Roubillac)*
> *representing Mr. Handel, in Spring Gardens, Vauxhall.*
>
> That *Orpheus* drew a grove, a rock, a stream
> By musick's power, will not a fiction seem;
> For here as great a miracle is shown –
> Fam'd *Handel* breathing, tho' transformed to stone.
> ....
> *To be written under the Effigies of Mr. Handel in*
> Vaux-Hall *Gardens.*
>
> ACROSTICK.
>
> High as thy *genius*, on the wings of *fame*,
> Around the *world* spreads thy *all-tuneful* name.
> Nature, who *form'd* thee with peculiar care,
> Did *art* employ, to *draw* a *copy here*,
> *Emblem of that great self!* whilst yet you live
> Lending such *helps*, your *better part* can give.
>   J. A. Hesse.

Upon Handel's *Statue being placed in* Spring-Garden *at* Vaux-Hall.

As in debate the tuneful sisters stood,
In what sequester'd shade, or hallow'd wood,
Should *Handel's* statue (musick's master!) stand,
In which fair art well mimicks nature's hand;
Thus spoke the god, that with enliv'ning rays,
Glads the whole earth, and crowns the bard with bays
"Here bid the marble rise, be this the place,
"The haunt of ev'ry muse, and ev'ry grace;
"Where harmony resides, and beauties rove:
"Where should he stand but in *Apollo's* grove?"

Handel was never official composer to any of the London pleasure gardens, and the only piece he is known to have written especially for them is a 'Hornpipe compos'd for the Concert at Vauxhall, 1740', to which is attached an amusing anecdote retailed by the grandson of the Rev. J. Fountayne in the *History of the Parish of Marylebone* (1833):

My grandfather, as I have been told, was an enthusiast in music, and culti-vated most of all the friendship of musical men, especially of Handel who visited him often, and had a great predilection for his society. This leads me to relate an anecdote, which I have on the best authority. While Marylebone Gardens were flourishing, the enchanting music of Handel, and probably of Arne, was often heard from the orchestra there. One evening, as my grandfather and Handel were walking together and alone, a new piece was struck up by the band. 'Come, Mr. Fountayne,' said Handel, 'let us sit down and listen to this piece; I want to know your opinion of it.' Down they sat; and after some time the old parson, turning to his companion, said, 'It is not worth listening to – it is very poor stuff.' 'You are right, Mr. Fountayne,' said Handel, 'it is very poor stuff; I thought so myself when I had finished it.' The old gentleman, being taken by surprise, was beginning to apologize; but Handel assured him there was no necessity, that the music was really bad, having been composed hastily, and his time for the production limited; and that the opinion given was as correct as it was honest.

In the course of various redevelopments, the 'grand Nich' was demolished and Handel's statue occupied various other settings in the Gardens. Before the site was finally razed in 1859, it had passed into private hands, and could be found standing at the head of the stairs in Novello's London premises until 1965, when it was sold to the Victoria & Albert Museum, where it can be seen today.*

Thus immortalized, Handel found himself as insecure in his ventures as before. Heidegger's new season had failed to take with the subscribers, and on 26 July the *Daily Post* carried his retraction.

---

*For full details of the statue and its history see Terence Hodgkinson, 'Handel at Vauxhall', *V&A Museum Bulletin Reprints* 1, HMSO.

PLATE IX A festival performance of *Messiah* in York Minster, 29 September 182

IX

X

Whereas the Opera's for the ensuing Season at the King's Theatre in the Hay-Market, cannot be carried on as was intended, by Reason of the Subscription not being full, and that I could not agree with the Singers th'I offer'd One Thousand Guineas to One of them: I therefore think myself oblig'd to declare, that I give up the Undertaking for next Year, and that Mr. Drummond will be ready to repay the Money paid in, upon the Delivery of his Receipt; I also take this Opportunity to return my humble Thanks to all Persons, who were pleas'd to contribute towards my Endeavours of carrying on that Entertainment.

J. J. Heidegger.

But Handel had seen the warning signs in time; two days earlier he had started work on the oratorio *Saul*. It is assumed that the libretto for this was the 'inclosed Oratorio' that Handel had received from Charles Jennens more than three years earlier (see p. 128). If so, his long reluctance to come to terms with its public potential was now offset by the determination with which he launched himself into the work. The condition of his working manuscript, particularly that for Act II, presents graphic evidence of the 'convulsive struggle that brought the oratorio to birth.'* Second, third and fourth thoughts crowd onto the staves, often superimposed; whole sections of arias are written out, then discarded, only to be recalled and reshaped. Eventually the struggle seems to have been too much for Handel. In early September he put the oratorio aside and started work on yet another Italian opera, *Imeneo*, for which he had neither cast, theatre nor public. At this point, with both opera and oratorio in confusion, Jennens called on him, and wrote to Lord Guernsey on 19 September:

> Mr. Handel's head is more full of maggots than ever. I found yesterday in his room a very queer instrument which he calls carillon (Anglice, a bell) and says some call it a Tubalcain, I suppose because it is both in the make and tone like a set of Hammers striking upon anvils. 'Tis played upon with keys like a Harpsichord and with this Cyclopean instrument he designs to make poor Saul stark mad. His second maggot is an organ of £500 price which (because he is overstocked with money) he has bespoke of one Moss [Jonathan Morse] of Barnet. This organ, he says, is so constructed that as he sits at it he has a better command of his performers than he used to have, and he is highly delighted to think with what exactness his Oratorio will be performed by the help of this organ; so that for the future instead of beating time at his oratorios, he is to sit at the organ all the time with his back to the Audience.

---

*Winton Dean, *Dramatic Oratorios*, p. 305.

PLATE X   Nicholas McGegan's production of *Orlando* in St Louis was an attempt to recreate the Baroque ethos on the stage as well as in the orchestral pit. A scene from Act I with (from left to right) Zoroaster, Angelica, Orlando and Medoro.

His third maggot is a Hallelujah which he has trump'd up at the end of his oratorio since I went into the Country, because he thought the conclusion of the oratorio not Grand enough; tho' if that were the case 'twas his own fault, for the words would have bore as Grand Musick as he could have set 'em to: but this Hallelujah, Grand as it is, comes in very nonsensically, having no manner of relation to what goes before. And this is the more extraordinary, because he refused to set a Hallelujah at the end of the first Chorus in the Oratorio, where I had placed one and where it was to be introduced with the utmost propriety, upon a pretence that it would make the entertainment too long. I could tell you more of his maggots: but it grows late and I must defer the rest till I write next, by which time, I doubt not, more new ones will breed in his Brain.

The tone of Jennens's letter betrays his self-importance and intolerance, the high-handed manner of a wealthy country gentleman, opinionated and cruel in his criticism, whose ostentation made many of his contemporaries his enemies. Dr Johnson (with whom he crossed swords over matters of Shakespearian scholarship when he insisted on publishing his own 'collated' versions of the plays) pronounced him 'a vain fool crazed by his wealth . . . verily, an English "Solyman the Magnificent"', and the nickname stuck.

But he was also a man of taste and learning. His country seat at Gopsall, in Leicestershire, was beautified in the Palladian style by the best architects from Lord Burlington's circle; he collected and commissioned fine paintings; he was well versed in the Classics; for some time he had subscribed to all Handel's publications and obtained manuscript copies of most of his output.* He had, moreover, a remarkable ability to construct the type of libretto that suited Handel best: whether dealing with the Scriptures or Milton, he could isolate and distil the drama and characterization without adopting a moralizing posture. Handel clearly respected his views, however conceited their expression. He restored the offending Hallelujah in *Saul* to Part I, for instance, where it forms a suitable climax to the jubilation on the fall of Goliath, as Jennens intended, rather than standing 'nonsensically' at the end of the oratorio.

Handel persisted in his other 'maggots', but returned to reorganize the remainder of *Saul* after Jennens's visit. With much effort he restructured Act III, in which he had intended to use large portions of Queen Caroline's Funeral Ode as an elegy for Saul and Jonathan, composing for it the Dead March and including the chilling encounter with the Witch at Endor, breathtakingly scored for two solo bassoons as the Ghost of Samuel arises. Perhaps to compensate for the lack of 'operatick' voices, Handel intended to make the maximum impact with his orchestra: flutes, three trombones, harp, theorbo and solo organ join the carillon as 'special effects', and the carillon was even induced to accompany a recitative ('harpeggiando piano ad libitum') as well as colouring the dance of the Israelite women. Such isolated effects apart, Handel's skill is most apparent

---

*This valuable primary material made up part of the Aylesford Collection, which was split up and sold in 1917. Much of the material is now housed in the Newman Flower Collection in Manchester.

in the restraint with which these symbolic colours are employed throughout the oratorio.

Several moments in *Saul* (including the Carillon Symphony) are Handel's revitalizations of borrowed material – in addition to one of his own trio sonatas, pressed into service for an overture, the main sources are keyboard music by Kuhnau and, more extensively, a mid-17th-century Te Deum by one Francesco Urio (which Handel may well have acquired in manuscript during his time in Italy). Percy Robinson's attempt to 'exonerate' Handel by suggesting that he composed the work himself while at the village of Urio, near Lake Como (*Handel and his Orbit*, 1908), is now discredited.

Within three days of finishing the score of *Saul*, Handel pushed on with yet another exploration into his newly gained oratorio territory. As the unashamed borrowings for *Saul* suggest, the dramatic experiment was, for him, clearly more urgent than any obligation to invent musical material. *Moses' Song*, as the new venture was first called, drew heavily for catalyst ideas on a serenata by Stradella, Urio's Te Deum again and a Magnificat for double chorus by Dionigi Erba, another souvenir of his Italian journey. The text, from Exodus XV, celebrating the deliverance of the chosen people from the wrath of Pharaoh, was ideal for a large-scale anthem. Sentiments like 'The Lord is a man of war' and 'Thou sentest forth thy wrath, which consumed them as stubble' were also in accord with the belligerent political mood, as both Whigs and Tories, poets as well as politicians, pressed for a war with Spain.

As the scheme of a great choral epic developed, with the *Song of Moses* as its culmination in Part III, Handel saw a new use for the *Funeral Ode* which had been rejected from *Saul*. Supplied with a fresh text it became Part I of the new oratorio, the *Lamentations of the Israelites for the Death of Joseph*. He began the central act, Exodus, the story of the plagues and tribulations of the captive tribe, immediately; and thanks to diligent use of existing material, finished it within two weeks. *Israel in Egypt*, as the completed work was called, seems deliberately designed to be the antithesis of *Saul* in its emphases: large choral sequences in four and eight parts instead of grand orchestral effect; a drama of nations rather than individuals; an almost total absence of solo arias; and a text taken literally from the Bible.

I think Handel never gets out of his wig, that is, out of his age: his Hallelujah Chorus is a chorus, not of angels, but of well-fed earthly choristers, ranged tier above tier in a Gothic cathedral, with princes for audience, and their military trumpets flourishing over the full volume of the organ. Handel's gods are like Homer's, and his sublime never reached beyond the region of the clouds. (Edward Fitzgerald, 1847)

With two new works different in so many ways from each other, and with two earlier compositions to supplement them (*Alexander's Feast* and *Il Trionfo del Tempo e della Verità*), Handel was fully equipped to test the public taste for oratorio. For his first oratorio season he hired the King's Theatre from Heidegger for a total of twelve days in the first half of 1739.

Saul opened on 16 January; word had already got around that it was heavily orchestrated: 'I hear Mr. Handell has borrow'd of the Duke of Argylle a pair of the largest kettle-drums in the Tower', wrote Lord Wentworth on 13 January 1739, 'so to be sure it will be most excessive noisy with a bad set off singers; I doubt it will not retrieve his former losses.'

36

The cast included the tenor John Beard (who created a scandal by marrying Lady Henrietta Powis on the day of the public rehearsal – 'there is no prudence below the girdle' sniffed Lord Egmont) and in the part of David, 'one Rusell, an Englishman that sings extreamly well' (Lord Wentworth). The *Daily Post* reported on 17 January that the piece 'met with general Applause by a numerous and splendid Audience' (including the Royal Family), and ran for five further nights that season. Handel added 'several new Concerto's on the Organ' to later performances, and on the final night (19 April) 'Sig. *Plantanida*, who is just arriv'd from Abroad', also played a violin concerto; it must have been a lengthy evening.

45

The great double drums from the artillery train (sounding an octave lower than the normal timpani) passed without further mention, but the architect William Kent was intrigued by the carillon, as he reported back to Burlington on 27 January.

The oratorio's goe on well, I was there with a handsom widow fatt, which has given much diversion to the looker on & whe was in the box you us'd to have – There is a pritty concerto in the oratorio there is some stops in the Harpsicord that are little bells, I thought it had been some squerrls in a cage.

On 17 February *Alexander's Feast* was revived with some alterations and at least three concertos added to the performance, and on 3 March, *Il Trionfo del Tempo e della Verità* 'with several Concerto's on the Organ and other Instruments' (*Daily Post*). Later in the month a special performance of *Alexander's Feast* was instigated by the composer. In spite of his own financial problems, Handel had been one of the first subscribers to the Fund for the Support of Decayed Musicians and their Families (now the Royal Society of Musicians), which had been set up the previous year – provoked, according to Burney, by the sight of the children of Jean Christian Kytch, the oboist, begging outside the coffeehouse in the Haymarket after their father's death. In support of this charity, Handel proposed a benefit performance of *Alexander's Feast* on 20 March. His lead was followed by Heidegger and some of the public, as the *Daily Post* reported: '. . . we hear, several of the Subscribers (tho' they had Tickets sent them Gratis for this Performance) were so generous as to pay at the Doors, and others have since sent Presents to the Fund; Mr. Handel gave the House and his Performance, upon this Occasion, Gratis, and Mr. Heidegger made a Present of Twenty Pounds to defray the other incident Expences'.

Israel in Egypt, introduced last in the season on 4 April, proved a flop. Inevitably in a society with strong puritanical elements, there was much debate over the propriety of singing scriptural words in the theatre, a controversy which continued for much of Handel's career. But it seems that the high density of choral writing and the scarce opportunities for solo virtuosity had so numbed the audience that even 'several Concerto's on the Organ, and particularly a new one . . .' (*Daily Post*, 4 April) could produce only a lukewarm response. (The 'new concerto' in F, finished only two days earlier, later became known as 'The Cuckoo and the Nightingale'; it must have been a curiously lighthearted episode before the tribulations of Exodus.)

A second performance, announced as the last, was 'shortned and Intermix'd with Songs' in an attempt to salvage the piece. La Francesina sang extracts from *Athalia* and Italian arias added earlier to *Esther* in place of deleted choruses, and the work would have rested there had not an anonymous letter appeared in the *Daily Post* on 13 April.

Sir,

Upon my Arrival in Town three Days ago, I was not a little surpriz'd, to find that Mr. Handel's last Oratorio, (*Israel in Egypt*) which had been performed but once, was advertis'd to be for the last time on Wednesday. I was almost tempted to think that his Genius had fail'd him, but must own myself agreeably disappointed. I was not only pleas'd, but also affected by it, for I never yet met with any Musical Performance, in which the Words and Sentiments were so thoroughly studied, and so clearly understood; and as the Words are taken from the Bible, they are perhaps some of the most sublime parts of it. I was indeed concern'd, that so excellent a Work of so great a Genius was neglected, for tho' it was a Polite and attentive Audience, it was not large enough I doubt to encourage him in any future Attempt. As I should be extreamely sorry to be depriv'd of hearing this again, and found many of the Auditors in the same Disposition; yet being afraid Mr. Handel will not undertake it without some Publick Encouragement, because he may think himself precluded by his Advertisement, (that it was to be the last time) I must beg leave, by your means, to convey not only my own, but the Desires of several others, that he will perform this again some time next Week.
     I am, Sir,
        Your very humble Servant,

                       A. Z.

A third performance was duly announced for 17 April, attended by the Prince and Princess of Wales and celebrated in a long, eloquent letter of approval printed in the *Daily Post* the following day. After congratulating the audience for its sense in being 'entertain'd by such a truly-spiritual Entertainment', the writer (possibly Richard Wesley, one of the subscribers to *Alexander's Feast*) continues with some advice for a future oratorio public, which is also a defence of the oratorio form itself:

If the Town is ever to be bless'd with this Entertainment *again*, I would recommend to every one to take the Book of the Drama with them: For tho' the Harmony be so unspeakably great of itself, it is in an unmeasurable Proportion more so, when seen to what Words it is adapted; especially, if every one who could take with them the Book, would do their best to carry a Heart for the Sense, as well as an Ear for the Sound.

The narrow Limits of your Paper forbids entering into Particulars: But they know not what they fall short of in the Perfection of the Entertainment, who, when they hear the Musick, are not acquainted with the Words it expresses; or, if they have the Book, have not the proper Spirit to relish them . . . 'Tis a sort of separate Existence the Musick has in these Places apart from the Words; 'tis Soul and Body join'd when heard and read together: And if People, before they went to hear it, would but retire a Moment, and read by themselves the Words of the Sacred Drama, it would tend very much to raise their Delight when at the Representation. The Theatre, on this occasion, ought to be enter'd with more Solemnity than a Church; inasmuch, as the Entertainment you go to is really in itself the noblest Adoration and Homage paid to the Deity that ever was in one. So sublime an Act of Devotion as this *Representation* carries in it, to a Heart and Ear duly tuned for it, would consecrate even Hell itself. – It is the Action that is done in it, that hallows the Place, and not the Place the Action . . .

I shall conclude with this Maxim, 'That in Publick Entertainments every one should come with a reasonable Desire of being entertain'd themselves, or with the polite Resolution, no ways to interrupt the Entertainment of others. And that to have a Truce with Dissipation, and noisy Discourse, and to forbear that silly Affectation of beating Time aloud on such an Occasion, is, indeed, in Appearance, a great Compliment paid to the divine Author of so sacred an Entertainment, and to the rest of the Company near them; but at the same time, in reality, a much greater Respect paid to themselves.' I cannot but add this Word, since I am on the Subject, 'That I think a profound Silence a much more proper Expression of Approbation to Musick, and to deep Distress in Tragedy, than all the noisy Applause so much in Vogue, however great the Authority of Custom may be for it.' I am, Sir, &c.

R. W.

Despite such enthusiastic support, the oratorio and the season languished. The Academy of Ancient Music tried an alternative on 10 May by performing only 'The Song of Moses, and the Funeral Anthem for her late Majesty', but eventually it was Parts II and III of *Israel and Egypt* that survived (our present day Parts I and II, which begin so awkwardly with a recitative). Handel, unconvinced by his experiments in oratorio, took refuge in an Italian *pasticcio, Jupiter in Argos*, which was advertised in the *Daily Post* as 'a Dramatical Composition . . . intermix'd with Chorus's, and two Concerto's on the Organ'. It ran for two nights, and was then forgotten for two hundred years.

The organ concertos that had become a regular feature of Handel's concerts remained a constant attraction up until the end of his life, when even despite a stroke and failing eyesight, his reputation as a player remained unchallenged. The first set of concertos to be published had appeared at the end of the

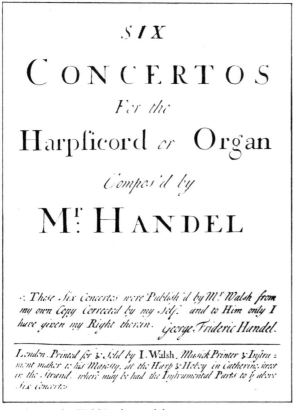

Title-page for Walsh's edition of the six organ concertos, op.4, published in October 1738.

previous year, apparently in retaliation to a pirated edition which has not survived. On 27 September 1738, Walsh had announced 'To all *Lovers of Musick*' in the *Daily Post*:

Whereas there is a spurious and incorrect Edition of Six Concerto's of Mr. Handel's for the Harpsicord and Organ, publish'd without the Knowledge or Consent of the Author,

This is to give *Notice*,

(That the Publick may not be imposed on with a mangled Edition)

That there are now printing from Mr. Handel's original Manuscript, and corrected by himself, the same Six Concerto's, which will be published in a few Days. Price 3s.

Other instrumental publications soon followed: a collection of 'Seven Sonat's, or Trio's, for two Violins, or German Flutes, and a Bass. Opera Quinta.' was announced on 18 January. The number is curious, suggesting that Walsh and Handel may have worked independently to assemble the set. Sonatas 1–3 derive from overtures to the *Chandos Anthems*, the autographs of which still show Handel's cues for the reworking; nos 5 and 6 were written specially for the publication. No. 7, which also derives from Chandos material, may have been intended as a replacement for Sonata 4, where the lack of an inner part, corresponding to the viola part in the original versions of the movements, is all too obvious.

Probably remembering the legal proceedings that Geminiani had been obliged to start against Walsh only a few years earlier, Handel issued his next publication only after he had secured himself anew against piracy. His earlier copyright of 1720 had expired in 1734, and while the operas had carried their own profits in performance, the fact that he now relied on the publication of instrumental works for his income placed him again at risk. The second Privilege of Copyright, dated 31 October, was issued in the name of John Walsh junior and first used to protect the '*Twelve Grand Concerto's*, in Seven Parts, for four Violins, a Tenor, a Violoncello, with a Thorough-Bass for the Harpsichord'.

These, the finest and most polished of Handel's instrumental works, were deliberately designed to compete in a field dominated by Corelli's Opus 6, still (in Roger North's phrase) 'to the musitians like the bread of life'.* English taste had been moulded on Corellian principles by his pupil, Geminiani, who had published several sets of his own *concerti grossi* in the previous ten years, together with concerto arrangements of all twelve of Corelli's violin sonatas. English imitators such as Festing and Woodcock helped to solidify the principles. Handel adopted the same scoring as Corelli (a trio sonata combination, with string *ripieno*), a typically loose Italian approach to fugal writing, and a similarly ambiguous attitude to dance movements; but added a purposeful drive, an eclectic wisdom and a mercurial wit to his more sober models. These concertos have little in common with the Venetian school of Vivaldi and Albinoni, whose works were also known in England, though less admired than Corelli's; nor with Bach's distillation of that pattern in his Brandenburg Concertos. The individual virtuosity of the fourth or fifth Brandenburg Concerto is not found in Handel's *Grand Concertos*, nor the exotic scorings of the second or sixth. Although Handel added oboe parts to nos 1, 2, 5 and 6 for use where appropriate, the printed material was considered complete without them.

The immediate object in writing a set of concertos was to provide instrumental interludes for the season of secular entertainment Handel was proposing for 1739–40. An air of cosmopolitan theatricality pervades them all, from the sturdy dialogue that opens the first concerto, through the mysterious and lengthy Musette of no.6, with its hushed moments of *sommeil* (a favourite of Handel's who, according to Burney, 'frequently introduced it between the parts of his Oratorios, both before and after publication'), to the invigorating final fugue, based on a theme from Zachow, that concludes the set. Some movements actually rework material from the unfinished opera *Imeneo*, temporarily set aside.

Handel's dated autographs show that he regarded the concertos from the start as a set of twelve suitable for publication, and also that he worked on them in a

*John Wilson, ed., *Roger North on Music*, p. 311.

burst of concentrated inspiration during the autumn of 1739. Apart from no. 9, which has a replacement last movement, the final page of each concerto bears the date of completion, a list giving proof of Handel's continued creative stamina:

Concerto I	September 29	Concerto VI	October 15
Concerto II	October 4	Concerto VIII	October 18
Concerto III	October 6	Concerto XII	October 20
Concerto IV	October 8	Concerto X	October 22
Concerto V	October 10	Concerto IX	[October 26]
Concerto VII	October 12	Concerto XI	October 30

Shortly before starting his month's work on the concertos, Handel set Dryden's *Ode for St Cecilia's Day*, drawing heavily for ideas on the recently published *Componimenti Musicali* of Gottlieb Muffat, a remarkable and neglected set of keyboard suites to which the *Grand Concertos* and later oratorios are indebted. The liaison between Handel and Muffat may be closer than has been thought. The familiar Chaconne in G from Handel's 1733 volume of keyboard music uses a bass going back to Purcell, which was also used by Bach in the Goldberg Variations, and by Muffat in the concluding Ciacona of his *Componimenti*; and there exists a heavily ornamented version of Handel's first collection of harpsichord suites in Muffat's hand, 'mises dans une autre applicature pour la Facilitè de la main', dated 1736.* Muffat's *Componimenti* was not the only keyboard collection which provided Handel with material for the concertos; Scarlatti's *Essercizi per cembalo* (published in London in 1738 and 1739), contributed several borrowings, most of them in the first six concertos.†

For his new season Handel hired the smaller theatre at Lincoln's Inn Fields from John Rich, and opened on St Cecilia's Day itself in a programme that included his new *Ode* and parts of *Alexander's Feast*. Both weather and the war contrived to lessen his chances of success. Against the exceptionally cold winter, when oxen were roasted on the frozen Thames, the management promised that 'Particular Preparations are making to keep the House warm; and the Passage from the Fields to the House will be cover'd for better Conveniency'; and when Handel repeated the *Ode* a month later, coupled with *Acis and Galatea*, 'Particular care will be taken to have Guards plac'd to keep all the Passages clear from the Mob' (*Daily Post*). Handel battled on, but he seems to have been alone. In a letter written on 13 December, Richard West reported grimly to Horace Walpole: 'Plays we have none, or damned ones. Handel has had a concerto [i.e. concert series] this winter. No opera, no nothing. All for war and Admiral Haddock'. The New Year was equally ill-fated. Even with 'Curtains plac'd before every Door, and constant Fires . . . in the House 'till the Time of Performance', a repeat of *Acis and Galatea* had to be postponed, 'two chief singers being taken ill'.

---

*See Wollenberg and Baselt.
†See Alexander Silbiger, 'Scarlatti Borrowings'.

While the London public stayed by their firesides, Handel seized the opportunity to set to work on a text supplied by Jennens for a third secular ode of the season. Although Handel himself was unfailingly complimentary about Jennens's work, the libretto this time did not meet with universal approval. As Jennens later wrote to Edward Holdsworth (4 February 1742):

> ... A little piece I wrote at Mr. Handel's request to be subjoyn'd to Milton's Allegro & Penseroso, to which He gave the Name of Il Moderato, & which united those two independent Poems in one Moral Design, met with smart censures from I don't know who. I overheard one in the Theatre saying it was Moderato indeed, & the Wits at Tom's Coffee house honour'd it with the Name of Moderatissimo ...

The notion of Moderation, 'Whom the wise God of Nature gave, mad mortals from themselves to save', while neither apt for Milton nor attractive to the present century, was a very Georgian ideal, and Handel's inspiration did not fail him in any of the three sections. *L'Allegro, il Penseroso ed il Moderato* is consistently inventive, richly scored* and filled with subtle responses to the pastoral imagery of the poems. According to Hawkins, Handel 'used to say, that, to an English audience, music joined to poetry was not an entertainment for an evening, and that something that had the appearance of a plot or fable was necessary to keep their attention awake'. Yet *L'Allegro*, like the two Dryden settings, is essentially undramatic. The two humours, delicately balanced for the first two parts, are resolved in Part 3, and differentiated by a range of mimetic effects in response to the variety of natural imagery in the poems. Perhaps only Handel had the genius to grasp this potential, and turn evocative poetry into powerfully evocative music; but 'never had music to depend upon herself so entirely'.† An anonymous poem appearing in the *Gentleman's Magazine* in May celebrated the work in terms that are conventional but nonetheless enthusiastic:

TO MR. HANDEL,

on hearing 'Alexander's feast,' 'L'Allegro, ed il Penseroso', etc.

If e'er *Arion's* music calm'd the floods,
And *Orpheus* ever drew the dancing woods;
Why do not *British* trees and forest throng
To hear the sweeter notes of *Handel's* song?
This does the falsehood of the fable prove,
Or seas and woods, when *Handel* harps, would move.
. . .
But *Handel's* harmony affects the soul,
To sooth by sweetness, or by force controul;

---

*Even the carillon makes another appearance (as it had done in the new version of *Acis* in the same season); its part is shown in the Halle Handel Edition.
†V. Schoelcher, *Life of Handel*, p. 229.

And with like sounds as tune the rolling spheres,
So tunes the mind, that ev'ry sense has ears.
    When jaundice jealousy, and carking care,
Or tyrant pride, or homicide despair,
The soul as on a rack in torture keep,
These monsters *Handel's* music lulls to sleep.
How, when he strikes the keys, do we rejoice!
Or when he fills a thousand tubes with voice,
Or gives his lessons to the speaking string,
And some to breathe the flute, and some to sing;
To sound the trumpet, or the horn to swell,
Or brazen cylinder to speak compel;
His art so modulates the sounds in all,
Our passions, as he pleases, rise and fall;
Their hold of us, at his command they quit,
And to his pow'r with pride and joy submit.
    Thou, sovereign of the lyre, dost so excel,
Who against thee, against thy art rebel.
But uncontested is in song, thy sway;
Thee all the nations where 'tis known obey:
E'en *Italy*, who long usurp'd the lyre,
Is proud to learn thy precepts and admire.
What harmony she had thou thence didst bring
And imp'd thy genius with a stronger wing;
To form thee, talent, travel, art, combine,
And all the powers of music now are thine.

The poet's enthusiasm was not misplaced; *L'Allegro* received five performances, opening on 27 February with 'the House secur'd against the Cold' (*Daily Post*). Before its last performance Handel had revived *Saul, Esther* and *Israel in Egypt*, each for a single night and each garnished with concertos from the Opus 6 set.

The set was published on 21 April, with a list of one hundred subscribers. They present an illuminating survey of contemporary support for Handel, ranging from the King's brother and all five Princesses, through the known Handelians (Granville, Jennens, James Harris), the impresarios John Rich and Jonathan Tyers (who bought respectively two and three sets, from which we may deduce the size of orchestras that might have performed the concertos in Covent Garden and Vauxhall), and a wide range of London and provincial amateur music societies: the Crown and Anchor Society (the Academy of Ancient Music), the Musical Society in Canterbury, the Academy of Musick at Dublin, the Ladies Concert in Lincoln, Salisbury Society of Musick and Monday Night Musical Society at Yᵉ Globe Tavern Fleet Street.

But no amount of support, however encouraging, could help Handel in his end-of-season dilemma. He had tried opera first, then oratorio and finally the ode – all appeared to have failed. The ode was a limited, undramatic form and suffered from a paucity of appropriate texts. The oratorio was disadvantaged, as Lord Shaftesbury put it in his *Memoirs of Handel*, by 'his Singers in general not being Capital, nor the Town come into a relies [relish] of this species of Musick'. The opera, his main love, had been proven untenable, yet it was still the only means of attracting the 'capital singers' with whom he was accustomed to work, and on whom all his other schemes depended.

It was perhaps in hopes of finding another set of operatic singers to resolve the dilemma that Handel took a trip abroad in the summer of 1740. Save for a single reference to his playing of the organ in Haarlem on 9 September, the journey is largely undocumented.

35 On his return he immediately took up *Imeneo*, begun two years earlier, finished it by 10 October, and on 27 October started another opera, *Deidamia*. For a second time he rented the Theatre Royal in Lincoln's Inn Fields and for the new season aimed at a more theatrical presentation. The serenata *Parnasso in Festa* opened on 8 November, and according to Burney was performed 'in its original oratorio manner, with the addition of scenes, dresses, and concertos on the organ, and several other instruments'. The next production did not occur until 22 November, when 'he put his stage in action' with *Imeneo*. The title role was sung by William Savage, now a bass, and with the castrato Andreoni, who had appeared at the Haymarket in the previous season, as Tirinto. (Burney ranked him as 'a good singer of the second class'; he was immensely fat and according to Horace Mann had no trill.) The new piece was described in the press as an operetta. Its plot is anti-heroic and uncomplicated, the mood verging on the comic; Handel's music is appropriately tuneful, with a preference for short phrases and an elegant simplicity. Only the feigned mad scene in Act III recalls the old-fashioned intensity of his Academy operas. Although in rehearsal it was declared 'very pretty', the public were not won over, and the opera ran for only two nights.

The libretto for *Deidamia* was an unexpectedly amusing version of the Achilles-Ulysses-Deidamia story written by his old colleague (and enemy) Rolli – a 'Dramatic Skeleton', as the librettist called all such pieces. He could also boast a new Italian voice, as Mrs Pendarves reported to her sister: 'Mr. Handel has got a new singer from Italy. Her voice is between Cuzzoni's and Strada's – strong, but not harsh, her person *miserably bad*, being very low, and *excessively* crooked'. This was Maria Monza, who had been expected to appear in *Imeneo*. When she failed to arrive, Handel had taken a safe course with the part of Nerea in *Deidamia* for which he originally made few technical demands. The extent of rewriting which he undertook when she finally reached London suggests that she was by no means 'below criticism', as Burney states; nor, for that matter, is her aria 'Quanto inganno' 'one of those subordinate airs of an opera for the under singers', as Burney condescendingly called them, 'which afford attentive hearers time to breathe, and discuss the merit of superior compositions and performance'. Burney's unbending distinction between the needs of *cadet* singers and *primarii* was certainly never shared by Handel, and can often be seen (as here) to vitiate his commentaries on the first-rate music of many smaller roles in Handel's operas.

Joseph Goupy's cruel cartoon, caricaturing Handel as a glutton, published in 1754.

The scoring of *Deidamia* was colourful enough, with the lute making its last appearance in an orchestral score; Burney was quick to note what he considered to be anticipations of Pergolesi's style. But this last-ditch attempt to lift the seriousness from *opera seria* failed. It was also Handel's last attempt to return to opera; when it closed after three performances, he finished the season with revivals of *L'Allegro*, *Parnasso*, *Acis and Galatea* and *Saul* (for one night only).

It was more than the apathy of the London public that doomed Handel's venture. An open letter in the *Daily Post* of 4 April solicits support on his behalf against active and malicious hostilities:

I wish I could ... persuade the Gentlemen who have taken Offence at any Part of this great Man's Conduct (for a great Man he must be in the Musical

World, whatever his Misfortunes may now too late say to the contrary:) I wish I could persuade them, I say, to take him back into Favour, and relieve him from the cruel Persecution of those little Vermin, who, taking Advantage of their Displeasure, pull down even his Bills as fast as he has them pasted up; and use a thousand other little Arts to injure and distress him. I am sure when they weigh the Thing without Prejudice, they will take him back into Favour; but in the mean time, let the Publick take Care that he wants not: That would be an unpardonable Ingratitude; and as this Oratorio of *Wednesday* next is his last for this Season, and if Report be true, probably his last for ever in this Country, let them, with a generous and friendly Benevolence, fill this his last House, and shew him on his Departure, that *London*, the greatest and richest City in the World, is great and rich in Virtue, as well as in Money, and can pardon and forget the Failings, or even the Faults of a great Genius.

Handel himself increased the suspicion that this would be a farewell by making special seating arrangements for the concert: 'This being the last Time of performing, many Persons of Quality and others, are pleas'd to make great Demands for Box Tickets, which encourage me (and hope will give no Offence) to put the Pit and Boxes together, at Half a Guinea each' (*Daily Post*). Rumour increased: 'I went to Lincolns Inn playhouse to hear Handel's music for the last time, he intending to go to Spa in Germany', wrote the Earl of Egmont in his diary on 8 April.

Although a mood of despondency is usually assumed to have settled over Handel at this time, a resignation to the 'cruel persecution' alluded to in the *Daily Post*, there is no outward evidence of depression under stress. On the contrary, on 30 July 1741 Thomas Dampier writes of him in high spirits, looking over new compositions from abroad with his friends Benjamin Tate and Robert Price, and apparently enjoying his freedom from the turmoils of opera:

They have had several conferences together, and I observed Fritz's musick* to lie before them, and that the great man frequently cried Bravo and sometimes bravissimo. He laughs very much at the opera which is preparing for next winter. He has refused to have anything to do in the matter. There are eight subscribers, each one 1,000 *l*. I can remember the names of some of them: Lord Middlesex, Lord Brooke, Lord Conway, Lord Holderness, Mr. Conway, Mr. Frederick, &c. Lord Middlesex it seems is the chief manager in the affair: the men of penetration give hints that his Lordship's sole aim is to make his mistress, the Muscovita, appear to great advantage upon the stage. With this intent, say they, he has taken care to hire singers with voices inferior to hers; and her's is not worth a farthing. Lord Brooke is quite easy in the matter. I believe he would pay a thousand pounds more rather than have anything to do in it in the character of manager.

---

*Presumably the four-part sonatas op.1 of Gaspard Fritz, which were about to be published by Walsh. Handel must have been reading from the separate parts.

That same month Handel could be found, apparently without commission, composing a series of Italian duets on lightly amorous texts – a repertoire that was highly acceptable in any German court. It is not impossible that rumour was correct, and that, despairing of the London public, he had decided to quit the country. If this is so, he was deflected by a surprising turn of fate.

It was Jennens who first tried to tempt Handel back to the oratorio, as he reported to his friend Edward Holdsworth on 10 July:* '. . . Handel says he will do nothing next Winter, but I hope I shall perswade him to set another Scripture Collection I have made for him, & perform it for his own Benefit in Passion week. I hope he will lay out his whole Genius & Skill upon it, that the Composition may excell all his former Compositions, as the Subject excells every other Subject. The Subject is Messiah . . .'. However attractive the subject, Handel never composed without a performance in mind, if not assured, and the book of *Messiah* might well have languished untouched for as long as that of *Saul* had it not been for an unexpected approach from Ireland.

William Cavendish, the Lord Lieutenant, was not a memorable diplomat. His impact on Dublin was limited to a few architectural improvements, and he might now be entirely forgotten but for his invitation to Handel, on behalf of several local charities, to take part in the following season of oratorio concerts. The prospect of a new public, a charitable cause and a series of concerts (instead of the single benefit that Jennens had proposed) galvanized Handel into planning a series of 'entertainments', to include his most recent secular successes – *L'Allegro*, *Acis and Galatea*, the *Ode for St Cecilia's Day* and *Alexander's Feast*. For the sacred component he immediately took up Jennens's new libretto, and began work on *Messiah* on 22 August. Part I was completed on 28 August, Part II on 6 September and Part III on the following Saturday, 12 September; two more days were spent in filling up the inner parts: 24 days in all, from start to finish.

The present-day standing of *Messiah* makes it difficult for us to realize that for Handel its composition was an offbeat venture, unsure in its rewards and probably unrepeatable. It is the only truly 'sacred' oratorio he ever wrote, it was the only one performed during his lifetime in a consecrated building, and yet it was intended, in Jennens's words, as 'a fine Entertainment'. Although quintessentially the work of a theatre composer, it contains no drama in the theatrical sense; there are no warring factions (no Israelites versus Philistines), no named protagonist; the text telescopes prophecy and fulfilment, and the drama is revealed obliquely, by inference and report, almost never by narrative.

---

*The important Jennens-Holdsworth correspondence was auctioned at Christie's on 4 July 1973, and is now in the Gerald Coke Collection.

The scheme was, of course, the responsibility of the librettist, and Jennens deserves more praise than he is sometimes allowed (one nineteenth-century denigrator would even have it that Jennens's chaplain, one Pooley, had done the work*). Avoiding the choral emphasis in *Israel in Egypt*, he opted for the same proportion of solos to choruses as had worked so well in *L'Allegro*; even so, *Messiah* has a higher choral element than any other of the oratorios, *Israel in Egypt* excepted. Old and New Testaments are skilfully blended, with some tactful adaptation and compression of the Authorized Version: 'He is the righteous Saviour', for instance, instead of 'He is just, and having salvation'; and 'Every valley shall be exalted, and every mountain and hill [shall be] made low; [and] the crooked [shall be made] straight, and the rough places plain' (Isaiah XL, v. 4). Most important of all is the clarity and confidence with which Jennens displays the divine scheme, a coherent progress from Prophecy, through Nativity, Crucifixion, Resurrection and Ascension to the promise of Redemption (Part III is based largely on the Anglican Burial Service). The work thus encompasses all the major festivals of the Christian year. Handel himself associated performances with Easter, but modern usage (particularly in North America) often prefers Christmas.

It is testimony enough to the soundness of Jennens's scheme that Handel wrote his score continuously, without any of the usual structural alterations. While Handel's speed of composition is indisputable, the legends which are accumulated around his 'whiteheat of inspiration' are a little hard to believe – of meals brought by his servant and taken away again untouched, of tears mingling with ink, and even the composer's own supposed words, 'I did think I did see all Heaven before me, and the great God Himself', which ring so false.

To counter this excess romanticism we can note Handel's unusual but very appropriate restraint in dealing with his theme. The original orchestration of *Messiah* was restricted to strings and a single solo instrument (the trumpet) used only once. Oboes and bassoons were added when the work was performed in London, doubling the strings throughout the choruses. The opportunity for vocal display is also slight – Handel composed four da capo arias at first and later reduced them to two ('He was despised' and 'The trumpet shall sound'). Both of these unusual features were in part due to his ignorance of conditions in Dublin, and Handel turned them to his advantage. Theatrical pictorialism is made the more telling by its discretion: two whole bars of trilling bird-song in 'Every valley', for instance, were cut at an early stage, and the symbolism of the heavenly trumpets on their first appearance with the angels in 'Glory to God' is enhanced by the instruction 'da lontano e un poco piano' ('from a distance and rather softly'). Handel originally wrote 'in disparte' ('in the wings'); they are heard from on stage for the first time in 'Hallelujah'.

A further antidote to the romantic belief in Handel's inspiration is to examine his compositional process in more detail. A sketch of the 'Amen' fugue is now in the Fitzwilliam Museum, Cambridge, along with other sketches of fugal examples dating from the 1730s; though the earlier sketches are not directly

---

*William Hone, *The Every-Day Book*.

related to the composition of *Messiah*, the juxtaposition suggests that Handel was clearly determined to exercise his contrapuntal cleverness in composing the 'Amen' to *Messiah*, where as Burney says, 'the subject is divided, subdivided, inverted, enriched with counter-subjects, and made subservient to many ingenious and latent purposes of harmony, melody and imitation'.

For a work composed in such haste, there is surprisingly little evidence of borrowings. The most important, and musically the most effective, are self-borrowings: Handel's transformations of some of his recent Italian duets into choruses. The lightness and antiphonal use of the voices ('All we like sheep', 'His yoke is easy', 'And He shall purify') is a valuable contrast to the grandiose manner of other choruses in the work, even though the adaptation led Handel to some unidiomatic word-stress ('*For* unto us a child is born' from 'Nò, di voi non vo fidarmi') and some rather irrelevant coloratura (the semiquavers of 'And He shall purify' and 'His yoke is easy', originating from 'Quel fior che all'alba ride' where they are entirely appropriate). 'And He shall purify' also contains borrowings from Telemann's *Harmonischer Gottes-Diens* and Buxtehude's G minor Praeludium (Bux WV 163), which has the same theme in the second fugal section. Other passages of questionable word-stress (in 'I know that my Redeemer liveth', for example, or 'The trumpet shall sound') went unaltered by Handel's singers during his lifetime, and in any case only cause distress when spoken.

Such small-scale, local problems of word-setting were only a part of Handel's difficulty with the text of *Messiah*. The characteristic antitheses of Biblical language contribute strongly to the epic by requiring a juxtaposition of musical ideas, but they were foreign to Handel's experience. In the traditional format of an opera libretto, and in his settings of Milton and Dryden, Handel had been given a single idea or *Affekt* on which to base a musical unit; Hebrew poetry commonly offered sudden contrasts rather than reiterations, so was at odds with Handel's own musical conditioning and with the very nature of aria form.

The flexibility of his choral procedures could accommodate such violent shifts, as in the last passage of 'All we like sheep' ('And the Lord hath laid on him . . .'), for instance; and the antiphony of 'Lift up your heads' came naturally to him. The aria was less malleable; in 'The people that walked in darkness', for example, the vision of 'a great light' can hardly be matched with a complementary move into a major key every time the mood of the text changes; and regardless of words, the aria must end in the minor.* With consummate pragmatism Handel therefore capitalizes on the change from minor to major between the aria and the succeeding chorus, 'For unto us a child is born', expanding the scope of a harmonic scheme that would otherwise have been limited to a single number.

Although the influence of the German Passion settings can be traced in Part II, only two choruses ('He trusted in God' and 'Let us break') represent the

---

*Could it have been such passages that William Shenston was remembering when he wrote that *Messiah* 'seems the best composer's best composition. Yet I fancied that I could observe *some parts* in it, wherein Handel's judgements failed him; where the music was not equal, or was even *opposite*, to what the words required . . .'? (letter to Richard Graves, 25 November 1758).

crowd. The first of these, as Burney points out, presents not 'the taunts and presumption of an individual, but the scoffs and scorn of a confused multitude'. George III took exception to this description in a 'critical note' to Burney, causing him to add the mollifying footnote: 'He [i.e. Handel] was so conscious of the merit of this movement, that he frequently performed it on key'd-instruments, as a lesson; and if he was pressed to sit down to play at such times as he felt no immediate impulse, this theme usually presented itself to his mind; when, making it the subject of extempore fugue and voluntary, it never failed to inspire him with the most sublime ideas, and wonderful sallies of imagination'.

38   The turbulent state of Handel's manuscript, the blots, erasures and emendations that litter the page right to the final bars give enough evidence of tempestuous creation to tempt any romantic biographer. But far from seeing Handel debilitated and exhausted, we find him within a few days of completing *Messiah* taking up his pen to begin a new work, intended for London rather than for Dublin. Act I of *Samson*, the biggest of all his oratorios, was finished by 29 September, and the whole was complete a month later. This work was the counterbalance to *Messiah* and an insurance against any possible criticism it might attract. If *Messiah* proved too contemplative, *Samson* was highly charged drama, with firmly-drawn characters and alternating choruses for the Philistines and the Israelites – although Handel makes only modest demands on the chorus. If *Messiah* were to be declared 'sacrilegious' because of its Biblical text, *Samson* stood on the safer ground of Milton's verse. Newburgh Hamilton, who had arranged the words for *Alexander's Feast*, defended his new libretto in a Preface:

> Several Pieces of *Milton* having been lately brought on the Stage with Success, particularly his *Penseroso* and *Allegro*, I was of Opinion that nothing of that Divine Poet's wou'd appear in the Theatre with greater Propriety or Applause than his SAMSON AGONISTES. That Poem indeed never was divided by him into Acts or Scenes, nor design'd (as he hints in his Preface) for the Stage; but given only as the Plan of a Tragedy with Chorus's, after the manner of the Ancients. But as Mr. *Handel* had so happily introduc'd here *Oratorios*, a musical Drama, whose Subject must be Scriptural, and in which the Solemnity of Church-Musick is agreeably united with the most pleasing Airs of the Stage: It would have been an irretrievable Loss to have neglected the Opportunity of that great Master's doing Justice to this Work; he having already added new Life and Spirit to some of the finest Things in the *English* Language, particularly that inimitable Ode of *Dryden's*, which no Age nor Nation ever excell'd . . .
>
> In adapting this POEM to the Stage, the Recitative is taken almost wholly from *Milton*, making use only of those Parts in his long Work most necessary to preserve the Spirit of the Subject, and justly connect it. In the Airs and Chorus's which I was oblig'd to add, I have interspers'd several Lines, Words, and Expressions borrowed from some of his smaller Poems, to make the whole as much of a piece as possible: Tho' I reduc'd the Original to so short an Entertainment, yet being thought too long for the proper Time of a

Representation, some Recitative must be left out in the Performance, but printed in its Place, and mark'd to distinguish it.

In dramatic scope, *Samson* is the natural successor to *Saul*, and like that work, begins with a festival and ends with an elegy. By pruning Milton's poem, and grafting on cuttings from other poems (his 'Paraphrases of the Psalms', the 'Ode on the Morning of Christ's Nativity' and others), Hamilton succeeds in removing the 'Agonistes' of Milton's title and creating a hero who is isolated, human, pitiable and eventually noble. He also creates suspense by asking a question the Bible could never allow: will God intervene in time?*

Handel responded to the text with a score of elaborate instrumental colouring, wonderfully sensual in the Dalila scenes, and a large number of borrowings – from Legrenzi, Telemann, Muffat and a curiously high percentage from Giovanni Porta's *Numitore*, the opera with which his first season with the Royal Academy had opened twenty-one years earlier. Even the germ of 'Let the bright Seraphims'† comes from this source.

Perhaps Handel's memories of that first season had been stirred by the opening of Lord Middlesex's extravagant new season at the Haymarket. Handel finished *Samson* on 29 October, saw the first night of *Alessandro in Persia* (compiled by Galuppi) on the 31st, when according to Walpole 'they were obliged to omit the part of Amorevoli [the tenor], who has fever', and left for Ireland immediately afterwards, much amused (see p. 173). He took with him, apparently, his copyist John Christopher Smith, and his material for the concert season ahead. Jennens had not been kept informed of these new developments and wrote, rather piqued, to Holdsworth: '. . . I heard with great pleasure at my arrival in Town, that Handel had set the Oratorio of Messiah; but it was some mortification to me to hear that instead of performing it here he was gone into Ireland with it. However, I hope we shall hear it when he comes back . . .'

En route for Dublin Handel passed through Chester, where Burney saw him for the first time and wrote the following account of his stay:

I was at the Public-School in that city, and very well remember seeing him smoke a pipe, over a dish of coffee, at the Exchange-Coffee-house; for being extremely curious to see so extraordinary a man, I watched him narrowly as long as he remained in Chester; which, on account of the wind being unfavourable for his embarking at Parkgate, was several days. During this time, he applied to Mr. Baker, the Organist, my first music-master, to know whether there were any choirmen in the cathedral who could sing *at sight*; as he wished to prove some books that had been hastily transcribed, by trying the choruses which he intended to perform in Ireland. Mr. Baker mentioned some of the most likely singers then in Chester, and, among the rest, a printer of the name of Janson, who had a good base voice, and was one of the best

*See Ruth Smith, 'Intellectual contexts'.
†The plural form is Milton's.

musicians in the choir . . . A time was fixed for this private rehearsal at the *Golden Falcon*, where HANDEL was quartered; but, alas! on trial of the chorus in the Messiah, '*And with his stripes we are healed*,' – Poor Janson, after repeated attempts, failed so egregiously, that HANDEL let loose his great bear upon him; and after swearing in four languages, cried out in broken English: 'You shcauntrel! tit not you dell me dat you could sing at soite?' – 'Yes, sir, says the printer, and so I can; but not at *first sight*.'*

At this time Dublin was in its 'golden age', the second city of the British Isles and a centre of the arts. Dr Johnson, in partisan spirit, thought that 'Dublin, though a place much worse than London, is not as bad as Iceland'; Jonathan Swift was Dean of St Patrick's Cathedral (although, as he put it, 'dying at the top'); Handel's friend the violinist Matthew Dubourg had been Master of the State Music since 1728; and many musicians well known in London were at some time involved with Dublin's musical life. Geminiani, Michael Arne and Giordani later lived there, and Thomas Arne, Castrucci, and Lampe paid the city extended visits.

Handel arrived in the packet-boat from Holyhead on 18 November and took rooms in Abbey Street. Three days later 'arrived in the Yatcht from Parkgate, Signiora Avolio, an excellent Singer, who is come to this Kingdom, to perform in Mr. Handel's Musical Entertainments'. While Handel set about organizing his concert series, his Utrecht Te Deum and Jubilate were quickly featured in a church service 'after the Cathedral Manner' in aid of the Mercer's Hospital. Handel himself agreed to play the organ, and was duly thanked in the Minutes of the Hospital.

From the start Handel's activities in Dublin may be reconstructed in some detail, not only from the press but also from his own correspondence; it is easy to appreciate his enthusiasm for such a welcome after the bickerings and jealousies of London. Handel's first series of 'Musical Entertainments' was opened to subscription in December, as Faulkner's *Dublin Journal* reported:

42   At the New Musick-hall in Fishamble-street, on Wednesday next, being the 23rd Day of December, Mr. Handel's Musical Entertainment will be opened; in which will be performed, *L'Allegro, il Penseroso, & il Moderato*, with two Concertos for several Instruments, and a Concerto on the Organ. To begin at 7 o'clock. Tickets for that Night will be delivered to the Subscribers (by sending their Subscription Ticket) on Tuesday and Wednesday next, at the Place of Performance, from 9 o'clock in the Morning till 3 in the Afternoon. – And Attendance will be given this Day and on Monday next, at Mr. Handel's House in Abbey-street, near Lyffey-street, from 9 o'clock in the Morning till 3 in the Afternoon, in order to receive the Subscription Money; at which Time each Subscriber will have a Ticket delivered to him, which entitles him to three tickets each Night, either for Ladies or Gentlemen. – NB.

---

*Doubt is cast on the latter part of this anecdote by Charles Cudworth in 'Mythistorica Handeliana'.

Subscriptions are likewise taken in at the same Place. Books will be sold at the said Place, Price a British Six-pence.

Dublin society responded willingly, as is shown by Handel's own account of his glowing reception, in a letter he wrote to Jennens on 29 December:

I am emboldned, Sir, by the generous Concern You please to take in relation to my affairs, to give You an Account of the Success I have met here. The Nobility did me the Honour to make amongst themselves a Subscription for 6 Nights, which did fill a Room of 600 Persons, so that I needed not sell one single Ticket at the door. and without Vanity the Performance was received with a general Approbation. Sig^{ra} Avolio, which I brought with me from London pleases extraordinary, I have form'd an other Tenor Voice which gives great satisfaction, the Basses and Counter Tenors are very good, and the rest of the Chorus Singers (by my Direction) do exceeding well, as for the Instruments they are really excellent. Mr. Dubourgh being at the head of them and the Musick sounds delightfully in this charming Room, which puts me in such spirits (and my Health being so good) that I exert my self on my Organ whit more then usual success. I opened with the Allegro, Penseroso, & Moderato, and I assure you that the Words of the Moderato are vastly admired. The Audience being composed (besides the Flower of Ladies of Distinction and other People of the greatest quality) of so many Bishops, Deans, Heads of the Colledge, the most eminents People in the Law as the Chancellor, Auditor general &tc. all which are very much taken with the Poëtry. So that I am desired to perform it again the next time. I cannot sufficiently express the kind treatment I receive here, but the Politeness of this generous Nation cannot be unknown to You, so I let you judge of the satisfaction I enjoy, passing my time with Honnour, profit, and pleasure. They propose already to have some more Performances, when the 6 Nights of the Subscription are over, and My Lord Duc the Lord Lieutenant (who is allways present with all his Family on those Nights) will easily obtain a longer Permission for me by His Majesty, so that I shall be obliged to make my stay here longer than I thought . . . I expect with Impatience the Favour of your News concerning your Health and wellfare, of which I take a real share, as for the News of Your Opera's, I need not trouble you for all this Town is full of their ill success, by a number of Letters from your quarters to the People of quality here, and I can't help saying but that it furnishes great Diversion and laughter. The first Opera I heard my self before I left London, and it made me very merry all a long my journey, and of the second opera, called Penelope, a certain noble man writes very jocosly, il faut que je dise avec Harlequin: nôtre Penelôpe n'est qu'une Sallôpe. but I think I have trespassed too much on your Patience.

The same programme was repeated on 13 January 1742, and three days later the *Dublin Journal* announced that on the 20th:

... will be performed, *Acis and Galatea*; to which will be added, an Ode for St. Cecilia's Day, written by Mr. Dryden, and newly set to Musick by Mr. Handel, with several concertos on the Organ and other Instruments. . . . To begin at 7 o'clock. N.B. – Gentlemen and Ladies are desired to order their Coaches and Chairs to come down Fishamble-street, which will prevent a great deal of Inconvenience that happened the Night before; and as there is a good convenient Room hired as an Addition to a former Place for the Footmen, it is hoped the Ladies will order them to attend there till called for.

A hitch occurred in arrangements for the next work when a licence granted by Swift for several of his Vicars Choral to perform in Handel's concerts was suddenly reversed. On 28 January, Swift wrote to the Sub-dean and Chapter of St Patrick's:

... I do hereby require and request the Very Reverend Sub-Dean, not to permit any of the Vicar Chorals, choristers, or organists, to attende or assist at any public musical performances, without my consent, or his consent, with the consent of the Chapter first obtained.

And whereas it hath been reported, that I gave a licence to certain vicars to assist at a club of fiddlers in Fishamble Street, I do hereby declare that I remember no such licence to have been ever signed or sealed by me; and that if ever such pretended licence should be produced, I do hereby annul and vacate the said licence; intreating my said Sub-Dean and Chapter to punish such vicars as shall ever appear there, as songsters, fiddlers, pipers, trumpeters, drummers, drum-majors, or in any sonal quality, according to the flagitious aggravations of their respective disobedience, rebellion, perfidy, and ingratitude.

This contretemps with the now unbalanced creator of Gulliver seems to have been ironed out, and the singing-men were able to contribute to 'an Oratorio called ESTHER, with Additions' on 30 January and to *Alexander's Feast*, which initiated a second series of concerts, on 13 February. A rather sad announcement in the *Dublin Journal* for 27 February shows that Handel could also call on all the best players in town: 'For the Benefit of Monsieur de Rheiner, a distress'd foreign Gentleman, at the Theatre in Smock-Alley, on Thursday the fourth of March. . . . The Constant Couple . . . N.B. Monsieur de Rheiner has been oblig'd to put off his Day, which was to have been on Tuesday next, on account of all the best Musick being engaged to Mr. Handel's Concert. . . .'

A concert version of *Imeneo*, introduced as 'a new Serenata called HYMEN', was performed on 24 March, with Susanna Cibber, singer and actress, and sister of Thomas Arne, prominent. She eventually became Garrick's leading lady, and an outstanding tragedienne; 'though her voice was a thread', as Burney unkindly put it, as a singer her expressive powers were matchless. An unsigned poem in the *Gentleman's Magazine* of 11 March specifically celebrated her Dublin performances:

40

To Mrs. CIBBER, on her Acting at *Dublin*.

. . . . .

Now tuneful as *Apollo's* lyre,
She stands amid the vocal choir;
If solemn measures slowly move,
Or *Lydian* airs invite to love,
Her looks inform the trembling strings,
And raise each passion, that she sings;
The wanton Graces hover round,
Perch on her lips, and tune the sound.

. . . . .

O wondrous girl! how small a space
Includes the gift of human race!

. . . . .

Even Burney had to admit, in a sly aside, that Handel himself had been enchanted by her: 'Handel was very fond of Mrs Cibber, whose voice and manners had softened his severity for her want of musical knowledge'.

She, amongst others, participated in the first performance of *Messiah*, announced in the *Dublin Journal* of 27 March.

For Relief of the Prisoners in the several Gaols, and for the Support of Mercer's Hospital in Stephen's Street, and of the Charitable Infirmary on the Inns Quay, on Monday the 12th of April, will be performed at the Musick Hall in Fishamble Street, Mr. *Handel's new Grand Oratorio, call'd the* MESSIAH, in which the Gentlemen of the Choirs of both Cathedrals will assist, with some Concertoes on the Organ, by Mr. Handell.

The performance was put off 'At the Desire of several Persons of distinction' until 13 April; the following instructions appeared in the *Dublin Journal* on the 10th: 'Many Ladies and Gentlemen who are well-wishers to this Noble and Grand Charity for which this Oratorio was composed, request it as a Favour, that the Ladies who honour this Performance with their Presence would be pleased to come without Hoops, as it will greatly encrease the Charity, by making room for more company'. At its public rehearsal the *Dublin Journal* reported that *Messiah* 'was allowed by the greatest Judges to be the finest Composition of Musick that ever was heard'. Its first public performance on 13 April was equally well received:

On Tuesday last [the 13th] Mr. Handel's Sacred Grand Oratorio, the MESSIAH, was performed at the New Musick-Hall in Fishamble-street; the best Judges allowed it to be the most finished piece of Musick. Words are wanting to express the exquisite Delight it afforded to the admiring crouded Audience. The Sublime, the Grand, and the Tender, adapted to the most

175

elevated, majestick and moving Words, conspired to transport and charm the ravished Heart and Ear. It is but Justice to Mr. Handel, that the World should know, he generously gave the Money arising from this Grand Performance, to be equally shared by the Society for relieving Prisoners, the Charitable Infirmary, and Mercer's Hospital, for which they will ever gratefully remember his Name; and that the Gentlemen of the two Choirs, Mr. Dubourg, Mrs. Avolio, and Mrs. Cibber, who all performed their Parts to Admiration, acted also on the same disinterested Principle, satisfied with the deserved Applause of the Publick, and the conscious Pleasure of promoting such useful, and extensive Charity. There were about 700 People in the Room, and the Sum collected for that Noble and Pious Charity amounted to about 400*l.* out of which 127*l.* goes to each of the three great and pious Charities. (*Dublin Journal*, 17 April)

One impromptu compliment was offered during the performance itself; the Rev. Dr Delany, a friend of Dean Swift (and later to marry Handel's friend Mrs Pendarves) was so transported by Mrs Cibber's singing of 'He was despised' that he rose from his seat and exclaimed, somewhat presumptuously for a divine, 'Woman, for this, be all thy sins forgiven!'

> *One night, while HANDEL was in Dublin, Dubourg having a solo part in a song, and a close to make,* ad libitum, *he wandered about in different keys a great while, and seemed indeed a little bewildered, and uncertain of his original . . . but, at length, coming to the shake, which was to terminate this long close, HANDEL, to the great delight of the audience, and augmentation of applause, cried out loud enough to be heard in the most remote parts of the theatre: 'You are welcome home, Mr. Dubourg!'*
>
> (Charles Burney, 1785)

Handel had made several alterations for this performance, possibly as a result of the public rehearsals that had preceded it on 9 April. In fact the oratorio was never performed exactly as it had been written in 1741. He wrote a new duet version of 'How beautiful are the feet', and either to compensate for the local male soloists, or to accelerate the drama for the benefit of the crowded concert hall (one hundred more people were admitted than it officially held), he reduced 'Why do the nations' to less than half its original length (a cut that he seems never to have rescinded), and reset 'But who may abide' and 'Thou shalt break them' as recitatives.

His chorus used twenty-six boys from the two cathedrals, which also provided the male soloists, including two countertenors, one for 'O Thou that tellest' and the other for the extended version of the duet 'O Death, where is thy sting?'

The only surviving blot on the event is the poetry offered up by Laurence Whyte in the *Dublin Journal* on 20 April.

What can we offer more in *Handel*'s praise?
Since his *Messiah* gain'd him groves of Bays;
Groves that can never wither nor decay,
Whose *Vistos* his Ability display: . . .
But our *Messiah*, blessed be his Name!
Both Heaven and Earth his *Miracles* proclaim.
His Birth, his Passion, and his Resurrection,
With his Ascension, have a strong Connection; . . .

A performance of *Saul* the next month, which at rehearsal was declared 'by all the Judges present, to have been the finest Performance that hath been heard in this Kingdom' (*Dublin Journal*) was followed by a repeat performance of *Messiah* on 3 June, with a public rehearsal two days earlier. It was the height of summer and the end of Handel's season, as the *Dublin Journal* announced: 'In order to keep the Room as cool as possible, a Pane of Glass will be removed from the Top of each of the windows. – N.B. This will be the last Performance of Mr. Handel's during his Stay in this Kingdom'.

After an all-Handel evening of solos and duets by Mrs Cibber and her sister-in-law, Cecilia Arne, and an evening which he may have spent watching Garrick play *Hamlet* in the little Smock-Alley Theatre, Handel prepared to leave for England. His farewell to Jonathan Swift, now sinking into insanity, occasioned the last sensible words that the Dean was heard to utter:

Mr. *Handel*, when about to quit *Ireland* went to take his leave of him: The Servant was a considerable Time, e'er he could make the Dean understand him; which, when he did, he cry'd, 'Oh! a *German*, and a Genius! A Prodigy! admit him.' The Servant did so, just to let Mr. *Handel* behold the Ruins of the greatest Wit that ever lived among the Tide of Time, where all at length are lost. (Mrs Laetitia Pilkington, *Memoirs*, 1754).

On 17 August the *Dublin Journal* succinctly records that: 'Last Week the celebrated Mr. Handel so famous for his excellent Compositions and fine Performance with which he entertained this Town in the most agreeable Manner, embarked for England'.

After some ten months away from London, his longest absence since first taking up residence there, Handel is supposed to have found the public's heart grown fonder of him. One powerful voice, at least, was in his favour. Alexander Pope, who admitted to having no ear for music, asked Dr Arbuthnot for his opinion of Handel's worth. The reply – 'Conceive the highest that you can of his ability and they [*sic*] are much beyond anything you can conceive' – allowed Pope to throw his weight behind Handel in the fourth book of *The Dunciad*, which appeared while Handel was in Dublin (see page 140). In the footnotes to his poem, Pope attacks 'the nature and genius of the *Italian* opera; its affected airs, its effeminate sounds, and the practice of patching up these Operas with favourite Songs, incoherently put together' and explains his strained metaphor of Handel, 'with a hundred hands': 'Mr. *Handel* had introduced a great number of Hands, and more variety of Instruments into the Orchestra, and employed even Drums and Cannon to make a fuller Chorus; which prov'd so much too manly for the fine Gentlemen of his age, that he was obliged to remove his Music into *Ireland*'.

> *The first time the serpent was used in a concert, at which Handel was in the habit of presiding, he was so disgusted with the powerful coarseness of its tones, that he called out in a rage, 'Vat de diffil be dat?' On being informed that it was an instrument called a serpent, 'O!' he replied, 'de serpent! – aye – but it not be de serpent vat seduced Eve.'*
>
> (Thomas Busby, 1825)

But Mainwaring's claim that 'The minds of most men were much more disposed in his favour' was made with hindsight, and from the standpoint of one who knew the future glories of oratorio and the gradual deification of its progenitor. Handel himself, buoyed up by his reception in Dublin and determined to return there, was in a state of indecision as to his career in England. He found Sir Robert Walpole had been forced from office as Prime Minister for opposing the general cry for war; yet another pleasure garden had opened, at Ranelagh, with a promise of weekly ridottos and 'much nobility, and much mob besides'; Lord Middlesex's opera was, predictably, losing money: 'there were but three-and-forty people last night in the pit and boxes', reported Horace Walpole on 26 May.

Handel had been approached with an offer of a thousand guineas to write two operas, but in his first letter from London (dated 9 September) to Jennens, whom he had failed to visit on his return journey, he denied any return to the theatre:

It was indeed your humble Servant which intended you a visit in my way from Ireland to London, for I certainly could have given you a better account by word of mouth, as by writing, how well your Messiah was received in that Country, yet as a Noble Lord, and no less then the Bishop of Elphin (a Nobleman very learned in musick) has given his observations in writing of this Oratorio, I send you here annexed the contents of it in his own words.
—— I shall send the printed Book of the Messiah to Mr. Sted for You. As for my success in general in that generous and polite Nation, I reserve the account of it till I have the Honour to see you in London. The report that the Direction of the Opera next winter is comitted to my Care is groundless. The gentlemen who have undertaken to middle with Harmony can not agree, and are quite in a Confusion. Whether I shall do something in the Oratorio way

(as several of my friends desire) I can not determine as yet. Certain it is that this time 12 month I shall continue my Oratorio's in Ireland, where they are a going to make a large subscription allready for that Purpose.

On 29 October Jennens passed this news on to Holdsworth, clearly hoping that he would be offered a chance to hear *Messiah*: 'You was misinformed about Mr. Handel, who does not return to Ireland till next Winter; so that I hope to have some very agreeable Entertainments from him this Season. His Messiah by all accounts is his Masterpiece . . .'.

One such account, until recently assumed lost, was that of the Bishop of Elphin (Dr Edward Synge). Its recent rediscovery allows us to share the immediate enthusiasm Dublin audiences felt for Handel's work.*

As Mr. Handel in his oratorio's greatly excells all other Composers I am acquainted with, So in the famous one, called The Messiah he seems to have excell'd himself. The whole is beyond any thing I had a notion of till I Read and heard it. It Seems to be a Species of Musick different from any other, and this is particularly remarkable of it. That tho' the Composition is very Masterly & artificial, yet the Harmony is So great and open, as to please all who have Ears & will hear, learned & unlearn'd . . . a Third reason for the Superior Excellence of this piece, 'Tis this there is no Dialogue. In every Drame there must be a great deal & often broken into very Short Speeches & Answers. If these be flat, & insipid, they move laughter or Contempt . . .

Synge's testimonial carries a short annotation by Handel, presumably addressed to Jennens: 'I send you this S^r only to show how zealous they are in Ireland for Oratorio's. I could send you a number of Instances more from others in Print and in writing'. Handel wisely ignored the Bishop's suggestion of a sequel to *Messiah* to be called *The Penitent* (one example of the flat-footed possibilities oratorio could offer), and apart from putting finishing touches to *Samson*, which had not been mentioned in Dublin, refrained from concert promotion for the rest of the year.

By the New Year 1743, Handel had resolved his indecision. An oratorio season of six performances by subscription was announced, following the plan that had been so successful in Dublin. The venue was Covent Garden, and the customary permission was sought from William Chetwynd, the government Inspector of Stage Plays, to present *Samson*; a manuscript word-book (now in the Huntington Library, California) was offered for perusal. On 5 February Handel completed the Organ Concerto in A (later published as op. 7 no. 2) to be performed on the 18th when *Samson* was first heard. The oratorio was an immediate success; even the cynical Horace Walpole, writing to Horace Mann on 24 February, was impressed: 'Handel has set up an Oratorio against the Operas, and succeeds. He has hired all the goddesses from farces and the singers of *Roast Beef*† from between the acts at both theatres, with a man with one note in his voice and a girl without ever an one; and so they sing, and make brave

---

*See the Christie's sale catalogue, *Autograph Letters*.   †A popular ballad.

hallelujahs; and the good company encore the recitative, if it happens to have any cadence like what they call a tune'.

> *The Oratorios thrive abundantly – for my part, they give me an idea of heaven, where everybody is to sing whether they have voices or not.*
> (Horace Walpole, 1743)

Walpole's criticism of the English voices is unfair. One of Handel's new decisions was to trust to native voices singing in their native language, and with the exception of Signora Avolio, who sang for Handel until the following year, to forego the stars of Italian opera. Handel's innovation of casting his hero as a tenor (the reliable Beard) marks a turning-point in the evolution of English oratorio. Another tenor, Thomas Lowe, who appeared in Handel's company in 1743, had 'the finest tenor voice I ever heard in my life', but 'for want of diligence and cultivation, he never could be safely trusted with any thing better than a ballad, which he constantly learned by his ear' (Burney).

Samson filled the theatre for all six nights of the subscription – helped by the fact that, as Lady Hertford reported to her son, 'the Ridotto was the worst that has been known. There was very little company of any kind, and not twenty people of distinction among them. The oratorio has answered much better, being filled with all the people of quality in town; and they say Handel has exerted himself to make it the finest piece of music he ever composed, and say he has not failed in his attempt'.

Handel pursued his success with 'six Entertainments more', beginning with *L'Allegro e il Penseroso* (but without *Il Moderato*, which cannot have pleased Jennens), and continuing two nights later with 'A NEW SACRED ORATORIO. With a *Concerto* on the *Organ*. And a Solo on the Violin by Mr. *Dubourg*' (*Daily Advertiser*, 19 March). Handel's reluctance to give *Messiah* its full title is quickly explained by an outspoken letter that appeared in the *Universal Spectator* on the same day (written therefore in advance of the performance).

SIR,

. . . My . . . Purpose . . . is to consider, and, if possible, induce others to consider, the Impropriety of *Oratorios*, as they are now perform'd.

Before I speak against them (that I may not be thought to do it out of Prejudice or Party) it may not be improper to declare, that I am a profess'd Lover of *Musick*, and in particular all Mr. *Handel's Performances*, being *one* of the *few* who never deserted him. I am also a great Admirer of *Church Musick*, and think no other equal to it, nor any Person so capable to compose it, as Mr. *Handel*. To return: An *Oratorio* either is an *Act* of *Religion*, or it is not; if it is, I ask if the *Playhouse* is a fit *Temple* to perform it in or a Company of *Players* fit *Ministers* of *God's Word*, for in that Case such they are made. . . .

In the other Case, if it is not perform'd as an *Act* of *Religion*, but for *Diversion* and *Amusement* only (and indeed I believe few or none go to an *Oratorio* out of *Devotion*), what a *Prophanation* of *God's* Name and Word is this, to make so light Use of them? I wish every one would consider whether, at the same Time they are *diverting* themselves, they are not accessory to the breaking the *Third Commandment*. I am sure it is not following the Advice of the *Psalmist, Serve the Lord with Fear, and rejoice unto him with Reverence*: How must it offend a devout *Jew*, to hear the great *Jehovah*, the *proper* and most *sacred Name of God* (a Name a *Jew*, if not a *Priest*, hardly dare pronounce) sung, I won't say to a light Air (for as Mr. *Handel* compos'd it, I dare say it is not) but by a Set of People very *unfit* to *perform* so *solemn* a *Service*. *David* said, *How can we sing the Lord's Song in a strange Land*; but sure he would have thought it much stranger to have heard it sung in a *Playhouse*.

But it seems the *Old Testament* is not to be prophan'd alone, nor *God* by the *Name* of *Jehovah* only, but the *New* must be join'd with it, and *God* by the most *sacred* the most *merciful Name* of *Messiah*; for I'm inform'd that an Oratorio call'd by that Name has already been perform'd in *Ireland*, and is soon to be perform'd *here*: What the Piece itself is, I know not, and therefore shall say nothing about it; but I must again ask, If the *Place* and *Performers* are fit?

PHILALETHES

This was stronger opposition than had greeted *Israel in Egypt* four years earlier. It can in part be attributed to the new wave of religious feeling stirred up by the Wesley brothers and William Law; two new chapels had opened in London that very year, noted for their 'swift singing' without organ accompaniment, and the initial puritanism of the movement placed particular blame on the playhouses as the source of corruption. It is curious that the very movement which was to create the middle-class fervour on which the growth of the oratorio tradition in England was founded should at first have opposed this particular work. John Wesley himself was an enthusiast for *Messiah*; after a performance in Bristol some years later he wrote: 'I doubt if that congregation was ever so serious at a sermon as they were during this performance. In many parts, especially several of the choruses, it exceeded my expectations' (*Journal*, August 1758). Criticism was to continue for many years; even Miss Catherine Talbot, a staunch supporter of Handel, had to admit after a performance of *Messiah* at Covent Garden in 1756 that 'the playhouse is an unfit place for such a solemn performance'.

Handel could easily weather this form of 'piety', assured that the general view was represented by the editor of the *Universal Spectator*, who took the precaution of prefacing the letter with a disclaimer: 'The following Letter may to many of my Readers, especially those of a gay and polite Taste, seem too rigid a Censure on a Performance, which is so universally approv'd: However, I could not suppress it, as there is so well-intended a Design and pious Zeal runs through the whole, and nothing derogatory said of Mr. *Handel's* Merit. Of what good Consequences it will produce, I can only say – *Valeat Quantum valere potest*'.* A more direct response came in some verses, 'Wrote extempore by a

---

*lit. 'Let it be worth as much as it is worth'.

Gentleman on reading the *Universal Spectator*' and printed in the *Daily Advertiser*
on 31 March.

> Cease, Zealots, cease to blame these Heav'nly Lays,
> For Seraphs fit to sing Messiah's Praise!
> Nor, for your trivial Argument, assign,
> 'The Theatre not fit for Praise Divine.'
>
> These hallow'd Lays to Musick give new Grace,
> To Virtue Awe, and sanctify the Place;
> To Harmony, like his, Celestial Pow'r is giv'n,
> T'exalt the Soul from Earth, and make, of Hell, a Heav'n.

Jennens may have been the anonymous author of those lines. If so, his private
opinion was rather different; upset that *Messiah* was first performed in Dublin,
he is aggressive in his criticism of Handel. If there was any direct communication
between the two at this period, it has disappeared, but the ill-nature of his
attacks can be judged from his correspondence with Holdsworth, who supplied
him with music and news from abroad. At the beginning of the year came an
accusation of plagiarism, and an expression of disappointment at *Messiah*,
which had not measured up to his expectations:

> ... I told you before that one of the Composers in my Box* [of music sent by
> Holdsworth] was good, I mean Scarlatti: & I shall not condemn the rest
> without a fair Trial. Handel has borrow'd a dozen of the pieces & I dare say I
> shall catch him stealing from them; as I have formerly, both from Scarlatti &
> Vinci. He has compos'd an exceeding fine Oratorio, being an alteration of
> Milton's Samson Agonistes, with which he is to begin Lent. His Messiah has
> disappointed me, being set in great hast, tho' he said he would be a year about
> it, & make it the best of all his Compositions. I shall put no more Sacred
> Words into his hands, to be thus abus'd . . .

Holdsworth appears to have heard bad reports of *Messiah* from other
correspondents, for in his reply of 16 February he says:

> ... I am sorry to hear yr. friend Handel is such a jew. His negligence, to say no
> worse, has been a great disappointment to others as well as yr. self, for I hear
> there was great expectation of his composition. I hope the words, tho'
> murther'd are still to be seen, and yt I shall have that pleasure when I return.
> And as I don't understand the musick I shall be better off than the rest of ye
> world . . .

---

*From a letter of Holdsworth to Jennens of 4 May 1742 we learn that the 'Box' contained 'part of
Cardinal Ottoboni's Collection; And most of it by celebrated hands, such as Scarlatti, Pollarolo,
Mancini, Bencini and Marcello'. See Michael Talbot, 'Jennens and Vivaldi'. Jennens might have
been surprised to find that some at least of this collection would have been familiar to Handel
already from his time in Rome.

Jennens warmed to his topic with an immediate reply (21 February), although he was large enough to admit his admiration for *Samson*.

> . . . I am sorry I mention'd my Italian Musick to Handel, for I don't like to have him borrow from them who has so much a better fund of his own. As to the Messiah, 'tis still in his power by retouching the weak parts to make it fit for a publick performance; & I have said a great deal to him on the Subject; but he is so lazy & so obstinate, that I much doubt the Effect. I have a copy, as it was printed in Ireland, full of Bulls; & if he does not print a correct one here, I shall do it my Self, & perhaps tell him a piece of my mind by way of Preface. I am a little out of humour, as you may perceive, & want to vent my Spleen for ease. What adds to my chagrin is, that if he makes his Oratorio ever so perfect, there is a clamour about Town, said to arise from the B^{rs} [Brothers, i.e. Methodists], against performing it. This may occasion some enlargement of the Preface . . . Last Friday Handel perform'd his Samson, a most exquisite Entertainment, which tho' I heard with infinite Pleasure, yet it increas'd my resentment for his neglect of the Messiah. You do him too much Honour to call him a Jew! a Jew would have paid more respect to the Prophets. The Name of Heathen will suit him better, yet a sensible Heathen would not have prefer'd the Nonsense foisted by one Hamilton into Milton's Samson Agonistes, to the sublime Sentiments & expressions of Isaiah & David, of the Apostles & Evangelists, & of Jesus Christ.

After hearing one of the London performances of *Messiah* at the end of March, Jennens extended his attack to include Handel's amanuensis Smith, a rare mention of this self-effacing man:

> . . . Messiah was perform'd last night, & will be again to morrow, notwithstanding the clamour rais'd against it, which has only occasion'd it's being advertis'd without its Name; a Farce which gives me as much offence as any thing relating to the performance can give the B^{rs} & other squeamish People. Tis after all, in the main, a fine Composition, notwithstanding some weak parts, which he was too idle & too obstinate to retouch, tho' I us'd great importunity to perswade him to it. He & his Toad-eater Smith did all they could to murder the Words in print; but I hope I have restor'd them to Life, not without difficulty.

Early in May Handel's health again gave way. 'Handel has had a palsy, and can't compose', wrote Walpole on 4 May; even Jennens retracted the severity of his censure: '. . . I hear Handel has a return of his Paralytick Disorder, which affects his Head & Speech. He talks of spending a year abroad, so that we are to expect no Musick next year; & since the Town has lost it's only Charm, I'll stay in the Country as long as ever I can'.

It was, luckily, a passing infirmity and by June Handel was planning his campaign for the next season. Still unsure of public reaction, he took notice of the success of Arne's setting of Congreve's masque *The Judgement of Paris* the previous year and now decided to follow the lead of the ever-popular *Acis and Galatea* with *The Story of Semele*, based on a libretto by Congreve which had been set by Eccles (but never performed) during the makeshift years before Italian opera had taken in London. Handel's work was neither opera nor oratorio, but the secular, erotic text was to be presented 'after the manner of an oratorio', in other words, on stage with a chorus and without action. This method of presentation had immediate effects on Congreve's libretto and Handel, probably with the assistance of Newburgh Hamilton, adjusted it accordingly: recitative was reduced, several aria texts were replaced and there were substantial interpolations for the chorus, which had hardly featured in Congreve's original.

Handel's composing speed had not slackened in the least because of his illness, and *Semele* was completed in four weeks. Restored to usual form, he would have gone on to prepare a second work for the new season had he not been anticipated by news of a major English victory near the village of Dettingen on the River Main, where the French armies had been routed by a combination of Hanoverian and English troops. The loss of two generals and some two thousand soldiers counted for little against the unexpected fact that George II had led his forces in person, trusting his own little legs, which he said 'he knew would not run away with him'. National rejoicing was declared, and Handel diverted his energies to setting the Te Deum and an anthem *The King shall rejoice* in his 'ceremonial manner' (and with heavy indebtedness to the Italian composer, Urio).

Jennens, hearing of Handel's return to health, went back on the attack:

> . . . I hear Handel is perfectly recover'd, & has compos'd a new Te Deum & a new Anthem against the return of his Master from Germany. I don't yet despair of making him retouch the Messiah, at least he shall suffer for his negligence; nay I am inform'd that he has suffr'd for he told Ld. Guernsey that a letter I wrote him about it contributed to the bringing of his last illness upon him; & it is reported that being a little delirious with a Fever, he said he should be damn'd for preferring Dagon (a Gentleman he was very complaisant to in the Oratorio of Samson) before the Messiah. This shews that I gall'd him: but I have not done with him yet . . .

But his friend Holdsworth found the renewed ferocity too much. From Florence on 28 October he wrote to Jennens in his country seat to remonstrate:

> . . . Pardon my speaking so freely of Leicestershire; but in truth I am angry with it. You have staid too long there already; it has had an ill effect upon you, and made you quarrel with your best friends, Virgil & Handel. You have contributed, by yr. own confession, to give poor Handel a fever, and now He is pretty well recover'd, you seem resolv'd to attack him again; for you say you have not yet done with him. This is really ungenerous, & not like Mr. Jennens. Pray be merciful; and don't you turn Samson, & use him like a Philistine . . .

33, 34 From 1732 Jonathan Tyers presented summer entertainment in Vauxhall Gardens, which he decked out with supper-boxes, a bandstand and shady walks. Handel's music was often heard there and at his own expense Tyers had a statue of the composer erected in 'a grand Nich' in the gardens (visible on the right of the picture). The monument (*right*), by Roubiliac, depicts Handel as Apollo but casually attired in nightcap and slippers.

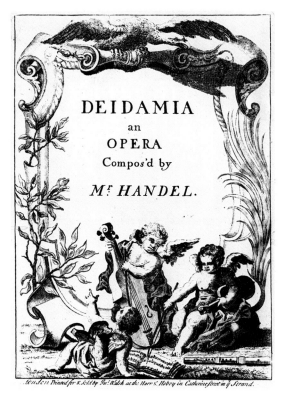

35, 36 Title-page of *Deidamia*, Handel's last opera, published by Walsh in 1741. It met a wall of indifference and hostility, and closed after three performances, Handel completing the season with revivals of oratorios including *Saul*. The indenture is for the hire of a pair of kettledrums from the Tower of London for a performance of *Saul* in 1739.

37 The beginning of 'I know that my Redeemer liveth', from *Messiah*, in Handel's autograph. The opening phrase is quoted on the composer's monument in Westminster Abbey.

38, 39 The bass recitative 'Thus saith the Lord' in Handel's autograph manuscript (*top*) and in Smith's fair copy – the earliest to be made. As the altered autograph shows, Handel subsequently revised and shortened the opening of this recitative into that familiar today.

M E S S I A H.

A N

O R A T O R I O.

Compos'd by Mr. *HANDEL*.

MAJORA CANAMUS.

*And without Controversy, great is the Mystery of Godliness :
God was manifested in the Flesh, justified by the Spirit,
seen of Angels, preached among the Gentiles, believed on in
the World, received up in Glory.
In whom are hid all the Treasures of Wisdom and Knowledge.*

DUBLIN: Printed by GEORGE FAULKNER, 1742.

(Price a British Six-pence.)

40, 41 An unexpected invitation from the Lord Lieutenant of Ireland to give concerts for the benefit of local charities earned Dublin the distinction of *Messiah*'s first performance. Among those taking part was Mrs Cibber. Also noted as a tragedienne, Susanna Maria Cibber was the sister of the composer Thomas Arne. *Right*, title-page of the word-book for *Messiah*.

The Old Music Hall in Fishamble St. Dublin, in which the first performance of the Messiah took place.

42 The newly opened Music Hall in Fishamble St, where the first performance took place.

T. MORELL, S.T.P - S.S.A.

43 John Christopher Smith the younger, Handel's pupil, amanuensis and friend.

44 The Rev. Thomas Morell was Handel's regular librettist from 1746, providing the words for such oratorios as *Judas Maccabaeus*, *Alexander Balus* and *Jephtha*.

SAMSON
Wed. March ye 11th

45 John Beard, one of the leading English tenors of the day, for whom Handel wrote parts in several oratorios. He succeeded Rich as manager of Covent Garden in 1761.

46 Decorative ticket for a revival of *Samson* at Covent Garden in 1752.

47–49 Handel's generous support for the Foundling Hospital resulted in an annual series of performances of *Messiah* there from 1750. *Left*, newspaper advertisement for a performance in 1758; *right*, Thomas Coram, the founder of the institution; *below*, the chapel where *Messiah* was given.

50 Portrait of Handel, English school, 18th century, after Hudson.

51 Cast of death mask by Roubiliac, now lost.

In the Name of god Amen.

I George Frideric Handel considering the Uncertainty of human Life doe make this my Will in manner following.
viz.

I give and bequeath unto my Servant Peter le Blond, my Clothes and Linnen, and three hundred Pounds sterl: and to my other servants a Year Wages.

I give and bequeath to Mr Christopher Smith my large Harpsicord, my Little House Organ, my Musick Books, and five hundred Pounds sterl:

Item I give and bequeath to Mr James Hunter

five hundred Pounds sterl:

52 First page of the private copy of Handel's will; the handwriting is his own. The bequest to John Christopher Smith (senior) includes the collection of autograph scores ('Musick Books') now in the British Library.

53 Handel's watch. The face is inscribed with the maker's name, Golling of Augsburg.

54 The Ruckers harpsichord (Antwerp, 1612) believed to be the instrument that Handel owned and bequeathed to Smith. It is now in Fenton House, London.

The analogy seems to have quieted Jennens for a few months, during which the London public were offered a somewhat mixed diet of Handel. *Roxana, or Alexander in India*, which the *Daily Advertiser* announced as 'compos'd by Mr Handel', opened at the Haymarket and ran, much to Lord Middlesex's delight, for twelve performances before the end of the year. This was a version of *Alessandro* which Handel himself may have offered to produce for the King's Theatre as compensation for his refusal to write a new opera for them.* The new house composer at the Haymarket, Lampugnani, probably made the arrangement. (Lampugnani's *Alessandro nell'Indie*, produced in 1746, is an entirely different work.) Whatever its origins, the compilation did not please a true Handelian, as Mrs Delany wrote on 18 November: 'I was at the opera of Alexander, which under the disguise it suffered, was infinitely better than any Italian opera; but it vexed me to hear some favourite songs mangled'.

The Dettingen Te Deum, on the other hand, she had pronounced to be 'excessively fine, I was all rapture and so was your friend D.D. [Dr Delany] as you may imagine; everybody says it is the finest of his compositions; I am not well enough acquainted with it to pronounce that of it, but it is heavenly'.

With the celebratory anthem out of the way, Handel was at liberty to produce a second novelty for the new season, the oratorio *Joseph and his Brethren*, to a libretto by the Reverend James Miller. This 'stage-struck cleric from Wadham College, Oxford', as Winton Dean describes him,† provided a book containing major faults of diction and structure; to what musical imagery could Handel be inspired by lines like 'Ah jealousy, thou pelican'? The story was complicated by the omission of vital features, and an almost deliberate avoidance of dramatic confrontation, and although Handel did his best with the music to overcome the shortcomings of his libretto, the plot could not be rescued from Miller's impenetrability – there was, alas, no sign of the author's 'gradual and artful Unravelling of his Subject, as well as the clear and full Explication of his Character' promised in the Dedication. An eighteenth-century audience was in one respect better served than a modern one, since for them many of the incomprehensibilities of an oratorio text would have been clarified by reference to the author's printed 'Advertisement', which appeared at the beginning of the word-book and gave a full synopsis – in the case of the libretto for *Joseph and his Brethren*, vital to an understanding of the plot and motivation.

The year 1744 began with a confident announcement in the *Daily Post*:

By *Particular* DESIRE,
Mr. HANDEL proposes to Perform, by *Subscription*, Twelve Times during next Lent, and engages to play two New Performances (and some of his former Oratorios, if Time will permit).

The venue was again Covent Garden, and the first of Handel's 'New

*For details of the offers made to Handel, see Smith's letter in Betty Matthews, 'Unpublished Letters'.
†*Dramatic Oratorios*, p. 398.

Performances' was *Semele*. In manuscript notes to his copy of Mainwaring's *Life*, Jennens caustically refers to *Semele* as 'No Oratorio, but a baudy Opera . . . An English Opera, but called *by fools* an Oratorio, and performed as such at Covent-Garden'. Taking her usual interest in Handel, Mrs Delany reported to her sister in a series of letters on the rehearsal, the first performance and subsequent productions of this and other oratorios Handel presented during the season.

24 January 1744

I was yesterday morning at Mr. Handel's to hear the rehearsal of Semele. It is a delightful piece of music, quite new and different from anything he has done . . . Francesina is improved, and sings the principal part in it.

11 February 1744

I was yesterday to hear Semele; it is a delightful piece of music. Mrs. Donnellan desires her particular compliments to all *but* to my brother; she bids me say 'she loses half her pleasure in Handel's music by *his not being here* to talk over the particular passages'. There is a four-part song that is delightfully pretty;* Francesina is extremely improved, her notes are more distinct, and there is something in her running-divisions that is quite surprizing. She was much applauded, and the house full, though not crowded; I believe I wrote my brother word that Mr. Handel and the Prince had quarelled, which I am sorry for. Handel says the *Prince* is quite out of *his* good graces! there was no disturbance at the play-house and the Goths were not so very absurd as to declare, in a public manner, their disapprobation of such a composer.

21 February 1744

Semele is charming; the more I hear it the better I like it, and as I am a subscriber I shall not fail one night. But it being a profane story D.D. [Dr Delany] does not think it proper for him to go; but when Joseph or Samson is performed I shall persuade him to go – you know *how much* he delights in music. They say Samson is to be next Friday, for Semele has a strong party against it, viz. the fine ladies, petit maîtres and *ignoramus*'s. All the opera people are enraged at Handel, but Lady Cobham, Lady Westmoreland, and Lady Chesterfield never fail it.

25 February 1744

I was last night to hear Samson. Francesina sings most of Mrs. Cibber's part and some of Mrs. Clive's: upon the whole it went off very well, but not better than last year. Joseph, I believe, will be next Friday, but Handel is mightily out of humour about it, for Sullivan, who is to sing Joseph, is *a block* with a very fine voice, and Beard has *no voice at all*. The part which Francescina is to have (of Joseph's wife) will not admit of much variety; but I hope it will be well received; the houses have not been crowded, but pretty full every night.

---

*'Why dost thou thus untimely grieve?' (Act I, Scene 1).

10 March 1744

The oratorios fill very well, not withstanding the spite of the opera party: nine of the twelve are over. Joseph is to be performed (I hope) once more, then Saul and the Messiah finishes; as they have taken very well, I fancy Handel will have a second subscription; and how do you think *I have lately been employed*? Why, I have made a drama for an oratorio, out of Milton's Paradise Lost, to give Mr. Handel to compose to; it has cost me a great deal of thought and contrivance; D.D. approves of my performance, and that gives me some reason to think it not bad, though all I have had to do has been collecting and making the connection between the fine parts. I begin with Satan's threatenings to seduce the woman, her being seduced follows, and it ends with the man's yielding to the temptation; I would not have a word or a thought of Milton's altered; and I hope to prevail with Handel to set it without having *any of the lines put into verse*, for that will take from its dignity. This, and painting three pictures, have been my chief morning employment since I came to town.

Like the Bishop of Elphin's libretto, this one was never set by Handel, but it has been suggested (by E. J. Dent) that the text may be related to that later given to Haydn for *The Creation*.*

The season did not contain everything that Mrs Delany wanted, as she lamented on 22 March – 'Last night alas! was the last night of the oratorio: it concluded with Saul: I was in hopes of the Messiah . . .' – but on 3 April we catch a glimpse of her delight as Handel relaxed after twelve performances in just over five weeks: 'To-day I shall have a treat that I shall most ardently wish you and my mother your share of. Handel, my brother, and Donnellan *dine here*, and we are to be entertained with *Handel's playing over Joseph to us*'. This first-hand evidence of Handel playing arrangements, rather than original compositions on the keyboard is complemented by Walsh's continued publication of sets of overtures in transcription, the latest having appeared in December, with *Messiah* still cautiously described as 'A Sacred Oratorio'.

Although nothing had caught the public imagination as *Samson* had the previous year – even *Semele* only had four performances – Handel was able to invest £1300 in annuities after paying his cast. At the Haymarket, the opera season had been unsuccessful, and 'on account of the [Jacobite] rebellion, and popular prejudice against the performers, who being foreigners, were chiefly Roman Catholics' the managers decided not to reopen that winter. Lord Middlesex's passion for opera had not diminished, however: in fact he had taken the precaution of marrying an heiress, Grace Boyle: 'She proves an immense fortune, they pretend a hundred and thirty thousand pounds – what a fund for making operas!' exclaimed Walpole.

Handel saw his chance, booked the Haymarket Theatre for the next season, and laid plans for another intense summer bout of composition. The follow-up

---

*The idea is an ingenious though slightly involved one, and the clearest account of the story appears in H. C. Robbins Landon, *Haydn: the Years of 'The Creation'*, pp. 118–19.

to *Semele* was to be *Hercules*, a secular 'Musical Drama'. His librettist, the Reverend Thomas Broughton, was a great improvement on his clerical colleague of the previous year. By mixing characterization from Sophocles, Ovid and his own imagination, Broughton fashioned a text of personal jealousies and formidably balanced tensions. Handel himself confused the structure by expanding the part of Lichas for Mrs Cibber, but completed within a month what Paul Henry Lang has described as 'the highest peak of late baroque music drama'.

For a sacred complement to this classical drama, Handel turned again to his collaborator and antagonist of the previous year, Charles Jennens. Whether there had been an open dispute between Handel and Jennens is uncertain, since no letters between the two have survived for this period, but if so they obviously met and were reconciled during the summer. Handel was soon elaborating his scheme for an unusually lavish season to take the place of the opera. On 9 June he wrote to Jennens:

It gave me great Pleasure to hear Your safe arrival in the Country, and that Your Health was much improuved. I hope it is by this time firmly established, and I wish You with all my Heart the Continuation of it, and all the Prosperity. As You do me the Honour to encourage my Musical undertakings, and even to promote them with a particular kindness, I take the Liberty to trouble you with an account of what Engagements I have hitherto concluded. I have taken the Opera House in the Haymarketh. engaged, as Singers, Sig^ra Francesina, Mr. Robinson, Beard, Reinhold, Mr. Gates with his Boyes's and several of the best Chorus Singers from the choirs, and I have some hopes that Mrs. Cibber will sing for me. She sent word from Bath (where she is now) that she would perform for me next Winter with great pleasure if it did not interfere with her playing, but I think I can obtain Mr. Riches's permission (with whom she is engaged to play in Covent Garden House) since so obligingly he gave Leave to Mr. Beard and Mr. Reinhold. Now should I be extreamly glad to receive the first Act, or what is ready, of the new Oratorio with which you intend to favour me, that I might employ all my attention and time, in order to answer in some measure the great Obligation I lay under. this new favour will great increase my Obligations.

The 'New Oratorio' was *Belshazzar*, and Handel's enthusiasm for the project continues in a rare sequence of letters from this summer. Immediately on his return from a country trip, and on the very day he started work on *Hercules* (19 July), he wrote anxiously about the length of the piece (and humbly about *Messiah*):

At my arrival in London, which was yesterday, I immediately perused the Act of the Oratorio with which you favour'd me, and, the little time only I had it, gives me great Pleasure. Your reasons for the Lenght of the first act are intirely Satisfactory to me, and it is likewise my Opinion to have the following Acts short. I shall be very glad and much obliged to you, if you will soon favour me with the remaining Acts. Be pleased to point out these passages in te Messiah which You think require altering . . .

A month later (21 August), having just completed *Hercules*, he wrote again, pressing for more material:

The Second Act of the Oratorio I have received Safe, and own my self highly obliged to You for it. I am greatly pleased with it, and shall use my best endeavours to do it Justice. I can only Say that I impatiently wait for the third Act . . .

So high was his excitement that he began work on *Belshazzar* before the words for Act III arrived, and in three weeks almost ran out of text. His next letter (13 September) anxiously requests the remaining act, and clearly reveals the composer's concern for overall planning, his delight in 'particular Ideas' (i.e. specific imagery) and the opportunity for employing the chorus effectively – and above all, at the age of nearly sixty, his infectious enthusiasm:

Your most excellent Oratorio has given me great Delight in setting it to Musick and still engages me warmly. It is indeed a Noble Piece, very grand and uncommon, it has furnished me with Expressions, and has given me Opportunity to some very particular Ideas, besides so many great Chorus. I intreat you heartily to favour me soon with the last Act, which I expect with anxiety, that I may regulate my Self the better as to the Lenght of it. I profess my Self highly obliged to you, for so generous a Present . . .

When Act III eventually arrived, Handel was faced with one of Jennens's faults: verbosity. Knowing that the librettist would be mortified if too many of his words remained unset, he proposed a drastic tightening up of the ceremonial choruses:

I received the 3ᵈ Act, with a great deal of pleasure, as you can imagine, and you may believe that I think it a very fine and sublime Oratorio, only it is realy too long, if I should extend the Musick, it would last 4 Hours and more. I retrench'd already a great deal of the Musick, that I might preserve the Poetry as much as I could, yet still it may be shortned. The Anthems come in very proprely, but would not the Words (tell it out among the Heathen that the Lord is King.) [be] sufficient for one Chorus? Te Anthem (I will magnify thee O God my King, and I will praise thy name for ever and ever, vers). the Lord preserveth all them that love him, but scattreth abroad all the ungodly. (vers and Chorus) my mouth shall speak the Praise of the Lord and let all flesh give thanks unto His holy name for ever and ever Amen) concludes well the Oratorio. I hope you will make a Visit to London next Winter. I have a good

197

Set of Singers. Sr Francesina performs Nitocris, Miss Robinson, Cyrus, Mrs. Cibber. Daniel, Mr Beard (who is recoverd) Belshazzar, Mr Reinhold, Gobrias, and a good Number of Choir Singers for the Chorus's. I propose 24 Nights to perform this Season on [Sa]turdays but in Lent on Wednesday's or fryday's. I shall open Ye 3^d of Novemb^r next with [Debo]rah.

Jennens's text would not in any case have been lost to his public, since it was normal to print the complete text in word-books and simply mark the cut passages with inverted commas.

Against the enthusiasm and reasonableness of Handel's requests can be set the casual arrogance which Jennens reveals in a letter to Holdsworth written on 26 September, shortly after the words of Act III were completed:

I have been prevaild with once more to expose my self to the Criticks, to oblige the Man who made me but a Scurvy return for former obligations; the truth is, I had a farther view in it; but if he does not mend his manners I am resolv'd to have no more to do with him. But the reason of my mentioning this was to excuse my delay of answering your letter dated almost 4 months ago. For my Muse is such a Jade, & Handel hurry'd her so, that I could not find time for writing letters. Our Operas are at an end, & He has taken the Opera House to perform Oratorios in this next Season. In your Letter of May 16 you suppose him in Ireland, where indeed he met with encouragement, but has had so much better since in England, that I believe he has had no inclination yet to go into Ireland again.

But his libretto was skilfully assembled, gaps in characterization (that of Nitocris, for example) ingeniously filled, the turning points of the story approached and relinquished with true dramatic skill. Both word-book and score contain 'stage directions', even though neither author nor composer was anticipating a stage production with action; such explanations were as great a help to the audience in appreciating the drama as to the composer in creating it.

Evidently full of exuberance after perhaps the greatest and most concentrated period of creation of his whole career, Handel decided to risk a season of twenty-four performances on subscription, and as the *Daily Advertiser* announced, 'engages to exhibit two new Performances, and several of his former Oratorios. The first Performance will be on Saturday the 3d of November, and continue every Saturday until Lent, and then on Wednesdays and Fridays'. It was a gruelling and, one might reasonably say, a foolhardy, proposition Intoxicated with the drama of *Hercules* and *Belshazzar*, Handel imprudently ignored the considerable opposition that still existed to him and his new ventures. The 'spite of the opera party' continued, although (perhaps because) he was occupying their territory; the 'fine ladies, petit maîtres and *ignoramus*'s' who had been a strong party against *Semele* protested as much at *Hercules*; the 'little Vermin, who . . . pull down even his Bills as fast as he has them pasted up' were still rampant; and the ladies of high society (led, so Burney tells us, by Lady Margaret Cecil Brown, granddaughter of the 3rd Earl of

Salisbury and wife of Sir Robert Brown, Paymaster of His Majesty's Works) organized a vicious boycott of the composer, mounting balls and card parties to clash with his performances.

The season was unfortunate from the start. *Deborah* opened on 3 November, but two days later the *Daily Advertiser* reported that 'as the greatest Part of Mr. Handel's Subscribers are not in Town, he is requested not to perform till Saturday the 24th Instant'. Obviously the house had been thin. After one more performance of *Deborah*, *Semele* was given twice, with 'additions and alterations', the additions including five Italian arias from *Alcina, Arminio* and *Giustino*.

There was a break in performances until 5 January, when *Hercules* first appeared. Mrs Cibber was indisposed for this first performance, but although perfectly recovered by the following Saturday, she was not enough to draw a sufficient house. Handel decided to abandon his series and wrote a dignified and eloquent letter to the *Daily Advertiser* which appeared on 17 January 1745.

> Sir.
> Having for a Series of Years received the greatest Obligations from the Nobility and Gentry of this Nation, I have always retained a deep Impression of their Goodness. As I perceived, that joining good Sense and significant Words to Musick, was the best Method of recommending *this* to an English Audience; I have directed my Studies that way, and endeavour'd to shew, that the English Language, which is so expressive of the sublimest Sentiments is the best adapted of any to the full and solemn Kind of Musick. I have the Mortification now to find, that my Labours to please are become ineffectual, when my Expences are considerably greater. To what Cause I must impute the loss of the publick Favour I am ignorant, but the Loss itself I shall always lament. In the mean time, I am assur'd that a Nation, whose Characteristick is Good Nature, would be affected with the Ruin of any Man, which was owing to his Endeavours to entertain them. I am likewise persuaded, that I shall have the Forgiveness of those noble Persons, who have honour'd me with their Patronage, and their Subscription this Winter, if I beg their Permission to stop short, before my Losses are too great to support, if I proceed no father in my Undertaking; and if I intreat them to withdraw three Fourths of their Subscription, one Fourth Part only of my Proposal having been perform'd.

The result was an immediate rallying of the subscribers, who replied the next day:

> Upon Reading Mr. Handel's Letter in your Paper this Morning I was sensibly touch'd with that great Master's Misfortunes, failing in his Endeavours to entertain the Publick; whose Neglect in not attending his admirable Performances can no otherwise be made up with Justice to the Character of the Nation, and the Merit of the Man, than by the Subscribers generously declining to withdraw the Remainder of their Subscriptions.

199

I would lament the Loss of the Publick in Mr. Handel, in Strains equal to his if I was able, but our Concern will be best express'd by our Generosity.

Notwithstanding the personal risk to his finances which a continuation of the season put him to, Handel relented and in a further letter to the *Daily Advertiser* said:

The new Proofs which I have receiv'd of the Generosity of my Subscribers, in refusing upon their own Motives, to withdraw their Subscriptions call upon me for the earliest Return, and the warmest Expressions of my Gratitude; but natural as it is to feel, proper as it is to have, I find this extremely difficult to express. Indeed, I ought not to content myself with bare expressions of it; therefore, though I am not able to fulfil the whole of my Engagement, I shall think it my Duty to perform what Part of it I can, and shall in some Time proceed with the Oratorios, let the *Risque* which I may run be what it will.

Jennens, who in spite of his acerbity was a first-rank 'Handelian', shows himself characteristically less sympathetic than the body of subscribers in his account of Handel's mismanagement to Holdsworth:*

. . . Handel has had worse success than ever he had before, being forc'd to disist after performing but 6 of the 24 Entertainments he had contracted for, & to advertise that the Subscribers might have 3 4ths of their money return'd. Most of them refus'd to take back their Money, upon which he resolv'd to begin again in Lent. His ill success is laid chiefly to the charge of the Ladies [   ] than a certain Anglo-Venetian Lady [   ] you may have been acquainted [   ] former Expeditions. But I believe it is in some measure owing to his own imprudence in changing the profitable method he was in before for a new & hazardous Experiment. For the two last years he had perform'd Oratorios in Covent-Garden Playhouse on Wednesdays & Fridays in Lent only, when there was no publick Entertainment of any consequence to interfere with him: & his gains were considerable, 2100 ll. one year, & 1600 ll the other, for only 12 performances. Flush'd with this success, the Italian Opera being drop'd, he takes the Opera-house in the Haymarket for this Season at the rent of 400 ll, buys him a new organ, & instead of an Oratorio produces an English Opera call'd Hercules, which he performs on Saturdays during the run of Plays, Concerts, Assemblys, Drums, Routs, Hurricanes,† & all the madness of Town Diversions. His

---

*Square brackets indicate missing words where the letter is torn.
†In a footnote to his poem *Advice*, Smollett defines some of these less familiar entertainments: '. . . a riotous assembly of fashionable people of both sexes, at a private house consisting of some hundreds, not inaptly styled a *drum*, from the noise and emptiness of the entertainment. There were also drum-major, rout, tempest and hurricane; differing only in degrees of multitude and uproar, as the significant name of each declares'.

Opera, for want of the top Italian voices, Action, Dresses, Scenes & Dances, which us'd to draw company, & prevent the Undertakers losing above 3 or 4 thousand pounds, had scarce half a house the first night, much less than half the second; & he has been quiet ever since.

The subscription series was eventually revived with *Samson* on 1 March. A note in the *Daily Advertiser* that 'Proper Care will be taken to keep the House warm' indicates that the English weather was assisting Lady Brown in her attempts to sabotage it. *Saul* and *Joseph* were also announced, and at Drury Lane the Arnes courteously avoided a clash, declaring on their own advertisements that 'This Day is fix'd on to avoid interfering with Mr. Handel'.

At its premiere *Belshazzar*, which should have equalled the success of *Samson*, suffered the ignominy of being applauded by only a small handful of supporters. Mrs Cibber was still indisposed, and the singers had to change roles at the last minute. On 2 April Elizabeth Carter wrote sadly to Catherine Talbot:

Handel, once so crowded, plays to empty walls in that opera house, where there used to be a constant *audience* as long as there were any dancers to be *seen*. Unfashionable that I am, I was I own highly delighted the other night at his last oratorio. 'Tis called Belshazzar, the story the taking of Babylon by Cyrus; and the music, in spite of all that very bad performers could do to spoil it, equal to any thing I ever heard. There is a chorus of Babylonians deriding Cyrus from their walls that has the best expression of scornful laughter imaginable. Another of the Jews, where the name, Jehovah, is introduced first with a moment's silence, and then with a full swell of music so solemn, that I think it is the most striking lesson against common genteel swearing I ever met with.

When Frasi told him, that she should study hard, and was going to learn Thorough-Base, in order to accompany herself: HANDEL, *who well knew how little this pleasing singer was addicted to application and diligence, says,* 'Oh – vaat may we not expect!' (Charles Burney, 1785)

This dramatic masterpiece ran for three performances; 'A Sacred Oratorio', which had not been given for more than a year, ran for two. For this season Handel made two alterations in *Messiah*: 'Rejoice greatly' was reworked in its more brilliant 4/4 form, and the arioso setting of 'Their sound is gone out' was replaced by the choral version. The first change was surely for the sake of Signora Frasi's agile gullet; the second might conceivably have been suggested by Jennens, who in a letter to Holdsworth later in the year claims partial success for his criticisms:

I shall show you a collection I gave Handel, call'd Messiah, which I value highly, & he has made a fine Entertainment of it, tho' not near so good as he might & ought to have done. I have with great difficulty made him correct some of the grossest faults in the composition, but he retain'd his Overture obstinately, in which there are some passages far unworthy of Handel, but much more unworthy of the Messiah . . .*

At this point, two-thirds of the way through his proposed season, Handel called a halt. Sixteen of the promised twenty-four concerts had been given, and although Handel was certainly not bankrupt (nor ever was, contrary to legend), he could have been severely compromised had he tried to continue, or had the subscribers insisted on their money back. Yet again he had misjudged his public; they simply did not want oratorio, although they were happy to support his music in several other concerts for the remainder of the season. Mrs Robinson offered items from *Alcina* in her benefit, and Miss Davis, 'a Child of eight Years of Age', performed at Hickford's Room in a concert that included 'several favourite organ concertos . . . with two remarkable Songs, Composed by Mr. Handel, entirely for the Harpsichord' (*Daily Advertiser*, 10 May). On 13 May Handel paid £150 to Jordan, the organ builder, presumably for the instrument mentioned by Jennens; Jordan's later advertisement (1 August), offering 'Two second-hand Chamber Organs . . . to be Sold a Pennyworth', surely implies that he was disposing of the redundant instruments that had seen such good service at Covent Garden. The traditional interpretation that Handel was unable to keep up the payments has no basis.

> About this time a bon mot of lord Chesterfield's was handed about by a nobleman, still living, who going one night to the Oratorio at Covent-Garden, met his lordship coming out of the theatre. 'What! my lord, are you dismissed? Is there no Oratorio to-night?' 'Yes, says his lordship, they are now performing; but I thought it best to retire, less I should disturb the king in his privacies.' (Charles Burney, 1785)

Not only had Handel misjudged and overspent, he had again overtaxed his health, and withdrew to the country to recuperate. In June he can be traced to Exton Hall in Leicestershire, the home of the Earl of Gainsborough, where he was drawn into 'family theatricals'. There was a proposal for an open-air performance of Milton's masque *Comus*, in which the Earl and his two daughters could take part; Handel was prevailed upon to add 'three songs . . . with the Chorus at the end of each' to supplement extracts taken from *L'Allegro* and *Alcina*; Arne's score was not used. This music, long thought lost, was rediscovered by Anthony Hicks in 1969, and shows a tactful regard on Handel's part for the Earl's limited abilities. From Leicestershire Handel moved on to Scarborough, but there was no more composing. Indeed, the attention of the

---

*His criticisms are not altogether without basis: the overture does contain some particularly scanty bars (32–36 for instance).

whole country had been turned from the arts to the sudden threat of invasion. from the north.

While George II was away in Hanover, Charles Edward the Young Pretender landed in Scotland and moved southwards. The English army was hastily recalled from Flanders to meet Bonnie Prince Charlie, London took to arms and Handel wrote 'A Chorus Song . . . for the *Gentlemen Volunteers* of the City of London'. As the Duke of Cumberland pressed northwards to earn his nickname of 'Butcher', he was supported musically from London with a patriotic musical drama, *La Caduta de' Giganti*, written by the young Gluck, who was resident composer at the revived Haymarket Theatre for that troubled season. Burney saw the piece and found the heroic manner overdone: 'Pompeati, though nominally second woman, had such a masculine and violent manner of singing, that few female symptoms were perceptible', and Handel is supposed to have commiserated with Gluck on the small success of his piece: 'what the English like is something they can beat time to, something that hits them straight on the drum of the ear'. Gluck later told Burney 'that he owed entirely to England the study of nature in his dramatic compositions', a debt which certainly would have included a perusal of Handel's works.

> *When Gluck came first into England, in 1745, he was neither so great a composer, nor so high in reputation, as he afterwards mounted; and I remember when Mrs. Cibber, in my hearing, asked HANDEL what sort of a composer he was; his answer, prefaced by an oath – was, 'he knows no more of contrapunto, as mein cook, Waltz.'* (Charles Burney, 1785)

Handel's health was still disordered: the Reverend William Harris (brother of Handel's Salisbury friend) had reported on 29 August: 'I met Handel a few days since in the street, and stopped and put him in mind who I was, upon which I am sure it would have diverted you to have seen his antic motions. He seemed highly pleased, and was full of inquiry after you . . . I told him I was very confident that you expected a visit from him this summer. He talked much of his precarious state of health, yet he looks well enough. I believe you will have him with you ere long'. At the end of October, the Earl of Shaftesbury wrote to his cousin that 'Poor Handel looks something better. I hope he will entirely recover in due time, though he has been a good deal disordered in his head'.

In this condition, it is not surprising that for his patriotic contribution to the emergency, an *Occasional Oratorio*, Handel had recourse to large-scale borrowing. But even the 'propaganda' style shows his usual sense of dramatic

Two folios from the Occasional Oratorio (performed 1746) exemplifying an interesting aspect of Handel's borrowing. The four-bar insertion marked 'No. 2' replacing the two deleted bars is not a reworking of borrowed material but a direct transplant of music from Telemann's Musique de table.

pace and his instinctive use of musical strength to overcome verbal weaknesses. Material from *Athalia*, *Israel in Egypt* and the Opus 6 concerti, as well as the *Comus* songs and passages from Telemann and Stradella can be identified in the oratorio; the vitality of the piece springs from their polishing and placing in the whole. On 8 February the Rev. William Morris wrote to Mrs Thomas Harris:

> Yesterday morning I was at Handel's house to hear the rehearsal of his new occasional Oratorio. It is extremely worthy of him, which you will allow to be saying all one can in praise of it. He has but three voices for his songs – Francesina, Reinholt, and Beard; his band of music is not very extraordinary – Du Feche is his first fiddle, and for the rest I really could not find out who they were, and I doubt his failure will be in this article. The words of his Oratorio are scriptural, but taken from various parts, and are expressive of the rebels' flight and our pursuit of them. Had not the Duke carried his point triumphantly, this Oratorio could not have been brought on. It is to be performed in public next Friday [14 February].

Writing to Holdsworth on 3 February, Jennens was critical of the whole conception:

> . . . The Oratorio, as you call it, contrary to custom, raised no inclination in me to hear it. I am weary of nonsense and impertinence; & by the Account Ld. Guernsey gives me of this Piece I am to expect nothing else. Tis a triumph for a Victory not yet gain'd, & if the Duke does not make hast, it may not be gain'd at the time of performance. 'Tis an inconceivable jumble of Milton & Spencer, a Chaos extracted from Order by the most absurd of all Blockheads, who like the Devil takes delight in defacing the Beauties of Creation. The difference is, that one does it from malice, the other from pure Stupidity . . .

Newburgh Hamilton, Handel's librettist, is again the victim of Jennens's scorn in a second letter to Holdsworth (3 March); nor is even Milton or Spenser acquitted of blame:

> . . . You are mistaken as to the Occasional Oratorio, which is most of it transcrib'd from Milton & Spenser, but chiefly from Milton, who in his Version of some of the Psalms wrote so like Sternhold & Hopkins that there is not a pin to choose betwixt 'em. But there are people in the world who fancy every thing excellent which has Milton's name to it. I believe Hamilton has done little more than tack the passages together, which he has done with his usual judgement & cook'd up an Oratorio of Shreds & patches. There is perhaps but one piece of Nonsense in all Spenser's Works, & that Hamilton has pick'd out for his Oratorio:
>
>> O who shall pour into my Swollen Eyes
>> A Sea of Tears – a brazen Voice –

And iron sides? or *An iron Frame* as Hamilton has it. I thought he had left out Something necessary to the connection, having observ'd some instances of the same kind in his Samson; but to my great surprize I found it as I give it to you in Spenser's Tears of the Muses . . .

Having struggled as far south as Derby, the Jacobite forces were now driven northwards again. But the rebellion was by no means quelled, and Handel waited until victory was announced in April before starting on the second of what came to be a quartet of oratorios with heavily militaristic overtones: *The Occasional Oratorio, Judas Maccabaeus, Joshua* and *Alexander Balus.*

In retrospect, Handel's career seems to contain a series of crossroads which the composer himself blithely ignored. Stubborn optimism and a reluctance to be proved wrong so often prevented him taking the proffered turning; a psychology that required challenge, that found its greatest power in retaliation, that even in musical terms required a 'borrowed' catalyst against which to react, meant that he produced his greatest works against a background of mishandled finances, misjudged public taste and missed opportunities. One can speculate on previous moments of despair, quickly brushed aside, and periods of indecision exorcised by activity; after three-score years, however, there are signs of healthy opportunism slipping into a slightly weary pragmatism. With growing evidence around him that no one ever lost a fortune by underestimating public taste, Handel seems to have been prepared to meet the public and the politicians in his music, while withdrawing from them in his person. Burney, who played in Handel's orchestra when he first arrived in London in 1745, says that although he had formerly been seen 'at the Playhouses, the Opera, and at St Martin's church, when the late Mr. Kelway played the organ . . . in his latter years, except when he went to pay his duty to the royal family at St James's, or Leicester-House, he seldom visited the great, or was visible, but at church, and the performance of his own Oratorios'.

HANDEL *wore an enormous white wig, and, when things went well at the Oratorio, it had a certain nod, or vibration, which manifested his pleasure and satisfaction. Without it, nice observers were certain that he was out of humour.* (Charles Burney, 1785)

Concerning the bagwigs of composers. Handel's was not a bagwig, which was simply so named from the little stuffed black silk watch-pocket that hung down behind the back of the wearer. Such were Haydn's and Mozart's — much less influential on the character: much less ostentatious in themselves: not towering so high, nor rolling down in following curls so low as to overlay the nature of the brain within. But Handel wore the Sir Godfrey Kneller wig: greatest of wigs: one of which some great General of the day used to take off his head after the fatigue of the battle, and hand over to his valet to have the bullets combed out of it. Such a wig was a fugue in itself. (Edward Fitzgerald, 1845)

The composition of *Judas Maccabaeus* began when Handel was sure there was a victory to celebrate; after the battle of Culloden in April 1746, he hurried into action with a new librettist, the cheerful and sympathetic Reverend Thomas Morell.* Morell's account of his collaboration with Handel (in a letter written around 1764) shows the great man as energetic and peremptory as ever: 44

> And now as to Oratorio's: – 'There was a time (says Mr Addison), when it was laid down as a maxim, that nothing was capable of being well set to musick, that was not nonsense.' And this I think, though it might be wrote before Oratorio's were in fashion, supplies an Oratorio-writer (if he may be called a writer) with some sort of apology; especially if it be considered, what alterations he must submit to, if the Composer be of an haughty disposition, and has but an imperfect acquaintance with the English language. As to myself, great a lover as I am of music, I should never have thought of such an undertaking (in which for the reasons above, little or no credit is to be gained), had not Mr Handell applied to me, when at Kew, in 1746 [*recte* 1745], and added to his request the honour of a recommendation from Prince Frederic. Upon this I thought I could do as well as some that had gone before me, and within 2 or 3 days carried him the first Act of *Judas Maccabaeus*, which he approved of. 'Well,' says he, 'and how are you to go on?' 'Why, we are to suppose an engagement, and that the Israelites have conquered, and so begin with a chorus as
>
> Fallen is the Foe
>
> or, something like it.' 'No, I will have this', and began working it, as it is, upon the Harpsichord. 'Well, go on', 'I will bring you more tomorrow.' 'No, something now',
>
> 'So fall thy Foes, O Lord'
>
> 'that will do', and immediately carried on the composition as we have it in that most admirable chorus.
>
> That incomparable Air, *Wise men flattering, may deceive us* (which was the last he composed, as *Sion now his head shall raise*, was his last chorus) was designed for *Belshazzar* but that not being perform'd he happily flung it into *Judas Maccabaeus*. N.B. The plan of *Judas Maccabaeus* was designed as a compliment to the Duke of Cumberland, upon his returning victorious from Scotland. I had introduced several incidents more apropos, but it was thought they would make it too long and were therefore omitted . . . The success of this Oratorio was very great. And I have often wished, that at first I had ask'd in jest, for the benefit of the 30th Night instead of a 3d. I am sure he would have given it me: on which night the[re] was above 400 *l*. in the House.

In his rush to get the piece set, Handel occasionally came to grief through his 'imperfect acquaintance with the English language': 'How vain is man' is set to

---

*Morell may indeed have been responsible for the text of the *Occasional Oratorio* since in the score of *Judas* he adds a footnote: 'The following Air "O Liberty, thou choicest treasure" was designed, and wrote for this Place, but it got I know not how, into the *Occasional Oratorio*, and was there incomparably Set, and as finely executed'.

an extrovert theme appropriate to 'conceited' but not to Morell's intended 'ineffectual', and the Chaucerian turn of 'Ashtoreth, yclep'd the Queen of Heav'n' stumped him completely even though he had met the word previously in *L'Allegro*. Perhaps it was Morell's handwriting which defeated him: he eventually wrote 'eclips'd'. Amongst the best music in the piece are the non-triumphal opening of Act I – the mourning of Israel, with lachrymose bassoons – and the air 'Pious orgies' which derives from a cunningly orchestrated funeral march for Mattathias, with recorders (instruments traditionally symbolic of death and the supernatural), drums and *pizzicato* strings. The famous number 'See, the conqu'ring Hero comes' was originally written for *Joshua*, from where it was transferred to *Judas* only at later performances. The march following it is taken from Muffat's *Componimenti*.

Both styles, warlike and sombre, were appreciated in a curious comparison by Catherine Talbot, who wrote to Mrs Carter on 18 April 1747: 'Those oratorios of Handel's are certainly (next to the *hooting of owls*) the most solemnly striking music one can hear. I am sure you must be fond of them, even I am who have no ear for music, and no skill in it. In this last oratorio he has literally introduced guns, and they have a good effect'. The 'guns' were probably 'great kettledrums' borrowed from the Royal Artillery.

For this 'victory oratorio season' Handel abandoned the subscription system and depended wholly on a walk-in public. *Judas* was doubly successful; not only did he hit the right mood of insistent rejoicing, but he offered a hero whom the Jewish population of London could also recognize as their own. Covent Garden's takings marked their response.

For his next text Handel again turned to Morell, who supplied a sequel, *Alexander Balus*, and another revealing anecdote:

In the first part there is a very pleasing Air, accompanied with the harp, *Hark, Hark he strikes the Golden Lyre*. In the 2d, two charming duets, O *what pleasure past expressing*, and *Hail, wedded Love, mysterious Law*. The 3d begins with an incomparable Air, in the affettuoso style, intermixed with the chorus Recitative that follows it. And as to the last Air, I cannot help telling you that, when Mr Handell first read it, he cried out 'D—n your Iambics'. 'Dont put yourself in a passion, they are easily Trochees.' *'Trochees, what are Trochees?'* 'Why, the very reverse of Iambics, by leaving out a syllable in every line, as instead of

> Convey me to some peaceful shore,
> Lead me to some peaceful shore.'

'That is what I want.' 'I will step into the parlour, and alter them immediately.' I went down and returned with them altered in about 3 minutes; when he would have them as they were, and set them most delightfully accompanied with only a quaver, and a rest of 3 quavers.

Morell's preference for iambics is corroborated by the writer John Lockman, who investigated the type of verse required by contemporary English composers for his 'Enquiry into the Rise and Progress of Operas and Oratorios' (printed as a preface to *Rosalinda*, an opera he produced with J. C. Smith in 1740) and found that 'smooth Verses of six or eight Syllables that run in Iambicks' were preferred.

Another of Lockman's findings was that in general 'the Flame of Poetry' should be avoided. For Morell this was not difficult – the level of inspiration in *Alexander Balus* left even Handel at a loss for strategy. But the piece is strong in local colour – the pagan East rather than the Hebraic scene – and the addition of harp, mandoline and flutes brings to mind a similarly evocative Asiatic scoring in *Giulio Cesare* written twenty-three years previously. The similarity to *opera seria* does not end there; Cleopatra's 'garden' aria in Act III is rudely interrupted by the entry of 'Ruffians' sent from Ptolomey, and Handel writes a vocal line which trails off to nothing to depict her being dragged away. (There is no evidence to suppose that Handel intended action to support this musically vivid scene, any more than Bach did in Cantata 106 when he used a similar device.) There are fewer choruses in *Alexander* than in any other of his English oratorios, and a love plot which rivals but hardly assists the religious protestations of the piece. Nowhere is it clearer how the idea of dramatic oratorio has become inseparably tied up with genuine choral involvement and contribution. As a contrast to *Judas*, Handel makes the most of a tragic ending, preferring to Morell's offer of jubilation the picture of Cleopatra 'forgetting and forgot', and a chorus that remains sombrely in the minor throughout.

> *I heard him [Morell] say that one fine summer morning he was roused out of bed at five o'clock by Handel, who came in his carriage a short distance from London. The doctor went to the window and spoke to Handel, who would not leave his carriage. Handel was at the time composing an oratorio. When the doctor asked him what he wanted, he said, 'What de devil means de vord billow?' which was in the oratorio the doctor had written for him. The doctor, after laughing at so ludicrous a reason for disturbing him, told him that billow meant wave, a wave of the sea. 'Oh, de vave,' said Handel, and bade his coachman return, without addressing another word to the doctor.* (John Taylor, 1832)

Joshua, Handel's next text from Morell, returns to the successful recipe of *Judas Maccabaeus*: a Jewish hero, more triumphing choruses and, as leaven to the rejoicings, a sub-plot with romantic tendencies which provides the foil for the battling Israelites that *Judas* lacked. As with the earlier collaborations, we may suspect that Handel wrote faster than Morell could supply him with text, and the result is a series of incidents rather than a developed plot. Joshua is a commanding hero, who stops the sun in its tracks – the violins, oboes and trumpet between them holding a high A for twenty-three bars – and Caleb a patriarchal bass; around the four distinctive and convincing characters is woven a sequence of picturesque choruses. A sure sign of Handel's financial security is the lavish orchestration that he was able to afford. In *Joshua* there are horns, flutes and side-drum (for the conquering hero), marked by Handel 'Drum ad libitum the second time drum warbling', in addition to the normal full orchestra with trumpets and timpani.

Before either of these rousing pieces was heard, the King's Theatre, still managed by the irrepressible Lord Middlesex and sustained by his wife's fortune, began its season with a compliment to Handel. It was an act of homage that would have been unthinkable ten years earlier; the rehearsal was reported in the *Daily Advertiser* in terms worthy of Sheridan's Critic himself:

> . . . the Opera of LUCIUS VERUS: This Drama Consists of Airs, borrow'd entirely from Mr. Handel's favourite Operas: and so may (probably) be justly styl'd the most exquisite Composition of Harmony, ever offer'd to the Publick. The lovers of Musick among us, whose Ears have been charm'd with Farinello, Faustina, Senesino, Cuzzoni, and other great Performers will now have an Opportunity of Reviving their former Delight; which, if not so transporting as then, may yet prove a very high Entertainment. Mr. Handel is acknowledged (universally) so great a Master of the Lyre; that nothing urg'd in Favour of his Capital Performances, can reasonably be considered as a Puff.

Although Handel seems to have had no hand in this *pasticcio*, his relations with the Opera were obviously more cordial. Burney found 'the richness of the harmony and ingenuity of the contrivance of several songs . . . very striking, compared with the light melodies and their accompaniments of what I had heard at the Opera-house before'; the piece was played fourteen times before Christmas and eight after, a success Handel might have viewed with rather mixed feelings.

His own season opened on 26 February, three days after his sixty-third birthday, with *Judas Maccabaeus*; *Joshua* followed on 9 March and *Alexander Balus* on the 23rd. The elaborate *Concerti a due cori*, featuring antiphonal wind bands, were almost certainly written as interval-fillers for performances of the three oratorios. There were in all thirteen performances (six of *Judas*, four of *Joshua* and three of *Alexander*), a pattern that was to become typical of Handel's Lenten activities for the remainder of his life.

Mrs Delany, whose acute commentary on Handel's fortunes provided a valuable record in previous years, had moved with her husband to Ireland. In her absence the most eloquent testimony to the success of the oratorios is Handel's bank statements: he deposited £300 after the first performance of *Judas*, £200 after the second and £100 after the third. There is little evidence of how and when he paid his performers although the statement records a withdrawal of £990 on 19 March, but at the beginning of May he was in a position to deal in annuities to the value of £4500.

The 1748 Lenten season inaugurated a regular series of some dozen performances, with revivals gradually outnumbering new works as Handel relaxed from his gruelling summer bursts of composition, although often 'a

New Concerto on the Organ' would be added to the programme. He supplemented his regular team of English singers with Italians borrowed from the Opera – another sign of lessening rivalry; from 1749 onwards, Frasi was a particular favourite and was declared to have a better singing accent in English than many natives.

To the public, oratorio-going became the norm, although motives varied. Henry Fielding's heroine in *The History of Amelia* (1751) arrives early to secure good seats and finds an additional attraction to Handel's music in the company she meets:

> Indeed there was only one Person in the House when they came: for *Amelia's* Inclinations, when she gave a Loose to them, were pretty eager for this Diversion, she being a great Lover of Music, and particularly of Mr. *Handel's* Compositions. Mrs. *Ellison* was, I suppose, a great Lover likewise of Music, for she was the more impatient of the two; which was rather the more extraordinary, as these Entertainments were not such Novelties to her as they were to poor *Amelia*.
>
> Tho' our Ladies arrived full two Hours before they saw the Back of Mr. *Handel*; yet this Time of Expectation did not hang extremely heavy on their Hands; for besides their own Chat, they had the Company of the Gentleman, whom they found at their first Arrival in the Galery; and who, though plainly, or rather roughly dressed, very luckily for the Women happened to be not only well-bred, but a Person of a very lively Conversation. The Gentleman on his part seemed highly charmed with *Amelia*, and in fact was so: for, though he restrained himself entirely within the Rules of Good-Breeding, yet was he in the highest Degree officious to catch at every Opportunity of shewing his Respect, and doing her little Services. He procured her a Book and Wax-Candle, and held the Candle for her himself during the whole Entertainment.
>
> At the End of the Oratorio, he declared he would not leave the Ladies till he had seen them safe into their Chairs or Coach; and at the same time very earnestly entreated that he might have the Honour of waiting on them. (Book IV, Chapter IX)

The French poetess Madame Anne-Marie Fiquet du Bocage was particularly taken with Handel's own contribution to the oratorio performances when she visited London in 1750:

> The Oratorio, or pious concert, pleases us highly. *English* words are sung by *Italian* performers, and accompanied by a variety of instruments. HANDEL is the soul of it: when he makes his appearance, two wax lights are carried before him, which are laid upon his organ. Amidst a loud clapping of hands he seats himself, and the whole band of music strikes up exactly at the same moment. At the interludes he plays concertos of his own composition, either alone or accompanied by the orchestra. These are equally admirable for the harmony and the execution. The *Italian* opera, in three acts, gives us much less pleasure . . .

In a letter to the poet William Shenstone, Lady Luxborough, whose steward was 'highly entertained' at *Judas Maccabaeus*, infers that a musical ear is no longer vital for an appreciation of these performances, so high has Handel's reputation grown: '. . . he speaks with such ecstasy of the music, as I confess I cannot conceive any one can feel who understands no more of music than myself; which I take to be his case. But I suppose he sets his judgment true to that of the multitude; for if his ear is not nice enough to distinguish the harmony, it serves to hear what the multitude say of it.'

> *Some days after the first exhibition of the same divine oratorio, Mr. Handel came to pay his respect to Lord Kinnoull, with whom he was particularly acquainted. His lordship, as was natural, paid him some compliments on the noble entertainment which he had lately given the town. 'My lord', said Handel, 'I should be sorry if I only entertained them, I wish to make them better.'*　　　　　　　　　　　　　　　　　　　　　(James Beattie, 1780)

The absorption of oratorio into the taste of the 'multitude' is one aspect of the phenomenon; even more potent was the assumption of moral uplift. When she heard *Samson* in December 1743, Catherine Talbot could not help thinking that 'this kind of entertainment must necessarily have some effect in correcting or moderating at least the levity of the age'. Eliza Heywood, finding herself 'transported into the most divine Extasy' by a rendering of *Joshua*, waxed even more evangelical in her *Epistles for the Ladies* (1749), declaring that such entertainments might 'go a great Way in reforming an Age, which seems to be degenerating equally into an Irreverence for the Deity, and a Brutality of Behavior to each other; but as this Depravity of Taste, of Principles, and Manners, has spread itself from *London* even to the remotest Parts of this Island, I should be glad there were *Oratorios* established in every City and great Town throughout the Kingdom; but even then, to be of general Service, they ought to be given *gratis*, and all Degrees of People allowed to partake of them, otherwise it is but an inconsiderable Number, in comparison with the whole, whose Fortunes would admit of their being improved this Way'. Her hopes of universal coverage were soon to be fulfilled, although the selection of the 'Entertainments' was somewhat limited. Handel's changed standing, and his sudden elevation to the unique position of a 'classic', was a result of the mobility and social adaptability of oratorio, which, once published, could become the repertoire of professional or amateur musicians at any point of the globe. The contrast with operas, limited to the London stage and by the purse-strings of society amateurs, is great – and the spread of oratorio is one of the first signs that 'English music' could at last mean something broader than 'London music'.

Having at last established a public liaison that was never again to be broken, Handel relaxed his selling-line of military triumph to prepare two complementary portrayals of a nation for his 1749 season. *Solomon* depicts a golden age which should surely be interpreted as the idealized spirit of Georgian England. Dealing with the aspirations of rulers – towards justice, true religion, and prosperity – and set in the most lavish and luxurious court the Bible could provide, the dramatic structure of *Solomon* is that of pageant rather than narrative. *Susanna*, a pastoral opera verging on the comic, immortalizes in contrast the charm of English village life, and takes a secular view of the lechery of the two Elders. Thus with a pageant and a comic opera Handel follows his normal pattern of composing in pairs; with these works, however, the contrast and balance is stronger and more conscious than with, for example, *Semele* and *Joseph* in 1743 or *Hercules* and *Belshazzar* in 1744.

It was also the last time Handel had the energy to write two oratorios in one summer; with a certain sense of precaution he began *Solomon* unusually early, on 5 May. It is imperial in every way, and almost profligate with its instrumental riches: for his 1749 performances Handel was anticipating 'above one Hundred Voices and Performers', who required special management (see p. 214). His borrowings were equally seigneurial; to take a single example, the Act III sinfonia (christened, inaccurately, 'The Arrival of the Queen of Sheba') draws on parts of Porta's *Numitore*, a Telemann concerto and a Muffat keyboard gigue.

The inspiration and catalyst for *Susanna* was found amongst more homely sources, the 'English opera' manner of Arne and Carey, with which Handel lightens the mutual love of the heroine and Joachim. An artless air like 'Ask if yon damask rose', which was in fact the result of endless rejection and rewriting, has the same feeling of inevitability as an English ballad; it is not surprising to find that Arne could later incorporate it into his ballad opera *Love in a Village*. Handel and the light opera composers may even have drawn from a common source, since Lady Luxborough records in a letter to Shenstone (16 October 1748) that 'The great Handel has told me that the hints of his very best songs have several of them been owing to the sounds in his ears of cries in the street'. The sources of the overture to *Susanna* are more specific; it is not, as Winton Dean has said, 'one of the few without a borrowing',[*] but is drawn *in extenso* from John Blow's St Cecilia Ode for 1684, *Begin the Song*. The skilful modernizing that Handel applied to the piece does him credit while flattering Blow; it has a calculated dramatic function in helping to establish the Englishness of the scene with a wistful hint of *temps perdu*.[†]

Lady Shaftesbury's judgment in a letter to James Harris after the first performance on 10 February was decided: 'it will not insinuate itself so much into my approbation as most of Handel's performances do, as it is in the light *operatic* style . . .', but it was not shared by the public: 'I think I never saw a fuller house. Rich told me that he believed he would receive near £400'. The work's

---

Dramatic Oratorios, p. 541.
†See Franklin B. Zimmerman, 'Musical Borrowings'.

initial success was never repeated, perhaps owing to its mixture of gravity and comedy: it was revived once only in Handel's lifetime, and has not often been heard since.

Solomon opened on 17 March with Signora Galli in the mezzo-soprano title role, one of countless instances where Handel showed no disinclination to cast a female singer in a male part. She also sang in a single performance of *Messiah* given (with its full title) on 23 March; it was the first time Handel had ventured the work since 1745. The exceptionally large orchestra that Handel had contracted for this season meant that many sections of the work, which had been designed for smaller forces, had to be 'marked down': the 'con ripieno' and 'senza ripieno' markings reproduced in some modern editions of *Messiah* originally applied to these exceptional circumstances, and should be observed nowadays only when dealing with similarly overweight forces. The performance appears to have been a last-minute idea on Handel's part, since there seems to have been no advertisement before the concert day itself. Somewhat tardily the word-book was advertised that same day by Watts, the publisher, as being ready 'Tomorrow'.

At this point Handel found himself involved in an immense demonstration of national jubilation. The War of the Austrian Succession (in which Dettingen had been the last notable victory) had finally been concluded in October the previous year with the signing of the Treaty of Aix-la-Chapelle. That November, bands of workmen had begun to erect in Green Park an enormous wooden structure in Palladian style, with a central triumphal arch and colonnades, statues of Greek gods and a bas-relief of the King. The 'machine', 410 feet long and 114 feet high, was devised by one Giovanni Servandoni (actually a Frenchman, Jean-Nicholas Servan), who worked in the London theatres, and it was to be the basis of an enormous firework display.

IV

By February, when peace was officially declared, it was almost completed, and Handel was called on to supply suitable music. 'Mr Handel's Fire Musick' from *Atalanta* had been for several years a regular accompaniment to pyrotechnics in the pleasure gardens, Cuper's in particular. Now something grander was needed. Royal taste for once ran counter to Handel's ideas of practicality and a sequence of irascible letters flew between the Duke of Montague, Master General of the Ordnance, and Charles Frederick, even more grandly dubbed 'Comptroller of his Majesty's Fireworks as well as for War as for Triumph'. Handel's own responses are missing; in the meantime he went ahead adapting and composing *Musick for the Royal Fireworks* to his own specification. On 28 March 1749, the Duke of Montague launched his first salvo:

I think Hendel now proposes to have but 12 trumpets and 12 French horns; at first there was to have been sixteen of each, and I remember I told the King so, who, at that time, objected to their being any musick; but, when I told him the quantity and nomber of martial musick there was to be, he was better satisfied, and said he hoped there would be no fidles. Now Hendel proposes to lessen the nomber of trumpets, &c. and to have violeens. I dont at all doubt but when the King hears it he will be very much displeased. If the thing war to be in such a manner as certainly to please the King, it ought to consist of no kind of instrument but martial instruments. Any other I am sure will put him out of humour, therefore I am shure it behoves Hendel to have as many trumpets, and other martial instruments, as possible, tho he dont retrench the violins, which I think he shoud, tho I beleeve he will never be persuaded to do it. I mention this as I have very lately been told, from very good authority, that the King has, within this fortnight, expressed himself to this purpose.

Some days later (on 9 April) the Duke wrote again telling Frederick to forward his own bad-tempered letter to Handel in another demand for clarification:

Sir, – In answer to Mr. Hendel's letter to you (which by the stile of it I am shure is impossible to be of his inditing) I can say no more but this, that this morning at court the King did me the honor to talke to me conserning the fireworks, and in the course of the conversation his Majesty was pleased to aske me when Mr. Hendel's overture was to be rehersed; I told his Majesty I really coud not say anything conserning it from the difficulty Mr. Hendel made about it, for that the master of Voxhall [i.e. Vauxhall Gardens], having offered to lend us all his lanterns, lamps, &c. to the value of seven hundred pounds, whereby we woud save just so much money to the office of Ordnance, besides thirty of his servants to assist in the illuminations, upon condition that Mr. Hendel's overture shoud be rehersed at Voxhall, Mr. Hendel has hetherto refused to let it be at Foxhall, which his Majesty seemed to think he was in the wrong of; and I am shure I think him extreamly so, and extreamly indifferent whether we have his overture or not, for it may very easily be suplyed by another, and I shall have the satisfaction that his Majesty will know the reason why we have it not; therefore, as Mr. Hendel knows the reason, and the great benefit and saving it will be to the publick to have the rehersal at Voxhall, if he continues to express his zeal for his Majesty's service by doing what is so contrary to it, in not letting the rehersal be there, I shall intirely give over any further thoughts of his overture and shall take care to have an other.

It appears that Mr Frederick had the good sense not to bait the composer with the letter as instructed.

The autograph score of the *Fireworks Music* shows some sign of these negotiations. Eventually deciding on 9 trumpets, 9 horns, 24 oboes, 12 bassoons and 3 pairs of kettle-drums (plus 'Contra Bassone et Serpent', deleted on second thoughts), Handel later added a note that strings should double the oboe and bassoon parts – contrary to royal wishes. But in some of the later movements, strings indicated at the start are then cancelled: it is impossible to say whether composer or monarch got his way.

Handel at least gave way over the public preview and apart from causing a traffic jam, the rehearsal on 21 April went off well; the band was 100 strong, and the audience 'above 12,000', the largest number ever seen at Vauxhall; the *Gentleman's Magazine* for April 1749 commented: 'So great a resort occasioned such a stoppage on *London Bridge*, that no carriage could pass for 3 hours'.

The event itself was less fortunate. John Byrom vividly sets the scene in a letter to his wife dated 'Green Park, 7 o'clock, Thursday night, before Squib Castle':

> Walking about here to see sights I have retired to a stump of a tree to write a line to thee lest anything should happen to prevent me by and by . . . they are all mad with thanksgivings, Venetian jubilees, Italian fireworks, and German pageantry. I have before my eyes such a concourse of people as to be sure I never have or shall see again, except we should have a Peace without a vowel. The building erected on this occasion is indeed extremely neat and pretty and grand to look at, and a world of fireworks placed in an order that promises a most amazing scene when it is to be in full display. His Majesty and other great folks have been walking to see the machinery before the Queen's Library;* it is all railed about there, where the lords, ladies, commons, &c. are sat under scaffolding, and seem to be under confinement in comparison of us mobility, who enjoy the free air and walks here.
>
> It has been a very hot day, but there is a dark overcast of cloudiness which may possibly turn to rain, which occasions some of better habits to think of retiring; and while I am now writing it spits a little and grows into a menacing appearance of rain, which, if it pass not over, will disappoint expectations. My intention, if it be fair, is to gain a post under one of the trees in St. James's Park, where the fireworks are in front, and where the tail of a rocket, if it should fall, cannot but be hindered by the branches from doing any mischief to them who are sheltered under them, so I shall now draw away to be ready for near shelter from either watery or fiery rain.

But the show fell short of expectations, as Walpole describes in a letter to Sir Horace Mann on 3 May: 'The rockets, and whatever was thrown up into the air, succeeded mighty well; but the wheels, and all that was to compose the principal part, were pitiful and ill-conducted, with no changes of coloured fires and shapes: the illumination was mean, and lighted so slowly that scarce any body had patience to wait the finishing; and then, what contributed to the awkwardness of the whole, was the right pavilion catching fire, and being burnt down in the middle of the show'. This mishap was too much for the impetuous designer, Servandoni, who drew his sword on poor Charles Frederick for having conspicuously failed in his role of 'Comptroller of the Fireworks'. No one mentions the music which was apparently played before the fireworks went off, rather than during them, and probably also while the Royal party made their tour of the Machine. Handel was unused to being so overlooked, and within a month scheduled a second hearing of his music for a very different cause.

---

*Demolished in the nineteenth century.

For some years a retired sea captain, Thomas Coram, had been labouring to   48
establish a refuge on the lines of the *Ospedali* of Venice 'for the reception,
maintenance, and education of exposed and deserted young children'. In 1739 a
Royal Charter had been granted to his Foundling Hospital, and building began
in 1742 on a site in Lamb's Conduit Fields. Coram had the support of many
artists – Hogarth (a Governor), Hudson, Reynolds, Ramsay and Wilson; and
the Minutes of the Hospital of 9 May 1749 thank Handel for having offered a
concert to raise money for the finishing of the chapel. George II had already   49
contributed £3000 and had proposed to make Handel a Governor. The concert,
which included the music 'for the late *Royal Fireworks*', selections from *Solomon*
relating to the dedication of the Temple and a new anthem *Blessed are they that
considereth the poor*, was given on 19 May in the chapel itself, unfinished but
'sash'd, and made commodious for the Purpose'. The King sent £2000, tickets
were half a guinea, and more than a thousand people managed to get in; 'there
was no collection', noted the *Gentlemen's Magazine* succinctly.

Handel's connection with the Foundling Hospital continued for the rest of
his life. When the chapel was completed the following year, he presented it with
an organ built by Morse of Barnet. The instrument has now disappeared, except
for the keyboard (which can be seen in the Thomas Coram Foundation);
Handel's practicality in matters of organ design is evident from a letter of advice
written on 30 September to Jennens, who at this time was equipping his palatial
residence at Gopsall.

Yesterday I received Your Letter, in answer to which I hereunder Specify my
Opinion of an Organ which I think will answer the Ends you propose, being
every thing that is necessary for a good and grand Organ, without Reed stops,
which I have omitted, because they are continually wanting to be tuned,
which in the Country is very inconvenient, and should it remain useless on
that Account, it wou'd still be very expensive, altho' that may not be your
Consideration. I very well approve of Mr. Bridge who without any Objection
is a very good Organ Builder, and I shall willingly (when He has finish'd it)
give You my Opinion of it. I have referr'd you to the Flute stop in Mr.
Freemans Organ being excellent in its kind, but as I do not referr you in that
Organ, The System of the Organ I advise is, (Vizt
     The Compass to be up to D and down to Gamut,
     full Octave,   Church work,
     one Row of Keys, whole stops and none in halves.

Stops

An Open Diapason – of Metal throughout to be in Front.
A Stopt Diapason – the Treble Metal and the Bass Wood.
A Principal – of Metal throughout.
A Twelfth – of Metal throughout.
A Fifteenth – of Metal throughout.
A Great Tierce – of Metal throughout.
A Flute Stop – Such a one as in Freemans Organ.

217

This instrument, with later modifications and alterations, can still be heard in St James's, Great Packington, in Warwickshire, where it was moved after Jennens's death.

Title-page of the manuscript word-book for Theodora, *inscribed by Handel for submission to the Inspector of Stage Plays.*

The exertions of the summer celebrations limited Handel to a single new oratorio for the following year. Having done his duty in terms of military pomposity in the four oratorios written during 1747 and 1748, he had moved closer to his own personal beliefs the year after with twin visions of a golden age and a natural tranquility. *Theodora*, written in June and July 1749, demonstrates personal faith in a Christian destiny; nobility, loyalty, sacrifice and eventual martyrdom are shown as facets of a courage very different from the bluster of military heroism. Handel presents Christianity and paganism as equally vital and attractive – Theodora's devotion and piety spring equally from her own youthful fervour and her young religion – and then declares the first as morally preferable. From this balanced struggle evolves a final mood of 'injured sublimity' (Winton Dean's ideal phrase) comparable with the close of the *St Matthew Passion*.

In the winter of that year Handel received what was for him an unusual commission. Although closely associated with the London theatre, he wrote very little incidental music for plays. A request from John Rich to provide airs and dances for Smollett's *Alceste* was undertaken, according to Hawkins, in repayment of a debt to Rich – nothing more of this tantalizing detail is known. According to Smollett himself, in a letter of 14 February, the production was to be lavish, with 'such magnificence of Scenery [by Servandoni] as was never exhibited in Britain before'. The score shows decided French influence and Handel's music for the celebratory scenes, two dream sequences (the first of which includes one of his finest *sommeils*, 'Gentle Morpheus'), and a melancholy scene in Hades, competes with Rameau on his own terms. In the event the production never materialized, possibly because of 'a dispute taking place between the author and the manager', possibly because of the widespread panic caused by a series of earthquakes in February. Many people fled from London; 'they say they are not frightened', observed Walpole, 'but that in such fine weather, Lord, one can't help going into the country'. Mrs Montague was amongst the more audacious, as she reports in a letter to her sister:

I was not under any apprehensions about the earthquake, but went that night to the Oratorio, then quietly to bed, but the madness of the multitude was prodigious. Near fifty of the people I had sent to, to play at cards here the Saturday following, went out of town to avoid being swallowed, and I believe they made a third part of the number I asked, so that you may imagine how universal the fright must be. The Wednesday night the Oratorio was very empty, though it was the most favourite performance of Handel's.

In 1749, Theodora *was so very unfortunately abandoned, that he was glad if any professors, who did not perform, would accept of tickets or orders for admission. Two gentlemen of that description, now living, having applied to* HANDEL, *after the disgrace of* Theodora, *for an order to hear the* MESSIAH, *he cried out, 'Oh your sarvant, Mien-herren! you are tamnaple tainty! you would not co to* TEODORA *– der was room enough to tance dere, when dat was perform.'*

Sometimes, however, I have heard him, as pleasantly as philosophically, console his friends, when, previous to the curtain being drawn up, they have lamented that the house was so empty, by saying, 'Nevre moind; de moosic vil sound de petter.'   (Charles Burney, 1785)

Theodora never recovered from the scare. In his letter of *c.* 1770 Morell, besides confirming Handel's high opinion of the work, shows the composer's sense of humour as sharp as ever:

. . . when I once ask'd him, whether he did not look upon the Grand Chorus in the Messiah as his Master Piece? 'No', says he, 'I think the Chorus at the end of the 2d part in Theodora far beyond it. He saw the lovely youth &c.'

The 2d night of Theodora was very thin indeed, tho' the Princess Amelia was there. I guessed it a losing night, so did not go to Mr Handell as usual; but seeing him smile, I ventured, when, 'Will you be there next Friday night,' says he, 'and I will play it to you?' I told him I had just seen Sir T. Hankey, 'and he desired me to tell you, that if you would have it again, he would engage for all the Boxes.' 'He is a fool; the Jews will not come to it (as to Judas) because it is a Christian story; and the Ladies will not come, because it [is] a virtuous one.'

A note from Handel to the Keeper of the Ordnance Office in the Tower of London shows that he had permission to borrow the 'Artillery Kettle Drums' for his oratorio season this year. Saul and Judas Maccabaeus were given together with a performance of Messiah which marked the first appearance in London of the castrato Gaetano Guadagni. Burney thought him 'a wild and careless singer', but Handel was moved by his coloratura to rewrite 'Thou art gone up on high' and 'But who may abide the day of His coming': this version with its showy 'refiner's fire' is entirely unsuited to the bass voice on which it has so frequently been imposed.

Another performance of Messiah inaugurated the Foundling Hospital organ on 1 May; the instrument was not quite ready, and Morse had to be pressed 'to have as many stops as he can, for chorus's'. In spite of instructions in the printed invitations that 'The Gentlemen are desired to come without Swords, and the Ladies without Hoops', many people were unable to get in. The General Advertiser placed the blame on 'Persons of Distinction' who had gate-crashed, and Handel offered a repeat performance in the Foundling Hospital on 15 May. Between the two performances he was elected a Governor, and from this year onwards gave annual performances of the oratorio for the benefit of Thomas Coram's foundation. Messiah, in Burney's words, 'fed the hungry, clothed the naked, fostered the orphan, and enriched succeeding managers of Oratorios, more than any single musical production in this or any country'. It is appropriate that this status should stem from Handel's charitable rather than commercial promotions, but sad that, although the Foundation itself still exists and thrives in London, the chapel in which Handel played, and to which he left score and parts of Messiah in his will to continue the performances, should have been declared unsafe and demolished as recently as 1926. It was the last remaining building in the capital in which he had promoted concerts. Handel Street (WC1) still survives near the site.

A few days after his second performance of Messiah, a ghost from Handel's past returned to cast a chill on his spirits. Cuzzoni, 'grown old, poor, and almost deprived of voice by age and infirmities', revisited her scenes of former glory and gave a benefit concert in Hickford's Room on 18 May. She was imprisoned shortly afterwards for owing £30, and bailed out, Walpole says, by the Prince of Wales. A concert she performed the following year included the love duet from Giulio Cesare, three arias from Ottone and, in an appeal to current taste, 'Return, O God of Hosts' from Samson. Thanking the nobility and gentry for their past

47

favours in a letter to the *General Advertiser*, she made an assurance that this concert 'shall be the last I will ever trouble them with, and is made solely to pay my Creditors'. 'There was but little company', Burney says: she finally left the country 'more miserable than she came', and died in poverty in Bologna, making buttons. Burney's account of Cuzzoni's last appearances may be one-sided; a manuscript note in the British Library copy of Mainwaring states that 'Her voice in 1750, when she was an Old Woman, was equal to that of the angelic M$_{iss}^{rs}$ Linley in her best days . . .'.

Handel's own health had improved along with his finances; earlier in the year the Earl of Shaftesbury had reported to James Harris that: 'I have seen Handel several times since I came hither, and think I never saw him so cool and well. He is quite easy in his behaviour, and has been pleasing himself in the purchase of several fine pictures, particularly a large Rembrandt, which is indeed excellent. We have scarce talked at all about musical subjects, though enough to find his performances will go off incomparably'.

That summer, Handel left for Germany, having taken the precaution of making his will on 1 June, shortly before his departure. Nothing is known of his destination – whether he took the waters at Aix or visited relatives – and the only evidence we have of his journeying is a chance mention of a coaching accident in the *General Advertiser*: 'Mr. Handel, who went to Germany to visit his Friends some Time since, and between the Hague and Harlaem [Haarlem] had the Misfortune to be overturned, by which he was terribly hurt, is now out of Danger'. If Handel had been injured, he said nothing to his old friend Telemann in a letter dated 25 December. Although they had first met almost fifty years previously, Handel still writes in formal French (to a fellow German) and remembers Telemann's reputation as a botanical enthusiast with a choice collection of rare tulips, hyacinths and anemones:

I was on the point of leaving the Hague for London when your most agreeable letter was delivered to me by Mr. Passerini. I had just enough time to be able to hear his wife sing* . . .

I thank you for the splendid work on the system of intervals† which you were good enough to send me; it is worthy of your time and trouble and of your learning.

I congratulate you on the perfect health that you are enjoying at your somewhat advanced age, and I wish you from my heart every prosperity for many years to come. If your passion for exotic plants etc. could prolong your days and sustain the zest for life that is natural to you, I offer with very real pleasure to contribute to it in some sort. Consequently I am sending you as a present (*to the address enclosed*) a crate of flowers, which experts assure me are very choice and of admirable rarity. If they are not telling the truth, you will [at least] have the best plants in all England, and the season of

---

*Signora Passerini sang in Handel's oratorio seasons from 1754.
†A treatise on chromatic notation, *Neues musicalisches System*, published by Mizler.

the year is still right for their bearing flowers. You will be the best judge of this . . .

The crate had a troubled journey. The captain to whom they were entrusted told Handel that Telemann had died, and this report was only corrected much later, when the same captain returned with a list of exotic plants that Telemann would like bought for him. Handel, in a letter of September 1754, explains how upset he was by the false news and adds, 'I have been at pains to have these plants found, and you shall have nearly all of them'.

Back in England the question was: 'Does Mr. Handel do anything new against next Lent?' Mrs Delany's sister felt that 'surely Theodora will have some justice at last, if it was to be again performed, but the generality of the world have ears and *hear not*' (letter to Bernard Granville, 3 December 1750). As the status of the ageing composer grew firmly into that of a classic, one can feel, in remarks like this, the beginnings of a division between Handelians and non-Handelians. In the event, Handel's supporters got a season of re-runs – *Belshazzar, Esther, Judas Maccabaeus, Alexander's Feast* – spiced with new organ concertos. For *Alexander's Feast* Handel provided an 'additional New Act', *The Choice of Hercules*: rather than wasting the music he had written for Smollett's abandoned *Alceste*, he adapted it to a morality text in which Hercules is faced with a choice between Pleasure and Virtue. The scoring (flutes, bassoons, horns, trumpets) is good, but the plot and characters remain stylized and two-dimensional. Much of the music, including Pleasure's infectious gavotte aria 'Turn thee, youth' is obviously better suited to its original dramatic purpose in *Alceste*.

It was unlike Handel to be so unadventurous and offer so little that was new; it was equally untypical of him to begin composition of another full-scale oratorio immediately prior to a busy season. With hindsight we can read deeper levels of fatalism into the first line of the text that Handel began setting in January: 'It must be so'. Whether it was a husbanding of resources, a generalized awareness of mortality or a more definite omen that caused the early start on *Jephtha*, the sudden onset of Handel's personal tragedy appears vividly in the margins of his autograph score. Part of the way through the final Act II chorus 'How dark, O Lord, are thy decrees' he breaks off with a note in German: 'reached here on 13 Febr. 1751 unable to continue owing to a relaxation of the sight of my left eye'. He then crossed out 'relaxation' and added at the end 'so relaxt'. On his sixty-sixth birthday, after a concert the evening before when he had directed *Belshazzar* and played a new organ concerto, he takes up his pen again: 'the 23 of this month rather better started work again'. At the end of the act he was obliged to stop. Act III was not begun until mid-June and by 30 August Handel had struggled to the conclusion of the work, adding his age after the final hard-won bar: *aetatis* 66.

During the summer he had lost the sight of his left eye, but still continued to play. 'Noble Handel hath lost an eye', wrote Sir Edward Turner on 14 March, 'but I have the Rapture to say that St. Cecilia makes no complaint of any Defect in his Fingers'. After an abrupt end to the oratorio season caused by the death of

Folio of autograph manuscript of Jephtha, 1751. In the early 1750s Handel's sight began to deteriorate. The calligraphy is markedly less disciplined than before and some of the note-heads are lacking stems. At the foot of this page of his last major work, he scribbled a note about the weakening of his left eye (see p. 222). The words of this closing chorus of Act II are particularly poignant in the circumstances: 'How dark O Lord are thy decrees, all hid from mortal sight!'

AT the Theatre Royal in Covent-Garden, this Day, being the 26th instant, will be perform'd a new Oratorio, called,

J   E   P   T   H   A.

Pit and Boxes put together, and no Person to be admitted without Tickets, which will be deliver'd this Day, at the Office in Covent Garden Theatre, at Half a Guinea each.
Firft Gallery 5 s.   Second Gallery 3 s. 6 d.
Galleries to be open'd at half an Hour after Four o'Clock,
Pit and Boxes at Five
To begin at Half an Hour after Six o'Clock.

For the Benefit of Signora FRASI,

AT the New Theatre in the Hay-Market, on Tuesday the 10th of March, will be perform'd a Concert of Vocal and Instrumental MUSICK.
Pit and Boxes to be put together, at Half a Guinea.
Tickets to be had of Signora Frasi in Gerrard-Street ; at Mr. Hickford's in Brewer-Street; and at Simpson's Musick Shop in Sweeting's Alley.

223

the Prince of Wales, Handel directed his usual performances of *Messiah* for the Foundling Hospital before going with Smith to take the waters at Bath and Cheltenham. These did nothing to improve his sight, and a consultation with Samuel Sharp at Guy's Hospital produced a verdict of *gutta serena* – this was not necessarily cataract, since the term was used to mean any form of blindness without external signs of disease.

Despite deteriorating sight in his right eye also, Handel was able to give the first performance of *Jephtha* in the 1752 Lenten season. Galli, Frasi and John Beard were amongst his singers, and he banked £600 after the first performance. When Mrs Delany first heard the piece in April 1756 she perceptively found it 'very fine . . . but very different from any of his others'. Morell, who constructed the libretto, claims the piece as his own favourite, and it drew from Handel some of the most profound and introspective music of his whole career, including one of his finest ensemble settings for the four solo characters. It also contains more borrowings than any of his other oratorios, *Deborah* excepted, the main source being a collection of masses by Habermann, possibly supplied by Telemann, or collected on his recent trip to Germany. Handel's working sketches now in the Fitzwilliam Museum, Cambridge, show him improving on Habermann even as he first copies down the theme in rough; here, as elsewhere in Handel, it is more profitable to admire the skill in construction and recreation than to question the source of each unit of inspiration.

> *When Handel was blind, and attending a performance of the Oratorio of* Jephtha, *Mr [William] Savage, my master, who sat next him, said, 'This movement, sir, reminds me of some of old Purcell's music'. 'O got te teffel', said Handel, 'if Purcell had lived, he would have composed better music than this.'*
>
> (R. J. S. Stevens, 1775)

The failure of Handel's eyesight closed his composing life. His depression is recorded in several sources, most of them derivative: all report him sunk 'for a time into the deepest despondency' (Mainwaring): 'that fortitude which had supported him under afflictions of another kind, deserted him upon being told that a freedom from pain in the visual organs was all that he had to hope, for the remainder of his days' (Hawkins). His condition worsened in August 1752 when he 'was seized . . . with a Paralytick Disorder in his Head, which has deprived him of Sight' (*General Advertiser*).

He applied again to a specialist and sometime around November he was 'couched' by William Bromfield, a surgeon to St George's and the Lock Hospitals, when according to the *General Advertiser* 'it was thought there was all imaginable Hopes of Success by the Operation'. The procedure, which had a high success rating in the eighteenth century, involved piercing the cornea with a sharp hooked needle or thorn, and manipulating or 'couching' (depressing) the opaque material below the level of the pupil. A modern authority describes it as 'relatively painless'.* Handel may have had some relief from it, since the *Cambridge Chronicle* reported that 'Mr. Handel has so much recovered his sight that he is able to go abroad [i.e. out of doors]'. But the cure was temporary, and on 27 January the London public read: 'Mr. Handel has at length, unhappily, quite lost his sight. Upon his being couch'd some time since, he saw so well, that his friends flattered themselves his sight was restored for a continuance; but a few days have entirely put an end to their hope'.

The oratorios continued with Handel unable to take an active part. In a letter of March 1753, Lady Shaftesbury testifies to his despondency during the first months of total blindness.:

> My constancy to poor Handel got the better of . . . my indolence, and I went last Friday to 'Alexander's Feast'; but it was such a melancholy pleasure, as drew tears of sorrow to see the great though unhappy Handel, dejected, wan, and dark, sitting by, not playing on the harpsichord, and to think how his light had been spent by *being overplied in music's cause*. I was sorry to find the audience so insipid and tasteless (I may add unkind) not to give the poor man the comfort of applause; but affectation and conceit cannot discern or attend to merit.

It was to be his natural fortitude, together with the phenomenal powers of improvisation that had served him so well as a young man, that now sustained Handel's last years. Burney recalled that 'He continued to play concertos and voluntaries between the parts of his Oratorios to the last, with the same vigour of thought and touch, for which he was ever so justly renowned. To see him, however, led to the organ . . . and then conducted towards the audience to make his accustomed obeisance, was a sight so truly afflicting and deplorable to persons of sensibility, as greatly diminished their pleasure, in hearing him perform'. According to Burney, improvisation filled many of the solo sections:

> During the Oratorio season, I have been told, that he practised almost incessantly; and, indeed, that must have been the case, or his memory uncommonly retentive; for, after his blindness, he played several of his old organ-concertos, which must have been previously impressed on his memory by practice. At last, however, he rather chose to trust to his inventive powers, than those of reminiscence: for, giving the band only the skeleton, or ritornels of each movement, he played all the solo parts extempore, while the other instruments left him, *ad libitum*; waiting for the signal of a shake [trill], before they played such fragments of symphony [*tutti*] as they found in their books.

Audiences at the ever-popular *Samson* did not fail to notice the parallel with Milton's own blindness. According to Coxe (*Anecdotes of Smith*, p. 45): 46

---

*David M. Jackson, 'Bach, Handel, and the Chevalier Taylor'.

When Smith played the organ at the Theatre, during the first year of Handel's blindness, Samson was performed, and Beard sung, with great feeling,

'Total eclipse – no sun, no moon,
All dark amid the blaze of noon.' –

The recollection that Handel had set this air to music, with the view of the blind composer then sitting by the organ, affected the audience so forcibly, that many persons present were moved even to tears.

Handel himself, Burney tells us, was 'always much disturbed and agitated' by this aria.

Despite his blindness, Handel continued to supervise the oratorio seasons to within a week of his death. Apparently new music was produced for all of them – Mainwaring mentions the 'Songs and Chorusses, and other Compositions, which from the date of them, may almost be considered as his parting words'. The suggestion that this late music was 'dictated to Mr Smith' originated with Burney, but until recently the role of Handel's amanuensis has been seriously underestimated. Research by Anthony Hicks* suggests that Handel had little and in some cases no creative responsibility for the late additions to his oratorios. Some are straight transfers from earlier material, or compilations with adapted texts, others can be deduced to have existed in earlier versions now lost. The close involvement of Smith in this process is proven both by style and by working composition copies in his hand. The peak of his activity occurred in 1757–8, when an unusually large quantity of 'new' work was offered to the public. Covent Garden presented a complete oratorio, described in the advertisements as 'The Triumph of Time and Truth. Altered from the Italian, with several new Additions'. It was, in fact, the third version of a piece which had begun life in 1707 in Rome, and was later revised (still in Italian) for London in 1737. For this new production Thomas Morell dubbed English words to the original. While Handel may have initiated its revival, there is nothing to 'rule out the possibility that the compilation of the oratorio was entirely the work of a collaborator' (Hicks).

Against the supposition that it was Smith who lay behind Handel's production of 'new' music, a letter from the Earl of Shaftesbury (8 February 1757) states: 'Mr Handel is better than he has been for some years and finds he can compose Chorus's as well as other music to his own (and consequently to the hearers) satisfaction. His memory is strengthened of late to an astonishing degree'. In fact, the only chorus from that year, 'Sion now her head shall raise', written for a revival of Esther, is the single piece that Burney names as having been dictated to Smith.

A slightly later letter from Shaftesbury (31 December) refers to the singer Cassandra Frederick: 'I saw Mr Handel the other day, who is pretty well and has just finished the composing of several new songs for Federica his new singer,

*'The late additions to Handel's oratorios'.

from whom he has great expectations. She is the girl who was celebrated a few years since for playing on the Harpsichord at eight years old'. Again, however, these new additional arias derive from old material by Handel, and show none of his finesse in the refashioning.

Various reports of the other oratorio revivals exist. Mrs Delany, back on a visit to London in March 1755, attended *Joseph and his Brethren* but found the house 'miserably thin – the Italian opera is in high vogue'. The following year she found *Judas* predictably 'charming and full', but the first revival of *Israel in Egypt* for sixteen years 'did not take, it is too solemn for common ears'. In Catherine Talbot's account, *Messiah*, given twice in 1756, 'made amends for the solitude of his other oratorios'.

In the provinces and abroad in Europe, oratorio performances laid the backbone of Handel's reputation. Regional music societies in towns such as Oxford, Cambridge, Lincoln, Canterbury, Exeter and Salisbury took up Handel's oratorios, and the choral festivals of Bath, Bristol and the Three Choirs followed. In December 1753 the Governors of the Edinburgh Musical Society communicated with Handel, requesting:

> a copy of the Recitatives and Choruses to some of your oratorios, which indeed they would not ask, were they not informed that you have allowed such copys to other Societys that have applyed for them. The Performers of our Society have hitherto been confined to the Compositions of Corelli, Geminiani and Mr Handel. We are already posest of most of your Oratorios and other works that are published, and we have particularly all the recitatives and songs of the Messiah excepting one namely (How beautiful are the feet of them that preach the Gospell of peace, and Bring Glad tidings of good things) and therefore could we obtain your order to Mr Smith, for writing out for us that Song and the Choruses to that Sacred Oratorio, and the Recitative and Choruses of any other of your works. We would ever retain the most Grateful Sense of the favour, and with pleasure reward Mr Smith to his Satisfaction . . .

According to the Minute Book, 'Mr. Handel's Return to the letter' directed them to Smith 'at the Blue Periwig in Dean Street', who was then sent precise orders for the copying:

> You will therefore make out for them in Score, the Recitatives, Chorus & Such other parts of his Oratorio of Deborah as are not printed. Let them be wrote upon paper of the Same Size with the printed Score, in such a manner as to be put in the proper place of the Score, so that a Compleat Copy thereof may be bound up altogether.*

In the eighteenth century availability of material was the composer's nearest approach to a copyright protection. Handel and his copyists maintained a large

---

*For full details see Phyllis Hamilton, 'Handel in the papers of the Edinburgh Musical Society'.

library of hire parts, as well as an archive of manuscripts dating back to the composer's earliest years, which were used extensively for later revivals. *Admeto*, first performed at the King's Theatre in 1727, was revived there on 12 March 1754, and although Handel himself did not participate, his material was presumably borrowed. The Opera may even fall under suspicion of not returning the music, since both autograph score and conducting score are now missing; material exists for every other opera Handel wrote in England as a testimony to his scrupulous administration.

One score was even endowed by Handel before he died. To ensure that the Foundling Hospital should continue its annual fund-raising *Messiahs* after his death, Handel left them 'a fair copy of the Score and all parts' in a codicil to his will. This material still exists in the Thomas Coram Foundation, and although copied after Handel's death, it provides important evidence of the conditions of performance that he expected in the 1750s. The division of solo parts allows for five singers (two sopranos) instead of the familiar quartet, and their parts indicate that they sang in the choruses as well. Taken in conjunction with the detailed accounts of payments made to all performers, Handel's vocal and instrumental resources can be reconstructed with some accuracy. From the 1754 accounts we find payments for a choir of 6 boy trebles supplied from the Chapel Royal by Bernard Gates, and 13 men. The orchestra comprised 14 violins (divided 8–6 according to a copyist's bill for Vinci's *Didone*), 6 violas, 3 cellos, 2 double basses, 4 oboes, 4 bassoons, 2 horns, 2 trumpets and timpani. The oboe parts of the Foundling Hospital material are specially allocated to give maximum support to the treble line; what the horns played is unknown. The total figures are very similar to those given by M. Fourgeroux for Handel's opera productions in 1728 and the Duke of Portland's account for 1720–21 (see page 79 for both), and can be safely taken as representing a 'typical' Handel orchestra for a medium-sized building when there were no financial restraints. The proportion of woodwind to strings is one of the more telling factors in performance, and should be observed where possible by present-day ensembles. The Three Choirs Festival of 1757 advertised a similar sized ensemble for performances of the Coronation Anthems, the Dettingen Te Deum, oratorios and *Acis and Galatea*: 'Three Trumpets, a Pair of Kettle-drums, Four Hautboys, Four Bassoons, Two Double basses, Violins, Violincelloes, and Chorus Singers in Proportion' (*Jackson's Oxford Journal*, 16 July).

A final attempt was apparently made to restore Handel's eyesight in the last years of his life by the notorious peripatetic English oculist John Taylor, self-styled 'Chevalier', who in the highly coloured account of his own career as an 'opthalmiater' (a word of his own devising) includes a paragraph remarkable for its inaccuracies:

I have seen a vast variety of singular animals, such as dromedaries, camels, &c and particularly at *Leipsick*, where a celebrated master of music, who had already arrived to his 88th year, received his sight by my hands; it is with this very man that the famous *Handel* was first educated, and with whom I once thought to have had the same success, having all circumstances in his favour, motions of the pupil, light, &c but upon drawing the curtain, we found the bottom defective, from a paralytic disorder.

The Leipzig musician was J. S. Bach, who was the same age as Handel and, far from educating him, had never even met him. Taylor's operation was in any case unsuccessful, and Bach became blind, but, like many itinerant surgeons, Taylor had moved on before the outcome of his 'cure' could be known. Both he and Handel were in Tunbridge Wells during the August of 1758 (John Baker's diary adds that Morell was with Handel), and on 24 August an extravagant poem was published anonymously in the *London Chronicle* 'On the Recovery of the Sight of the Celebrated Mr. Handel, by the Chevalier Taylor'. The Muses inform Apollo that

> in yon villa, from pleasures confin'd
> Lies our favourite, Handel, afflicted and blind,

and implore the healing aid of Aesculapius. Not necessary, Apollo replies, for Taylor is already there:

> Then with Handel's Concerto concluding the day,
> to Parnassus they took their aerial way.

Apart from Taylor's own claims, this over-optimistic effusion is the only evidence that any operation took place.

Not only was there no cure for his eyes, but Handel's general health now began to deteriorate. Mainwaring mentions a loss of appetite, and incidentally defends Handel from any accusation of earlier gluttony: 'It would be as unreasonable to confine HANDEL to the fare and allowance of common men, as to expect that a London merchant should live like a Swiss mechanic . . . Nature had given him so vigorous a constitution, so exquisite a palate, and so craving an appetite . . .'.

He was in his person a large made and very portly man. His gait, which was ever sauntering, was rather ungraceful, as it had in it somewhat of that rocking motion, which distinguishes those whose legs are bowed. His features were finely marked, and the general cast of his countenance placid, bespeaking dignity attempered with benevolence, and every quality of the heart that has a tendency to beget confidence and insure esteem. Few of the pictures extant of him are to any tolerable degree likenesses, except one painted abroad, from a print whereof the engraving given of him in this work is taken: in the print of him by Houbraken, the features are too prominent; and in the mezzotinto after Hudson there is a harshness of aspect to which his countenance was a stranger; the most perfect resemblance of him is the statue on his monument, and in that the true lineaments of his face are apparent. (Sir John Hawkins, 1776)

His last oratorio season opened with *Solomon* on 2 March, and was well supported. Burney records that 'the money he used to take to his carriage of a night, though in gold and silver, was as likely to weigh him down and throw him into a fever, as the copper-money of the painter Coreggio, if he had had as far to carry it'. After a final performance of *Messiah* on 6 April, 'at which he attended and performed', he proposed setting out for Bath to take the waters, but was unable to make the journey. On the 11th he dictated the last of the four codicils to his will; in the previous three he had adapted his original testament as members of his family died, and disposed of his organ, which stood in Covent Garden, to John Rich (it remained there until the fire of 1808); his paintings had been allocated: two Denners to Jennens, the Rembrandts returned to Bernard Granville; his librettists had been remembered. In his final bequests he gave £1000 to the Society for the Support of Decayed Musicians and their Families, a charity which he had assisted for several years, remembered his friends, many of whom are now scarcely more than names, and gave 'to my Maid Servants each one years wages over and above what shall be due to them'.

Burney records that 'He had most seriously and devoutly wished, for several days before his death, that he might breathe his last on *Good-Friday*, "in hopes, he said, of meeting his Good God, his sweet Lord and Saviour, on the day of his resurrection"'. In the event he died on the Saturday morning, 14 April 1759. On the 17th James Smyth wrote to Bernard Granville:

According to your request to me when you left London, that I would let you know when our good friend departed this life, *on Saturday last at 8 o'clock in the morn died the great and good Mr. Handel.* He was sensible to the last moment; made a codicil to his will on Tuesday, ordered to be buried privately in Westminster Abbey, and a monument not to exceed £600 for him. I had the pleasure to reconcile him to his old friends; he saw them and forgave them, and let all their legacies stand! In the codicil he left many legacies to his friends, and among the rest he left me £500, and has left to you the two pictures *you formerly gave him.* He took leave of all his friends on Friday morning, and desired to see nobody but the Doctor and Apothecary and myself. At 7 o'clock in the evening he took leave of me, and told me we 'should meet again'; as soon as I was gone he told his servant '*not* to let me come to him any more, for that he had *now done with the world'.* He died as he lived – a good *Christian,* with a true sense of his duty to God and man, and in perfect charity with all the world.

His death was reported widely in the press, many newspapers anticipating the event by a couple of days and almost all emphasizing that he died worth upwards of £20,000. He was denied the private funeral he had requested, and according to the *London Evening Post* on 24 April 'it is computed there were no fewer than 3000 Persons present' on the evening of the 20th in Westminster Abbey, when he was buried in the South Cross. The undertaker's book adds practically: 'N.B. There may be made very good graves on his Right and Left by Digging up a Foundation of an old Staircase; Room at the feet'. The room was filled, 110 years later, by the body of Charles Dickens.

> *They buried Dickens in the very next grave, cheek by jowl with Handel. It does not matter, but it pained me to think that people who could do this could become Deans of Westminster.*
>
> (Samuel Butler, *Notebooks* 1874–1902)

William Croft's Burial Service was sung by the combined choirs of the Chapel Royal, St Paul's and the Abbey, and 'a monument is also to be erected for him, which there is no doubt but his works will outlive' (*Universal Chronicle*, 28 April). Pending the arrival of the Roubiliac memorial, which was unveiled three years later, the most elegant tribute appeared anonymously in the *Universal Chronicle* of 21 April, entitled 55

'An Attempt towards an EPITAPH.':

Beneath this Place
Are reposited the Remains of
GEORGE FREDERICK HANDEL.
The most excellent Musician
Any Age ever produced:
Whose Compositions were a
Sentimental Language
Rather than mere Sounds;
And surpassed the Power of Words
In expressing the various Passions
Of the Human Heart.

6

Handel and Posterity

His is the music for a great active people. (Edward Fitzgerald)

The legacies of Handel the Man, in addition to the bequests he himself intended and the manuscripts remaining with Smith in Brook Street, also included a large portion of Myth and Memories. Just as his itemized bequests proved to be larger than the sums indicated in his will (thanks to his judicious investments £1000 worth of stock had on Handel's death appreciated to a value of £1254), so the myths and memories grew out of all proportion to the truth.

Handel's manuscripts were well served. The 'Musick Books' bequeathed to John Christopher Smith (senior) in the will probably included some of the material now to be found in Hamburg and elsewhere, but the greater part was preserved intact, passed to Smith junior in 1763 and from him to the Royal Family, via Princess Augusta, the Dowager Princess of Wales in the 1770s. While seven volumes (those that appeared to consist mainly of rough sketches) were separated and became part of the Founder's Collection in the Fitzwilliam Museum, Cambridge, together with Handel's bookcase, the remaining eighty-eight volumes remained in various royal residences until 1911, when they were deposited on loan in the British Museum as part of the Royal Music Library. In 1957, two hundred years after George II had presented the Old Royal Library to the Trustees, Elizabeth II donated the music collection. The Royal Library collection of manuscripts is the largest assembly of autographs of any great composer to be housed in a single institution anywhere in the world, and represents 90 per cent of all the autograph material that survives. Handel's own working habits explain why he found it useful to keep all his material intact and available to himself for easy reference and loaning. The coherence of this collection has always proved an inestimable boon to scholars, to whom it has been continuously available: Charles Burney in the 1770s, William Crotch from 1843 to 1858, Victor Schoelcher in the 1850s, assisted by Rophino Lacy, and Chrysander in the latter half of the nineteenth century. Only Dr Samuel Arnold, curiously, seems not to have made use of this source for his planned complete edition, despite dedicating the whole project to the king in 1786.

In 1856 Schoelcher acquired 129 contemporary manuscript scores of Handel's works from a Bristol bookshop – the 'conducting scores' which represent many of the changes of mind made during or as a result of performances. Failing to persuade the British Museum to buy them, Schoelcher disposed of them, on Chrysander's advice, to a group of Hamburg businessmen, who later presented them to the State Library, where they remain today.

Another major collection was formed by Charles Jennens, and passed to his great-nephew the third Earl of Aylesford on Jennens's death in 1773; it was eventually sold at Sotheby's in 1918. The greater part of this important collection was bought by Sir Newman Flower and is now housed in the Henry Watson Music Library in Manchester. Other important manuscripts were bought by Barclay Squire and are now in the British Library. Four other contemporary collections of Handel's manuscripts are extant in Britain: those formed by Bernard Granville (now in the British Library) and the 4th Earl of Shaftesbury; the Malmesbury collection, originally formed by Elizabeth Legh and acquired by James Harris; and the collection eventually acquired by Henry Barrett-Lennard, now in the Fitzwilliam Museum, Cambridge. In addition the Santini collection in Münster contains important Italian manuscripts, including a number of cantatas and the conducting score of *La Resurrezione*.

Handel's less tangible legacies were not to be so easily controlled. Impressions of the man, his speech, anecdotes and fictions, proliferated and became absorbed into the Myth of Handel. Between the man and the music there was always a natural congruency; his generosity in life is reflected authentically in his annual concerts for the Foundling Hospital. Between the Man and the Myth there was a growing rift. One of the basic misconceptions stems from Handel's own apparent unconsciousness of public feeling. At several junctures in his life he held out stubbornly or even unwittingly against the wishes of his audiences, and in his final works it is clear that while he doggedly pursued the dramatic ideals of oratorio, with or without an essentially Christian theme, his public were invariably smitten by its sacred concept.

Another legacy of Brook Street, the oratorio industry, moved into action in the years after Handel's own death with a constant stream of *pasticcii* for the Lenten seasons. Thomas Morell continued as librettist, as he explained in a letter of *c.* 1770: 'To oblige Mr Handell's successor, I wrote *Nabal* in 1764, and *Gideon.* The Music of both are entirely taken from some old genuine pieces of Mr Handell. In the latter is an inimitable Chorus – *Gloria Patri, Gloria filio,* which at first sight I despaired of setting with proper words; but at last struck out *Glorious Patron, glorious Hero &c.* which did mighty well. . . .' Other *pasticcio* oratorio titles were *Israel in Babylon* (1765), *The Cure of Saul* (1766), *Omnipotence,* and *Redemption* (1786), the latter two described as 'adjusted by Dr. Arnold'. J. C. Smith, as well as carrying on the direction of the oratorio season and taking over Handel's position as Royal Music Master, also contributed *Paradise Lost* (not on the text devised by Mrs Delany), *Rebecca* (1761) and *Nabal* (1764), and his lead was followed by Worgan, Arnold and others.

During his lifetime Handel had acquired the status of a classic and his statue had been erected in Vauxhall Gardens. After his death, the corpus of his works came to be seen as a source of musical authority comparable to the works of a poet or writer of antiquity; his association with classic literary figures such as Dryden and Milton and the classical basis of many opera plots assisted this process. (A statue of Milton, cast in lead, did in fact stand in Vauxhall Gardens balancing the Handel effigy; it is now lost.) Handel was the first musician to be the subject of a biography and, as Peter Kivy points out,* the 'Observations on the Works' which conclude Mainwaring's *Memoirs of the life of the Late George Frederic Handel* (written by Robert Price) established a coherent critical point of view for the appreciation of Handel's music.

Price fixed Handel within the romantic aesthetic of sublimity in art, a tide which rose in the last half of the eighteenth century leaving neo-classicism and the pursuit of beauty stranded. As early as 1744 James Harris characterized Handel's 'Genius' as 'having been cultivated by continued Exercise, and being itself far the sublimest and most universal now known . . .' (*Concerning Music, Painting and Poetry*). A decade later William Hayes in his *Remarks on Mr. Avison's Essay* (1753) called Handel 'the truly Great and Heroic' composer; Charles Avison, whose *Essay on Musical Expression* (1751) was Hayes's target, added a critical note to the simple appellation of greatness: 'Mr. HANDEL is in Music, what his own DRYDEN was in Poetry; nervous, exalted, and harmonious; but voluminous, and, consequently, not always correct. Their Abilities equal to every Thing; their Execution frequently inferior . . . both their Characters will devolve to latest Posterity, not as Models of Perfection, yet glorious Examples of those amazing Powers that actuate the human Soul' (*Reply to the Author of Remarks on the Essay on Musical Expression*, 1753). It was the idea of Handel overcoming artistic flaws through his own greatness that Price adopted, and which became the standard approach to Handel for the next twenty-five years.

Handel's commanding position in the musical life of the country was in any case secure before philosophy found an aesthetic basis for it, and rested on the interest in 'Ancient' music which flourished in mid-eighteenth-century England. Many anecdotes remain which show Handel's admiration for earlier composers (see, for example, p. 224). Despite this he was seen during his life as an opponent of 'that indefatigable society, the gropers into antique music, and hummers of madrigals' (*Harmony in an Uproar*, 1734), and it is ironic that after his death, his music should have become the backbone of programmes given by the Academy of Ancient Music and the Concerts of Antient Music. Both these institutions succeeded not only in keeping Handel's music alive, but also in preserving the social élite which had grown around him during the last few years of his life. The Subscribers to the Antient Concerts, founded in 1768 and granted royal patronage in 1785, were amateurs from the highest London society, whose wealth ensured that the orchestras comprised 'the best hands in Town'.

The first great display of public devotion initiated by the Handelians was conceived early in 1783, when three influential musical amateurs, Sir Watkin Williams Wynn, the Earl of Sandwich, and his enthusiastic secretary Joah Bates, were struck with the idea of celebrating the centenary of Handel's birth (which they mistakenly believed fell in 1784) with performances of his works 'on such a scale of magnificence, as could not be equalled in any part of the world'. George

*'Mainwaring's *Handel*'.

LIST of the Compofitions felected from the Works of
HANDEL,

For the firft Commemoration Performance.

The CORONATION ANTHEM.

PART I.

OVERTURE—ESTHER.
The Dettingen TE DEUM.

PART II.

OVERTURE, with the DEAD MARCH in SAUL.
Part of the FUNERAL ANTHEM.
When the ear heard him.
He delivered the poor that cried.
His body is buried in Peace.
GLORIA PATRI, from the JUBILATE.

PART III.

ANTHEM—*O fing unto the Lord.*
CHORUS—*The Lord fhall reign,* from ISRAEL IN EGYPT.

LIST of the Pieces felected for the Second Performance.

PART I.

SECOND HAUTBOIS CONCERTO.

Sorge infausta, AIR in ORLANDO.

Ye Sons of Israel—CHORUS in JOSHUA.

Rende il sereno—AIR in SOSARMES.

Caro vieni—in RICHARD THE FIRST.

He smote all the first-born. CHORUS, from ISRAEL IN EGYPT.

Va tacito e nascosto. AIR in JULIUS CÆSAR.

SIXTH GRAND CONCERTO.

M'allontano sdegnose pupille. AIR in ATALANTA.

He gave them hail-stones for rain. CHORUS—ISRAEL IN EGYPT.

PART II.

FIFTH GRAND CONCERTO.

Dite che fà—AIR in PTOLEMY.

Vi fida lo spofo—in ÆTIUS.

Fallen is the foe, CHORUS, in JUDAS MACCHABÆUS.

OVERTURE OF ARIADNE.

Alma del gran Pompeo. Accompanied Recitative in JULIUS CÆSAR.

Followed by

Affanni del pensier— AIR in OTHO.

Nasco al bosco — —- in ÆTIUS.

Io t'abbraccio —DUET in RODELINDA.

ELEVENTH GRAND CONCERTO.

Ah! mio cor!—AIR in ALCINA.

ANTHEM. *My heart is inditing of a good matter.*

III was enthusiastic and recommended Westminster Abbey as an appropriate setting. From the start, the Commemoration took on an aspect of overt nationalism. As *The European Magazine* pompously asserted in March 1784: 'The English nation have seldom been wanting in gratitude to those who have contributed either to the glory or to the entertainment of the country.'

The unprecedented size of chorus and orchestra was seen as a proof of the musicality of the nation: 'From all the information with which my musical readings and inquiries have furnished me', wrote Burney, the official chronicler of the event, 'it seems not too much to say, that the musicians assembled on this occasion exceeded in abilities, as well as number, those of every band that has been collected in modern times'. As elaborate preparations went on at Westminster Abbey under the supervision of James Wyatt, expectation grew into intense excitement at the sheer size of the venture: 'The number of voices and instruments which are to unite in the performance of this Oratorio will produce an effect, that those best versed in the power of sounds can have but a very imperfect idea of; and even such as are auditors will never have language to express the sensations they must feel, if they have *music* in their souls!' (*The European Magazine*).

Originally the organizers had planned a two-day celebration, but 'it was at his majesty's instigation that the celebrity was extended to three days instead of two, which he thought would not be sufficient for the display of HANDEL's powers' (Burney). The events were planned for 26 May, when a selection from the anthems and oratorios would be performed in the Abbey; for 27 May, with a programme of secular orchestral music and arias in the Pantheon; and for 29 May, with a performance of *Messiah* at Westminster. Tickets went on sale at a guinea each for all three evenings at the end of February, and were soon sold out.

As well as being 'a more numerous Band than was ever known to be collected in any country, or on any occasion whatever', the orchestra promised some unusual sonorities. 'In order to render the band as powerful and complete as possible', wrote Burney, 'it was determined to employ every species of instrument that was capable of producing grand effects in a great orchestra, and spacious building'. Among the rarities were six 'Tromboni, or Sacbuts', played by members of his Majesty's military band; a double bassoon, 'made with the approbation of Mr. HANDEL, by Stainsby, the Flute-maker, for the coronation of his late majesty, George the Second', but never used in any band in England 'till now, by the ingenuity and perseverance of Mr. Ashly, of the Guards'; and to supplement the kettle-drums from the Tower (often heard in Handel's own oratorio performances) 'The Double-Base Kettle Drums . . . much longer, as well as more capacious, than the common kettle-drum'. Most marvellous of all was the combined organ and harpsichord from which Joah Bates was to direct the performers:

The excellent ORGAN, erected at the west end of the Abbey, for the commemoration performances only, is the workmanship of the ingenious Mr. Samuel Green, of Islington . . . The keys of communication with the harpsichord, at which Mr. Bates, the conductor, was seated, extended nineteen feet from the body of the organ, and twenty feet seven inches below the perpendicular of the set of keys by which it is usually played. Similar keys were first contrived in this country for HANDEL himself, at his Oratorios; but to convey them to so great a distance from the instrument, without rendering the touch impracticably heavy, required uncommon ingenuity and mechanical resources.

60   The musicians were to be disposed at the west end of the Abbey nave, the King and court at the east, 'and the public in general, to the number of between three and four thousand persons, in the area and galleries' between them.

Each performance was preceded by a single rehearsal, 'an indisputable proof of the high state of cultivation to which practical Music is at present arrived in this country', although a '*drilling Rehearsal*' had been held in the preceding week to audition volunteers – only two were turned away. The first general rehearsal in the Abbey was disrupted by the crowd of spectators, but produced 'small mistakes, and great effects', so that for subsequent rehearsals an admission price of half a guinea was charged. What surprised the audiences at the rehearsals above all was the accuracy and precision of the performers, without even a conductor to beat time: 'When all the wheels of that huge machine, the Orchestra, were in motion, the effect resembled a clock-work in every thing, but want of feeling and expression' (Burney).

By 26 May the city was crowded with people for the celebration. Many, so Burney tells us, found themselves at nine o'clock in front of the Abbey doors: 'such a croud of ladies and gentlemen were assembled together as became very formidable and terrific to each other'. For a description of the performance itself, Silas Neville's diary account, free from the constraints of royal approval which bound Burney, is vivid and immediate:

Wed. May 26. Commemoration of Handel – first part in Westminster Abbey, one of the greatest musical performances I ever heard, indeed with regard to the number of the bands the greatest; 513 performers. The effect of the first crash of such a band was astonishing. Wonder mixed with pleasure appeared in every countenance. They played in time – excellent time – contrary to all expectations. Hey* was the leader; his manner is graceful & easy to be observed by the band.

Le spectacle bien magnifique. The great aile of the Abbey was converted into a most superb theatre with very rich & elegant decorations; at the west end the orchestra in the gallery *vis-à-vis* the Throne or Royal box, in front of which seats for the Lords & Ladies of the Court, hung with white satin with festoons of gold fringe; behind these on each side the Throne seats for my Lords the Bishops & the clergy of the Abbey with purple; the two side galleries & the body of the aile which formed the pit hung with crimson damask & festoons of the same colour. The audience was splendid to a

---

*Mr. Hay and Mr. Cramer are listed as principals of the first violins.

degree. It consisted chiefly of the first persons in the Kingdom of both sexes. I was so lucky as to sit near a lady of uncommon beauty.

The next evening's performance at the Pantheon was generally agreed to be rather an anti-climax: not disappointing in itself, as Neville's description shows, but only in comparison to the unique splendours of the day before:

Thurs. May 27. This evening at the 2nd performance in Commemoration of Handel. This at the Pantheon & like the other consisted entirely of pieces selected from the works of this great composer. This was a grand concert but did not strike so much as that at the Abbey. We have had many grand concerts at the Pantheon, but the performance at the church was entirely new & from the dignity of the place, the immense band & other circumstances the first of its kind. Here there was not room for more than half the band. Cramer was the leader. Madame Mara has an exquisite voice of great power and variety, but is very ugly. Miss Cantelo has a sweet voice & a very pretty person. They sung delightfully both here & at the Abbey, but if I was to do justice to all the great vocal & instrumental performers who generously assisted at this Commemoration I should fill many pages. So many voices, such prodigious kettle drums, that most powerfull instrument the trombone & the loftiness of the place so well adapted to give the highest effect to musical sound – all conspired to make the choruses at the Church grand indeed. What would have been the effect of the same entertainment in a magnificent Italian Church!

Mr Wyat has great merit in the building erected on this occasion. It is all mortice work. He was not permitted to drive a nail in the Church.

The Pantheon was quite full & the company of the first water – a box for the royal family in the gallery opposite the Orchestra. George & his consort & several of their children at both performances.

Neville seems not to have attended the final scheduled performance of *Messiah* on the next day but one, which began after the Royal Family had made its stately entrance at midday; but *The European Magazine* records what must have been a general sense of wonder at the grandeur of the whole thing: 'The immense volume and torrent of sound was almost too much for the head or the senses to bear – we were elevated into a species of delirium . . .'. So great was the success of the two scheduled performances in the Abbey that a further two repeat performances were given, on 31 May and 5 June. Miss Mary Hamilton, attending the repeat of *Messiah* in the august company of Boswell, Burney and Sir Joshua Reynolds, confirms in her diary the effect that this grand rendering of the work produced: 'I was so delighted that I thought myself in the heavenly regions. 513 Performers, the Harmony so unbroken that it was like the fall of Waters from one source, imperceptibly blended. The Spectacle too was sublime, So universal a silence, So great a number of People'.

Some more sceptical members of the audience in the Abbey, expecting 'little more than noise and confusion' from such a vast array of forces, were surprised despite themselves. Burney's private opinion before the performances, in sharp contrast to his reaction after them, was that so many musicians could produce nothing but chaos. His fears were only heightened by the fact that the Directors of the Commemoration ignored his advice; as he wrote to his long-standing confidant, Thomas Twining, 'I was invited to meet them . . . to 5 or 6 Dinners; but so far from doing any good, I c^d not edge in a Word – all I had to do was to stuff – drink – & be a witness to their importance & blunders'.*

As it turned out, the performances made a great effect on him and Twining reports that he 'had been *worked* prodigiously' by them. His enthusiasm was channelled into a plan for writing an account of the Commemoration – a plan which coincided with the wishes of the King and the Directors. Somewhat reluctantly he agreed to donate the profits from his book to the Fund of Decayed Musicians (which had already benefited to the tune of £6000 from the Commemoration). Worse was to come, as the King and Joah Bates imposed their conditions: '*one key* of Panegyric is all they want. – fine! – very fine! – charming! exquisite! grand! Sublime!!!. These are all the notes (a Hexachord) I must use'. What angered Burney most of all was the unreasoning devotion to Handel which both Bates and the King displayed in themselves, and required of others; Burney's deepest musical convictions were flouted and outraged: 'my God! – what contraction, & childish prejudices – how deaf, as well as how blind are both to real Genius!' The constraints of writing under the 'Royal Eye' and the tempting prospect of a position in the King's pay forced Burney to suppress his real sentiments. As a record of the five performances, his *Account* is sincere enough; as a considered view of Handel it is decidedly incomplete.

Burney has often and misleadingly been represented as the champion of Handel. The chapter on 'Italian Opera in Eighteenth Century England' in his *History* is longer than the rest of Book IV put together, and is dominated by an exhaustive account of Handel's operas; in a notebook he testifies that he had been for many years 'a blind admirer of Handel'. In fact Burney's devotion to the composer was partial and his admiration qualified by a preference, growing more decided with the years, for the Neapolitan style. The emphasis placed on Handel in the *History* arose partly because Handel's operas were available to the public in the editions published by Walsh, supplemented by new editions prepared by Samuel Arnold during the years when Burney was writing his *History*, and partly to satisfy royal taste; the *Account* was a project in which the King took a close personal interest, insisting on seeing the pages in manuscript as they proceeded from Burney's pen.

A study of Burney's unpublished notebooks shows that his private feelings were far more critical than his published opinions could ever suggest.† Handel in Burney's notebooks was 'grand, masterly, full, and flowing', unsurpassed in the breadth of orchestration and harmonic resources open to him; but set against the Neapolitan masters of the 1730s and '40s he could be found wanting:

---

*Quotations from Burney's correspondence with Twining come from R. Lonsdale: *Dr. Charles Burney*.
†See K. F. Grant: *Dr Burney as Critic*.

his melodies show 'a want of Delicacy'; he was guilty of 'crowding a score'; 'almost all his songs seem *scientific*'. Handel's merits were evident: 'That Handel was superior in the strength and boldness of his style, the richness of his Harmony, and complication of parts, to every Composer who has been most admired for such excellencies cannot be disputed . . .'. But, as Burney finally admitted in print in 1811, 'We will not assert that his vocal melodies were more polished and graceful than those of his countryman and contemporary Hasse; or his recitatives, or musical declaration, superior to that of his rivals, Bononcini and Porpora'.

Such heretical ideas ill-suited the musical temper of the times, fired as it was by the success of the 1784 Commemoration. Certainly someone in Burney's delicate position, conscious that his immediate audience would accept only unqualified devotion to Handel and that his wider readership would tolerate only small deviations from the royal line, could not have expressed them publicly. There were dissenting voices however. From his refuge in Olney, the devout, depressive poet William Cowper sent a letter to the Reverend William Unwin containing a 'short drama' to 'set the musical business in so clear a light that you will no longer doubt the propriety of the censure':

Scene opens, and discovers the Abbey filled with Hearers and Performers. An ANGEL *descends into the midst of them.*

> *Angel.* What are you about?
> *Answer.* Commemorating Handel.
> *Angel.* What is a commemoration?
> *Answer.* A ceremony instituted in honour of him whom we commemorate.
> *Angel.* But you sing anthems?
> *Answer.* Yes, because he composed them.
> *Angel.* And Italian airs?
> *Answer.* Yes, and for the same reason.
> *Angel.* So then because Handel set anthems to music, you sing them in honour of Handel; and because he composed the music of Italian songs, you sing them in a church. Truly Handel is much obliged to you, but God is greatly dishonoured.
> [*Exit* ANGEL, *and the music proceeds without further impediment.*

Like many other serious-minded moralists, Cowper objected not to the music of Handel, nor even to the circumstance of its having been performed at Westminster: it was the air of reverence and even of worship surrounding the Commemoration that was so distasteful:

> Lo Albion's sons, her nobles and her King
> To deck thy name eternal honors bring:
> Approach with awe thy venerable urn,
> And o'er thy embers with affection burn!

Nor deem their debt discharg'd or cancel'd now,
But to thy shrine perpetual homage vow:
Thus more than loftiest pyramids decree,
More than triumphal monuments to thee.

(John Ring, *The Commemoration of Handel*)

To Cowper the use of *Messiah* as a vehicle for Handel worship was idolatry:

Remember Handel? Who that was not born
Deaf as the dead to harmony, forgets,
Or can, the more than Homer of his age?
Yes – we remember him; and while we praise
A talent so divine, remember too
That His most holy book from whom it came
Was never meant, was never used before,
To buckram out the memory of a man.

(*The Task*, Book VI)

Cowper's friend and spiritual adviser, John Newton, who in 1784 and 1785 preached a series of fifty sermons on the 'Scriptural Passages, Which form the Subject of the Celebrated Oratorio of Handel', condemned the spirit in which the whole event had been conceived and executed: 'The gratification of the *Great*, the *Wealthy*, and the *Gay*, was chiefly consulted in the late exhibitions in Westminster-Abbey'.

But a tradition had been established and the Commemorations continued. In 1785 Mrs Delany's nephew went to the first of four 'grand performances of sacred music from the works of Handel' in the Abbey and reported that it was 'by far *the finest thing* both for *sight* or *sound* I *ever saw or heard*; I think you and Bernard would have been full *as well* entertained with it as with the best day's fly-fishing you ever had! . . .' This year the number of performers was increased to 616, and it went on growing. The next year there were 640, which caused the aging Horace Walpole some discomfort: 'The sight was really very fine, and the performance magnificent; but the chorus and kettle-drums for four hours were so thunderfull, that they gave me a head-ache, to which I am not at all subject'. These already considerable forces were augmented to 806 in 1787, when Harriet Granville wrote that the performance of *Messiah* 'fully answered every grand idea I had formed of it'. The violinist and composer Giardini (whose disposition according to an anonymous contemporary was 'truly diabolical') had another opinion. In the words of William Shield: 'He hated Handel, and the modern "German compositions". – When the performance of Handel's composition was proposed to be in Westminster Abbey Giardini so far from encouraging affected to sneer at the proposal, and said He would go 2 or 3 miles from the town, as He could then sufficiently hear the effect'. Some thousands of miles away from the town, Joseph Fowke – who had made his fortune in India, lost it in England, then returned to India to retrieve his losses – wrote to his daughter from Calcutta that he welcomed the 'Handel Jubilee' and hoped that 'sensible music may revive':

I feel a great Miss of Handel Overtures in 4 parts which I could not avoid returning to Messink for his amusement in the Voyage [the journey by boat back to England]. The more I study this great Author the more I am smitten with his superior excellencies. There is no end to the fertility of his imagination and his judgement keeps pace with it. He is sublime whenever he chuses to be so, and is never trifling. In short he seems to have the whole world of harmony at his command, with an exact knowledge of the powers of every instrument which he never introduces but with Effect. What a pity he is so seldom executed with any tolerable degree of correctness? In his own lifetime he was continually mortified by the want of steadiness & firmness in the performers, who were even then prone to run riot in the time.

In a subsequent letter, Fowke instructed his daughter to 'Take notice that in Handel's C time Allegro the Crotchet may be nearly valued by the beat of an old Man's pulse . . . . I have a perfect remembrance of Handel's manner, whose greatest beauty in these movements was a very even finger; so that in the subdivisions the semiquavers were precisely of the same value.'*

In 1791 the trial of Warren Hastings was postponed so that the Commemoration could proceed unhindered. A total of 1068 musicians were employed (including the young Hummel, who stood at the right shoulder of Joah Bates, helping him with the registration of the organ), and the audience was as lofty as ever. W. T. Parke called it 'a dignified display of the British court, united with the brilliant assemblage of the most beautiful and fashionable women of the Island'. For the performance of Messiah on 1 June, Haydn had a box near the royal family, and two of his biographers testify to the effect which this first experience of Handel performed in the English manner had on him: 'At this last Abbey Meeting, there was present one auditor, of all men the most capable of appreciating its excellence, the immortal Haydn, then on his first visit to this country; and from it he derived a confirmation of that deep reverence for the mighty genius of Handel, which, to the honour no less of his candid modesty than of his judgment, he was ever prone to avow' (William Shield). To Giuseppe Carpani Haydn confessed '. . . that when he heard the music of Hendl in London, he was struck as if he had been put back to the beginning of his studies and had known nothing up to that moment. He meditated on every note and drew from those most learned scores the essence of true musical grandeur'.

It was the Commemorations also that made possible a scheme to publish the entire corpus of 'those most learned scores'. As a result of Handel's business arrangements with Walsh and Cluer, many of his works had appeared wholly or partially in print during his lifetime, albeit most often without his personal

---

*From Fowke's collection of letters in the India Office Library, London. Fowke MS vol. 26, Eur E. 5. 53; vol. 24 Eur E. 5 66.

supervision. In the years just before and after Handel's death, Walsh's catalogues assumed more and more the appearance of a repository of the best of Handel, and with the issue of sixty overtures in arrangement for keyboard (publication completed *c.* 1755), Walsh produced the largest single corpus of any composer's music at that time. The Commemorations gave fresh impetus to a subscription scheme proposed by Birchall in 1783, but it was Dr Samuel Arnold, organist and composer to the Chapel Royal and official conductor of the Academy of Ancient Music, who rationalized the project and issued in 1785 a prospectus soliciting subscriptions for 'The Works of Handel, in Score; correct, uniform, and complete'. The influence of George III, who put his name down for twenty-five sets of the projected edition, was perhaps crucial. According to Thomas Busby, writing in 1825: 'The New interest given to the productions of the Prince of Modern Musicians, by this *royal* celebration of German genius, suggested to Dr. Arnold the idea of furnishing the public with a complete edition of Handel's works'.

Arnold's folio full-score editions were preceded by a continuo vocal-score edition of *The Songs of Handel Compleat*, published in 1786 by Harrison 'under the Direction of Doctor Arnold'. Between 1787 and 1797 Arnold issued 180 separate parts of his own edition, which the subscribers could bind as they chose. *Athalia*, *Theodora* and *Messiah* were the first works to appear, *Theodora* with a frontispiece representing the 'Apotheosis of Handel'. After eleven years the series was discontinued 'in consequence of the many deaths that have happened, as well as other losses sustained by those who have seceded &c.&c.'

Whilst preparing his editions, Arnold had been much perplexed by the problem of variants and adaptations, a problem of collation which has faced all subsequent editors. In a letter of 1797 to one of the subscribers, Joseph Cator, he explained that he had been unable to find definitive versions of many oratorios, and that many of the songs which Walsh had published were drawn from other works. But his editions include a number of variant readings which have never been reprinted since, and in some cases Arnold clearly had access to important manuscript versions which have since disappeared, though for some reason he did not use the autographs in the Royal Library. Issues 146–149 (*Agrippina*) include a facsimile of a page of the manuscript score used by Arnold, mistakenly thought by him to be Handel's autograph.*

Shortly after the Handel project was brought to a close Arnold fell from the steps of his library, and this accident, compounded by the fact that his 'general habits were not the most abstemious', hastened his death in 1802. His work deserves more praise than later editors, notably Chrysander, have deigned to give it; it was the first attempt at a *Gesamtausgabe* (Complete Edition) of any composer, and it remained the standard edition until the formation of the German Handel Society in 1858. It was, even so, very much a product of its time in including nineteen oratorios, but only five of Handel's Italian operas, a reflection not only of national pride in the English language but also of contemporary taste, which rejected the older forms of *opera seria*.

57

---

*See P. Hirsch: 'Dr. Arnold's Handel Edition'.

The last of the great eighteenth-century Handel Commemorations was held in 1791. Perhaps the organizers were conscious of the criticism voiced by Burney in the same year: 'It cannot reasonably be supposed, that there is a sufficient number of persons in this kingdom, whose wealth, or zeal for the honour of this great and favourite master, will continue much longer to enable or incline them to attend such an expensive performance year after year, merely to hear the same pieces repeated'. But the damage had already been done. The ripples of the 1784 Commemoration spread throughout England as festivals in Birmingham, York, Manchester and Sheffield imitated the grand performing style and provoked the ecstatic reactions of their London original. It was this widespread 'Handelomania', in Burney's private opinion, that threatened the vitality of English music. At the bottom of a page in one of his notebooks appears a confession that could never have been allowed to pass outside its covers: 'I dare not say what I have long thought. That it is our reverence for old authors and bigotry to Handel, that has prevented us from keeping pace with the rest of Europe in the cultivation of Music'.

> *The distinction due to Shakespeare in energy of poetry, to Michelangelo in sculpture and painting, Handel may justly claim in the sister art; to him belongs the Majesty of Music. The merit of Handel is not confined; it is of universal cast, that he may be styled the great musician of nature.*

Eighteenth-century programmes of the Three Choirs Festival show how deeply the reverence went. *Messiah* had been first performed at the 1757 Festival in Gloucester, where 'it was received . . . with rapturous applause, and has been repeated at every succeeding meeting of the Three Choirs' (Rev. Daniel Lyons, *Origin & Progress of the Meeting of the Three Choirs*, 1812). For the rest of the century Handel's oratorios dominated the meetings, together with a small core of other works: *Zadok the Priest*, the Dettingen Te Deum, *Acis and Galatea*, *Alexander's Feast* and *L'Allegro*. The same core of secular vocal works and oratorio extracts, together with occasional opera numbers, formed the basic repertoire of the Concerts of Antient Music which kept the Handel flame alive in London. Programme books indicate that almost two-thirds of the concerts were devoted to Handel, with over a half of this figure being oratorio extracts; not a surprising imbalance given that Samuel Arnold was Director of the Concerts from 1789 until his death, and Joah Bates a frequent conductor.

If Handel became in England a figure of nationalistic pride and religious fervour, his classic status ensured him varying degrees of recognition and popularity elsewhere in the world. Even during his lifetime his music had been performed on the Continent. After his death, Michael Arne, touring Germany with a singing pupil, gave the first public performance of *Messiah* in Hamburg on 21 May 1772, following a private performance on 15 April; in 1775, C. P. E. Bach conducted the work in a German version. Mozart, along with the rest of the Mannheim public, was bored by a *Messiah* which Vogler gave there in 1777; but Goethe, hearing it for the first time in Weimar three years later, was deeply impressed. Over forty years later, he confessed that it was *Messiah* 'which earlier led me to the most serious in musical art'.

The greatest eighteenth-century advocate of Handel's music in Germany was Johann Adam Hiller, an intellectual writer and musician with strong views on German song and aesthetics; he taught the young Gertrud Schmeling, who later became Madame Mara and sang so effectively in the 1784 London Commemoration. For a performance of *Messiah* in Berlin in 1786, Hiller's approach was pragmatic rather than reverential: 'Many improvements may be made in Handel's compositions by the employment of the wind instruments, according to the fashion of the present day'. Nor did his adaptations stop at reorchestrating Handel's score; he shortened and altered the original to produce 'an entirely new score, as far as may be what Handel would himself have written at the present day'. Some of the results might have surprised Handel; 'If God be for us', for instance, was transformed from a violin solo to an elaborate and quite incongruous solo for bassoon.

Hiller's cavalier treatment of Handel was pursued with increasing enthusiasm as subsequent editors presented his works to their publics in a form adapted to the tastes and techniques of their own times. In Vienna during the 1780s Baron van Swieten introduced a wider selection of Handel's music to the public at his informal Sunday concerts in the Hall of the Imperial Library. Mozart attended regularly and in 1788 reorchestrated *Acis and Galatea* for one of the programmes. The following year it was the turn of *Messiah*, and in 1790 of the *St Cecilia Ode* and *Alexander's Feast*. Apart from the obvious choice of *Messiah*, Mozart had picked those works of Handel which exploit atmospheric colouring, and avoided those which display militaristic fervour or epic choral activity. His ability to update Handel without destroying the essential character of the music was crucial to its success in late eighteenth-century Vienna, and evidence of Mozart's own genius, as Baron van Swieten said: 'He who can clothe Händel so solemnly and so tastefully that he pleases the modish fop on the one hand and on the other still shows himself in his sublimity, has felt his worth, has understood him, has penetrated to the well-spring of his expression, from which he can and will draw confidently'. Mozart's 'additional accompaniments' were never intended to replace a keyboard continuo; it is notable, however, that they continue seamlessly and without pause through those cadential moments where earlier soloists would have been expected to halt for an impromptu cadenza, and thus indicate a major shift in stylistic practice. Possibly the intimacy of Van Swieten's concerts discouraged lavish display. From the extant performance material it appears there was a chorus of twelve singers in all, who shared the solos.

If Mozart's intervention served to make Handel more palatable in Vienna, his 'improvements' were not so well received in England, where Handel's own scoring (though not the size of his forces) was more carefully respected. After the first performance of Mozart's version at Covent Garden in March 1805, the reviewer for *The Sun* wrote: 'We entertain a very high respect for the genius of

Mozart, but we also hold the unrivalled powers of Handel in due reverence, and therefore must enter our protest against any such alterations in works that have obtained the sanction of time and of the best musical judges'. Mozart's touching-up work on Handel's scores certainly implied no disrespect, and he showed in any case a full appreciation of Handel's strengths. 'Handel knows better than any of us what will make an effect', he once said to Rochlitz; 'when he chooses he strikes like a thunderbolt'.

> It was from Handel that I learned that style consists in force of assertion. If you can say a thing with one stroke unanswerably you have style; if not, you are at best a marchand de plaisir, a decorative littérateur or a musical confectioner, or a painter of fans with cupids and cocottes. Handel had this power . . . You may despise what you like; but you cannot contradict Handel.   (George Bernard Shaw, 1913)

Haydn, another regular member of Van Swieten's musical circle in Vienna, had been particularly struck by the large-scale Handel performances in Westminster Abbey during his first visit to England in 1791. William Shield travelled with him from London to Taplow, 'and having (the preceding evening) observed his countenance expressing rapturous astonishment during the Concert of Ancient music, I embraced the favourable opportunity of enquiring how he estimated the Chorus in Joshua "The Nations tremble at the dreadful sound." The reply: "He had long been acquainted with [the] music, but never knew half its powers before he heard it, and he was perfectly certain that only one inspired Author ever did, or ever would pen so sublime a composition"' (*An Introduction to Harmony*, 1800). When Shield later complimented Haydn on the recitatives in *Il Ritorno di Tobia*, Haydn returned that 'Deeper and deeper' from *Jephtha* 'greatly surpassed them in Pathos and Contrast'. As the pre-eminent composer of the Austrian Empire, Haydn used his influence with Joseph II to ensure that Handel was well represented in the Imperial Library, and instructed his own copyist, Johann Elssler, to make copies of Handel oratorios (in the Mozartian orchestration).

When Haydn left England for the second time in 1795, he took with him, as a present from Salomon, the libretto for a possible future oratorio to be called *The Creation*. This text, which has since disappeared, provided the basis for Van Swieten's translation, which he hoped to lay 'in front of the excellent Haydn for him to compose in the spirit and manner of Handel's.' According to Griesinger, the English original had been written by one 'Lidley' (= Linley?), and tradition asserts that it had been intended for Handel (see p. 195n).* When the full score of Haydn's masterpiece was eventually published in 1800, it carried a bilingual text, showing that the composer intended the English to have equal authority with the German. After the first English performance of *The Creation* at Covent

---

*See N. Temperley: 'New light'.

Garden on 28 March 1800, the *Morning Herald* was complimentary if slightly defensive: 'It is certainly a fine composition, in every respect worthy of its great author . . . and although not equal in grandeur to the divine compositions of the immortal HANDEL, is, nevertheless, on the whole, a very charming production'. Just over a week later, following a repeat performance of the oratorio, the *Herald* printed another review in which the tone had distinctly chilled from the defensive to the challenging: ' – it is correctly scientific, for all we know, and certainly not devoid of impressive harmonies; but it breathes no more the sacred inspiration of HANDEL, than KOTZEBUE does of that which immortalized our own SHAKESPEARE!' This was the spirit in which Haydn's presumptuous incursions into Handelian territory would be regarded by the English for many years to come.

Both Mozart and Haydn had paid Handel the compliment of imitation. Beethoven, who of all the great Viennese classical composers was warmest in his expressed admiration for Handel, wrote a two-part fugue on the 'Harmonious Blacksmith' as an examination piece for the post of second court organist when he was thirteen years old. In 1796, he composed a set of variations for piano and cello on 'See the conqu'ring hero comes' from *Judas Maccabaeus*; and only months before his death, thirty years later, announced to Holz: 'In future I shall write in the manner of my grand-master Handel annually only an oratorio or a concerto for some string or wind instrument'. According to Schindler, Handel was the inspiration for Beethoven during the composition of his Overture to *Die Weihe des Hauses* (1822): 'he had long cherished the plan to write an overture in the strict, expressly in the Handelian, style'. In a letter of 1819 Beethoven urged his patron and pupil the Archduke Rudolph 'not to forget Handel's works, as they always offer the best nourishment for your ripe musical mind, and will at the same time lead to admiration for this great man'. To Edward Schulz, who visited him in 1823, Beethoven asserted 'very distinctly in German, "Handel is the greatest composer that ever lived". I cannot describe to you with what pathos, and I am inclined to say, with what sublimity of language, he spoke of the *Messiah* of this immortal genius. Every one of us was moved when he said, "I would uncover my head, and kneel down at his tomb!"'

The next year Johann Stumpff had the following written exchange with the deaf composer:

'Whom do you consider the greatest composer that ever lived?'

'Handel,' was his instantaneous reply; 'to him I bow the knee', and he bent one knee to the floor.

. . . I took the liberty of writing: 'As you yourself, a peerless artist in the art of music, exalt the merits of Handel so highly above all, you must certainly own the scores of his principal works.'

'I? How should I, a poor devil, have got them? . . .'

. . . At that moment I made a secret vow: Beethoven, you shall have the works of Handel for which your heart is longing if they are anywhere to be found.

Two years later Stumpff fulfilled his vow and presented to Beethoven (via

Andreas Streicher) Samuel Arnold's edition of Handel's works. Gerhard von Breuning remembered its effect: 'When I entered his room at noon as usual, he at once pointed out these works piled up on the piano, while his eyes glowed with joy. 'Look, these were given to me to-day. These works have given me great pleasure. For a long time I've been wishing to have them; for Händel is the greatest, the most capable of composers; there is still much to be learned from him. Just hand me those books again!'''

> *One morning, after I had been singing with him [Gluck], he said, 'Follow me upstaires, Sir, and I will introduce you to one whom all my life I have made my study and endeavoured to imitate.' I followed him into his bedroom, and opposite to the head of the bed saw a full-length picture of Handel in a rich frame. 'There, Sir,' said he, 'is the portrait of the inspired master of our art. When I open my eyes in the morning I look upon him with reverential awe and acknowledge him as such, and the highest praise is due to your country for having distinguished and cherished his gigantic genius.'* (Michael Kelly, 1826)

In England during the early years of the nineteenth century 'Grand Musical Festivals' continued to be promoted throughout the provinces, largely through the industry of the Ashley family, five of whom had been amongst the performers in the Commemoration of 1784. In 1815 Charles Ashley was invited to direct the first Edinburgh Musical Festival and agreed to provide 'efficient orchestral performers from England, both vocal and instrumental, together with the requisite music, and the use of an excellent organ from Covent-garden theatre'. Handel filled most of the programme, with the usual oratorio extracts and selections from *Messiah*; and if the number of musicians was small by English standards (58 vocal, 61 orchestral performers), the size of the audience for *Messiah* made up for it: 'The number of persons who attended the performance this morning was very great; and consequently the struggle for admission was considerable, and occasioned a good deal of personal inconvenience to the female part of the company, some of whom fainted in consequence of fright and pressure'.

When Handel festivals resumed in London in 1834, it was against a background of nationalism strikingly reminiscent of the previous century. There may have been only 644 musicians in the Abbey but:

> When the company and the performers were assembled, the *coup d'oeil* presented a magnificent spectacle, that made the observer think of chivalrous times; of that assemblage of the nobles and the better classes of society, which so frequently took place within the walls of a gothic edifice on high days of festival and rejoicing . . .
>
> It was a gratifying sight to look on the royal party; – to see the king and the youthful successor to his crown, the Princess Victoria, now our gracious and

beloved sovereign, thus seated in the Abbey, the most venerable and historical building in the kingdom, surrounded by so many of the people, to attend a commemoration of Handel, in the performance of some of his greatest works.

(Mrs Bray, *Life, Personal and Professional . . . of . . . Handel*)

The organist was Vincent Novello and his daughter Clara, just sixteen, sang 'How beautiful are the feet' with a 'quiet truthfulness, that pure, firm, silvery voice, precisely suited to the devout words'.

By this time public response to Handel's works, especially *Messiah*, was primarily religious: reactions to the music were filtered through a thick gauze of devotional sentiment. A pamphlet of 1843, *Remarks upon the Use and Abuse of Musical Festivals*, written by 'An English Churchman', shows to what extent the established Church had taken over the biggest events in the musical calendar. The practice of holding music festivals in churches, according to this anonymous writer, 'has gradually, we almost said imperceptibly, grown to so full a stature, as to include in its grasp, or involve under its influence, the whole body of Christ's church in this land.' Even Handel's secular music was appropriated for the Church; one writer voiced the surprising conviction that 'all Handel's fine Italian airs [are] essentially of a sacred character.'

In 1842, a new publication to supply choral societies with cheap and appropriate music was founded in London. The *Musical Times* was the brainchild of Joseph Mainzer, a German educationist who came to England in 1841 and who saw choral singing as 'a powerful auxiliary in the religious and moral education of the people'. In May 1844 the *Musical Times* was taken over by Novello and two years later octavo editions of sacred music began to be published, starting with Vincent Novello's vocal score reduction of *Messiah*, advertised as 'the cheapest musical publication ever offered to the public' (it cost 6s). It was quickly followed by *Judas Maccabaeus* and Haydn's *Creation*, both so popular that J. Alfred Novello was soon able to publish the choruses alone at half price 'for the poorer Choral Societies, who want a large number of the Choruses'. In 1849 the price was lowered still further to prevent Societies from doing their own copying, and to protect the Novello copyright: 'All separate Vocal Parts are now published for THREE HALF-PENCE PER PAGE, which will be found less costly than the blank music paper necessary to copy out the same quantity of music'.

These cheap, well-printed and conveniently sized editions of Handel's oratorios assisted the popularization of a small core of Handel's works immeasurably. A century before, his music had been the province of an élite determined to buttress itself from modern music behind the finest orchestras money could provide and a social cachet sealed by royal involvement. Arnold's edition of Handel had been the backbone of provincial performances for over fifty years, but its cost and its size together limited its usefulness as a vehicle for widespread dissemination. Novello's editions undoubtedly fired the enthusiasm for oratorio in general and *Messiah* in particular which foreign visitors to England often noted. Wagner, in London during 1855 at the invitation of the

Philharmonic Society, was struck by the ritual element in the Sacred Harmonic Society's performances of *Messiah* at Exeter Hall, where Novello's scores were much in evidence:

> It was here that I came to understand the true spirit of English musical culture, which is bound up with the spirit of English Protestantism. This accounts for the fact that an oratorio attracts the public far more than an opera. A further advantage is secured by the feeling among the audience that an evening spent in listening to an oratorio may be regarded as a sort of service, and is almost as good as going to church. Every one in the audience holds a Handel piano score in the same way as one holds a prayer-book in church. These scores are sold at the box-office in shilling editions, and are followed most diligently – out of anxiety, it seemed to me, not to miss certain points solemnly enjoyed by the whole audience. For instance, at the beginning of the 'Hallelujah Chorus' it is considered proper for everyone to rise from his seat. This moment, which probably originated in an expression of enthusiasm, is now carried out at each performance of the *Messiah* with painfull precision . . . (*My Life*, English edition, 1911, pp. 634–5)

We have all had our Handelian training in church, and the perfect church-going mood is one of pure abstract reverence. A mood of active intelligence would be scandalous. Thus we get broken in to the custom of singing Handel as if he meant nothing; and as it happens that he meant a great deal, and was tremendously in earnest about it, we know rather less about him in England than they do in the Andaman Islands, since the Andamans are only unconscious of him, whereas we are misconscious.

(George Bernard Shaw, 1890)

As in England, it was the choral societies and musical festivals which spread performances of Handel oratorios throughout Germany in the first half of the nineteenth century. Moritz Hauptmann, cantor of the Thomas-Schule at Leipzig during the middle years of the century, reported on performances of *Israel in Egypt*, *Judas Maccabaeus* and *Jephtha*, as well as *Messiah*, in the city. A rehearsal of *Israel* in the Thomaskirche on 14 April 1854 particularly impressed him: 'There's health and strength for you! What poverty-stricken stuff is our best modern music, by the side of it! How we strain for effect, and miss all the simplicity and repose, which one associated with every bar of this oratorio, even in its most vigorous movements!' In 1857 Liszt, who disliked the 'Hallelujah-perruque of a Handel', called *Messiah* 'a *chef-d'oeuvre* which has been for years the "daily bread", so to speak, of great and small vocal societies both in England and Germany'.

The previous year, the music scholar Friedrich Chrysander and the literary historian Gottfried Gervinus had together founded the Händel-Gesellschaft in Leipzig, with the intention of publishing a collected edition of Handel's works both to complete and supersede the Arnold edition, now eighty years old. The first volume (*Susanna*) appeared in 1858 with an introduction setting out Chrysander's editorial method. Four sources were specified as the basis of the editions, and although Chrysander planned to publish Handel's rough drafts and variants at a later date, these were not used systematically in his edition. Of these four one in particular, the set of conducting scores discovered in 1856, assumed prominence over Handel's autographs and the Smith copies in the Royal Collection. In all a total of ninety-five volumes was published by Chrysander; in many cases they remain the standard edition although their authoritativeness has been seriously challenged with reference to the eclecticism of method and the fact that Chrysander carried out none of the detailed comparison of sources which alone could clarify Handel's revisions. His industry and dedication is undoubted however: when his grant from the Hanoverian crown ceased on the annexation of Hanover by Prussia, Chrysander continued production himself in a printing shop near his home, and obtained funds by selling produce from his own garden. There is even a story, possibly apocryphal, that while studying the manuscripts in London, Chrysander kept going for sixteen or eighteen hours a day by drinking black coffee and immersing his feet in ice-cold water.*

One target for Chrysander's sometimes savage attacks was the London Handel Society, founded in 1843 'for the production of a superior and standard edition of the works of Handel'. Although the Society was disbanded five years later, the publishers (Cramer, Beale & Co.) continued production until 1858, issuing twelve major works, mostly oratorios, and two collections. In its aim of producing an edition based on the autographs, the Handel Society was both truer and on sounder bibliographical ground than Chrysander. Mendelssohn, who had performed *Israel in Egypt* in Düsseldorf in 1833, was asked by the Society to prepare an edition and was entirely scrupulous in his approach; as he wrote to Ignaz and Charlotte Moscheles in March 1845: '. . . I cannot possibly introduce my marks of expression into a score of Handel's, nor my tempi, nor anything else, unless it is to be made perfectly clear what is mine and what Handel's; and as he has put his pianos and fortes and his figured basses where he thought them necessary, I must either omit them or leave the public in doubt as to which is his marking and which mine'.

If the German public sustained sufficient interest in Handel to warrant the preparation of a new complete edition, France seems to have been indifferent or actively hostile. In 1784 Mme Mara sang 'I know that my Redeemer liveth' in Paris, but according to an Englishman present in the audience, 'the French had not the taste to like it'. Some enthusiasm was shown in 1827 for a performance of selections from *Messiah*, in Mozart's orchestration; 'Handel's *Alleluia* woke the audience'. The more academic and didactic of French musicians granted Handel his contrapuntal skill. Reicha, professor of counterpoint at the Conservatoire in the early nineteenth century, based a six-part fugue in his didactic method on the Handel theme 'I will sing unto the Lord'; Grétry,

---

*See A. Hyatt King: *Handel and his Autographs*, p. 14.

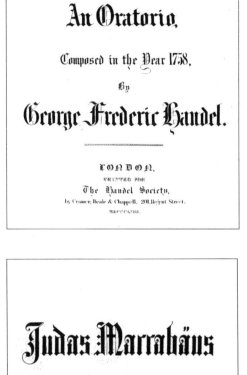

Edition of the English Handel Society (founded 1843): title-pages for the series and for Jephtha.

Title-page of Judas Maccabaeus in Chrysander's edition for the Händel-Gesellschaft in Leipzig (initiated in 1858).

writing in 1789, insisted that 'like everyone else, I love Handel's fugues, the most worked-out fugues I know; but in listening to them, in admiring them, I hunt for the melody with the impatience of a lover hunting his mistress in a thick wood' (*Essai sur la musique*, 1789, p. 389). Berlioz, objecting like Liszt to Handel's wig, was rudely dismissive of 'ce tonneau de porc et de bière qu'on appelle Haendel', although, curiously, he included a scene from *Athalia* in a benefit concert at the Opéra.* *Messiah* was never performed complete in Paris until 1873, when a performance under the direction of Charles Lamoureux inspired Arthur Pougin to urge his countrymen: 'Let us try at least to recapture the past, and prove to the musical world that France is ready to love, understand and admire everything!' His plea was heard; *Messiah* was performed more frequently in the next thirty years, and in 1900 gained the official seal of approval by being performed at the opening of the Paris Exposition.

No doubt acceptance of Handel in France was inhibited by her political enmity with England; after all, civic organizations in parts of Austria performed Handel's oratorios dealing with Israel's liberation from captivity at the height of the Napoleonic wars. On the other side of the Atlantic, Handel began to be known just as the Americans were on the point of asserting their own rights to independence. On 16 January 1770, according to the *New York Journal*, 'a Gentleman just arrived from Dublin' played a concerto on the French horn in the Gèorge Burns' Music Room, New York; he was followed in part two of the concert by another import from Dublin: 'A SACRED ORATORIO, on the Prophecies concerning CHRIST, and his Coming; being an Extract from the late Mr. HANDEL'S GRAND ORATORIO, called the MESSIAH, consisting of the Overture, and sixteen other Pieces, viz. Airs, Recitatives, and Choruses. Never performed in America'. Two other performances of *Messiah* extracts followed in October 1770 and April 1772. During the 1780s selections from *Messiah* became a regular feature of concert life in New York. In Boston a chorus of seventy performed selections from *Samson* and *Messiah* in January 1773; a decade later, choruses from several oratorios were performed in Bethlehem, Pennsylvania, where manuscript scores of *Messiah* from 1780 and 1790 (in Mozart's version) still survive. Two years after the 1784 Commemoration in London, Maria Storer came to New York from England, where she sang regularly in Handel festivals, and performed arias from *Messiah* in imitation of 'Handel's Sacred Music, as performed in Westminster Abbey'. Not to be outshone in its emulation of London, Philadelphia gathered together that same year a band of 230 vocal and 50 instrumental performers, which *The Pennsylvania Packet* for 30 May called 'the most complete, both with respect to number and accuracy of execution, ever, on any occasion, combined in this city, and, perhaps, throughout America'.

Another way in which American practice echoed English was in giving performances of *Messiah* for charity. William Selby's 'Concert of sacred Musick' (including extracts from *Messiah*) given in Boston in 1784 was organized 'for the benefit and relief of the poor prisoners confined in the jail of

---

Memoirs, ed. D. Cairns, p. 314.

this town'. Early next year Selby, who was an organist trained in England, put on another '*Spiritual Concert* for the benefit of those among us who have known better days', for which the *Boston Gazette* gave special instructions to its readers: 'At the performance of this Divine Chorus [the 'Hallelujah'], called by way of eminence the *Thunder Chorus*, it is usual for the whole audience to rise from their seats, and be upon their feet the whole time of the Chorus, in testimony of the humble adoration of the Supreme Governor of the Universe, our great and universal Parent, and in honor of our blessed Redeemer'.

In the early years of the nineteenth century, Boston was the artistic capital of America, and its musical life was dominated by the emigré Gottlieb Graupner, a Hanoverian by birth who had been an oboist in Haydn's London orchestra and who settled in Boston in 1797. As well as being a founder member of the Boston Philharmonic and the Handel and Haydn Societies, Graupner taught, published and sold music: in 1807 his stock included *Messiah*, *Judas Maccabaeus* and *Acis and Galatea* as well as music by Haydn and Mozart. It was through his influence that the first American edition of *Messiah* was published, 'under the patronage and inspection of the Handel and Haydn Society, Boston'.

> *I only ever met one American who seemed to like and understand Handel. How far he did so in reality I do not know, but* inter alia *he said that Handel 'struck ile with the* Messiah,' *and that 'it panned out well, the* Messiah *did.'*　　　　　　　(Samuel Butler, *Notebooks* 1874–1902)

The opening concert of the Society took place on Christmas Eve, 1815, and included selections from *Messiah*. Exactly three years later, the first complete performance of the work in America was given in Boylston Hall, initiating a tradition of Christmas Eve performances which continues to this day. The performers, according to one member of the audience, were not uniformly up to standard: 'The violins apparently played with no confidence (steadiness) in time or tune, the chorus was more than once completely thrown out by them, and the efforts of the vocal performers completely paralyzed by their want of spirit'. Eager to improve, the Society engaged the English tenor Charles Incledon to instruct them in the authentic London manner. At the first rehearsal, one of the singers records, Incledon 'bluntly remarked, the choir knew nothing about the grand and peculiar characteristics of that chorus ['For unto us a child is born']. He then, by request, told the Society what he knew by tradition, and proceeding to drill the singers, insisted on the unexcited progress of the semi-chorus portions till the climax was reached with the words, "Wonderful!" "Counsellor," etc., which should burst upon the ear with the square and solid stroke of a vast explosion'. Emerson, attending the Christmas *Messiah* in 1843, was particularly struck by the choruses: 'I walked in the bright paths of sound, and liked it best when the long continuance of a chorus had made the ear sensible to the music, made it as if there was none; then I was quite solitary and at ease in the melodious uproar. . . '.

In England, the 'astonishing rage' for Handel oratorios was growing. In 1856 the Crystal Palace Company approached the Sacred Harmonic Society with a suggestion that a Festival of the People in honour of Handel should be held in the enormous glass building recently transferred from Hyde Park to Sydenham. A preliminary 'Rehearsal' was arranged for the next year: 'From every large town in England came numbers of intelligent young persons, of the highest respectability, carefully trained under the new system of choral singing, and having an intellectual and personal enjoyment of the sublime strains they were to render'. The 'wonderful assembly of 2000 vocal and 500 instrumental performers' (Charles Greville) performed *Messiah*, *Judas Maccabaeus* and *Israel in Egypt*; but despite these impressive numbers, 'the volume of sound was dispersed and lost in the prodigious space'. The Queen and Consort of course attended: 'It was observed that the Queen beat time with a fan, and Prince Albert with a roll of music'.

63   For the Second Grand Handel Festival in 1859, things had improved. The main hall of the Crystal Palace was turned into an auditorium proper, with a false roof (or 'volarium') and special resonators to improve the acoustics. The choir, augmented to 2765 singers and the orchestra of 460, all under the direction of Sir Michael Costa, performed *Messiah*, *Israel* and a programme of selections – an arrangement which remained constant for most subsequent festivals in the second half of the nineteenth century. The total attendance (including one rehearsal) was 81,319, and the receipts amounted to £33,000, of which £18,000 went on expenses. From 1859 onwards, Handel Festivals were repeated triennially (with a special festival in 1885 to mark the bicentenary of Handel's birth). In terms of numbers the climax came in 1883, when the orchestra numbered 500, the choir 4000 and the total audience 87,769.

The massiveness of such forces, quite disproportionate to the scale of Handel's music, was justified in the opinion of the audiences by its effects. It was not to render Handel's score that 4500 people gathered to perform *Messiah*, but rather to participate in a ceremony whose basis was an assertion of power. To an observer of 1784, *Messiah* in Westminster Abbey had 'seemed like a great act of national assent to the fundamental truths of religion' (Rev. Robert Hall).

He (Handel) was a good old Pagan at heart, and (till he had to yield to the fashionable Piety of England) stuck to Opera, and Cantatas, such as Acis and Galatea, Milton's Penseroso, Alexander's Feast, etc., where he could revel and plunge without being tied down to Orthodoxy. And these are (to my mind) his really great works: these, and his Coronation Anthems, where Human Pomp is to be accompanied and illustrated.

(Edward Fitzgerald, 1863)

Audiences at the Crystal Palace in the second half of the nineteenth century were witness to an equally naked act of national assent to the nation. As Dean Ramsay proudly stated: 'The Handel commemorations have become identified with national feelings' (*Two Lectures on the Genius of Handel*, 1862).

GEORGE FREDERICK HANDEL Efqr.
born February XXIII. MDCLXXXIV.
died April XIV. MDCCLIX. L.F.Roubiliac inv! et sc!

55 The Handel monument by Roubiliac in Westminster Abbey, executed
in 1761. Handel's contemporary Sir John Hawkins considered it 'the most
perfect resemblance . . . in that the true lineaments of his face are
apparent'. His birth is inscribed as a year too early.

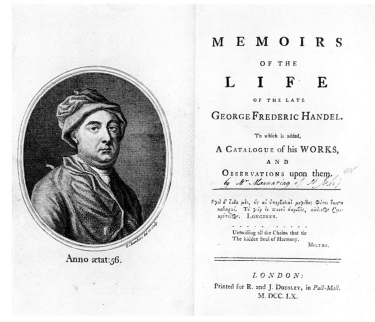

M E M O I R S

OF THE

L I F E

OF THE LATE

GEORGE FREDERIC HANDEL.

To which is added,

A CATALOGUE of his WORKS,

AND

OBSERVATIONS upon them.

by Mr Mainwaring of St John's

Ἐγὼ δ᾽ ἴσθα μὲν, ὡς αἱ ὑπερβολαὶ μεγίϛει Θώϛι ϊκετα
κοϑαρα. Τὸ γὰρ ἐν παντὶ ἀκριβὲς, κόϑινϙ Ϲω
μερτ᾽ϙ᾽. LONGINUS.

- - - - - -

Untwisting all the Chains that tie
The hidden Soul of Harmony.   MILTON.

LONDON:

Printed for R. and J. DODSLEY, in *Pall-Mall*.
M. DCC. LX.

Anno ætat:56.

56 Title-page of Mainwaring's Life of Handel (1760), the first biography
devoted to a composer.

APOTHEOSIS of HANDEL.

57 'Apotheosis of Handel', by Biagio Rebecca,
published in connection with the Commemoration
of 1787.

58 Mary Granville met Handel when she was ten. As Mrs Delany, in 1784, she was observed listening to 'I know that my Redeemer liveth' with 'tears . . . trickling down her venerable cheeks'.

59 Charles Burney, whose account of the 1784 Commemoration reflected, against his better judgment, the prevailing mood of idolatry.

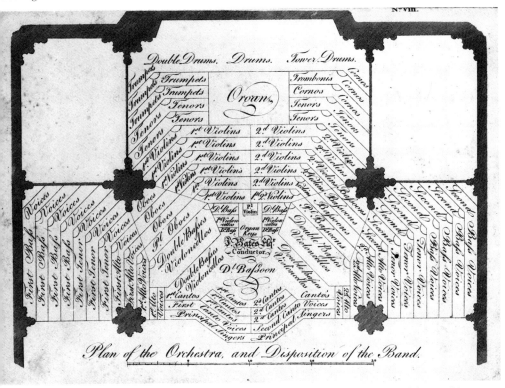

60 Seating plan of the performers for the Commemoration in Westminster Abbey, 1784.

61 The story that Handel's E major air and variations was inspired by one William Powell (the 'Harmonious Blacksmith') is a legend that publishers did nothing to discourage. The cover of Potter's edition shows St Lawrence, Whitchurch, adjacent to Cannons. The tombstone of Powell, the Parish Clerk, is prominent on the right.

62 Sheet music cover by John Brandard (1812–63) for a trio from *Acis and Galatea*.

63 The Great Handel Festival at Crystal Palace, 1859.

64, 65 Two Teutonic images of Handel in the twenties: *left*, announcement of the Leipzig 'Workers' Handel Festival' in 1926; *below*, powerful masonic structures and youthful athleticism feature in this staging of *Radamisto* (Göttingen Handel Festival, 1926–8).

66, 67 The harbour scene from *Giulio Cesare*: *above*, design for 1725 Hamburg production; *below*, Reinking's set for 1935–8 production at the Hamburg Staatsoper.

69 (*opposite*) Still from Norman Walker's film *The Gre[at]*
Mr. Handel (1942), starring Wilfrid Lawson as Hande[l]
Elizabeth Allan as Mrs Cibber (Gladys Ripley as vocali[st])
and A. E. Matthews as Jennen[s]

68 Handel ripe in years; one of Batt's celebrated series of drawings of the great composers.

70, 71 Halle market-place. Handel looks down on a production of *Orlando* (by Peter Sellars for the American Repertory Theatre at Harvard University) treating the work as a science-fiction fantasy. For a strikingly different approach to the same work at the same time elsewhere in America, see colour plate X.

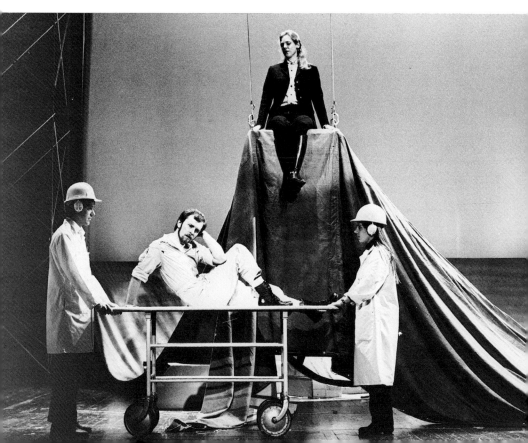

Victorian participants in Handel festivals assumed that immensity of numbers was a sure route to sublimity. In fact, the true correlation of such vast forces was with the current of covert militarism, the doctrine of 'might is right', which ran so strongly through the national psychology at this time. As Dean Ramsay said: 'It has always appeared to me that nothing is a stronger proof of the vastness of Handel's conceptions, and the colossal character of his choral productions, than their suitableness to such immense numbers of performers. They seem beyond all compositions to crave power to set them off . . .'.

> *Handel was the Jupiter of music; . . . his hallelujahs open the heavens. He utters the word 'Wonderful', as if all their trumpets spoke together. And then, when he comes to earth, to make love amidst nymphs and shepherds (for the beauties of all religions find room in his breast), his strains drop milk and honey, and his love is the youthfulness of the Golden Age.*
>
> (Leigh Hunt)

Some at length grew weary of such extravagance, on artistic as well as moral grounds. When Sir Michael Costa, stalwart director of the vast Crystal Palace performances, died in 1884, George Grove wrote under the guise of 'A Correspondent' in the *Pall Mall Gazette* (1 May 1884):

Some of the biographers have mentioned his interpolations in great works. They were shameful; it is the only word! The additions to choruses in the 'Dettingen Te Deum' and 'Israel in Egypt', the prelude added to 'Wretched Lovers' in 'Acis and Galatea', are enough to make your hair stand on end – so vulgar, so unnecessary, so out of keeping are they. The 'big drum' – 'enormous' it should be called, for it was the biggest ever made – so freely laid on all through the Handel festivals, is not more inconsistent with Handel's score than it was brutal and monotonous. His ignorance was astounding.

But even after the First World War, 'monster performances' (as Grove put it) continued. 'The Great Handel Festival' of 1920 at Crystal Palace promised a choir and orchestra of 4000 performers under the direction of Sir Frederic Cowen. 'Strong contingents of specially selected voices came from Sheffield, Leeds and Huddersfield' to reinforce the 2500-strong London contingent; the band was equally diverse, consisting of the London Symphony Orchestra as 'Solo Band' together with 'the most talented professionals of the London and provincial orchestras, reinforced by amateurs of great musical ability, thus representing the instrumental, as the chorus represents the vocal, forces of the Kingdom' (Festival Programme). Handel, it seems, could still be relied upon to evoke sentiments of national cohesion: the last Crystal Palace Festival took place six years later, in 1926, the year of the General Strike.

Victorian England's veneration for Handel had turned him into a musical showpiece and an icon of national pride. The obstacle of Handel's origins was easily overcome by a simple assertion of national supremacy:

> True, Handel was not an Englishman by birth, but no one was ever more thoroughly English in respect of all the best and most distinguishing features of Englishmen. As a young man, though Italy and Germany were open to him, he adopted the country of Purcell, feeling it, doubtless, to be, as far as he was concerned, more Saxon than Saxony itself. He chose England; nor can there be a doubt that he chose it because he believed it to be the country in which his music had the best chance of being appreciated. And what does this involve, if not that England, take it all round, is the most musically minded country in the world? That this is so, that it has produced the finest music the world has known, and is therefore the finest school of music in the world, cannot be reasonably disputed. (Samuel Butler, *Notebooks*)

Apart from his nationality, the question of the morality rather than the musicality of Handel's 'borrowings' continued to trouble early twentieth-century writers on Handel. The evidence for constructing a case against him was assembled by the indefatigable Chrysander in a series called 'Sources for Handel's Works' compiled around 1890. It was left to an Englishman, Sedley Taylor, to prosecute the composer in a book called *The Indebtedness of Handel to Works by other Composers* (1906). For Taylor, Handel was simply dishonest: 'as matters stand, the fact remains that he accepted, indeed practically claimed, merit for what he must have known was not his own work.' E. J. Dent, who helped Taylor with his book, testifies that the root of his objection to Handel's borrowings was simply his abnormal sensitivity to a code of proper conduct: 'I, who knew him so well, always remember the tiny old man who practically turned himself into a martyr, so far as normal life was concerned, in his fanatical regard for absolute truth and justice.'

Taylor's verdict attracted hostile replies from defenders of the faith. A. J. Balfour, a lifelong Handelian who financed a Handel Festival at the Albert Hall and founded the Handel Society in 1882, took a resolute stand suitable to his grounding in British Imperialism: 'If the main objection to robbery consists in the fact that the victim of the robbery is injured by it, Handel's appropriation of the music of his predecessors would seem to be innocent, if not meritorious. So far from their being injured by it in the quarter in which injury was alone possible, namely, their reputation, it is not too much to say that their whole reputation is entirely founded on it. . . . The fact is that Handel has not cheated them *out of* their due meed of fame, he has cheated them *into* it.'

He takes other men's pebbles and polishes them into diamonds.
(attrib. William Boyce)

Another line of defence was mounted by Percy Robinson, who, according to Dent, 'has a vast knowledge of Handel and his works, but he is a man with but a single idea in his head' – i.e. his insistence that Handel had himself composed those works from which he borrowed most. Such theories of authorship are now discredited.

Since the early years of this century, many further instances of Handel's borrowings have come to light, but the question of how to regard them is still open. After devoting several closely-argued pages of his notebook to the problem, it was Samuel Butler who came up with the pragmatic dictum of the creative artist: 'Honesty consists not in never stealing but in knowing where to stop in stealing, and how to make good use of what one does steal'.

Butler's addiction to Handel was, admittedly, extreme: 'with me everything in the last century (and a good deal in this) groups itself round Handel'. He collected material for a biography (never written) and collaborated with Henry Festing Jones, who claimed to be a descendant of the Michael Festing who had played the violin in Handel's orchestras, on a number of pieces 'in the Handelian form': a cantata (*Narcissus*) and an oratorio (*Ulysses*) were both published. Small wonder that when at a loss for words he turned to musical quotation from his hero; he even dreamed of Handel's music (*Alps and Sanctuaries*, chapter 6); and, of course, he regularly attended the Handel Festivals.

> *Above all things, let no unwary reader do me the injustice of believing in me. In that I write at all I am among the damned. If he must believe in anything, let him believe in the music of Handel, the painting of Giovanni Bellini, and in the thirteenth chapter of St. Paul's First Epistle to the Corinthians.* (Samuel Butler, *Notebooks* 1874–1902)

Another regular festival-goer, and a 'convinced and ardent admirer of Handel' was George Bernard Shaw. As with Grove, admiration was tempered, however, by his dislike of the massed choirs and huge orchestras of Costa and Manns, which he criticised in a characteristically acidic vein:

People think that four thousand singers must be four thousand times as impressive as one. This is a mistake: they are not even louder. You can hear the footsteps of four thousand people any day in the Rue de Rivoli – I mention it because it is the only street in Paris known to English tourists – but they are not so impressive as the march of a single well-trained actor down the stage of the Théâtre Français. It might as well be said that four thousand starving men are four thousand times as hungry as one, or four thousand slim *ingénues* four thousand times as slim as one . . . If I were a member of the House of Commons, I would propose a law making it a capital offence to perform an oratorio by Handel with more than eighty performers in the chorus and orchestra, allowing forty-eight singers and thirty-two instrumentalists.

Shaw's desire to hear the music played in a form closer to Handel's own performances was not an isolated whim; since the start of the nineteenth century voices had been raised in protest at the changes made to the composer's original scoring. Samuel Wesley was one of the first to insist that Handel's works needed no other orchestration beyond 'what their immortal author deemed proper and necessary' (*Lectures on Music*, 1811). In 1835 Mendelssohn declared his intentions of restoring Handel's original scoring to *Messiah*, without the 'tedious imitations and sentimental dissonances' or the 'flutes and clarinets which make me shudder'. Audiences noted the difference: that same year, Von Raumer records that in a performance at Drury Lane 'The old Handelian score was used, with a few exceptions, without the added accompaniments'. Some performers, such as the great nineteenth-century bass James Bartelman, refused to sing *Messiah* if Mozart's accompaniments were used: there was in some quarters considerable support for Hauptmann's view, expressed in a letter of 1856, that Mozart's instrumentation 'resembles elegant stucco work upon an old marble temple, which might easily be chipped off again by the weather'.

A further hazard to which some nineteenth-century performers of Handel subjected their audiences was the gradual slowing-down of tempi, partly as a result of overweight forces. The trend had begun, however, at the start of the century and was reflected in metronome markings suggested by the composer William Crotch in his 'Remarks on the Terms at present used in Music, for regulating Time' (1800). Although himself concerned at the slowing of tempi, Crotch gave even slower markings to the same pieces in a piano score of *Messiah* published thirteen years later. The decline in speed continued through Chrysander and Ebenezer Prout; only relatively recently has the trend been reversed to prevent a complete standstill.*

In the event it was the twin rediscovery, of neglected repertory and reconstructed instruments, that led to the restoration of Handel to his pre-nineteenth-century state. In 1890 the young Arnold Dolmetsch published an edition of six Handel sonatas for violin and piano, welcomed by the *Musical Times* as 'very acceptable, not only to violin players but to students of Handel's works'. Handel's chamber music, neglected for over a hundred years, was becoming known again. Three years later, Chrysander wrote to Dolmetsch promising to 'sketch out a number of pieces for your forthcoming Handel concert, including entirely unknown compositions for the harpsichord'. The *Times* critic wrote after the concert: 'Handel is known to so many people only as a composer of oratorio that there is an element of novelty in a programme which includes none but his instrumental works'. Shaw, surfeited with Crystal Palace renderings of *Messiah*, slyly hailed Dolmetsch's clavichord (and by implication the rediscovered repertory of Handel) 'as, on a modern computation, about forty thousand times as important as the Handel Festival'.

---

*For some of the available evidence on Handel's own speeds and the related question of ornamentation, see W. Malloch, 'The Earl of Bute's machine organ'; David Fuller, *G. F. Handel: Two Ornamented Organ Concertos*; Barry Cooper, 'Keyboard Sources in Hereford'.

In the early decades of the twentieth century, some of Handel's large-scale music other than the usual oratorios and anthems began to be performed by the BBC. Julian Herbage edited *Acis and Galatea*, using the original instrumentation as far as possible, for performances conducted by Adrian Boult. *Giove in Argo*, a *pasticcio* from 1739, was refurbished as *Perseus and Andromeda*. In 1938 a series of concerts was broadcast under the title 'Handel in Rome', including the cantatas *Handel non può mia musa* and *Apollo e Dafne*, and the oratorio *La Resurrezione*.

Unfamiliar oratorios were also resurrected, but in a form which did not reflect Handel's own performances of them. *Semele* was one of the first (in March 1925), and Percy Scholes reported for the *Musical Times*:

> Cambridge is to be warmly congratulated. It was a bold thing to revive this work, and the boldness has been justified. As an opera 'Semele' gives opportunity for the spectacular, and advantage was taken of this in the planning of a number of stage pictures which by their grouping and colour were very pleasant to the eye. It gives less opportunity for dramatic expression. It is to be doubted whether any of Handel's operas could be given with the life and movement which go to the making of 'drama', and 'Semele' was not originally an opera, but a secular oratorio – if this contradiction in terms is to be permitted. However, if we think Wagner's Wotan speeches dramatic there is no reason why we should not also think Handel's *da capo* arias dramatic, and when these are reduced in length, as was done at Cambridge, by decapitating the *da capo*, progress to the next thing is not so long delayed as to become painful.

The abundant misconceptions in this notice spring from a hopeless confusion of oratorio and opera: drama was to be achieved by weighting the production with 'stage pictures' and lightening the music by butchering the arias. Four years later, *Samson* was produced by the Falmouth Opera Singers, and the *Times* observed sagely in its review that there was 'no difficulty whatever in presenting the oratorio as an opera, so long as the right dramatic *tempo* is chosen, except possibly the treatment of the choruses. This production had the great merit of unfolding the plot in a series of conventionalized stage pictures in which very little movement or gesture was used. This allowed the chorus to appear on the stage, while some choral numbers were cut and some were sung off the stage – so was the balance of interest shifted from the oratorio centre of gravity to the operatic.'

Throughout the 1930s, staged performances of Handel's oratorios became a vogue in England, generating notions of drama wholly alien to the eighteenth century. The crowd, inevitably prominent in oratorio, moved onto the stage with the kind of elaborate, cumbersome mechanics described in the *Times*; the chorus loudly proclaimed moralistic sentiments; the actions of the main characters were set against a religious background, rather than the atmosphere of emotional crisis which provided the mainspring of Handel's drama in the operas. It is true that a staged performance of *Esther* may have been planned in

1732, at the start of Handel's career as an oratorio composer, but the scheme did not come off and all subsequent performances of his oratorios during his lifetime held to the pattern of concert performances established in 1732. The twentieth-century English tradition of staging has, in the words of a recent historian of the form, 'little to do with the practice of oratorio performance in the Baroque era'.*

It is curious that given the widespread interest in turning Handel's oratorios into operas, little effort was made to explore the operas themselves. Occasional productions were mounted – *Giulio Cesare* (in an English translation) in 1930, *Rinaldo* in 1933 and *Rodelinda* in 1939 – but it was left to the other claimant of Handel's birthright, Germany, to resurrect the central part of his output.

In 1920, a teacher of art history at the University of Göttingen, Oskar Hagen, staged a production of *Rodelinda* in the Stadttheater. It was the first performance of a Handel opera since 1754. Five other operas followed in the course of the decade, and during the late 1920s another four German cities (Halle, Münster, Berlin and Leipzig) began to stage Handel's operas on a regular basis. By 1930 eleven separate Handel operas had been revived in Germany. Hagen's arrangement of *Giulio Cesare* 'had 222 performances in 34 different cities in less than five years'.† This remarkable renascence of interest was more the result of a coincidence than of any new appraisal of Handelian opera itself. Baroque opera was almost entirely unknown to German audiences, and the German producers used Handel as a vehicle for their reaction against Wagnerian music-drama, whose influence was still unbreakable on its own ground. It was difficult to stage Wagner outside the accepted conventions of naturalism; but whereas audiences would resist abstraction in Wagner they were happy to accept it in Handel. The German approach was at the other end of the spectrum from that of Dolmetsch: interpretation set against historicism.

The choice of Handel was not fortuitous; his operas embodied structural qualities to which Hagen and later producers were especially attracted. They saw the aria as a strict musical form in which emotion would be transformed and stylized rather than naturalistically expressed; the Baroque use of a proto-type form in which individualism was contained appealed to them. The strictness both of text and music meant an objective, formal expression in contrast to the looseness of music-drama. The action of Handel's operas was thought to be similarly tight, and fell into 'tension-fields' which were considered to be impossible to stage naturalistically, but which responded well to abstract scenery and symbolic staging. The sets and productions of the 1920s, which featured displays of youthful athleticism in front of mausoleums and neo-Hellenic stadiums, were imagined to reflect the strength of form which Handel's operas possessed. Lighting emphasized the static qualities of the staging and the play of power between the singers, which was seen as a main theme.

It is hardly surprising that these opera productions, built upon an aesthetic wholly alien to the eighteenth century, would also betray Handel's music.

*Howard E. Smither, *A History of the Oratorio*.
†Winton Dean, 'The recovery of Handel's operas'.

Sketch by Paul Thiersch for his stage set for Rodelinda, Göttingen, 1920.

Hagen adopted a cavalier approach: he shortened the operas, to the detriment of the drama, and interpolated new passages that held up what action remained. Although on the whole Handel's instrumental scorings were respected, his allocation of vocal lines was not. High male parts, which Handel gave to castrati or female sopranos irrespectively, offended against the Teutonic concept of the Hero and were routinely transposed down an octave, thus ruining both texture and harmonic structure. Hagen had the opera texts translated from Italian to German, sometimes altering the music so as to give preference to the verbal sense. Recitatives were cut or even recomposed entirely.

The liberties taken in the 1920s and early 30s were in the direction of a new and heavily symbolic German music theatre. Reinterpretation of a more sinister kind had first showed itself in 1914 when *Judas Maccabeus* was turned into a blatantly nationalist oratorio *Der Feldhern*, in which according to the arranger Hermann Stephani, the hero is not an individual but 'das Volk'. The nationalist tendency broke out again at the Halle Festival in 1935 (the 250th anniversary of Handel's birth). A performance of the *St Cecilia Ode* on the eve of Handel's birthday was 'broken in two parts by long political–mystical–

musical orations by Herr Rosenberg, Germany's cultural dictator, and other local Nazi leaders'. Richard Capell, reporting from Halle for the *Daily Telegraph*, described Rosenberg's Handel as 'a German Viking', and his anti-Semitism was patent. According to Rosenberg, 'The Messiah of Judaism and Handel's *Messiah* have in the last analysis inwardly nothing in common. This was probably already felt by his contemporaries, who often called him "the great pagan". The mighty fanfares of this work are a victory jubilation, delighting in struggle, which will always be understood by the European mind, whether in England or Germany.' One Englishman in the audience was E. J. Dent, who delivered the Handel Memorial Lecture in the University Hall, surrounded by citizens of Halle and political leaders, many in uniform: 'In the midst of this elaborate Meistersinger-like gathering, one saw the representative of the University of Cambridge, Professor Dent, tall, urbane, imperturbable, rise to deliver in German an eloquent lecture on Handel, teeming with scholarship, wit, and skilful allusions to certain political virtues at present under a cloud in Nazi Germany.'

The Festival proper began at midnight on 22/23 February, with a mass rally around the Handel statue in the market place. Handel's biographer, Newman Flower, was there:

It was a clear night with cold stars in the sky and a bitter wind. Some thousands of people had gathered about the Handel statue to await the midnight hour which would bring in the two hundred and fiftieth birthday of Handel. Thirty-six uniformed youths held their blazing torches aloft about the statue. A hundred yards away the church where Handel had learned his first notes on the organ, stood out, a creation of white beauty in the floodlights. Musicians waited in the gallery between the spires to play to the waiting thousands when the midnight hour had struck. A black sea of people seemed to reach across the square to the steps of the church. There was no sound, no movement. But with midnight came a great clangour of bells. Presently the crowd began to shuffle and whisper. The vast human sea became restless. Hitler was expected. He would be here in five minutes. Hitler was asleep in the train which drew in to Halle at this very hour. Overworked and driven, he was sleeping on his journey from Berlin to Munich. Four officials of Halle went to the station to meet the train, to beg him to come – if only for ten minutes – to greet this city of Handel in her hour of celebrations. They were told that Hitler slept and must not be disturbed, and the train swept on into the night.

Seven years later, a programme for rewriting the texts of Handel's oratorios was begun. Under a headline 'MUSICAL POGROM', *The Times* for 16 February 1942 reported:

ORATORIOS ARYANIZED BY
NAZIS From our Special Correspondent
GERMAN FRONTIER, Feb. 15

The expurgation of the masterpieces of German art from Jewish contamination is reported to be making rapid progress, and it is pointed out that this is all the more remarkable as Germany is engaged in a life and death struggle in which the concentration of the nation's entire strength on essentials is imperative. The texts of all the oratorios of Handel are being rewritten. After the acknowledged success of the conversion of *Judas Maccabeus* into *William of Nassau* by Klöcking and Harke, these two collaborators have been entrusted with the still more difficult task of transforming *Israel in Egypt* into *Mongolensturm* (Mongol Fury), which is to be performed for the first time in Hamburg towards the end of this year.

It is expected that the 'Aryanization' of all the works of the German classical composers, notably Bach, will take many years.

When the war ended, Handel's operas began to be staged again in Germany and although the freedom of Hagen's pre-war approach was slightly modified, his methods were still generally followed, and the traditions whose main lines were drawn in Germany in the 1920s are still visible in the Halle festivals today.

After the war, it was at last the turn of Handel's operas to be revived in their country of origin. The initial stimulus resulted in the formation of the Handel Opera Society in 1955, which first in St Pancras Town Hall and later Sadler's Wells has produced annual performances of Handelian opera under its conductor Charles Farncombe. An equally important venture began four years later at the Unicorn Theatre in Abingdon (near Oxford), where Alan and Frances Kitching produced fourteen Handel operas, notably *Agrippina* in a British premiere and four others (*Floridante, Giustino, Sosarme* and *Lotario*) which had never been staged since their first London performances over two hundred years previously. For the bicentenary of Handel's death in 1959, a major festival in London included a production of *Samson* by the Royal Opera at Covent Garden and a series of opera productions directed by Anthony Lewis was inaugurated at the Barber Institute of Fine Arts, Birmingham.

But even though the experience of Handel's music broadened out in concert halls and opera houses during the course of the present century, his popular appeal still rests, as it did in 1900, on a few favourite pieces. One guide to the progress of popular taste is the history of Handel recordings, which began on 30 June 1888, four days after a 'perfected phonograph' had arrived in England from the USA. A cylinder made on an Edison phonograph at the Crystal Palace Handel Festival of 1888 featured four thousand performers in a chorus from *Israel in Egypt* conducted by Sir August Manns and was both the earliest location recording and the first recording of classical music ever. (The cylinder is now in the Edison Museum, New Jersey.) The remainder of the century was surprisingly bare of Handel recordings, but the 1900 HMV catalogue offered Mr Wills Page singing 'Ev'ry Valley', and Mr G. H. Snazelle's version of 'Why do the Nations', balanced by his humorous recitation of 'How Bill Adams won the Battle of Waterloo'. In 1902 Sousa's Band recorded the 'Largo' for the American Victor label and initiated a concentration on Handel 'pops' which has never faltered.

A first attempt to record a 'potted' version of *Messiah*, including all the major arias and choruses, was made in 1905–6 and issued on twenty single-sided discs. In 1910, Master Hubert Langley, 'Boy Soloist, Eton College', recorded 'Rejoice greatly' for HMV, and the beginnings of seasonal promotions can be seen in the selection of Easter records which included Clara Butt's performance of 'He shall feed his Flock'. A near-complete *Messiah* was recorded by Sir Thomas Beecham in June–October 1927, the first of three versions he was to record. The second (1947) included a spoken introduction by the conductor and the last (1959) was reorchestrated by Eugene Goossens (the extended cymbal-roll in the ritornello of 'Thou shalt break them' is only one of many exotic incidents). Beecham defended his theory in an accompanying essay:

> I do seriously consider that if Handel is to be brought back into popular favour some reasonable compromise must be effected between excessive grossness and exaggerated leanness of effect, and this is what has been aimed at in the present version.
>
> Sixty years' study of his life and works have led me to think that he would have raised little objection to some modernisation of the instrumental portion of his oratorios as well as his operas. We do know that, like Mozart, he revelled in great demonstrations of sound, to the point of sighing on one occasion for the assistance of a cannon. I also entertain the fear that without some effort along these lines the greater portion of his magnificent output will remain unplayed, possibly to the satisfaction of drowsy armchair purists, but hardly to the advantage of the keenly alive and enquiring concertgoer.

Another firm favourite of the record companies was the 'Largo', recorded by Clara Butt (1909 and 1915), Caruso (1920), Tauber (1939), Flagstad (1948) and by other singers under various titles and in various languages, including a recording by Sigurdur Birkis in Icelandic for HMV. The 'Harmonious Blacksmith' recorded by Backhaus (1908) and Rachmaninoff (1936) was the staple keyboard piece until HMV released the harpsichord suites performed by Wanda Landowska in their 'Handel Society' series. In 1936 Boyd Neel recorded all the op. 6 concertos on fifty sides (twenty-five discs). Other notable recordings were *Alcina*, with Joan Sutherland, from Zeffirelli's Covent Garden production where the plot had been 'sensitively re-ordered'; and the *Royal Fireworks Music* under Charles Mackerras, performed with its original wind forces and recorded at midnight – the only time when all the players were free. Most bizarre were some renderings of the 'Hallelujah' Chorus: on a Swiss music-box, in three Rock interpretations (one by the 'One Experience Choir and Revelation Philharmonic Orchestra'), by the Portsmouth Sinfonia, 'featuring inaccuracies in notes, time and intonation', and by two no less intriguingly named brass bands, the Ever Ready Band and Hammond's Sauce Works Band.

The pious hope that the recording industry might take advantage of its freedom from box-office constraints to expand the range of Handel's music available to the public has not in general been realized. Only in the field of 'historically aware' performances have the record companies taken the lead:

two complete Handel operas have been recorded recently, and others will follow, but this foray into unexplored territory hardly constitutes an attempt to encompass Handel's works – as Bach's, for instance, have been encompassed in recordings over the past two decades. Instead, recordings of Handel simply reflect what public taste has selected over the years: several 'major' oratorios, a handful of orchestral pieces, the ceremonial music that has become closely identified with occasions of state and grandeur, and a few instrumental favourites. Since the late eighteenth century Handel has suffered from the strong impression that a few standard pieces – together with the acquired social functions which they now possess – have made on his public.

Handel's predicament is underlined by Joseph Kerman's recent writings on the methodology of music history and criticism, in which he examines the distinction between the 'canon' of historical music (a type of Great Composers Club initiated and defined by critics and historians) and the 'repertory' – those pieces which have held a secure place in the public's affection.* 'A canon is an idea: a repertory is a program of action.' Handel, granted classic status during his lifetime, and immediate apotheosis on his death, was the first composer to retain his stature posthumously. But this was achieved by the allocation of many works to the canon, few to the repertory. Thanks to the facility of sound recording, Kerman now proposes a new paradigm for music – one that starts with the listener rather than the composer or performer, and which can retrieve works from the canon much as it has retrieved historical methods of performance as part of a new 'program of action'. Several recent recordings of *Messiah*, for instance, at last live up to Bernard Shaw's requirements (see page 267) and present the sonorities, style and number of performers that Handel prescribed.

While 'authentic recordings' cannot acquire canonical status, they serve well to extend and clarify the repertory of historical music, and preserve the modern listener from the overlap of nineteenth-century sentiment and the patina of Romanticism. A similar twentieth-century outlook has saved us from the outbursts of moral indignation that Handel's borrowing once attracted. With a new 'paradigm of literacy' we can again subscribe to Jonathan Richardson's defence of borrowings in the arts:

Nor need any Man be asham'd to be sometimes a Plagiary, 'tis what the greatest Painters, and Poets have allowed themselves . . . indeed 'tis hard that a Man having had a good Thought should have a Patent for it for Ever. The Painter that can take a Hint, or insert a Figure, or Groupes of Figures from another Man, and mix these with his Own, so as to make a good Composition, will thereby establish such a Reputation to himself, as to be above fearing to suffer.

A Discourse on the Dignity, Certainty, Pleasure and Advantage of the Science of the Connoisseur (1719)

---

*See two articles in *Critical Inquiry*.

It is the amalgamation of ingredients and skills, enhanced by our interest and enquiry into their origins and characters that lends power to the greatest art. The interrelationships between 'manufacture' and 'fabric' in the creative process so typical of Handel can be traced with equal fascination in, for example, the 'fabrick' of Dryden's verse or the ambiguities of Picasso's bull-fights.* Handel's orchestration of a conjunction of Muffat's music with Dryden's verse to produce the 1739 *Ode for St Cecilia's Day* is an instance where 'the act of composition is the perception of this conjunction, the fabric of a transformation'.

Since we, both listeners and performers, must marvel at the transformation in the music itself, albeit enhanced by a knowledge of the man and his life, the exhortation of William Hayes (in his *Remarks on Mr. Avison's Essay on Musical Expression*) is as apt at this point as it was in 1753:

Perhaps, as I have been so particular in delivering my sentiments concerning the Hero of the Essay, You may expect me to give you a Detail of the various Excellencies, which still remain unmentioned in HANDEL; and to point out wherein he excels *all others* of his Profession: The Man, who hath so bravely withstood the repeated Efforts of *Italian Forces*: – Who hath maintained his Ground against all Opposers: – Who at the Age of *Seventy*, with a broken Constitution, produced such a Composition [*Jephtha*], which no Man mentioned in the Essay beside, either is, or ever was (so far as it hath appeared to us) equal to, in his highest Vigour; – And, to the Astonishment of all Mankind, at the same Period – I say, perhaps you may expect me to enter into *Particulars*, to *defend* and *characterize* this Man: – but the first would be an endless Undertaking; – his Works being almost out of Number. – The second, a needless one, the Works themselves being his best Defence: – And the third, I must acknowledge is above my Capacity; and therefore once more refer you to his Works, where only his true character is to be found.

---

*Richard Luckett, 'The Fabric of Dryden's Verse'.

Afterword

Nearly a quarter-century on from the first publication of this biography, we have seen a rapid acceleration in the worldwide dissemination of Handel's music – particularly his operas – and scholars have become increasingly adventurous and meticulous in researching new areas and revising old positions. Much of this activity was galvanized by the 1985 Tercentenary celebrations which, although shared with J. S. Bach, Domenico Scarlatti and Heinrich Schütz, seemed to give greatest impetus to Handel, with his dramatic insight and musical impact spread across an international array of genres.

1985 was a gift for record companies: major operas appeared that had been neglected ever since the invention of the gramophone, but also many other special projects including The Academy of Ancient Music's premiere recordings of *Esther* and *Athalia*. The development of the CD boosted Handel's vast corpus of neglected (or at least, comparatively unfamiliar) music with influential recordings of operas *Alcina* and *Tamerlano* notably rare special treats. English National Opera celebrated Handel's birthday with Nicholas Hytner's chirpy production of *Serse* (in English). All three operas are now staple baroque opera fare all over the world two decades later. Even television joined in with the drama-documentary *God Rot Tunbridge Wells!* and *The Sorceress*, a film of operatic set-pieces sung by Kiri Te Kanawa (remembered for her recent performance of 'Let the bright seraphims' from *Samson* at the wedding of Prince Charles and Lady Diana Spencer).

At a far remove from such glamour, the musicological world was also changing. Peter Williams' collection of essays devoted to the three 1685 composers featured significant articles about Handel's brief time working in Hanover (Donald Burrows) and Handel's connections with James Brydges (by Graydon Beeks, who has emerged as the leading scholar working on Handel's Cannons period). Stanley Sadie and Nigel Fortune organized an ambitious conference devoted solely to Handel at the Royal Society of Arts, which led to a ground-breaking collection of essays published two years later (edited by Sadie and Anthony Hicks). It was already well known that Handel recycled his own musical material and occasionally that of other composers but John Roberts' bombshell was the discovery of many more borrowings from works by others than had previously been supposed. Instead of denouncing Handel's plagiarism, Roberts made a serious attempt to consider why Handel borrowed material and to place the practice into a fair historical context. His investigations continue to reveal the germs of many familiar

Handelian musical ideas in works by Keiser, Bononcini, Alessandro Scarlatti, Lotti and others.

Handelian iconography was considerably furthered in 1985 by the National Portrait Gallery's exhibition and finely researched catalogue devoted to Handel, his colleagues and associates (edited by Jacob Simon), which introduced unfamiliar portraits of important contemporaries including Baron Kielmansegge and Cardinal Ottoboni. 1985 was also the opportune moment for Reinhard Strohm to publish his pioneering studies of Handel's *pasticcios* and research on the source librettos on which Handel's London operas were based (*Essays on Handel and Italian Opera*). A certain over-excitement roused by the Latin psalm settings Handel composed in Rome led to the notion that they could all be strung together to form the so-called 'Carmelite Vespers', followed by two editions and a fine recording – only to be dampened a few years later when Donald Burrows showed that Handel could have composed no more than some short antiphons for the Carmelites.

Since 1985 there has been an explosion of interest in Handel's Italian operas and dramatic oratorios. Results of research published in journals such as *Early Music*, *The Musical Quarterly*, *Musical Times*, *Music & Letters* and the recently inaugurated *Eighteenth-Century Music* have led the way, although competition has pushed some of the most interesting Handel research to the annual *Händel-Jahrbuch* and the slightly less predictable *Göttinger Händel-Beitrage*. Many diverse and illuminating articles by Donald Burrows have appeared in most or all of these journals; Burrows has been author, co-author or editor of several books that have become instantly essential for all other Handel scholars: an attentive scholarly biography published in 1994, a catalogue of all the composer's extant musical autographs (with Martha Ronish) which details rastra, watermarks, foliation, and annotations; a detailed study of Handel's connections with and music for the English Chapel Royal; a collection of illuminating letters written by Handel's friends the Harris family; music editions of neglected repertoire such as Handel's English songs for soprano and basso continuo – all these have helped transform the landscape of Handel studies.

Burrows and other leading British scholars were also instrumental in establishing The Handel Institute in 1987, 'to advance education by promoting the study and appreciation of, and supporting and publishing research on, the music and life of George Frideric Handel and his contemporaries'. An international conference is held in London every three years, and new research is disseminated in its newsletter published twice yearly. The Handel Institute, like its transatlantic counterpart the American Handel Society, is also responsible for nominating two members to participate in the management of the Hallische Händel-Ausgabe. Initiated in the 1950s before critical scholarly standards were widely used, there is some concern that the earliest attempts to improve on Chrysander's monumental 19th-century complete edition of Handel's works already need revision. Although volumes published since 1984 have generally been excellently researched and edited, progress is slow and only a few volumes have been re-edited. Surprisingly few of Handel's major English works are yet published by the HHA, but progress on the Italian operas has been good, with one or two major editions every year; the absence of *Giulio Cesare* and *Alcina* conceals the fact that Bärenreiter have been hiring out performance material of editions in progress for some time, although at the current rate, the HHA will not be complete for at least another two decades, if not longer.

With the HHA understandably slow to complete its mammoth task, Novello confining itself to occasional new editions of English vocal works aimed principally at the choral market, and Chrysander's edition generally out of print apart from a few reprinted volumes, musicians on a budget have found solace in Clifford Bartlett's King's Music editions. His cottage-industry approach – to make modern typeset scores based on Chrysander with enhancements from some of the primary sources – has been an important practical ingredient in performing Handel's music in the early 21st century: all the major international baroque groups and opera houses have started to use King's Music as a cheap and necessary alternative to the incomplete HHA.

For those researching Handel's variant performance versions and making reliable scholarly editions, the 1991 Handel Institute Conference's survey of Handel Collections was manna from heaven. The papers giving the history and catalogue details of music manuscript collections once belonging to Handel's friends and staunchest supporters were edited by Terence Best and published two years later by Oxford University Press. David Ross Hurley has undertaken revelatory work about Handel's compositional methods in his English dramas from *Semele* through to *Jephtha*, and Richard Luckett, Donald Burrows and Teri Noel Towe have all found fresh approaches to *Messiah*.

In the most vital book about Handel's English oratorios since Winton Dean's seminal 1959 work, Ruth Smith makes an utterly convincing and extremely detailed argument that we should take the moral and philosophical subtexts of the English oratorios much more seriously as reflections of intellectual ideas. Ellen Harris has ploughed a variety of furrows, ranging from controversial speculations of a possible homosexual subtext in Handel's Italian chamber cantatas, to some of the most important concrete factual work in recent Handel studies, such as a series of opera libretto facsimiles and research into Handel's personal bank accounts.

The steady and reliable work of such projects as Manfred Rätzer's database of all staged productions and concert performances of Handel's operas (and some discreetly inserted English works) since Handel's own and the work of Hans Joachim Marx and Steffen Voss at Hamburg University in examining spurious and misattributed works, and hitherto little examined collections (producing some individual arias that may relate to *Rodrigo*), was off-set by the media-frenzy that greeted the unveiling of a setting of *Gloria in excelsis Deo* found in the Royal Academy of Music's library (heralded sight unseen in one quality newspaper as 'the new *Messiah*'), which fuelled an unseemly race to present the premiere. Three commercial recordings were rushed out to exploit the publicity, but once the dust had settled it was declared very unlikely that

Handel composed the *Gloria*, and extremely implausible that it dates from his time in Italy. Once burnt, twice shy: a hitherto unknown version of the cantata 'Crudel tiranno amor' for keyboard and voice was recently discovered in Munich which is certainly written in Handel's own hand, and uniquely features his full realization of the continuo keyboard part in the two secco recitatives: yet little attention has so far been paid to this discovery which, although small, sheds light on an enigmatic problem faced by all continuo players.

Handel's actual keyboard instruments have also made news: Michael Cole reported (*Early Music*, February 1993) on a harpsichord in the Bate Collection at the University of Oxford that bears more than a passing resemblance to the instrument upon which Handel leans in the famous Mercier portrait (see the cover illustration of this book). The organ at St Lawrence's Church, Whitchurch, has been restored to the condition Handel would have known when performing the *Chandos Anthems* and has been used by Paul Nicholson for a recording of Handel's organ concertos (opp. 4 and 7).

Among the most influential literary achievements since 1984 is Winton Dean and J. Merrill Knapp's *Handel's Operas, 1704–1726*, volume 1. Notwithstanding Dean's early book *Handel and the Opera Seria* (1969), Handel's operas had long awaited the sort of descriptive detail and analysis commonly devoted to Mozart, Verdi and Wagner. Indeed, the authors made the bold claim that in their view Handel ranks alongside the three great opera composers as one of the finest musical dramatists. Their book went a long way to proving their argument, and certainly provided a resource for budding musicians and opera directors (each opera was allocated a large chapter including information on synopsis, libretto, composition, analysis of the music, observations about characterization, performances, editions and sources). Despite the success of the book, each author decided to pursue his own independent draft for the next installment and Dean has recently completed his *Handel's Operas, 1726–1741*. Ursula Kirkendale's research on the Marquis Ruspoli, which has shown the patron's importance to Handel throughout most of his years in Italy to have been much greater than previously suspected, has also made an important iconographic contribution by suggesting that a painting of a procession outside the Ruspoli palace in Rome might feature the young Handel nonchalantly holding his hat under his arm. Edwin Werner, the recently retired director of the Handel House in Halle, has been engaged in a massive iconography project for years that will presumably bear fruit in print or on the internet.

Although Handel's operas, after being avoided for so long, have (in rather less time than the bicycle has taken to become an honorary biped) achieved repertoire status in opera houses throughout the world, many major houses will only attempt them with the security of a celebrity soloist who happens to be attracted to Handel amidst the Verdi and Puccini. Glyndebourne, resistant to Handel for so long despite having a perfect-sized theatre and a tradition for both earlier 17th- and later 18th-century opera, has only recently started to treat Handel seriously. Their most powerful and influential effort to date, however, has been an oratorio full of choruses – Peter Sellar's unremittingly

intense *Theodora* (1996). This gave those in favour of staging English oratorios an unusually successful example to emulate (it is difficult to imagine that
Welsh National Opera would have tackled *Jephtha* without the success of
Theodora to pave the way), although challenges such as how to integrate the
choruses into a stage drama without entrance and exit-music from the composer have remained unresolved in most cases.

As the modern-day heirs of John Rich's Covent Garden, the Royal Opera
House regrettably still marginalizes Handel in comparison to other established opera composers, apart from an occasional *Giulio Cesare*, *Semele* and a
recent production of *Orlando*. English National Opera has made occasional
forays, with popular productions of *Semele*, *Ariodante* and *Alcina* receiving
several runs. At the time of writing, a new production of *Agrippina* is scheduled for early 2007, but it seems a pity that so many of the thirty or so other
operas are neglected in favour of over-frequent revivals of *Serse*. However, one
of the most creative and innovative imports in recent years (also at the ENO),
the Mark Morris Dance Group's flamboyant depiction of mirth and melancholy in a ballet version of *L'Allegro, il Penseroso ed il Moderato* sets a high standard for balletic interpretation which should be followed up.

One caveat, however, applies to this happy activity: all the examples cited
above are essentially modernistic stage productions, with approximately contemporary sets, costumes, props and behaviour. If this indicates a management
assumption that baroque-style staging is boring, then the public have scarcely
had any opportunity to prove it otherwise. Instead, staged productions are
predominantly located in an aesthetic world totally alien to their conception
and first performances, with the result that the moral tone and characterization of Handel's dramatic ideas suffer. ENO's *Alcina* and Glyndebourne's
Giulio Cesare (both directed by David McVicar) are perfect illustrations of
how arias intended to be concentrated and solo expressions of a character's
emotions can be upstaged by the activities of ballet dancers, with chorus
members' antics in the foreground and assorted gimmicks 'to keep the audience interested'. Handel seldom included dances or choruses in his operas,
and the modern habit of injecting unasked-for eye candy into Handel staging
merely confesses an unwillingness to trust the audience to stay with Handel
for an entire evening. No such reservations are felt about Mozart, Verdi or
Wagner, even in operas that contain little real incidental action compared to
Serse or *Alcina* – so why Handel? There is clearly still work to be done in per-
suading opera companies and directors (and, perhaps, even musicians) that
Handel was a perceptive dramatist who deserves to be trusted a little more.
Baroque-style staging with 18th-century costumes, acting incorporating an
impression of baroque gesture, elegant sets, and literal faith in the original
content and morality of the libretto is not necessarily the only solution, but
such approaches are astonishingly rare. Even Drottningholm and Göttingen,
renowned in the 1980s and 1990s for 18th-century style productions, now regularly alternate annually between the baroque and the modern in their productions. The Halle festival has always pursued a more modernist approach
to Handel's operas, and the annual student-based Handel opera production at

the Royal College of Music's Britten Theatre varies its styles according to the practical possibilities of each London Handel Festival.

The arrival of DVD has encouraged a spate of Handel opera productions being made available for an unexpected venue – domestic viewing. When the production is as insightful and intelligent as Michael Hampe's Dresden production of *Serse* (TDK) the medium has a future, though hardly one the composer would have anticipated. Opera, like religious ritual, is essentially a corporate activity.

Commercial recordings are no longer made with the same kind of financial and moral support from the record companies that was common before the mid-1990s, but the variety of new Handel recording projects proves that the format is still an effective way to disseminate the music. In sharp contrast to 1984, every one of Handel's oratorios and extant operas has now been commercially released on CD (although quite a few so poorly performed in ruthlessly cut versions that they beg to be replaced). Much of the most admirable pioneering work is to be found in the recordings by Nicholas McGegan of *Giustino, Ottone, Ariodante, Agrippina, Il Floridante, Il Pastor Fido* and *Radamisto* (Handel's second version), made fresh on the back of baroque-style stagings at the Göttingen Handel Festival (of which he has been artistic director since 1990). These complement a series of oratorio recordings made in California, including the premiere recording of *Susanna*, a version of *Messiah* featuring a vast assortment of appendices of music for different versions and the first complete *Theodora*. Alan Curtis was one of the pioneers of Handel opera performances using period instruments, and in recent years he has made not only a complete recording of *Rodelinda*, but premiere recordings of *Rodrigo, Arminio, Deidamia, Radamisto* (first version), *Lotario* and *Fernando* (the first draft version of *Sosarme*). Several of these have won the Stanley Sadie Handel Recording Prize, which was initiated in 2002 by an international panel of scholars and critics to reward important recordings of Handel's music.

Handel's operas have also been championed on disc by the French school of baroque performers (notably William Christie's Les Arts Florissants, Marc Minkowski's Les Musiciens du Louvre, and Christophe Rousset's Les Talens Lyriques), although the greatest number of important recordings of oratorios, odes and masques since 1984 have been made by John Eliot Gardiner, Paul McCreesh, Peter Neumann and Robert King, the latter having produced a series of the lesser-known oratorios, including *Deborah, Joseph and his Brethren, The Occasional Oratorio* and *Alexander Balus*. The cantatas *con strumenti*, most of them composed in Italy, are seldom publicly performed – sufficient reason to be excited about a new ambitious series to record them all by the Italian group La Risonanza. In contrast, the large number of cantatas for solo voice and basso continuo still languish in obscurity.

New recordings of orchestral works (notably the *Water Music* and *Music for the Royal Fireworks*) and smaller scale repertoire (violin sonatas, recorder sonatas, trio sonatas, and keyboard music – including clavichord) continue, but one particular fad that has dominated recent Handel recording projects is the aria recital: anthologies of arias intended to display the showcased soprano or countertenor in a selection of their favourite numbers. The result can be exhilarating with an experienced baroque singer and a flowing programme (Sandrine Piau with Rousset, Emma Kirkby with Goodman), but all too often these recital discs contain predictable selections and offer very little other than an opportunity to massage the singer's ego. Perhaps that in itself is a peculiarly authentic element with which Handel's celebrated castrati and prima donnas would have sympathized, but a steady stream of vanity recitals (including 'Ombra mai fu', 'Lascia ch'io pianga' and 'Where'er you walk' which show little regard for which voice Handel originally intended them or for the dramatic context of the words) does not do the composer justice.

Since 1984 there has been a dramatic increase in the number of star countertenor soloists (also in the amount of vibrato) who have cultivated careers specializing in singing Handel castrato roles, and indeed stolen roles Handel actually composed for women, such as Sesto in *Giulio Cesare*. A similar pattern has developed in oratorio performances, where *Solomon* has been recorded on at least two occasions with the title-part sung by a countertenor; a feminine fight-back is surely called for here.

Whatever the scale of repertoire, Handel is at the moment very much the preserve of period instrument groups. That is not to say that presence of gut strings and natural trumpets is any longer an indication of an 'early music' approach to stylistic principles. Amongst the new generation of performers who use period instruments for the very creditable reason that 'they sound good', some have declared themselves no longer 'bound by historical considerations', and as a result stray far from the aesthetic or personality of Handel's music, a phenomenon that has been termed 'HUP' ('historically uninformed performance'). There are the cosmetic surgeons who chop out unwanted parts, insert fanciful flourishes in the name of dramatic verisimilitude, compose interludes that have little place in Handel's structure and rearrange Handel's orchestration. Then there are the 'silly pluckers', specially fond of the unclubbable guitar, who would deploy a different sonority for each character or situation. The results are undeniably colourful, and such approaches are justified by their practitioners as 'dramatically motivated', but a continuo team perpetually changing gears creates a manic rather than a theatrical effect. There is no reason why Handel's known practice of two harpsichords, theorbo and single cello providing simple support throughout all recitatives cannot be the most naturalistic, dramatic, flowing and stylistically plausible approach. There is rightly no single proscribed way to perform Handel's music 'correctly', but some solutions gaining currency since 1984 are as harmful to Handel's musical personality and ideas as anything done by the early German opera pioneers mentioned in Chapter 6. Indeed, in the light of some period-instrument led aberrations, it seems odd that modern chamber orchestras, which have reclaimed Mozart and Beethoven in recent years, are still reluctant to return to Handel.

Thanks to the internet the popularity of Handel's music is now globally unlimited. Websites such as GFHandel.org and the Yahoo discussion list Handel-L are not designed solely for scholars, but are actively offering information about Handel and his music to all comers. GFHandel.org in particular contains links with every other Handel organization and website, including groups in Italy, the Czech Republic, Japan, Australia and Poland, plus some important bibliographies.

In London, the Handel House Museum opened in 2001 as a physical focal point for Handelian pilgrims at 25 Brook Street, where all Handel's major works from 1723 onwards were composed. The house has been sensitively restored to fulfil all the functions of a modern museum despite its small size, and regularly presents live music in the room where Handel probably rehearsed his operas and oratorios; the upper floors of no. 23 (shockingly found to have been home to rock legend Jimi Hendrix in 1968–9) provide a space for changing exhibitions and educational events. The Foundling Museum (housed in the institution now unhappily rechristened Coram Family) has become an even more important centre for Handel studies since the Gerald Coke Handel Collection (long in storage at Hampshire Record Office after Gerald Coke's death) took up the new purpose-designed library on the top floor in June 2004.

The Handelian world of 2007 has been transformed from what it was in 1984 largely as a result of active research and debate, both professional and amateur. The last twenty years of research have shown that there is always more to discover, whether it be new insights on old friends such as *Messiah*, or innovative studies of neglected repertoire, new information about Handel the man, or deeper considerations of interdisciplinary cultural contexts. Familiar music can be given a new lease of life with help from new discoveries; my recent handbook on the *Water Music* and the *Music for the Royal Fireworks*, for example, benefited significantly from the discovery of the earliest known source of the *Water Music*, which clarifies the order and organization of the numbers, and has been patiently sitting in a London institution for more than a century. Instead of the implausible (though popular) grouping into three suites, and speculation that Handel created these for different occasions, the manuscript confirms the *Water Music* as one long sequence of movements; Chrysander was right.

Unless dedicated researchers find music for the three lost Hamburg operas or some very early autographs of music from Handel's Halle apprenticeship, it seems there is not much music left to discover. New finds such as the debatable *Gloria* or the Halifax arrangement of *Judas Maccabaeus* (with alleged elements of reorchestration that might be by Mozart) have been over-hyped but are transitory. Yet there remains, for example, a rich seam of untapped music in Handel's own revivals of his theatre works: a considerable number of arias, duets and choruses lie undetected or unknown to almost all except a few scholars, but hopefully will be published as appendices of each relevant HHA volume. Performers – especially singers determined to make aria recital programmes – should have no excuse not to be more adventurous in exploring the alterations Handel made for his revivals, all well worth performing in their own right. While one can pick and choose movements from all versions to assemble a mongrel score, there has been very little attempt to preserve and perform Handel's own versions of his operas and oratorios (other than *Messiah*, which since the AAM's Foundling Hospital version recorded in 1980 has received several other distinct reconstructions).

While works such as *Theodora* and *L'Allegro* have been restored to rude health, casual opera-goers might be forgiven for thinking that Handel only composed eight good operas (*Rinaldo, Giulio Cesare, Tamerlano, Rodelinda, Orlando, Ariodante, Alcina* and *Serse*). One has to attend smaller-budget chamber-scale performances of Handel's operas, or productions associated with festivals (Buxton is a fine British example), to find that *Agrippina, Amadigi, Ottone, Admeto, Partenope, Ezio, Atalanta* and *Imeneo* are also distinctive music dramas in their own right.

Some important non-theatrical repertoire remains neglected: *Parnasso in Festa* has been pushed aside for far too long as being a mere pasticcio of *Athalia*, but in fact it contains much new music. The Chapel Royal anthems have been scandalously neglected, even though most *Messiah*-trained audiences think of Handel as a fine English choral composer of sacred texts. Handel's *pasticcio* operas (both those using his own music and those featuring arias by Vinci, Hasse, Orlandini and Leo) deserve a fair reappraisal, and the cantatas for solo voice and basso continuo (a forthcoming HHA edition) are waiting to be explored (hopefully without technicolour accompaniments). It is also time to investigate and perform the music of Handel's closest artistic colleagues: Caldara's Carmelite church music, Bononcini's *Griselda*, Ariosti's *Coriolano*, Keiser's Hamburg operas and the odes and oratorios of Arne and Stanley will all shed further light on our view of Handel. In short, no moment for Handelian relaxation before the next anniversary already on the horizon in 2009.

Chronological Table

compiled by Anthony Hicks

The chart summarizes the events of Handel's life that can be dated with a reasonable degree of certainty, emphasis being given to his activities as a composer and performer (as well as traveller). Column 1 shows the events of the life, together with key historical events, and mentions all major works for which composition dates are known. Column 2 gives dates of performances, and also indicates when new music was included in revivals of operas, oratorios, etc., the exact composition dates of such additions seldom being known. Taken together, the two columns convey some impression of the extent of Handel's day-to-day activities.

CG – *Covent Garden*   KT/QT – *King's/Queen's Theatre, Haymarket*   LIF – *Lincoln's Inn Fields*
‡ *signifies undatable events*

BIOGRAPHICAL	PERFORMANCES
1685 *23 Feb* Born in Halle, at what is now 5 Grosse Nikolaistrasse. *24 Feb* Christened Georg Friederich Händel at Liebfrauenkirche, Halle.	
1694 Composition lessons under F. Zachow.	
1697 *11 Feb* Father dies. *18 Feb* His poem in memory of his father published.	
1699–1700 Earliest extant datable composition (trio sonata op.2 no.2), 'composed at the Age of 14' (Jennens).	
1701 Meets Georg Philipp Telemann	
1702 *10 Feb* Registers at University of Halle. *13 Mar* Appointed organist at Domkirche, Halle.	
1703 *9 July* Meets Mattheson in St Mary Magdalene, Hamburg. *17 Aug* Visits Lübeck with Mattheson.	
1704 Joins opera orchestra at Gansemarkt Theatre, Hamburg, playing violin and harpsichord. *5 Dec* Fights duel with Mattheson after refusing to yield place at the harpsichord during perf of Mattheson's *Cleopatra*.	

1705

8 *Jan Almira*, his 1st opera, opens at Gänsemarkt Theatre. *25 Feb Nero* opens at Gänsemarkt Theatre.

1706

Travels to Italy, probably visiting Florence at invitation of Ferdinand de' Medici before moving on to Rome.

1707

First Roman patron probably Cardinal Pamphili. *Feb* Sets Pamphili's cantata *Il delirio amoroso*. *Apr* Completes *Dixit Dominus*. ‡Joins household of Marquess Ruspoli at Bonelli Palace primarily as a composer of cantatas for the meetings of the Arcadian Academy. *June* Goes with Ruspoli to Vignanello; composes cantata *Diana Cacciatrice* and Latin motets. *8 July* Completes *Laudate Pueri* (in D major). *13 July* Completes *Nisi Dominus*. ‡Moves to Florence.

1707

Il *trionfo del Tempo e del Disinganno* perf for Pamphili.

15–16 July His settings of the 2 psalms, a motet and 2 antiphons perf during services for Our Lady of Mount Carmel at Church of Santa Maria di Monte Santo.

Oct Clori, Tirsi e Fileno, a *cantata a tre*, perf. Goes to Florence for production of his first Italian opera *Rodrigo*. *Nov Rodrigo* opens at Via di Cocomero Theatre, Florence.

1708

Returns to Rome. Moves to Naples. *16 June* Completes *Aci, Galatea e Polifemo*, a *cantata a tre* probably intended for perf at wedding of Duke of Alvito on 16 July. ‡Returns to Ruspoli at Rome.

1708

Jan Florindo and *Daphne* perf in Gänsemarkt Theatre, Hamburg. *8 Apr* (Easter Sunday) *La Resurrezione* perf at Bonelli Palace (repeated next day). *14 July* Cantata *Aminta e Fillide* perf. *9 Sep* Cantata *O come chiare e belle* perf.

1709

Probably moves to Venice and then returns to Florence. *9 Nov* Ferdinand de' Medici provides note of recommendation to Prince Karl von Neuburg, Governor of the Tyrol, at Innsbruck. ‡Moves to Venice.

1710

Returns to Germany. *9 Mar* Prince Karl reports to Ferdinand that Handel did not need his help. *4 June* Entertains the court at Herrenhausen in Hanover. *10 June* The Electress Sophia reports Handel's arrival, mentioning the rumour that he was the 'lover of Victoria'. *16 June* Appointed Kapellmeister to Georg Ludwig, Elector of Hanover. ‡Completes cantata *Apollo e Dafne*. *Aug* Visits court of Elector Palatine at Düsseldorf. *13 Sep* The Elector Palatine reports to Ferdinand his good opinion of Handel. *Nov* Arrives in London

1710

Jan Agrippina opens as 2nd opera of winter carnival season at S. Giovanni Crisostomo. *10 Jan* His music first heard in London when orchestral movements from *Rodrigo* are played as incidental music in *The Alchemist* at QT.

BIOGRAPHICAL

PERFORMANCES

1711
Returns to Germany, visiting Düsseldorf on way to Hanover. *17 June* The Elector Palatine writes a note of apology to Elector of Hanover for having detained Handel.

1711
24 Feb Rinaldo opens at QT (15 perfs to 2 June).

1712
Returns to Hanover but comes back to England for next opera season, staying at London home of 'Mr. Andrews, of Barn-Elms' (Hawkins) and later at Burlington House (until 1716). *24 Oct* Completes *Il Pastor Fido*. *19 Dec* Completes *Teseo*.

1712
23 Jan Rinaldo revived at QT (9 perfs to 1 Apr).

22 Nov Il Pastor Fido opens at QT (6 perfs to 27 Dec; also 21 Feb).

1713
13 Jan Completes Utrecht Te Deum.
‡*Birthday Ode for Queen Anne* composed for perf on 6 Feb, but perhaps not perf. *Silla* composed for perf (probably at QT) on 2 June, but perhaps not perf.

1713
10 Jan Teseo opens at QT (10 perfs to 17 Feb; also 17 Mar, 18 Apr, 16 May). *19 Mar* Rehearsal of Utrecht Te Deum at the Banqueting House, Whitehall (then a Royal chapel). *6 May Rinaldo* revived (also 9 May). *16 May Teseo* perf for Handel's benefit includes 'entertainment' for harpsichord. *7 July* Utrecht Te Deum perf at St Paul's.

28 Dec Granted pension of £200 p.a. by Queen Anne.

1714
1 Aug Queen Anne dies; Elector of Hanover proclaimed King George I.

1714
26 Sep Te Deum (probably the 'Caroline') and anthem (probably no.4a, O *Sing unto the Lord*) perf at Chapel Royal, St James's Palace. *17 Oct* His Te Deum repeated at Chapel Royal. *30 Dec Rinaldo* revived at KT (10 perfs to 19 Feb; also 25 June).

1715

1715
25 May Amadigi opens at KT (6 perfs to 9 July)

10 Oct His arrears of salary for 1712 (half-year) paid by Hanover treasury.

1716
13 Mar Directs payment of dividend on £500 South Sea Stock.

1716
16 Feb Amadigi revived (4 perfs to 6 Mar; also 16 June and 7 July).

1717

1717
5 Jan Rinaldo revived at KT with several new arias (7 perfs to 9 Mar; also 2 May, 18 May and 5 June). *16 Feb Amadigi* revived at KT, probably with some new music (also 21 Mar, 11 Apr, 30 May). *21 Mar Amadigi* perf includes 'a New Scene' for Nicolini and Anastasia Robinson.

29 June Opera season ends; no more opera

in London until 1720. *17 July* The King goes by barge on the Thames from Whitehall to Chelsea; the *Water Music* is played three times during the trip. *25 Sep* James Brydges, Earl of Carnarvon (later Duke of Chandos) reports that Handel has composed 2 anthems for him at Cannons and is at work on 2 more, together with some overtures.

1718
27 May Sir David Dalrymple reports to Earl of Loudon that Handel is composing a 'little opera' (*Acis and Galatea*) for the Earl of Carnarvon at Cannons. ‡The oratorio *Esther* is probably composed and perf about this time.

1719
14 May Commissioned by the newly-formed Royal Academy of Music to engage singers for the operas. ‡Leaves for the continent, visiting Düsseldorf and Halle, and reaching Dresden in July. *15 July* Writes to the Earl of Burlington, hoping that he will be able to engage Senesino and other singers. *30 Nov* The Royal Academy appoints him 'Master of the Orchester with a Sallary'.

1720
Returns to London after engaging a number of singers in the Dresden perfs. *14 June* Granted royal warrant for sole right to publication of his music for 14 years. *14 Nov* His 1st volume of keyboard music (*Suites des Pièces*) published on his behalf by Christopher Smith. *19 Nov* Opera season at KT opens with Bononcini's *Astarto*; début of Senesino in London.

1721
23 Mar Completes Act III of *Muzio Scevola*.

28 Nov Completes *Floridante*.

1722
10 Aug Completes *Ottone*, but the score is later substantially revised before 1st perf.

1718
16 May An 'entirely new' concerto (unidentified) perf at Theatre Royal, Drury Lane.

1719
23 Mar Brockes Passion perf in refectory of Hamburg Cathedral.

1720
2 Apr First season of the Royal Academy opens at KT with Giovanni Porta's *Numitore*. *27 Apr* Radamisto opens at KT (8 perfs to 21 May; also 8, 22 June).

28 Dec Radamisto revived at KT in revised version with much new music (5 perfs to 25 Jan 1721; also 21, 25 Mar).

1721
15 Apr Muzio Scevola (Act I by Amadei, Act II by Bononcini, Act III by Handel) opens at KT (9 perfs to 17 May; also 7 June). *5 July* New cantata (probably *Crudel tiranno amor*) sung by Durastanti at KT. *25 Nov* Radamisto revived at KT (4 perfs to 6 Dec). *9 Dec* Floridante opens at KT (9 perfs to 5 Jan 1722; also 13, 20 Feb, 25, 28 Apr, 23, 26 May).

1722
9 Feb First recorded concert perf of *Water Music* at Stationer's Hall. *27 Oct* Opera

1723
25 Feb Appointed 'Composer of Musick for
His Majesty's Chapel Royal'.

Apr Plans are made to take opera company
to Paris in July but fall through. *7 May*
Completes *Flavio*. ‡*Giulio Cesare* probably
begun during summer.

1724
Handel now living in house in Lower Brook
Street, present day no. 25.

3 July Begins *Tamerlano*. *24 July* Completes
1st version of *Tamerlano*; score substantially
revised before 1st perf. *24 Aug* Plays organ
at St Paul's in the presence of his pupils, the
Princesses Anne and Caroline.

1725

6 May 'Rodelinda an Opera' published, the
first Handel score to be issued on
subscription.

1726

2 Mar Completes *Scipione*. *11 Apr*
Completes *Alessandro*.

10 Nov Completes *Admeto*.

season opens with revival of *Muzio Scevola* (5
perfs to 13 Nov). *4 Dec Floridante* revived
with 5 new arias (3 from cantata *Crudel
tiranno amor*).

1723
12 Jan Ottone opens at KT (11 perfs to 16
Feb; also 26 Mar, 4, 8 June); Cuzzoni's
début in London. *20 Mar* 'New Concerto
for French Horns' (probably the Concerto in
F, related to the *Water Music*) perf at Drury
Lane. *26 Mar Ottone* perf for Cuzzoni's
benefit includes 4 new arias. *14 May Flavio*
opens at KT (8 perfs to 15 June). *11 Dec
Ottone* revived (6 perfs to 1 Jan 1724).

1724
11 Jan His Te Deum and new anthem
(probably the Te Deum in A and *Let God
arise*, A major version) perf at Chapel Royal,
St James's, on the King's return from
Hanover. *20 Feb Giulio Cesare* opens at KT
(14 perfs to 11 Apr).

31 Oct Tamerlano opens at KT, beginning the
opera season (9 perfs to 28 Oct); début of
Borosini in London.

1725
2 Jan Giulio Cesare revived at KT with
several revisions, including 4 new arias (7
perfs to 9 Feb). *23 Jan Giulio Cesare* perf
includes 2 new arias for the soprano
Sorosina. *13 Feb Rodelinda* opens at KT (14
perfs to 6 Apr). *1 May Tamerlano* revived
(3 perfs to 8 May). *9 May Elpidia*, a
pasticcio arranged by Handel, opens at KT
(12 perfs to 19 June). *30 Nov* Opera season
opens with revival of *Elpidia* (4 perfs to 11
Dec). *18 Dec Rodelinda* revived with 4 new
arias and new duet (8 perfs to 11 Jan 1726).

1726
8 Feb Ottone revived with 5 new arias (9
perfs to 8 Mar). *12 Mar Scipione* opens at
KT (13 perfs to 30 Apr). *5 May Alessandro*
opens at KT (14 perfs to 7 June); début of
Faustina Bordoni in London.

1727
31 Jan Admeto opens at KT (19 perfs to 18

1727

20 Feb Act for naturalizing Handel receives Royal Assent. *11 June* George I dies at Osnabrück. George II proclaimed King in London on 15 June.

Apr). *7 Mar Admeto* perf for Faustina's benefit includes new arias. *11 Apr Ottone* revived at KT (also 13 Apr). *29 Apr Floridante* revived at KT (also 2 May). *30 Sep* Opera season opens with revival of *Admeto* (5 perfs to 17 Oct; also 4 Nov). *11 Oct* His anthems perf at coronation of King George and Queen Caroline at Westminster Abbey. *30 Oct* His minuets perf at Court ball. *11 Nov Riccardo Primo* opens at KT (11 perfs to 16 Dec). *26 Dec Alessandro* revived at KT (at least 4 perfs).

1728

29 Jan The Beggar's Opera opens at Lincoln's Inn Fields. *5 Feb* Completes *Siroe*. *19 April* Completes *Tolomeo*.

1728

Jan Radamisto revived at KT. *17 Feb Siroe* opens at KT (18 perfs to 27 Apr). *30 Apr Tolomeo* opens at KT (7 perfs to 21 May). *25 May Admeto* revived with new aria for Mrs Wright (3 perfs to 1 June). *1 June* Perf of *Admeto* ends last season of Royal Academy of Music.

1729

18 Jan Enters agreement with Heidegger to continue operas at KT for 5 years. *4 Feb* Leaves for Italy to seek new opera singers. *Mar* Meets Owen Swiney in Bologna. *June* Visits Hamburg, Hanover and Halle. *29 June* Returns to London, having engaged 7 singers. *10 Oct* Gives concert with opera singers at Kensington Palace. *16 Nov* Completes *Lotario*.

1729

2 Dec Lotario opens at KT (9 perfs to 13 Feb 1730).

1730

12 Feb Completes *Partenope*.

1730

17 Jan Giulio Cesare revived at KT (9 perfs to 21 Feb; also 21, 31 Mar). *21 Feb Partenope* opens at KT (7 perfs to 10 Mar). *21 Mar Giulio Cesare* perf includes 2 new arias for Strada. *4 Apr Ormisda (pasticcio)* opens at KT (13 perfs to 14 May; also 9 June; '12 songs changed' at perf of 21 Apr, for Strada's benefit). *19 May Tolomeo* revived at KT (7 perfs to 13 June). *3 Nov* Opera season opens at KT with revival of *Scipione*, including 2 new arias for Fabri and 12 additions from other operas (6 perfs to 21 Nov). *28 Nov Ormisda* revived at KT with several arias changed (5 perfs to 8 Dec). *12 Dec Partenope* revived at KT with new aria for Senesino (7 perfs to 9 Jan 1731).

8 Aug Tries new organ at Westminster Abbey.

16 Dec Mother dies at Halle.

BIOGRAPHICAL

PERFORMANCES

1731
16 Jan Completes *Poro*.

1731
12 Jan Venceslao (pasticcio) opens at KT (4 perfs to 23 Jan). *2 Feb Poro* opens at KT (14 perfs to 27 Mar). *26 Mar Acis and Galatea* perf at LIF for Rochetti's benefit. *6 Apr Rinaldo* revived at KT with new accompanied recitative, 2 new symphonies and 6 arias from other operas (6 perfs to 1 May). *4 May Rodelinda* revived at KT with 4 items from other operas (8 perfs to 29 May). *13 Nov* Opera season at KT opens with revival of *Tamerlano* including new aria for Montagnana (3 perfs to 20 Nov). *23 Nov Poro* revived at KT with 3 additional arias from other operas (4 perfs to 4 Dec). *7 Dec Admeto* revived at KT with 3 new arias (6 perfs to 11 Jan 1732).

1732

4 Feb Completes *Sosarme*.

1732
11 Jan Ezio opens at KT (5 perfs to 29 Jan). *1 Feb Giulio Cesare* revived at KT (4 perfs to 12 Feb). *15 Feb Sosarme* opens at KT (11 perfs to 21 Mar). *23 Feb* (47th birthday) *Esther* perf by members of Chapel Royal at Crown & Anchor Tavern, The Strand (also 1, 3 Mar). *18 Apr Flavio* revived at KT (4 perfs to 29 Apr). *20 Apr* Unauthorized perf of *Esther* at York Buildings, Villiers St. *2 May* His new expanded version of *Esther*, presented without action, opens at KT (6 perfs to 20 May). *17 May* Unauthorized perf of *Acis and Galatea* at Little Theatre, Haymarket (also 19 May). *10 June* His new English/Italian version of *Acis and Galatea*, presented as 'Serenata', opens at KT (4 perfs to 20 June). *25 Nov Alessandro* revived at KT (6 perfs to 30 Dec). *2 Dec Acis and Galatea* revived at KT (4 perfs to 16 Dec).

20 Nov Completes *Orlando*. *2 Dec* Aaron Hill writes, pleading for operas in English. *7 Dec* John Rich's new theatre at Covent Garden opens.

1733
Initiatives for a new opera company, the 'Opera of the Nobility'. *21 Feb* Completes *Deborah*.

7 June Completes *Athalia*. June/July Goes to Oxford for the Act. Returns to London.

1733
2 Jan Tolomeo revived at KT (4 perfs to 16 Jan). *27 Jan Orlando* opens at KT (6 perfs to 20 Feb; resumed 21 Apr for 4 more perfs to 5 May). *3 Mar Floridante* revived at KT (4 perfs to 13 Mar; resumed 8 May for 3 more perfs to 19 May). *17 Mar Deborah* opens at KT (6 perfs to 10 Apr). *14 Apr Esther* revived at KT (also 17 Apr). *5 July Esther* perf at Sheldonian Theatre (also 7 July). *10 July Athalia* given 1st perf at Sheldonian. *11 July Acis and Galatea* at Christ Church Hall; *Athalia* at Sheldonian. *12 July Deborah* perf at

Oct Completes *Arianna in Creta*. *29 Dec* The 1st season of the 'Opera of the Nobility' opens at LIF with Porpora's *Arianna in Nasso*.

Sheldonian. *13 Nov Ottone* revived at KT (4 perfs to 24 Nov).

1734

12 Feb Publication of *Harmony in an Uproar*, a satirical pamphlet attacking Handel's rivals. *Apr* (between 4 and *12*) Mrs Pendarves gives an evening party during which Handel plays lessons on the harpsichord and accompanies Strada.

1734

26 Jan Arianna in Creta opens at KT (14 perfs to 12 Mar; also 16, 20 Apr). *13 Mar Parnasso in Festa*, a serenata mostly arranged from *Athalia* but with 10 new items, opens at KT (4 perfs to 23 Mar). *14 Mar* His anthem *This is the Day* (also mostly arranged from *Athalia*) perf during the wedding of William, Prince of Orange, and Anne, Princess Royal, at the Queen's Chapel, St James's Palace. *2 Apr Deborah* revived at KT, sung partly in Italian (3 perfs to 9 Apr). *27 Apr Sosarme* revived at KT (3 perfs to 4 May). *7 May Acis and Galatea* (English/Italian version) revived at KT (1 perf). *18 May Il Pastor Fido* revived at KT in substantially revised version with 2 new arias and items from *Parnasso in Festa* (13 perfs to 6 July, the end of the season).

12 Aug Begins composing *Ariodante*. *27 Aug* Writes to Sir Wyndham Knatchbull on his return 'from the Country', refusing an invitation as he is 'engag'd with Mr. Rich to carry on the Operas at Covent Garden'. *24 Oct* Completes *Ariodante*. *31 Oct* The Royal bounty of £1000 for operas is ordered to be paid directly to Handel; he receives it on 19 Dec.

9 Nov His new opera season at CG opens with revival of *Il Pastor Fido*, revised with new prologue *Terpsicore*, 2 new arias and new dances for Marie Sallé (5 perfs to 23 Nov); début of John Beard. *27 Nov Arianna in Creta* revived at CG with new dances (5 perfs to 11 Dec). *10 Dec* An arrangement of his *Ottone* perf at KT by the 'Opera of the Nobility', with Farinelli in the role of Adalberto (5 perfs to 23 Dec). *18 Dec Oreste* (all-Handel *pasticcio* with new dances) opens at CG (3 perfs to 28 Dec).

1735

1735

8 Jan Ariodante opens at CG (11 perfs to 3 Mar). *5 Mar Esther* revived at CG with 2 new organ concertos: op.4 nos 2 and 3 (6 perfs to 21 Mar). *26 Mar Deborah* revived at CG with new organ concerto: op.4 no.5 (3 perfs to 31 Mar). *1 Apr Athalia* revived at CG with several items recomposed and new organ concerto: op.4 no.4 (5 perfs to 12 Apr). *16 Apr Alcina* opens at CG (18 perfs to 2 July, the end of the season).

28 July Writes to Jennens, thanking him for an unidentified oratorio libretto and saying he is about to leave for Tunbridge (Wells).

1736
5–17 Jan Completes *Alexander's Feast*. *25 Jan* Completes Concerto Grosso in C major ('Concerto in *Alexander's Feast*'). *13 Mar* His publisher John Walsh dies; the younger John takes over the business. *9–22 Apr* Completes *Atalanta*.

14 Aug–7 Sep Drafts *Giustino*. *17 Aug* Writes to Michaelsen, glad to learn of the forthcoming marriage of his niece Johanna and saying he is sending gifts to bride and groom. *15 Sep–14 Oct* Composes *Arminio*. *15–20 Oct* Revises and fills out *Giustino*. *18 Dec–18 Jan* Drafts *Berenice*.

1737
27 Jan Completes revision and filling out of *Berenice*.

14 Mar Completes extensive revision of his first Italian oratorio, now called *Il Trionfo del Tempo e della Verità*. *30 Apr* His recovery from an attack of 'rheumatism' reported. *14 May* Reported to be 'very much indispos'd . . . with a Paraletick Disorder, he having at present no use of his Right Hand'. *11 June* The last season of the 'Opera of the Nobility' ends at KT. *Sep* Goes to Aix-la-Chapelle for about 6 weeks, taking the baths as a cure for his paralysis. *7 Nov* (approx) Returns to London. *18 Nov–4 Dec* Composes Acts I and II of *Faramondo*. *20 Nov* Queen Caroline dies. *12 Dec* Completes the Funeral Anthem *The Ways of Zion do Mourn*. *24 Dec* Completes *Faramondo*. *26 Dec–6 Feb* Composes *Serse*.

1738

1736
19 Feb Alexander's Feast opens at CG, with cantata *Cecilia volgi*, concerto grosso in C, harp/lute concerto op.4 no.6, and organ concerto op.4 no.1 (5 perfs to 17 Mar). *24 Mar Acis and Galatea* (English/Italian version) revived at CG (also 31 Mar). *7 Apr Esther* revived at CG, probably with Italian airs (also 14 Apr). *27 Apr* His anthem *Sing unto God* perf at the German Chapel, St James's Palace, during the wedding of Frederick, Prince of Wales, and Princess Augusta of Saxe-Gotha. *5 May Ariodante* revived at CG. *12 May Atalanta* opens at CG (8 perfs to 9 June). *6 Nov Alcina* revived at CG to open Handel's new opera season (3 perfs to 13 Nov). *20 Nov Atalanta* revived at CG (also 27 Nov). *8 Dec Poro* revived at CG in revised version (4 perfs to 5 Jan 1737).

1737
12 Jan Arminio opens at CG (5 perfs to 26 Jan; also 12 Feb). *29 Jan Partenope* revived at CG (4 perfs to 9 Feb). *16 Feb Giustino* opens at CG (6 perfs to 4 Mar; also 4, 11 May, 10 June). *28 Feb* James Miller's comedy *The Universal Passion* opens at Drury Lane with Handel's new song 'I like the am'rous youth that's free' sung by Catherine Clive. *9 Mar Parnasso in Festa* revived at CG (also 11 Mar). *16 Mar Alexander's Feast* revived at CG (also 18, 30 Mar, 5, 25 June). *23 Mar Il Trionfo* opens at CG (4 perfs to 4 Apr). *6 Apr Esther* revived at CG (also 7 Apr). *18 May Berenice* opens at CG (3 perfs to 25 May; also 15 June). *10 June Alcina* revived at CG, (also 21 June). *25 June* His season at CG ends with *Alexander's Feast*. *17 Dec The Ways of Zion* perf in King Henry VII's Chapel, Westminster Abbey, during the funeral of Queen Caroline.

1738
3 Jan Faramondo opens at KT to begin a new season of operas by Handel and others (7 perfs to 24 Jan; also 16 May). *24 Feb*

Alessandro Severo (all-Handel *pasticcio* with new overture and recitatives) opens at KT (5 perfs to 11 Mar; also 30 May). *28 Mar* 'An Oratorio' (actually a selection from Handel's oratorios and anthems, including a newly expanded version of *As pants the hart*) perf for his own benefit at KT; 'he got this night £1000' (Earl of Egmont). *15 Apr Serse* opens at KT (5 perfs to 2 May).

8 Mar Full score of *Alexander's Feast* published by subscription. *23 Apr* 1st meeting of subscribers to the Fund for the Support of Decayed Musicians, of which Handel is a founder member, held at Crown & Anchor Tavern. *1 May* Season at Vauxhall Gardens opens, with the new statue of Handel by Louis François Roubiliac on display. *23 July–15 Aug* Drafts *Saul*. *9–20 Sep* Drafts *Imeneo*. *18 Sep* Is visited by Jennens, who makes various suggestions for revising *Saul*. *19 Sep* Jennens reports to Lord Guernsey that Handel has obtained a carillon and a new organ for his oratorio performances. *27 Sep* Completes *Saul*, taking account of some of Jennens's suggestions. *1 Oct–1 Nov* Composes *Israel in Egypt* (using *The Ways of Zion*, with modified words, as Part 1); filling out completed 28 Oct. *4 Oct* His organ concertos op.4 published in solo keyboard transcriptions.

1739

1739

16 *Jan Saul* opens at KT (4 perfs to 10 Feb; also 27 Mar, 19 Apr). *22 Jan Saul* perf, announced as containing 'several new Concertos on the Organ'. *17 Feb Alexander's Feast* revived at KT (also 24 Feb, 20 Mar). *3 Mar Il Trionfo del Tempo e della Verità* revived at KT (1 perf). *20 Mar Alexander's Feast* perf with new organ concerto (no.2 of the 'Second Set') at KT for the benefit of the Fund for the Support of Decayed Musicians. *4 Apr Israel in Egypt* opens at KT with the new organ concerto in F (3 perfs to 17 Apr). *7 Apr Israel in Egypt* perf with the addition of 4 Italian and English airs from earlier works. *1 May Giove in Argo* opens at KT (also 5 May, ending the season). *22 Nov* (St Cecilia's Day) *Ode for St Cecilia's Day* first perf with *Alexander's Feast* at LIF, opening a season of oratorios and odes (also 27 Nov). *13 Dec Acis and Galatea*, restored to its original all-English form and with a new additional chorus, revived at LIF; the perf includes 2 of the new Grand Concertos and the *St Cecilia Ode* (also 20 Dec, 21 Feb).

28 Feb His Trio Sonatas op.5 (partly new, partly compiled from earlier works) published. *2 Apr* Completes organ concerto in F (no.1 of 'Second Set'). *24 Apr* Completes *Giove in Argo* (*Jupiter in Argos*), using much material from earlier works. *15–24 Sep* Composes Dryden's ode *A Song for St Cecilia's Day*. *29 Sep* Completes no.1 of the Grand Concertos, op.6, and continues with the composition of the other 11, finishing the last (published as no.11) on 30 Oct. *19 Oct* Great Britain declares war on Spain. *31 Oct* Granted 2nd copyright privilege for 14 years.

BIOGRAPHICAL

PERFORMANCES

1740

19 Jan–4 Feb Composes *L'Allegro, il Penseroso ed il Moderato*. Severe frost in London causes postponement of Handel's performances. *17 Feb* Completes organ concerto op.7 no.1.

‡Visits Continent. *9 Sep* Plays organ at Haarlem. Returns to London and resumes work on *Imeneo*, begun 2 years earlier. *27 Oct–7 Nov* Composes Acts I and II of *Deidamia*. *8 Nov* 'Second Set' of concertos published in transcriptions for solo keyboard; they comprise the 2 organ concertos of 1739 and 4 of the Grand Concertos. *14–20 Nov* Composes Act III of *Deidamia*.

1741

1 July Completes duet *Quel fior ch'all'alba ride*. *3 July* Completes duet *No, di voi non vuo fidarmi* (G major setting). *22 Aug* Begins composing *Messiah*; Part 1 completed in draft on 28 Aug, Part 2 on 6 Sep and Part 3 on 12 Sep; filling out completed on 14 Sep. *29 Sep–29 Oct* Drafts *Samson*. In response to an invitation from the Lord Lieutenant of Ireland goes to Dublin for the winter season; delayed for a few days at Chester, where he is seen by the 15-year-old Charles Burney. *18 Nov* Arrives in Dublin.

1742

27 Mar Announcement of perf of *Messiah* for the benefit of 3 charities, 'in which the Gentlemen of the Choirs of both Cathedrals will assist'. ‡Returns to London after last concert in Dublin.

1740

27 Feb *L'Allegro* opens at LIF, with new organ concerto and 1st perf of 2 of the Grand Concertos (4 perfs to 14 Mar; also 23 Apr). *21 Mar* *Saul* revived at LIF, with 1st perf of another Grand Concerto (1 perf). *26 Mar* *Esther* revived at LIF (1 perf). *28 Mar* *Acis and Galatea* perf with *St Cecilia Ode* for benefit of the Fund for the Support of Decayed Musicians. *1 Apr* *Israel in Egypt* revived at LIF, with 1st perf of one of the Grand Concertos (1 perf). *23 Apr* Perf of *L'Allegro* includes 1st perfs of 2 more of the Grand Concertos. *8 Nov* *Parnasso in Festa* revived at LIF to open new season of operas, odes and oratorios (1 perf). *22 Nov* *Imeneo* opens at LIF (also 13 Dec).

1741

10 Jan *Deidamia* opens at LIF (also 24 Jan and at Little Theatre, Haymarket, on 10 Feb, the last perf of a Handel opera under the composer's direction). *31 Jan* *L'Allegro* revived with several new items, some of the airs being sung in Italian (also 7, 21 Feb). *28 Feb* *Acis and Galatea* revived at LIF (also 11 Mar). *14 Mar* *Parnasso in Festa* perf at KT (perhaps not under Handel) for the benefit of the Fund for the Support of Decayed Musicians. *18 Mar* *Saul* revived at LIF (1 perf). *8 Apr* *L'Allegro* (probably without Part 3) perf with *St Cecilia Ode* to end Handel's last season at LIF. *10 Dec* Plays the organ at a service at St Andrew's Church, during which his Utrecht Te Deum and Jubilate and a Coronation Anthem are performed. *23 Dec* Subscription series of 6 concerts at the New Music Hall, Fishamble St, opens with a revival of *L'Allegro* (also 13 J

1742

20 Jan *Acis and Galatea* and *St Cecilia Ode* revived at New Music Hall (also 27 Jan). *3 Feb* *Esther* revived at New Music Hall (also 10 Feb). *17 Feb* *Alexander's Feast* revived at New Music Hall, with new solo for Mrs Cibber and new duet, opening a second series of 6 concerts (also 2 Mar). *17 Mar* *L'Allegro* revived at New Music Hall (1 perf). *24 Mar* *Imeneo* revived in revised version as Italian 'serenata' at New Music Hall (also 31 Mar). *7 Apr* *Esther* revived at New Music Hall (1 perf, ending Handel's second series). *9 Apr* Public rehearsal of

Messiah. *13 Apr Messiah* first performed at New Music Hall. *25 May Saul* revived at New Music Hall by special request. *3 June Messiah* again perf there as Handel's last concert in Dublin.

12 Oct Completes *Samson* (drafted in Sep 1741). *31 Oct* Completes duet *Beato in ver chi può.* *2 Nov* Completes duet *No, di voi non vuo fidarmi* (E flat major setting).

1743

10 Jan Sends MS of *Samson* libretto to Inspector of Stage Plays. *5 Feb* Completes organ concerto op.7 no.2. *19 Mar* 1st London perf of 'A New Sacred Oratorio' (i.e. *Messiah*) announced for 23 Mar; a correspondent to *The Universal Spectator* condemns the singing of sacred texts in a 'Playhouse'. *11 Apr* Report that 'Mr. Handel, who has been dangerously ill, is now recover'd'. *29 Apr* Jennens, writing to Holdsworth, says that 'Handel has a return of his Paralytic Disorder, which affects his Head & Speech'. *3 June–4 July* Composes *Semele.* *27 June* British and Hanoverian troops under the direct command of King George II are victorious over the French at Dettingen. *17 July* Begins composing the Dettingen Te Deum, completing it before the end of the month. *30 July–3 Aug* Composes the Dettingen Anthem (*The King shall Rejoice*). *26 Aug–12 Sep* Composes *Joseph and his Brethren.*

1743

18 Feb Samson opens at CG, beginning a Lenten subscription series of oratorio concerts (7 perfs to 16 Mar; also 31 Mar). *18 Mar L'Allegro* and *St Cecilia Ode* revived at CG. *23 Mar Messiah* revived with new soprano and tenor solos at CG (3 perfs to 29 Mar). *31 Mar Samson* perf ends Handel's season.

8 Nov Lord Middlesex's opera company revives *Alessandro* at KT in new version entitled *Rossane.* *27 Nov* Dettingen Te Deum and Anthem perf at Chapel Royal, St James's Palace, during a service to celebrate King's safe return to England.

1744

21 Feb Mrs Delany reports to Mrs Dewes that 'Semele has a strong party against it . . . All the opera people are enrag'd at Handel'. *9 June* Writes to Jennens, saying that he intends giving perfs at KT every Saturday in the forthcoming season; he is looking forward to receiving Jennens's new oratorio libretto. ‡Leaves London, presumably to stay in the country with one of his patrons; returns *18 July.* *19 July–17 Aug* Composes *Hercules.* *23 Aug–23 Oct* Composes *Belshazzar.* *20 Oct* Announcement of subscription series of 24

1744

10 Feb Semele opens at CG to begin new Lenten subscription series of concerts (4 perfs to 22 Feb). *24 Feb Samson* revived at CG (also 29 Feb). *2 Mar Joseph and his Brethren* opens at CG (4 perfs to 14 Mar). *16 Mar Saul* revived at CG (also 21 Mar, last concert of series). *3 Nov* Revival of *Deborah* at KT begins the subscription series; next perf is postponed to 24 Nov 'as the greatest Part of Mr. Handel's subscribers are not in Town'. *1 Dec Semele* is revived at KT, with Italian arias from Handel's operas interpolated (also 8 Dec).

concerts 'every Saturday till Lent, and then on Wednesdays and Fridays'.

1745

17 Jan Announces that despite his attempts in setting English words to music he now finds that his labours 'are become ineffectual' and he can 'proceed no farther' in his undertakings; a fourth of the subscription having been performed, he proposes to return three-quarters of the money subscribed. *18 Jan* Letter of support published, urging subscribers not to withdraw the remainder of their subscriptions. *21 Jan* Anonymous poem published in support of Handel hints that his audiences have been kept low by the intrigues of a society lady ('Whene'er he play'd, she'd make a *Drum* [give a party]/Invite her Neighbours all to come'), probably Lady Brown, wife of former British Resident in Venice. *25 Jan* Announces resumption of concerts, in view of support offered. *Summer* Leaves London to visit Exton, Leics., seat of the Earl of Gainsborough. *13 June* (approx) Leaves Exton for Scarborough. ‡Returns to London. *21 July* Prince Charles Edward Stuart, the Young Pretender, lands at Eriksay, beginning the second Jacobite rebellion. *31 Aug* Completes duet *Ahi, nelle sorte umane*. *17 Sep* The Young Pretender enters Edinburgh. *24 Oct* Lord Shaftesbury reports to James Harris that Handel is better, but 'has been a good deal disordered in his head'. *17 Nov* The Young Pretender captures Carlisle. *4 Dec* The Young Pretender reaches Derby, then begins to retreat.

1746

Jan–Feb Composes *Occasional Oratorio*. *16 Apr* Jacobite forces defeated by the Duke of Cumberland's armies at Culloden. ‡Composes *A Song on the Victory obtained over the Rebels* ('From scourging rebellion'), sung by Thomas Lowe at Vauxhall Gardens. *'8 or 9' July* (Handel's dating)–*11 Aug* Composes *Judas Maccabaeus*.

1747

16 Mar Trial of the Jacobite Lord Lovat opens, causing postponement of some concerts. *8 Apr Judas Maccabaeus*

1745

5 Jan Hercules opens at KT (also 12 Jan).

1 Mar Samson revived at KT with new air for Miss Robinson (also 8 Mar). *13 Mar Saul* revived at KT (1 perf). *15 Mar Joseph and his Brethren* revived at KT (also 22 Mar). *27 Mar Belshazzar* opens at KT (also 29 Mar, 23 Apr). *9 Apr Messiah* ('A Sacred Oratorio') revived at KT, probably with new settings of 'Rejoice greatly' and 'Their sound is gone out' (chorus) (also 11 Apr). *23 Apr* Perf of *Belshazzar* ends Handel's series, 16 concerts out of the promised 24 having been given. *9 June* (approx) His 3 songs and chorus for *Comus*, newly composed, conclude a private perf of the masque at Exton. *14 Nov* His new *Song for the Gentlemen Volunteers of the City of London* ('Stand round my brave boys') perf at Drury Lane.

1746

14 Feb His *New Occasional Oratorio* 'expressive of the rebels' flight and our pursuit of them' (William Harris) opens at CG (3 perfs to 26 Feb).

1747

24 Feb Lord Middlesex's company revive *Rossane* (their version of *Alessandro*) at KT announced with 'additions' (probably the air 'O liberty' and the March). *1 June–4 July* Composes *Alexander Balus*. *19 July–19 Aug* Composes *Joshua*.

1748

5 May–13 June Composes *Solomon*. *11 July–24 Aug* Composes *Susanna*. *7 Oct* Peace of Aix-la-Chapelle concludes the War of the Austrian Succession.

1749
Completes the *Music for the Royal Fireworks* in celebration of the peace treaty; it is rehearsed in Handel's house in Brook St (*17 Apr*) and in public in Vauxhall Gardens (*21 Apr*) for the perf, with firework display, in Green Park (*27 Apr*). *7 May* Attends General Committee of the Foundling Hospital and offers a perf for the benefit of the charity at the newly built Chapel. *28 June–31 July* Composes *Theodora*. *July* Contracts with Dr Morse of Barnet for a new organ to be put in the Foundling Hospital Chapel. Goes to Bath. Returns to London. *27 Dec* Begins composing the music for Tobias Smollett's *Alceste*, intended for perf at CG.

1750
8 Jan Completes the music for *Alceste* (but two airs probably recomposed later). *31 Jan* Completes the organ concerto op.7 no.5. *13 Feb* Lord Shaftesbury reports to James Harris that Handel has been buying pictures, 'particularly a large Rembrandt'.

6 Mar Occasional Oratorio revived at CG to open new series of Lenten concerts (3 perfs to 13 Mar). *20 Mar Joseph and his Brethren* revived at CG (also 25 Mar). *1 Apr Judas Maccabaeus* opens at CG with a 'new Concerto' (probably the *concerto a due cori* no.3) (6 perfs to 15 Apr). *15 Apr* Last perf of *Judas Maccabaeus* ends the season. *14 Nov* Lord Middlesex's opera company open their season at KT with *Lucio Vero*, a *pasticcio* based on arias from Handel's operas.

1748
20 Feb Rossane revived at KT. *9 Mar* Joshua opens at CG to begin Handel's new series of Lenten concerts; it is perf with a 'New Concerto' (probably the *concerto a due cori* no.1) (4 perfs to 18 Mar). *23 Mar Alexander Balus* opens at CG with a 'New Concerto' (probably the *concerto a due cori* no.2) (3 perfs to 30 Mar). *7 Apr Judas Maccabaeus* revived at CG to close Handel's season (1 perf).

1749
10 Feb Susanna opens at CG to begin series of Lenten concerts (4 perfs to 22 Feb). *3 Mar Samson* revived at CG (4 perfs to 15 Mar). *17 Mar Solomon* opens at CG (3 perfs to 22 Mar). *23 Mar Messiah* revived at CG (1 perf, ending the season). *25 Apr* His Anthem on the Peace (*How Beautiful are the Feet*, partly compiled from earlier works) perf at the Chapel Royal, St James's Palace, during the official service of thanksgiving. *7 May* His concert at the Chapel of the Foundling Hospital includes the 1st perf of his new anthem (*Blessed are they that considereth the Poor*, partly compiled from earlier works).

1750
The planned performances of *Alceste* are cancelled. *2 Mar Saul* revived at CG, opening new series of Lenten concerts (also 7 Mar). *9 Mar Judas Maccabaeus* revived at CG (4 perfs to 30 Mar). *16 Mar Theodora* opens at CG, with the new organ concerto

9 May Elected a Governor of the Foundling Hospital. *1 June* Makes his Will, including a bequest to Christopher Smith of 'my large Harpsicord, my little House Organ, my Musick Books and five hundred Pounds sterl:'; his niece Johanna Floerken is the residual legatee. *28 June* Begins composing *The Choice of Hercules* (partly adapted from the unperformed music to *Alceste*), completing it on July 5. ‡Visits Germany for last time. *21 Aug General Advertiser* reports that he was hurt in a coach accident between The Hague and Haarlem, but 'is now out of Danger'. Returns to London. *14 Dec* Writes to Telemann, commenting on the singer Passerini and thanking him for the copy of *Das neue musikalische System*; he says he is sending a crate of rare plants as a gift.

op.7 no.5 (3 perfs to 23 Mar). *4 Apr Samson* revived at CG (also 6 Apr). *12 Apr Messiah* revived at CG with new settings of 'But who may abide' and 'Thou art gone up' composed for Guadagni (1 perf, ending the season). *1 May Messiah* perf at the Chapel of the Foundling Hospital for the benefit of the charity. *15 May Messiah* repeated at Foundling Hospital.

1751

1–4 Jan Composes the organ concerto op.7 no.3. *21 Jan–2 Feb* Drafts Act I of *Jephtha*. *13 Feb* During the composition of the chorus 'How dark, O Lord, are thy decrees' in Act II of *Jephtha* he records that he is unable to continue because of the loss of sight in his left eye. *23 Feb* Resumes composition of *Jephtha* feeling 'etwas besser', completing it on 27 Feb. Leaves for Bath and Cheltenham. *13 June* Returns to London after taking the waters at Cheltenham. *18 June–'15 or 17' July* Drafts Act III of *Jephtha*. *30 Aug* Completes *Jephtha*.

1751

1 Mar Alexander's Feast revived at CG with *The Choice of Hercules* and the organ concerto op.7 no.3, opening new series of Lenten concerts (4 perfs to 13 Mar). *15 Mar Esther* revived at CG (1 perf). *20 Mar Judas Maccabaeus* revived at CG (1 perf). *20 Mar* Death of Prince of Wales causes cancellation of the rest of Handel's season. *18 Apr* and *16 May Messiah* at Foundling Hospital; Handel plays a voluntary on the organ.

1752

1752

14 Feb Joshua is revived at CG to open a new series of Lenten concerts (also 19 Feb). *21 Feb Hercules* revived at CG (1 perf). *26 Feb Jephtha* opens at CG (3 perfs to 4 Mar). *6 Mar Samson* revived at CG (3 perfs to 13 Mar). *18 Mar Judas Maccabaeus* revived at CG (also 20 Mar). *25 Mar Messiah* revived at CG (also 26 Mar, ending the series). *9 Apr Messiah* at Foundling Hospital.

17 Aug Announcement that he was 'seiz'd a few days ago with a Paralytic Disorder in his Head which has deprived him of Sight'. [British Calendar changes to Continental style, 2 Sep being followed by 14 Sep] *3 Nov* Undergoes operation by William Bromfield, Surgeon to the Princess of Wales, to restore his sight.

1753

23 Jan Reported to be well enough to go out of doors. *27 Jan* Further report that he has 'quite lost his Sight'.

Dec The Musical Society of Edinburgh apply to Handel for copies of the unpublished sections of *Messiah* and other oratorios; he authorizes Christopher Smith to meet their requirements.

1754

25 June General Committee of the Foundling Hospital notes Handel's approval of the younger John Christopher Smith being appointed organist of the Chapel, and 'on Account of his Health he excused himself from giving any further Instructions relating to the Performances'. *20 Sep* Dictates and signs letter to Telemann, rejoicing that rumours of his death have proved false and promising him another set of exotic plants.

1753

9 Mar Alexander's Feast and *The Choice of Hercules* revived at CG to begin a new series of Lenten concerts; Lady Shaftesbury reports Handel 'dejected, wan and dark, sitting by, not playing on the harpsichord'. *16 Mar Jephtha* revived at CG with the additions of an air adapted from *Agrippina* and a new quintet (also 21 Mar). *23 Mar Judas Maccabaeus* revived at CG (3 perfs to 30 Mar). *4 Apr Samson* revived at CG (3 perfs to 11 Apr). *13 Apr Messiah* revived at CG (1 perf, ending the season). *1 May Messiah* at Foundling Hospital; Handel plays organ concerto and voluntary.

1754

1 Mar Alexander Balus revived at CG to open new series of Lenten concerts (also 6 Mar). *8 Mar Deborah* revived at CG (also 13 Mar). *12 Mar Admeto* revived in an altered version at KT (5 perfs to 6 Apr, the last perf of any Handel opera on the stage before the 20th century). *17 Mar Saul* revived at CG (also 20 Mar). *22 Mar Joshua* revived at CG (1 perf). *27 Mar Judas Maccabaeus* revived at CG (also 3 Apr). *29 Mar Samson* revived at CG (1 perf). *5 Apr Messiah* revived at CG (1 perf, ending the season). *15 May Messiah* at Foundling Hospital, probably the last time under Handel's direct supervision.

1755

14 Feb Alexander's Feast and *The Choice of Hercules* revived at CG, opening a new series of Lenten concerts (also 19 Feb). *21 Feb L'Allegro* and the *St Cecilia Ode* revived at CG (1 perf). *26 Feb Samson* revived at CG

BIOGRAPHICAL

PERFORMANCES

(also 7 Mar). *28 Feb Joseph and his Brethren* revived at CG (1 perf). *5 Mar Theodora* revived at CG (1 perf), with new solo and chorus and new air dictated to (and perhaps partly composed by) the younger Smith. *12 Mar Judas Maccabaeus* revived at CG (also 14 Mar). *19 Mar Messiah* revived at CG (also 21 Mar, ending the season). *1 May Messiah* at Foundling Hospital.

1756

1756

5 Mar Athalia revived in a substantially revised version, with 2 additional airs adapted from *Parnasso in Festa* (3 perfs to 12 Mar). *17 Mar Israel in Egypt* revived at CG with new Part 1, compiled from the Anthem on the Peace, the *Occasional Oratorio* and *Solomon* (also 24 Mar). *19 Mar Deborah* revived at CG with added aria adapted from *Tolomeo* (1 perf). *26 Mar Judas Maccabaeus* revived at CG (also 31 Mar). *2 Apr Jephtha* revived at CG (1 perf). *7 Apr Messiah* revived at CG (1 perf), ending the season). *19 May Messiah* at Foundling Hospital.

6 Aug Adds first Codicil to his Will, making bequests to Thomas Morell and Newburgh Hamilton, and adding £1500 to Christopher Smith's bequest.

1757

1757

8 Feb Lord Shaftesbury reports to James Harris that Handel 'is better than he has been for some years and finds he can compose Chorus's as well as other music to his , . . satisfaction'. *22 Mar* Adds second Codicil to his Will.

25 Feb Esther revived at CG with new duet and chorus 'Sion now her head shall raise' ('his last chorus' – Morell) and 2 new airs (perhaps not Handel's), opening new series of Lenten concerts (also 2 Mar). *7 Mar Israel in Egypt* revived at CG (1 perf). *9 Mar Joseph and his Brethren* revived at CG (1 perf). *11 Mar The Triumph of Time and Truth* (mainly adapted from *Il Trionfo del Tempo e della Verità* and other works, with new recitatives perhaps by the younger Smith) opens at CG (4 perfs to 23 Mar). *25 Mar Judas Maccabaeus* revived at CG (1 perf). *30 Mar Messiah* revived at CG (also 1 Apr, ending the season). *5 May Messiah* at Foundling Hospital.

4 Aug Adds third Codicil to his Will, bequeathing his theatre organ at CG to John Rich, pictures to Jennens and Bernard Granville, and a 'fair copy of the Score and all Parts' of *Messiah* to the Foundling Hospital. *31 Dec* Lord Shaftesbury reports to James Harris that Handel 'is pretty well and has just finished the composing of several new songs' for Cassandra Frederick, 'his new singer'.

1758
10 Feb The Triumph of Time and Truth revived at CG with 5 additional airs for Cassandra Frederick, partly based on material from earlier works, opening new Lenten season of concerts (also 15 Feb). *22 Feb Belshazzar* revived at CG with 2 additional airs for Frasi, partly based on material from earlier works (1 perf). *24 Feb Israel in Egypt* revived at CG (1 perf). *1 Mar Jephtha* revived at CG (1 perf). *3 Mar Judas Maccabaeus* revived at CG with 2 additional airs for Cassandra Frederick, partly based on material from earlier works (also 8 Mar). *10 Mar Messiah* revived at CG (also 15 and 17 Mar, the end of the season). *27 Apr Messiah* at Foundling Hospital.

1759

1759
2 Mar Solomon revived at CG in a revised version prepared by the younger Smith and containing 5 additional airs and a chorus adapted from earlier works by Handel (also 7 Mar). *9 Mar Susanna* revived at CG (1 perf). *14 Mar Samson* revived at CG (3 perfs to 21 Mar). *23 Mar Judas Maccabaeus* revived at CG (also 28 Mar). *30 Mar Messiah* revived at CG (3 perfs to 6 Apr). *3 May Messiah* at Foundling Hospital under the younger Smith's direction. *24 May* A concert of sacred music (the Foundling Hospital Anthem and Coronation Anthems) given at the Hospital Chapel under Smith's direction in memory of Handel.

11 Apr Adds fourth Codicil to his Will, bequeathing £1000 to the Society for the Support of Decayed Musicians and desiring burial in Westminster Abbey and the erection there of a monument for him. *14 Apr* Dies at Brook St at about 8 am. *20 Apr* Buried at Westminster Abbey; 'it is computed there were no fewer than 3000 Persons present on this Occasion' (*London Evening Post*). *27 Aug* Contents of Handel's house sold by order of Handel's executors to his servant John Duburk. *10 Oct* George Amyand, one of the executors, pays residue of estate to his niece, Johanna Floerken. *31 Oct* Amyand completes execution of the Will with payments of individual bequests.

1762
15 July Roubiliac's monument in memory of Handel unveiled at Westminster Abbey.

Select Bibliography

ABRAHAM, Gerald, ed.: *Handel: a Symposium* (London, 1954)

ADDISON, Joseph: Articles in *The Spectator* (1710–12)

——: *Remarks on Several Parts of Italy &c. In the Years 1701, 1702, 1703* (London, 1705)

AVISON, Charles: *An Essay on Musical Expression* (London, 1752)

——: *A Reply to the Author of Remarks on the Essay on Musical Expression* (London, 1753)

BAKER, C. H. Collins and Muriel: *The Life and Circumstances of James Brydges, First Duke of Chandos* (Oxford, 1949)

BALFOUR, A. J.: *Essays and Addresses* (Edinburgh, 1893)

BASELT, Bernd: 'Miscellanea Handeliana', *Der Komponist und sein Adressat*, ed. S. Bimberg (Halle, 1976), 60

——: 'Muffat and Handel: a two-way Exchange', *Musical Times*, cxx (1979), 904

——: 'Wiederentdeckung von Fragmenten aus Händels verschollenen Hamburger Opern', *Händel-Jahrbuch 1983*, 7

BEEKS, Graydon: 'Handel's Chandos Anthems: the "Extra" Movements', *Musical Times*, cxix (1978), 621

BERLIOZ, Hector: *The Memoirs of Hector Berlioz*, trans. and ed. David Cairns (London, 1969)

BEST, T.: 'Handel's harpsichord music: a checklist', in C. Hogwood and R. Luckett, eds: *Music in Eighteenth-Century England* (Cambridge, 1983), 171

——: 'Handel's Keyboard Music', *Musical Times*, cxii (1971), 845

BLAINVILLE, Monsieur de: *Travels through Holland, Germany, Switzerland and other parts of Europe; but especially Italy*, 3 vols (London, 1743–5)

BUELOW, George J. and Marx, Hans Joachim, eds: *New Mattheson Studies* (Cambridge, 1983)

BURNEY, Charles: *A General History of Music from the Earliest Ages to the Present Period*, 4 vols (London, 1776–89; rev. edn 1935, repr. 1957)

——: *An Account of the Musical Performances in Westminster Abbey and the Pantheon May 26th, 27th, 29th; and June the 3rd and 5th, 1784: in Commemoration of Handel* (London, 1785, repr. 1965)

——: *Articles for The Cyclopaedia: or, Universal Dictionary of Arts, Sciences, and Literature*, ed. Abraham Rees, 39 vols (London 1802–19)

BURROWS, Donald: 'Handel and "Alexander's Feast"', *Musical Times*, cxxiii (1982), 252

——: 'Handel and the Foundling Hospital', *Music & Letters*, lviii (1977), 269

——: 'Handel's Peace Anthem', *Musical Times*, cxiv (1973), 1230

——: 'Handel's Performance of "Messiah": the Evidence of the Conducting Score', *Music & Letters*, lvi (1975), 319

BUSBY, Thomas: *Concert Room and Orchestra Anecdotes of Music and Musicians, Ancient and Modern*, 3 vols (London, 1825)

BUTLER, Samuel: *Alps and Sanctuaries of Piedmont and the Canton Ticino* (London, 1881)

——: *The Note-Books of Samuel Butler*, ed. Henry Festing Jones (London, 1912, repr. 1930)

——: *Further Extracts from the Note-Books of Samuel Butler*, ed. A. T. Bartholomew (London, 1934)

CAMPBELL, Margaret: *Dolmetsch: the Man and his Work* (London, 1975)

CHRYSANDER, Friedrich: *G. F. Händel* (Leipzig, 1858–67, repr. 1966); index, S. Flesch (Leipzig, 1967)

CLAUSEN, H. D.: *Händels Direktionspartituren ('Handexemplare')* (Hamburg, 1972)

COOPER, Barry: 'Keyboard Sources in Hereford', *RMA Research Chronicle*, no. 16 (1980), 135

COOPERSMITH, J. M.: 'The First Gesamtausgabe: Dr. Arnold's Edition of Handel's Works', *Notes*, iv (1946–7), 277, 439

——: 'A List of Portraits, Sculptures, etc of Georg Friedrich Handel', *Music & Letters*, xii (1932), 156

[W. COXE]: *Anecdotes of George Frederick Handel and John Christopher Smith* (London, 1799, repr. 1980)

COZENS-HARDY, Basil, ed.: *The Diary of Sylas Neville* (London, 1950)

CUDWORTH, Charles: 'Mythistorica Handeliana', *Festskrift Jens Peter Larsen* (Copenhagen, 1972), 161

DEAN, Winton: 'Charles Jennens's Marginalia to Mainwaring's Life of Handel', *Music & Letters*, liii (1972), 160

——: 'A French Traveller's View of Handel's Operas', *Music & Letters*, lv (1974), 172

——: 'Handel and Keiser: Further Borrowings', *Current Musicology*, no. 9 (1969), 73

——: *Handel and the Opera Seria* (Berkeley and Los Angeles, 1969; London, 1970)

——: *Handel's Dramatic Oratorios and Masques*

(London, 1959)
——: 'Handel's *Sosarme*, a Puzzle Opera', in *Essays on Opera and English Music in Honour of Sir Jack Westrup* (Oxford, 1975), 115
——: 'How Should Handel's Oratorios be Staged?', *Musical Newsletter*, i/4 (1971), 11
——: 'Masque into Opera [*Acis and Galatea*], *Musical Times*, cviii (1967), 605
——: 'The Performance of Recitative in Late Baroque Opera', *Music & Letters*, lviii (1977), 389

DELANY, M.: *Autobiography and Correspondence of Mary Granville, Mrs Delany* (London, 1861–2)

DENNIS, John: *Essay on the Operas after the Italian Manner. . .* (London, 1706)

DENT, Edward J.: *Handel* (London, 1934)

DEUTSCH, Otto Erich: *Handel: a Documentary Biography* (London, 1955, repr. 1974)

DORRIS, George: *Paoli Rolli and the Italian Circle in London* (The Hague, 1967)

DOWNES, John: *Roscius Anglicanus, or an historical review of the Stage* (London, 1708, repr. 1928)

EWERHART, R.: 'Die Händel-Handschriften der Santini-Bibliothek in Münster', *Händel-Jahrbuch* 1960, 111
——: 'New Sources for Handel's *La Resurrezione*', *Music & Letters*, xli (1960), 127

FARMER, H. G.: *Handel's Kettledrums, and Other Papers on Military Music* (London, 1950

FISKE, Roger: *English Theatre Music in the Eighteenth Century* (London, 1973)
——: 'Handel's Organ Concertos: Do they Belong to Particular Oratorios?', *Organ Yearbook*, iii (1972), 15

FITZGERALD, Edward: *Letters and Literary Remains*, ed. William Aldis Wright, 7 vols (London, 1902)

FLOWER, Newman: *George Frederic Handel: his Personality and his Times* (London, 1923, rev. 3/1959)

FOSS, Michael: *The Age of Patronage* (London, 1971)

FULLER, David: *G. F. Handel: Two Ornamented Organ Concertos* (Hackensack, New Jersey, 1980)

GRANT, K. S.: *Dr Burney as Critic and Historian of Music* (Ann Arbor, 1983)

GRÉTRY, André: *Mémoires, ou Essais sur la musique* (Paris, 1789)

HALL, J. S.: 'Handel among the Carmelites', *Dublin Review* (1959), No. 233, 121
——: 'The Problem of Handel's Latin Church Music', *Musical Times*, c (1959), 197

HAMILTON, Phyllis: 'Handel in the papers of the Edinburgh Musical Society (1728–1798)', *Brio*, i (1964), 19

HANDEL, G. F.: *Autograph Letters of George Frideric Handel and Charles Jennens* (London, 1973) [Christie's sale catalogue, 4 July]

HARRIS, Ellen: *Handel and the Pastoral Tradition* (London, 1980)

HARRIS, James: *Three Treatises . . . the Second concerning Music, Painting, and Poetry* (London, 1744)

HARRIS, John: *The Palladians* (London, 1981)

HATTON, Ragnhild: *George I* (London, 1979)

HAWKINS, Sir John: *A General History of the Science and Practice of Music*, 5 vols (London, 1776; rev. edn 1853, repr. 1963)

HERBAGE, Julian: *Messiah* (London, 1948)

HERIOT, Angus: *The Castrati in Opera* (London, 1956, repr. 1975)

HICKS, Anthony: 'Handel and Il Parnasso in festa', *Musical Times*, cxii (1971), 339
——: 'Handel's Early Musical Development', *Proceedings of the Royal Musical Association*, ciii (1976–7), 80
——: 'Handel's *La Resurrezione*', *Musical Times*, cx (1969), 145
——: 'Handel's Music for Comus', *Musical Times*, cxvii (1976), 28
——: 'The late additions to Handel's oratorios and the role of the younger Smith', in C. Hogwood and R. Luckett, eds: *Music in Eighteenth-Century England* (Cambridge, 1983), 147

HIGHFILL, Philip H., et al.: *A Biographical Dictionary of Actors, Actresses, Musicians, Dancers, Managers, and Other Stage Personnel in London, 1660–1800* (Southern Illinois, 1973–)

HIRSCH, P.: 'Dr. Arnold's Handel Edition', *Music Review*, viii (1947), 106

HODGKINSON, Terence: *Handel at Vauxhall* (London, 1969)

HOGWOOD, Christopher, and Luckett, Richard, eds: *Music in Eighteenth-Century England* (Cambridge, 1983)

HONE, William: *The Every-Day Book: and Table Book* (London, 1827)

HUME, Robert, ed.: *The London Theatre World 1660–1800* (Southern Illinois, 1980)

HURD, Michael: *Vincent Novello – and Company* (London, 1981)

JACKSON, David M.: 'Bach, Handel, and the Chevalier Taylor', *Medical History*, xii (1968), 385

JOHNSON, M. Earle: *Hallelujah, Amen! The Story of the Handel and Haydn Society of Boston* (Boston, 1965, repr. New York, 1981)

KELLY, Michael: *Reminiscences . . . of the King's Theatre*, 2 vols (London, 1826)

KERMAN, Joseph: 'A Few Canonic Variations', *Critical Inquiry*, x (1983), 107
——: 'How We Got into Analysis and How to

Get Out', *Critical Inquiry*, vii (1980), 311

KERSLAKE, John: 'The Likeness of Handel', *Handel and the Fitzwilliam* (Cambridge, 1974), 24

KEYNES, Milo: 'Handel and his Illnesses', *Musical Times*, cxxiii (1982), 613

——: 'Handel's Illnesses', *The Lancet*, 20–27 December 1980, p. 1354

KIMBELL, David: 'The "Amadis" Operas of Destouches and Handel', *Music & Letters*, xlix (1968), 329

——: 'Aspekte von Händels Umarbeitungen und Revisionen eigener Werke', *Händel-Jahrbuch 1977*, 45

——: *A critical study of Handel's early operas* (diss. Oxford University, 1968)

——: 'The Libretto of Handel's *Teseo*', *Music & Letters*, xliv (1963), 371

KING, Alec Hyatt: *Handel and his Autographs* (London, 1967)

KIRKENDALE, Ursula: 'The Ruspoli Documents on Handel', *Journal of the American Musicological Society*, xx (1967), 222–73, 518

KIVY, Peter: 'Mainwaring's Handel: its Relation to English Aesthetics', *Journal of the American Musicological Society*, xvii (1964), 170

KNAPP, J. Merrill: 'Handel, the Royal Academy of Music, and its First Opera Season in London (1720)', *Musical Quarterly*, xlv (1959), 145

——: 'Handel's First Italian Opera', *Music & Letters*, lxii (1981), 12

——: 'Handel's *Tamerlano*: the Creation of an Opera', *Musical Quarterly*, lvi (1970), 405

LANDON, H. C. Robbins: *Haydn: the Years of 'The Creation'* (London, 1977)

LANG, Paul Henry: *George Frideric Handel* (New York, 1966, repr. 1977)

LARSEN, Jens Peter: *Handel's Messiah: Origins, Composition, Sources* (London, 1957, rev. 2/1972)

LE HURAY, Peter, and Day, James, eds: *Music and Aesthetics in the Eighteenth and Early Nineteenth Centuries* (Cambridge, 1981)

LONSDALE, Roger: *Dr. Charles Burney: A literary Biography* (Oxford, 1965)

LUCKETT, Richard: 'The Fabric of Dryden's Verse', Chatterton Lecture on an English Poet, *Proceedings of the British Academy*, lxvii (1981), 289

LYONS, Rev. Daniel: *Origin and Progress of the Meetings of the Three Choirs* (London, 1895)

[MAINWARING, J.]: *Memoirs of the life of the Late George Frederic Handel* (London, 1760, repr. 1964, 1967)

MALLOCH, W.: 'The Earl of Bute's machine organ', *Early Music*, xi (1983), 172

MATTHESON, J.: *Georg Friedrich Händels Lebensbeschreibung* (Hamburg, 1761, repr. 1976)

MATTHESON, J.: *Grundlage einer Ehren-Pforte* (Hamburg, 1740); ed. M. Schneider (Berlin, 1910, repr. 1969)

MATTHEWS, Betty: 'Unpublished Letters Concerning Handel', *Music & Letters*, xl (1959), 261; see also p. 406

——: 'Handel: more Unpublished Letters', *Music & Letters*, xlii (1961), 127; see also p. 395

MILHOUS, Judith, and HUME, Robert: 'Box Office Reports for Five Operas Mounted by Handel in London, 1732–1734', *Harvard Library Bulletin*, xxvi (1978), 245

——: 'Handel's Opera Finances in 1732–3', *Musical Times*, cxxv (1984), 86–9

——: 'New Light on Handel and the Royal Academy of Music in 1720', *Theatre Journal*, xxxv (1983), 149

MILLER, Miriam: 'The early Novello octavo editions', in O. Neighbour, ed.: *Music and Bibliography: Essays in Honour of Alec Hyatt King* (London, 1980)

MOSCHELES, Felix, ed.: *Letters of Felix Mendelssohn* (Boston, 1888, repr. 1970)

MUELLER VON ASOW, H. and E. H.: *Georg Friedrich Händel: Briefe und Schriften* (Lindau, 1949) [incl. Mattheson's trans. of Mainwaring's Life]

MYERS, Rollo: *Handel's Messiah: a Touchstone of Taste* (New York, 1948)

NALBACH, Daniel: *The King's Theatre, 1704–1867* (London, 1972)

NEWTON, John: *Messiah. Fifty Expository Discourses . . .* (London, 1786)

NICHOLS, John: *Literary Anecdotes*, 9 vols (London, 1812–15)

OBER, William B.: 'Bach, Handel, and "Chevalier" John Taylor, M.D. Ophthalmiater', *New York State Journal of Medicine*, lxix/12 (1969), 1797

PÖLLNITZ, Karl Ludwig Freiherr von: *The Memoirs of Charles-Lewis, Baron de Pollnitz* (London, 2/1739)

POTTER, John: *Observations on the Present State of Music and Musicians* (London, 1762)

PRICE, Curtis: 'The Critical Decade for English Music Drama, 1700–1710', *Harvard Library Bulletin*, xxvi/1 (1978)

PROUT, Ebenezer: 'Graun's Passion Oratorio and Handel's Knowledge of it', *Monthly Musical Record*, xxiv (1894), 94, 121

——: 'Handel's Obligations to Stradella', *Monthly Musical Record*, i (1871), 154

——: 'Urio's Te Deum and Handel's Use thereof', *Monthly Musical Record*, i (1871), 139

RACKWITZ, W. and STEFFENS, H.: *George*

Frideric Handel: a Biography in Pictures (Leipzig, 1962)

RAMSAY, E. B.: *Two Lectures on the Genius of Handel* (London, 1862)

RAUMER, Frederick von: *England in 1835* (Philadelphia, 1836)

ROBERTS, J. H.: 'Handel's Borrowings from Telemann: An Inventory', in H. J. Marx, ed.: *Göttinger Händel-Beiträge* I (Kassel, Basle and London, 1984)

ROBINSON, Percy: *Handel and his Orbit* (London, 1908)

ROCKSTRO, W. S.: *The Life of George Frederick Handel* (London, 1883)

RING, John: *The Commemoration of Handel. A Poem* (London, 1786)

SADIE, Stanley: *Handel* (London, 1962)
——: *Handel Concertos* (London, 1972)

SANDS, Mollie: 'The Problem of "Teraminta"'. *Music & Letters*, xxxiii (1952), 217

SASSE, K.: 'Opera Register from 1712 to 1734 (Colman-Register)', *Händel-Jahrbuch 1959*, 199

SCHMIDGALL, Gary: *Literature as Opera* (New York, 1977)

SCHOELCHER, Victor: *The Life of Handel* (London, 1857)

SERAUKY, W.: *Georg Friedrich Händel: sein Leben, sein Werk* (Kassel, 1956–8) [only vols iii–v published]

SHAW, George Bernard: 'Causerie on Handel in England', repr. in *How to Become a Musical Critic*, ed. Dan Laurence (London, 1960)

SHAW, Watkins: *A Textual and Historical Companion to Handel's Messiah* (London, 1965)

SHIELD, William: *An Introduction to Harmony* (London, 1800)

SIEGMUND-Schultze, W.: *Georg Friedrich Händel: Leben und Werk* (Leipzig, 1954, rev. 3/1962)

SILBIGER, Alexander: 'Scarlatti Borrowings in Handel's Grand Concertos', *Musical Times*, cxxv (1984), 93–5

SMITH, Ruth: 'Intellectual contexts of Handel's Oratorios', in C. Hogwood and R. Luckett, eds: *Music in Eighteenth-Century England* (Cambridge, 1983), 115

SMITH, W. C.: *Concerning Handel, his Life and Works* (London, 1948)
——: 'George III, Handel and Mainwaring', *Musical Times*, lxv (1924), 789
——: *Handel: a Descriptive Catalogue of the Early Editions* (London, 1960, rev. 2/1970)

——: *A Handelian's Notebook* (London, 1965)

SMITHER, Howard, E.: *A History of the Oratorio*, 2 vols (North Carolina, 1977)

STREATFEILD, R. A.: *Handel* (London, 1909; rev. 2/1910, repr. 1964)

STROHM, Reinhard: 'Händel in Italia: nuovi contributi', *Rivista italiana di musicologia*, ix (1974), 152
——: 'Händels Pasticci', *Analecta musicologica*, no. 14 (1974), 208–67

TALBOT, Michael: 'Jennens and Vivaldi', *Vivaldi Veneziano Europeo*, ed. Degrada (Florence, 1980), 73.

TAYLOR, Carole: 'Handel and Frederick, Prince of Wales', *Musical Times*, cxxv (1984), 89–92

TAYLOR, John (jnr): *Records of My Life*, 2 vols (London, 1832)

TAYLOR, Sedley: *The Indebtedness of Handel to Works by other Composers* (Cambridge, 1906, repr. 1979)

TEMPERLEY, Nicholas: 'New light on the libretto of *The Creation*', in C. Hogwood and R. Luckett, eds: *Music in Eighteenth-Century England* (Cambridge, 1983), 189

TIMMS, C.: 'Handel and Steffani', *Musical Times*, cxiv (1973), 374

TROWELL, Brian: 'Handel as a Man of the Theatre', *Proceedings of the Royal Musical Association*, lxxxviii (1961–2), 17

WALPOLE, Horace: *Essay on Modern Gardening* (London, 1785)

WEBER, William: 'Intellectual Bases of the Handelian Tradition, 1759–1800', *Proceedings of the Royal Musical Association*, cviii (1981–2),

WILLIAMS, P. F.: 'Händel und die englische Orgelmusik', *Händel-Jahrbuch 1966*, 51

WILSON, John, ed.: *Roger North on Music* (London, 1959)

WOLFF, H. C.: *Die Händel-Oper auf der modernen Bühne* (Leipzig, 1957)

WOLLENBERG, Susan: 'Handel and Gottlieb Muffat', *Musical Times*, cxiii (1972), 448

YOUNG, Percy: *George Grove 1820–1900: A Biography* (London, 1980)
——: *Handel* (London, 1946, rev. 3/1975)

ZIMMERMAN, Franklin B.: 'Musical Borrowings in the English Baroque', *Musical Quarterly*, lii (1966), 493
——: 'Purcellian passages in the compositions of G. F. Handel', in C. Hogwood and R. Luckett, eds: *Music in Eighteenth-Century England* (Cambridge, 1983)

Select Bibliography Since 1985

Contributions to journals and yearbooks such as *Musical Times*, *Music & Letters*, *Early Music*, *Göttinger Händel-Beiträge*, and *Händel-Jahrbuch* are mostly omitted. See also JSTOR, http://gfhandel.org/references.htm and http://www.newolde.com/handel.htm

BEEKS, Graydon: 'Handel and Music for the Earl of Carnarvon', *Bach, Handel, Scarlatti: Tercentenary Essays*, ed. Peter Williams (Cambridge, 1985), 1

BEST, Terence, ed.: *Handel Collections and their History* (Oxford, 1993)
Includes essays on all the principal collections of music manuscripts containing music by Handel: Clausen on the Hamburg Collection, Dean on the Malmesbury Collection, Roberts on the Aylesford Collection, Hicks on the Shaftesbury Collection, Burrows on the Barrett Lennard Collection, Beeks on the Chandos Collection, and useful essays by Keiichiro Watanabe about the types of music-paper Handel and his copyists used in Italy, 1706–1710, and by Baselt on early German Handel editions during the 18th century.

BURROWS, Donald: *Handel* (Oxford, 1994)

——: *Handel: Messiah*, Cambridge Music Handbooks (Cambridge, 1991)

——: *Handel and the English Chapel Royal* (Oxford, 2005)

——: 'Handel's 1735 (London) Version of *Athalia*', *Music in Eighteenth-Century Britain*, ed. David Wyn Jones (Ashgate, 2000), 193

——, ed.: *The Cambridge Companion to Handel* (Cambridge, 1997)
Useful reference book for Handelians thirsty for reliable academic introductions to a variety of topics written by several leading experts: John Butt on Handel's Germanic education, Carlo Vitali on political and musical contexts in Italy, Milhous and Hume on London theatres during Handel's career, Lowell Lindgren and Ruth Smith on librettists, Beeks on Handel's sacred music, Malcolm Boyd on the chamber music, Best on keyboard music and Handel's relationship with the Italian language, and Burrows on Handel's concertos and oratorio performances.

BURROWS, Donald and Dunhill, Rosemary: *Music and Theatre in Handel's World: the Family Papers of James Harris 1732–1780* (Oxford, 2002)

BURROWS, Donald and Ronish, Martha: A

Catalogue of Handel's Musical Autographs (Oxford, 1994)

CHARLTON, David and Hibberd, Sarah: '"My father was a poor Parisian musician": A Memoir (1756) concerning Rameau, Handel's Library and Sallé', *Journal of the Royal Musical Association*, cxxviii/2 (2003), 161

DEAN, Winton: *Essays on Opera* (Oxford, 1990)

——: *Handel's Operas, 1726–1741* (Woodbridge, 2006)

DEAN, Winton and Knapp, J. Merrill: *Handel's Operas, 1704–1726*, i (Oxford, 1987)

GIBSON, Elizabeth: *The Royal Academy of Music, 1719–1728: the Institution and Its Directors* (New York and London, 1989)

HARRIS, Ellen T.: *Handel as Orpheus: Voice and Desire in the Chamber Cantatas* (Harvard, 2001)

——, ed.: *The Librettos of Handel's Operas*, 13 vols (London and New York, 1989)

HOGWOOD, Christopher: *Handel: Water Music and Music for the Royal Fireworks* (Cambridge, 2005)

HURLEY, David Ross: *Handel's Muse: Patterns of Creation in his Oratorios and Musical Dramas, 1743–1751* (Oxford, 2001)

KIRKENDALE, Ursula: 'Handel with Ruspoli: New Documents from the Archivio Segreto Vaticano, December 1706 to December 1708', *Studi musicali*, xxxii (2003), 301

LARUE, C. Steven: *Handel and his Singers: the Creation of the Royal Academy Operas, 1720–1728* (Oxford, 1995)

LEDBETTER, David, ed.: *Continuo Playing According to Handel – His Figured Bass Exercises* (Oxford, 1990)

LUCKETT, Richard: *Handel's Messiah: a Celebration* (London, 1992)

MANN, Alfred: *Handel: the Orchestral Music* (London, 1996)

PARKER, Mary Ann: *G. F. Handel: a Guide to Research* (London, 2005)

RÄTZER, Manfred: *Szenische Aufführungen von Werken Georg Friedrich Händels vom 18. bis 20. Jahrhundert: eine Dokumentation* (Halle, 2000)

ROBERTS, John: 'Handel and Charles Jennens's Italian opera manuscripts', *Music and Theatre: Essays in Honour of Winton Dean*, ed. Nigel Fortune (Cambridge, 1987), 159

——, ed.: *Handel Sources Series: Materials for the Study of Handel's Borrowing*, 9 vols (London and New York, 1986)
Contains scores of works by Keiser, Porta, Graun, Lotti, Alessandro Scarlatti, Bononcini and Steffani from which Handel borrowed substantial ideas.

SADIE, Stanley and Hicks, Anthony: *Handel Tercentenary Collection* (London, 1987)
Essays by Baselt, Dean, William D. Gudger, Lowell Lindgren, Curtis Price, Roberts, Carole Taylor and Colin Timms.

SIMON, Jacob, ed.: *Handel: a Celebration of his Life and Times* (London, 1985)

SMITH, Ruth: *Handel's Oratorios and Eighteenth-Century Thought* (Cambridge, 1995)

STROHM, Reinhard: *Dramma per Musica: Italian Opera Seria of the Eighteenth Century* (London 1997)

——: *Essays on Handel and Italian Opera* (Cambridge, 1985)

——: 'Vivaldi and Handel's settings of Giustino', *Music and Theatre: Essays in Honour of Winton Dean*, ed. Nigel Fortune (Cambridge, 1987), 131

TOWE, Teri Noel: 'A Collector's *Messiah*: Historic Handel Oratorio Recordings, 1899–1930', http://www.npj.com/homepage/teritowe/gfhacm00.html

WILLIAMS, Peter, ed.: *Bach, Handel, Scarlatti: Tercentenary Essays* (Cambridge, 1985)
Essays by Beeks, Paul Brainard, Burrows, Dean, Fuller, Gerald Hendrie, Robert Hill, Mark Lindley, Mann, Giorgio Pestelli and Williams.

ZÖLLNER, Eva: *English Oratorio after Handel: the London Oratorio Series and its Repertory, 1760–1800* (Marburg, 2002)

List of Illustrations

Index

Numbers in italics refer to illustration numbers.

Index of Handel's Works

Index

323